A CONCISE HISTORY OF
THE AMERICAN PEOPLE

Volume 2: Since 1865

A CONCISE HISTORY OF THE AMERICAN PEOPLE

Volume 2
Since 1865

ARTHUR S. LINK
Princeton University

ROBERT V. REMINI
University of Illinois at Chicago

DOUGLAS GREENBERG
Princeton University

ROBERT C. McMATH, JR.
Georgia Institute of Technology

Harlan Davidson, Inc.
Arlington Heights, Illinois 60004

Library of Congress Cataloging in Publication Data
Main entry under title:

A Concise history of the American people.

    Rev. and condensed ed. of: The American people. 1981.
    Includes bibliographies and indexes.
    Content: v. 1. To 1877—v. 2. Since 1865.
    1. United States—History. I. Link, Arthur Stanley.
II. American people.

                             83-23184

[E178.1.A493 1984b]   973
ISBN 0-88295-817-8 (pbk.)
ISBN 0-88295-818-6 (pbk. : v. 1)
ISBN 0-88295-819-4 (pbk. : v. 2)

A Concise History of the American People is available in
one-volume and two-volume paperbound editions. Volume 1
treats the period from European origin through Reconstruction
(chapters 1-17), and Volume 2 includes Reconstruction to the
present (chapters 17-33). This arrangement is made to provide
greater classroom flexibility for planning one- and two-semester
American history courses. Pagination and chapter numbers remain
the same in the two-volume edition, and the general index appears
at the end of both volumes.

PRINTED IN THE UNITED STATES OF AMERICA

84 85 86 87 88 CM 10 9 8 7 6 5 4 3 2 1

PREFACE

This book, a revision and condensation of *The American People* (1981), is about people making their own history. In the last decade (within which most of today's college students first became aware of events beyond their immediate surroundings) many Americans have come to have a sense of powerlessness about their ability to shape their own lives. The experience of the American people, viewed whole, belies that fear. Not only do we encounter in that experience the high drama of public figures shaping the political, diplomatic, and military history of the nation, but we also see ordinary men and women in their families, communities, and workplaces influencing the course of human events.

In telling the story of a people making its own history, we have not simply celebrated, uncritically, the nation's past. Rather, we have measured our history against the highest ideals which the American people themselves have expressed; and we have attempted to discuss frankly their failures to live up to those high standards, as well as their successes. For we believe that we can be set free to deal with the challenges of the present and future only if we confront the full truth of our history.

As for the particular format of this book, *A Concise History of the American People* is written for readers who, for a variety of reasons, would like to have a more concise account than is found in the standard American history textbooks. We believe the reader will find here a clear, concise narrative of political, diplomatic, and military events, coupled with analysis of major social and economic trends, including the dramatic developments of the 1980s. Throughout, one can see women and minorities making their own history, even while laboring under the influence of historical forces beyond their control.

The authors thank Susannah Hopkins Jones for her superb editing of the text and Maureen Gilgore Trobec for her general (and genial) supervision. The authors also thank Harlan Davidson for continuing encouragement and support.

The Authors

CONTENTS

23 WOODROW WILSON AND THE TRIUMPH OF PROGRESSIVISM

24 THE UNITED STATES AND THE FIRST WORLD WAR

25 THE UNITED STATES IN THE 1920s

26 THE GREAT DEPRESSION AND THE NEW DEAL

27 THE UNITED STATES AND THE SECOND WORLD WAR

28 POLITICS AND PROBLEMS OF THE TRUMAN ERA

APPENDICES

INDEX

CHAPTER 17
THE ERA OF
RECONSTRUCTION

1. STRUGGLES OVER RECONSTRUCTION POLICIES

The Status of the Southern States

The Civil War determined that secession by one or more states from the United States was not only unconstitutional but also militarily impossible. It also ended the old debate about the nature of the Union and established the ultimate sovereignty of the federal government. Finally, the Union victory put an end to slavery forever in North America. The Thirteenth Amendment, which abolished slavery, was approved by Congress and sent to the states before Lee's surrender, and it was ratified on December 18, 1865. But the northern victory also raised difficult questions.

One of the most pressing of these questions involved the status of the former Confederate states. Lincoln had claimed that the war was a rebellion of individual citizens and that the states, irrespective of their resolutions of secession, had never left the Union. Lincoln proclaimed in 1863 that, when at least 10 per cent of those persons who had voted in the election of 1860 in any of the seceded states took an oath of loyalty to the United States, these persons might then form a government without slavery, which he would recognize.

But Congress rejected Lincoln's plan in 1864 and substituted its own, more stringent conditions for readmission in the Wade-Davis bill. The war ended without any decision on basic reconstruction policies, except, of course, on the abolition of slavery and the restoration of national sovereignty in the former Confederacy. Lincoln was a masterful politician and might well have maintained a congressional majority behind a fairly moderate program by strategic concessions. His successor was less adroit, however, and he suffered for it.

Andrew Johnson and the Radicals

Andrew Johnson lacked Lincoln's tact, sympathy, and political skill. Johnson hated the great planters who, he believed, had dragged the poor people of the South into a senseless war. And, although a state-rights Democrat, he was intensely devoted to the Union.

There appears to have been a high degree of unity within the Republican party in support of a policy that would bring the defeated South back into the Union fairly quickly. The basic policy included a constitutional amendment affirming the sovereignty of the national government over the states and a guarantee of at least basic civil rights for the freed blacks. The most extreme element in the Republican party—the so-called Radicals—demanded a more thoroughgoing reconstruction of southern politics and society by the elimination of secessionist leaders from politics and by economic assistance, especially the grant of lands, to black people. A second Republican group—the so-called Moderates—did not want to go as far as the Radicals in social and economic reconstruction. Yet these Moderates, too, wanted to protect the civil and, to some degree, the political rights of the recently freed slaves.

The new President enjoyed a reputation as an extreme Radical and, during the first days of his tenure, indicated that he favored stern measures toward former Confederates. For reasons which are still not entirely clear, Johnson then issued a proclamation on May 29, 1865, which granted amnesty to all persons who had engaged in rebellion against the United States, except Confederate officers and persons with property worth more than $20,000. Even the exempted groups were invited to apply to the President for individual pardons. Next, Johnson appointed provisional civilian governors in the Carolinas, Georgia, Florida, Alabama, Mississippi, and Texas. He stipulated that constitutional conventions should be elected which had to repeal the ordinances of secession, frame new constitutions, and ratify the Thirteenth Amendment.

The suggestion by leading southern politicians that the federal government should assume Confederate debts received prominent attention in northern newspapers. The South Carolina constitutional convention refused either to repudiate the state's wartime debt or to ratify the Thirteenth Amendment. Southern voters elected many former Confederate officials to the United States Congress. Most galling of all to Northerners, southern legislatures began to adopt "black codes" which included vagrancy and apprenticeship laws. They assigned blacks without jobs to "guardians"—sometimes their former masters—for work without pay. South Carolina's code made theft of a mule or housebreaking by a black person a capital crime. No southern state under the Johnson government permitted black men to vote or to hold office. To Northerners, who felt some obligation to the people freed by the Civil

War, it seemed that the black codes were nothing more than a device to return black people to slavery.

2. RADICAL RECONSTRUCTION

The Beginnings of Radical Reconstruction

Johnson woefully underestimated the opposition that his program would arouse. Thaddeus Stevens of Pennsylvania, leader of the Radicals in the House of Representatives, obtained adoption of a resolution which instructed the clerk to omit from the roll call the names of the newly elected representatives from the former Confederate states. The Senate, led by Charles Sumner, took the same course.

Stevens next called for the appointment of a special Joint Committee of Fifteen on Reconstruction to inquire into the right to representation of the states of the "so-called late Confederacy." Actually, the committee would try to find a new plan of reconstruction acceptable to northern opinion. The battle between Johnson and the Radicals was now joined.

Stevens maneuvered skillfully and cautiously. Within the Committee of Fifteen, he permitted policy to be determined by the Moderates. The committee's first measure was a bill to extend indefinitely the life of the Freedmen's Bureau, which provided freed slaves (and many whites as well) with food, clothing, and shelter. It helped freedmen to find employment at fair wages, founded schools and colleges, and was primarily responsible for beginning free public education for black people in the South. Then Congress passed a civil-rights bill, which granted citizenship to blacks and guaranteed the same civil rights to all persons born in the United States.

The Joint Committee of Fifteen next turned to the problem of guaranteeing permanently the basic civil rights of blacks. Its solution was the Fourteenth Amendment. It declared that "all persons born or naturalized in the United States" were "citizens of the United States and of the state wherein they reside," and it forbade any state to deprive such persons of their rights as citizens. It did not enfranchise black men, but it required a reduction in the representation in Congress of any state which denied the vote to black men. The Fourteenth Amendment also forbade the payment of the Confederate debt and guaranteed payment of the public debt of the United States. Finally, it disqualified Confederate leaders from holding state and federal offices. This disqualification, however, could be removed by a two-thirds vote of Congress.

This was the minimum northern program for Reconstruction; Moderates insisted upon it as avidly as did Radicals. It offered a speedy process of self-reconstruction by the southern states. Now Johnson had to decide whether to accept this congressional plan or to insist upon his own. He made his decision known in a violent attack against Stevens and Sumner. He accused them of seeking to enslave the South, to invade the constitutional powers of the presidency, and to encourage his assassination. Johnson vetoed the bill which extended the life of the Freedmen's Bureau. He outraged Moderates by also vetoing the civil-rights bill. Finally, he urged the southern states to refuse to ratify the Fourteenth Amendment. Congress passed both the Freedmen's Bureau and the civil-rights bills over Johnson's vetoes.

Radical Reconstruction Is Launched

The Freedmen's Bureau bill, the civil-rights bill, and the Fourteenth Amendment provided the issues for the congressional campaign of 1866. In an effort to carry his fight with Congress to the people, Johnson undertook a long speaking tour of the East and Middle West, but the voters in November returned a Congress with an overwhelming anti-Johnson majority.

The Radicals, with the support of their Moderate allies, now took complete control. Congress adopted over Johnson's veto what was later called the First Reconstruction Act (there were others in 1867 and 1868). It wiped out the governments created under presidential reconstruction and grouped the ten southern states which had refused to ratify the Fourteenth Amendment into five military districts. The military governors were to summon conventions in the states under their control to frame new constitutions. Blacks could vote freely for members of these conventions, while former Confederate leaders were disqualified from voting. State constitutions with provisions for black male suffrage had to be framed and then approved by Congress; in addition, the legislatures elected under these constitutions had to ratify the Fourteenth Amendment. Once this was done, the states would be received into the Union.

The striking fact about this program was its leniency. Some Radicals wanted to impose thoroughgoing economic and social revolution on the South. Stevens and other extreme Radicals in Congress, if they had controlled sufficient votes, probably would have confiscated the land of former Confederates and tried to establish a large class of independent black landowners. Republican Moderates still held the balance of power, and they insisted that blacks receive the power to protect themselves at the polls. Beyond that, they were unwilling to go.

Radical Reconstruction in the South

It is not easy to characterize the Reconstruction governments in the southern states because they varied so greatly. A few general statements, however, can be made.

1. Blacks participated enthusiastically as voters and officeholders, but it is completely inaccurate to speak of Reconstruction as a time of black rule in the South. No black governor was elected, and only two black United States senators were sent to Washington. Conservative native whites controlled Reconstruction governments in some states. Native whites, derisively called "scalawags" by some of their neighbors, cooperated with Reconstruction authorities when it suited their interests to do so. In no state did blacks ever use their power to dominate or to punish their former masters.

2. Many of the northern whites who moved to the South (dubbed "carpetbaggers") and cooperated with blacks to control the Republican party in some states were not very well trained for political leadership. Many black officeholders had little education, since most southern states had made it a crime for slaves to learn to read and write. Even so, Reconstruction

*Woodcut of freedmen voting in New Orleans in 1867. In
imposing suffrage for black men upon the former Confederate states,
the Radicals in Congress set in motion the forces behind the
movement for national suffrage for blacks that resulted in the
passage of the Fifteenth Amendment. (The Bettmann Archive)*

governments in the southern states left a record of constructive work which
has endured to this day.

3. Many of the Reconstruction governments in the South were flagrantly
corrupt. But corruption permeated American politics generally in this
period, and southern states had no monopoly on it. Also, no single party
accounted for all the political corruption and public immorality of the
period. Further, corruption was not confined to carpetbaggers and blacks.
White Southerners were just as eager to profit from outright bribery as
anyone else. Furthermore, the major beneficiaries of bribery during Reconstruction were not the politicians, but southern businessmen and plantation
owners who obtained rights to railroad franchises, lands, and convict labor.
Moreover, the terms "carpetbagger" and "scalawag" were epithets used by
former Confederates to condemn those who helped former slaves—much as
civil-rights activists were condemned later.

The White South Strikes Back

Most southern whites objected to the Reconstruction regimes mainly
because they were based in large part upon black suffrage. The older ruling
class struck back in secret organizations, principally the Ku Klux Klan. Bands
of masked men on horseback, robed in white sheets, spread terror through
Negro quarters at night. Klansmen burned fiery crosses and posted warnings

During Reconstruction, members of the Ku Klux Klan used such devices as warnings to bring terrorism to the South. (Picture Collection, The Branch Libraries, The New York Public Library)

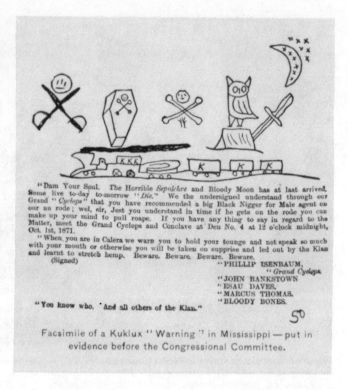

"Dam Your Soul. The Horrible *Sepulchre* and Bloody Moon has at last arrived. Some live to-day to-morrow "*Die.*" We the undersigned understand through our Grand "*Cyclops*" that you have recommended a big Black Nigger for Male agent on our nu rode ; wel, sir, Jest you understand in time if he gets on the rode you can make up your mind to pull roape. If you have any thing to say in regard to the Matter, meet the Grand Cyclops and Conclave at Den No. 4 at 12 o'clock midnight, Oct. 1st, 1871.

"When you are in Calera we warn you to hold your tounge and not speak so much with your mouth or otherwise you will be taken on surprise and led out by the Klan and learnt to stretch hemp. Beware. Beware. Beware. Beware.
(Signed)
                              "PHILLIP ISENBAUM,
                                          "*Grand Cyclops.*
                                "JOHN BANKSTOWN.
                                "ESAU DAVES.
                                "MARCUS THOMAS.
                                "BLOODY BONES.
"You know who. "And all others of the Klan."

Facsimile of a Kuklux "Warning" in Mississippi — put in evidence before the Congressional Committee.

of what would happen to all persons who aided the freedmen. They also whipped, tarred and feathered, and murdered at will.

Meanwhile, reports of this violence profoundly disturbed northern opinion. Congress adopted laws to protect black voters and to outlaw the Klan. The President suspended the writ of *habeas corpus* in nine South Carolina counties in the summer of 1871, and a joint congressional committee launched a full-scale investigation. These efforts were on the whole ineffective. Emboldened whites continued to use force to intimidate and defraud blacks in order to deprive them of political rights. Such tactics were supplemented by economic coercion—an even more effective weapon of racial control. Most freedmen had no alternative but to work as sharecroppers or tenants on plantations.

The Impeachment of Johnson

The Radicals were determined to drive Johnson from the White House. The same day on which it passed the First Reconstruction Act, Congress adopted the Tenure of Office Act. This measure was designed to prevent the President from dismissing members of his own cabinet without the prior approval of the Senate. It was designed not only to prevent Johnson from removing adversaries within his administration but also as a trap in the event that Johnson should violate the law. The act specifically defined any violation as a misdemeanor, and a President can be impeached only for committing high crimes and misdemeanors.

The High Court of Impeachment in the Senate for the trial of Andrew Johnson with John A. Bingham, Chairman of the House Committee of Impeachment Managers, reading the Articles of Impeachment. This engraving is from Frank Leslie's Illustrated Newspaper *(1868). (Culver Pictures, Inc.)*

Johnson dismissed Secretary of War Edwin M. Stanton, a virtual spy in the cabinet, who was in close alliance with the congressional Radicals. Thereupon the House impeached Johnson. The Senate tried the case from March 30 to May 26, 1868. In spite of frantic efforts by the Radicals to secure a conviction, the vote fell one short of the two thirds necessary for conviction.

3. NATIONAL POLITICS AND PROBLEMS

The Election of 1868

As the impeachment trial drew to an end, the Republican national convention nominated General Grant for President. Johnson and the Reconstruction Acts were the main issues in the campaign. Grant won a decisive victory over his Democratic opponent, former Governor Horatio Seymour of New York. However, without the approximately 700,000 blacks who voted for him in the South, Grant would have fallen behind Seymour. These figures made it clear to the Radicals that it was absolutely necessary to retain the black vote if the GOP was to remain in power. Congress, therefore, in 1869 adopted and submitted the Fifteenth Amendment. It forbade the states to deny the right to vote to any citizen on account of "race, color, or previous condition of servitude." It was ratified on March 30, 1870.

Grant as President

Ulysses S. Grant yielded to the flattery of his Radical friends and permitted his election to an office for which he was totally unprepared. A professional soldier with no political experience, he became little more than a puppet for the dominant faction in his party. He was personally honest, but he was also gullible and naive. His administration was riddled by corruption. Historians rate him one of the worst failures among American Presidents.

Fortunately for Grant, most of the important policies of his administration had already been adopted before he assumed office. By 1869, Radical Reconstruction was well under way. The Republican program of free homesteads, protective tariffs, the National Banking System, and lavish assistance to western railroads seemed to enjoy the support of an overwhelming majority of the people. Hence most partisan controversy revolved around Radical Reconstruction. The main body of Republicans continued to support it; in 1868, the Democrats tried, unsuccessfully, to overturn it.

The Prostrate South

No political leader seems to have given any serious attention to the nation's most important problem at this time—the economic reconstruction of the South. The real wealth of the South—buildings, railroads, livestock, factories, and roads—had been destroyed during the war. Financial institutions suffered bankruptcy when the Confederate bonds and currency that they were holding turned out to be worthless and when a high proportion of borrowers were obliged to default on loans. The greatest loss, however, was the 265,000 men who might have rebuilt the ravaged section had they not died for the Confederacy.

Northerners were in no mood to pay taxes to rebuild the South. Former slaves received little in the way of material aid. Except for the efforts of the Freedmen's Bureau, blacks were left to shift for themselves—and so was the rest of the population of the former Confederate States of America.

Enough capital came from the North and from Great Britain to put railroads into running condition, but manufacturing did not revive. Planters broke their plantations up into small holdings farmed by sharecroppers, who paid a part of their crop for food, seed, fertilizer, and rent of the land. They generally were in debt at high interest rates to the village storekeepers and money lenders, who, in turn, usually owed money at high interest rates to suppliers in the North. It would have been wise to grow a variety of crops, but cotton could not be stolen or eaten, and creditors therefore insisted on its cultivation to the exclusion of fruit or grain. Thus a one-crop system, immensely costly both to human beings and to the soil, was fastened along with an expensive credit system, upon large sections of the South.

The Greenback Controversy

The only other issue which excited national controversy during the Grant administration was monetary policy. It stemmed from the methods used by the federal government to pay for the war. Tax revenues were inadequate, and Congress resorted to paper money, called "greenbacks." They were based, not on gold or silver, but on the good faith of the United States Government and were legal tender for the payment of all debts except import duties. Naturally, this currency rose and fell in value and depended upon the confidence of holders, both at home and abroad, in the successful outcome of the federal war effort.

When the war ended, the government proposed to call the greenbacks in for payment in gold or bonds. Consequently, the value of the greenbacks rose sharply. The Secretary of the Treasury had already begun this process when a cry went up from many debtors, including certain manufacturers, railroad builders, and many farmers, who wanted cheap paper money. They had borrowed depreciated paper and now found themselves obliged to repay in dear money or gold. As paper money disappeared into the Treasury in Washington, businessmen suddenly found that it was difficult to obtain loans.

Arrayed against the idea of cheap money were most of the national banks; creditors in general; exporters and importers, who had an interest in a stable currency; and academic economists. Most of the latter argued for a sound currency to stimulate economic growth and foreign confidence. To be sure, many of the devotees of hard money were not averse to the enhancement of their own economic interests.

Greenback sentiment permeated both parties. The Democrats, desperate for an additional national issue, endorsed cheap money in their platform of 1868. However, their nominee, Seymour, was a hard-money man. The Republican platform demanded payment of greenbacks and bonds in gold, and Grant supported this program.

Congress accepted the election returns as something of a mandate and provided for the payment of United States bonds in gold in the Public Credit Act of 1869. When the Democrats, in the mid-term election of 1874, captured the House for the first time since the war, the Republicans made haste in their lame-duck session to settle the greenback issue, once and for all. They adopted the Resumption Act, which reduced the volume of greenbacks in circulation. Moreover, the act stipulated that greenbacks might be redeemed in gold on and after January 1, 1879. Champions of cheap money put the Greenback party into the field in the presidential election of 1876. The Greenbackers won only about 80,000 votes. But demands for cheap money were only temporarily silenced. They would be heard again.

4. THE EAGLE SCREAMS

Nationalism Rampant Again

Bitter enemies in domestic controversies showed surprising willingness to forget partisan advantage when foreign policy was involved. The expansive nationalism rampant during the 1840s reappeared in both sections after the end of the violent controversy between the North and the South. Agreement on foreign policy was also encouraged by William H. Seward and Hamilton Fish of New York, two of the ablest Secretaries of State in American history.

America's distress during the Civil War had tempted Spain and France to throw down, in the Dominican Republic and Mexico, the first serious challenges to the Monroe Doctrine. But Seward was a clever diplomat. He skillfully used the principles of the Monroe Doctrine to repel what he took to be European interference in the western hemisphere. The Monroe Doctrine came of age with Seward's successes. Now the whole world knew that it was the keystone of American foreign policy and that the United States would fight to defend it and the interests it protected.

A New Manifest Destiny?

A new movement for overseas expansion emerged in the United States during the immediate postwar era. As it turned out, it quickly subsided. However, it was a harbinger of what was to become—a generation later—a nationwide drive to achieve a new Manifest Destiny and to extend American dominion and civilization overseas.

Seward's project for the acquisition of Russian Alaska succeeded only because of an unusual sequence of events. Russia and the United States had always enjoyed good relations. When the Russian ambassador in Washington intimated that the Czar might be willing to sell Alaska to the United States, Seward responded enthusiastically. After some mild haggling, the Secretary of State signed a treaty on March 30, 1867, for the purchase of Alaska for $7.2 million. For a time it seemed that the Senate would reject the treaty. But the Senate approved it on April 9. There was much public outcry against "Seward's folly," and considerable condemnation of his search for any available real estate. But the acquisition of Alaska turned out to be an excellent bargain.

Settling an Old Score with Great Britain

The longest and most nagging diplomatic controversy of the postwar era involved American claims against Great Britain for damages done to American shipping by Confederate cruisers built in British shipyards. Anti-British feeling still ran high in the United States. A jingoistic speech by Senator Sumner and the favorable reaction which it evoked in the country greatly complicated the problems of the new Secretary of State, Hamilton Fish. Fish negotiated patiently, and American and British commissioners signed a treaty at Washington on May 8, 1871. It provided for the settlement of an old fisheries dispute and a boundary quarrel in Vancouver Bay and arbitration of the other claims by a tribunal to meet in Geneva in December 1871.

5. A NADIR OF NATIONAL POLITICS

The Campaign and Election of 1872

Discontent with Republican party leadership had spread in reaction against the apparent failure of Radical Reconstruction and its local excesses, signs of corruption in high places of government, the generally low tone of public morality, and the mania for speculation which had swept the country from one end to the other. A group of Republicans, led by Carl Schurz, began a movement for party reform in Missouri in 1870. The movement gained strength among Republicans throughout the nation. They advocated amnesty for the South, reduction of the tariff, and a thoroughgoing purge of the corrupt elements in the Republican party.

These Liberal Republicans, as they called themselves, held a convention, but dissension within their own ranks prevented them from nominating a strong candidate. They chose Horace Greeley, editor of the New York *Tribune*, an ardent protectionist, and a champion of reconciliation with the South. The Democratic convention also nominated Greeley. The Republicans renominated Grant. The campaign which followed was one of the most abusive in American history. Grant carried eight former slave states, as well as the entire North and West. The Republicans retained control of Congress by comfortable majorities.

Corruption Riddles the Grant Administration

The second Grant administration failed to distinguish itself with much constructive legislation. It was notable mainly for a series of scandals which nearly toppled the Republican party from its preeminent position. The first major scandal broke at the very end of the presidential campaign. The managers of the Union Pacific Railroad had formed a company called the Crédit Mobilier to construct the line, and then awarded themselves contracts for construction. They charged the railroad exorbitant prices and received huge profits from the arrangement. Moreover, they bribed Schuyler Colfax, Vice-President during Grant's first term, and several influential congressmen. The New York *Sun* exposed the skulduggery, and a congressional committee uncovered all the details early in 1873.

In the same year, greedy congressmen not only voted themselves a 50 per cent increase in salary but also made the increase retroactive to the session just coming to an end. Public indignation forced Congress to repeal this law in 1874.

In 1875 came the revelation of the so-called Whiskey Ring. A group of distillers and internal revenue officers had cheated the government out of hundreds of thousands of dollars in taxes. Grant's private secretary, General Orville E. Babcock, was involved and escaped conviction only because the President intervened. But the most shocking scandal came to light the following year. Secretary of War William W. Belknap was charged with reaping large profits from the sale of licenses to corrupt agents who stole supplies destined for Indian posts in the West. When the House of Representatives impeached Belknap on March 2, 1876, he resigned the same day to escape trial.

Scandal was not confined to Washington. In New York, the Tammany boss, William Marcy Tweed, plundered the city treasury of millions of dollars during the same period. Eventually he went to prison, where he died. Corrupt politicians all over the country sold public rights to businessmen who wanted control of such interests as natural resources, franchises for street railways, public utilities, and building contracts.

As severe panic in 1873 deepened the general mood of despair. The depression dragged on for five years; it caused sharp and widespread distress all over the country. It was little wonder that the administration suffered a stunning defeat in the mid-term election of 1874.

The Republican-controlled Forty-third Congress (1873–1875) adopted two measures before passing out of existence; the Resumption Act, already discussed, and the Civil Rights Act, sponsored by Senator Sumner and approved on March 1, 1875. The Civil Rights Act prohibited discrimination on account of race in inns, public transportation, and theaters. It forbade the exclusion of blacks from juries on account of color. Many congressmen who voted for the bill did so as a sop to black voters and white advocates of civil rights, not as an expression of national determination to abolish the color line. The Grant administration made only feeble efforts to enforce the law. In the Civil Rights Cases of 1883, the Supreme Court declared the measure unconstitutional on the ground that the Fourteenth Amendment (on which the Civil Rights Act was based) prohibited only official or state, not individual, discrimination against a person on account of race.

The End of Radical Reconstruction

Every year saw more lurid reports about the alleged incompetence of the Radical regimes. The Democrats, in their platform of 1868, had already declared that the issues of slavery and secession were "settled for all time." They demanded the restoration of all the states to their former rights in the Union. Virginia, North Carolina, and Georgia were "redeemed," as white Southerners put it, from Radical rule between 1869 and 1871. In 1875, Democrats won control of Alabama, Arkansas, and Texas. That same year, Mississippi went Democratic after a notorious campaign of terror and intimidation against black voters. Only Louisiana, South Carolina, and Florida remained under Radical Republican rule in 1876.

The Election of 1876

The Republicans were in deep trouble in 1876. They selected Governor Rutherford B. Hayes of Ohio, a former Union general. A man of unquestioned honesty, Hayes also entertained conciliatory views on the southern question. The Democrats nominated Governor Samuel J. Tilden of New York as their candidate.

The presidential election of 1876 was the most exciting one since the election of 1860. Late in the evening of election day, it seemed almost certain that Tilden was the victor. He had won enough states to give him 184 electoral votes—one short of a majority. Hayes had carried states with a total electoral count of 165. Twenty votes were in dispute.

The election hung on returns from South Carolina, Louisiana, and Florida. Congress, with one house Democratic and the other Republican, had to decide which of the double sets of returns to count. As weeks passed without a solution to the dilemma, it seemed that, for the second time in sixteen years, a presidential election would lead to a dire national crisis.

The Compromise of 1877

Conservatives in both parties were determined not to repeat the mistakes of 1860. After a series of meetings, congressmen agreed to create a commission

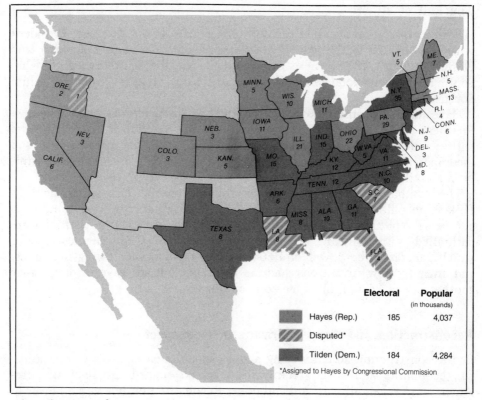

The Election of 1876

of fifteen members to determine which of the sets of disputed returns should be accepted. The commission consisted of eight Republicans and seven Democrats. Not surprisingly, in every case of the disputed twenty electoral votes, the commission voted eight to seven to accept the Hayes certificates.

But the crisis had not ended, because both houses of Congress had to approve the commission's decision before a President could be sworn in. Many of the northern Democrats wanted to hold out in the House of Representatives and thereby prevent Hayes' inauguration. However, a group of conservative southern Democrats in the lower house negotiated with spokesmen for Hayes and reached an informal understanding that the Southerners would vote to accept the commission's report. In return, Hayes would remove the last federal troops from the South, include at least one Southerner in his cabinet, give conservative Southerners control of part of the local patronage, and support generous appropriations for internal improvements, particularly railroads, in the South.

Hayes himself did not take part in the negotiations, and no one knows to this day whether a formal bargain was made. But southern conservatives did join with Republicans in the House of Representatives to approve the commission's report on March 2, 1877—only two days before the scheduled inauguration. The Republican Senate, of course, concurred at once, and the crisis ended. The other side of the alleged bargain, however, was not kept completely. Although administration forces tried, they were unable to persuade Congress to deliver the expected railroad subsidies to the South.

The End of an Era

Hayes' inauguration signaled the end of Reconstruction. The new President withdrew the last of the federal troops from South Carolina, Louisiana, and Florida in April 1877. These three states immediately returned to what Southerners were fond of calling "home rule," that is, rule by white Southerners.

Hayes named a former Confederate officer as Postmaster General. The new President also set out to rebuild and reunite the Republican party. And the entire administration applied itself vigorously to cleaning up graft and incompetence in the federal civil service, while Hayes pressed, unsuccessfully, for civil-service reform.

The symbol of the new era was the Centennial Exposition held in Philadelphia during the summer of 1876 to celebrate the one hundredth anniversary of the Declaration of Independence. Millions of visitors were enthralled by the whirling wheels of Machinery Hall. Giant engines—one of which generated the power of 1,600 horses—rapid home sewing machines, and amazing new inventions such as the telephone all gave evidence that another era of economic expansion lay ahead.

Reconstruction and Afro-Americans in Retrospect

Did Reconstruction actually bring about fundamental changes in the political, economic, and social relationships which shaped the lives of Afro-Americans? When all was said and done, Reconstruction left much power in the hands of the southern landed aristocracy, which, by combining agribusiness with commercial and industrial pursuits, managed to dominate much of the South for generations. In such a situation, improvement in the status of ex-slaves was inevitably limited. There was never any serious prospect of transferring economic and political control to blacks, even in those states where they were a majority.

Yet, by any measure, the gains registered during Reconstruction were remarkable. Between 1860 and 1880, the percentage of black children attending school rose from two to thirty-four. By 1870, over 1,000,000 blacks could vote, and 15 per cent of all public officials in the South were black, as compared to 3 per cent in 1979. Educational and political gains did not evaporate with the Compromise of 1877. Literacy rates and the number of black children in school continued to climb.

How can we account for these gains? It *did* make a difference that blacks were no longer slaves. More important, black institutions and community leaders emerged which enabled the freedmen to shape their own destiny. White Southerners were continually amazed during Reconstruction by the appearance of black preachers, teachers, and other community leaders. Quite often, these freedmen, and the network of kin and neighbors which they represented, were simply the "invisible" community of antebellum blacks, slave and free, coming into the open. These communities would prove resourceful and resilient bulwarks in preserving blacks' circumscribed freedom, even after bargains had been struck between the white North and the white South.

SUGGESTED READINGS

In addition to McPherson, *Ordeal by Fire*, and Randall and Donald, *Civil War and Reconstruction*, already cited, there are a number of good general surveys of Reconstruction: Kenneth M. Stampp, *The Era of Reconstruction* (1964); John Hope Franklin, *Reconstruction: After the Civil War* (1961); Rembert W. Patrick, *The Reconstruction of the Nation* (1967); E. Merton Coulter, *The South during Reconstruction* (1947); David Herbert Donald, *The Politics of Reconstruction* (1965); and W. R. Brock, *An American Crisis* (1963). A good social and economic history of the period is Allan Nevins, *The Emergence of Modern America, 1865–1878* (1927).

More recent studies have been extremely critical of Johnson. See, for example, Hans L. Trefousse, *The Radical Republicans: Lincoln's Vanguard for Racial Justice* (1969); Eric L. McKitrick, *Andrew Johnson and Reconstruction* (1960); and LaWanda and J. H. Cox, *Politics, Principle, and Prejudice: 1865–1866* (1963).

On the problems faced and occasioned by the emancipated Negro, see Willie Lee Rose, *Rehearsal for Reconstruction: The Port Royal Experiment* (1964), and Joel R. Williamson, *After Slavery* (1965). On the South's difficulties after the Civil War, see C. Vann Woodward, *Origins of the New South, 1877–1913* (1951), a stimulating analysis. On the Ku Klux Klan, the most recent work is Allen W. Trelease, *White Terror: The Ku Klux Klan Conspiracy and Southern Reconstruction* (1971). Thomas D. Clark and Albert D. Kirwan, *The South since Appomattox* (1967), is an adequate general survey with an excellent selective bibliography.

There is no satisfactory survey of the Grant administration. The best introduction is Allan Nevins, *Hamilton Fish: The Inner History of the Grant Administration* (1936). Useful on the Grant presidency is William B. Hesseltine, *Ulysses S. Grant: Politician* (1935). On the disputed election of 1876, see C. Vann Woodward, *Reunion and Reaction* (1951). Two excellent studies of the reform movement of the period are John G. Sproat, *"The Best Men": Liberal Reformers in the Gilded Age* (1968), and Earle D. Ross, *The Liberal Republican Movement* (1919).

CHAPTER 18
THE INDUSTRIAL
REVOLUTION, 1850–1900

1. THE INDUSTRIAL REVOLUTION IN THE UNITED STATES

Causes of Industrialization

Most of the forces which triggered America's industrial growth were present before the Civil War, even though their full impact would not be felt until much later. The story of the industrialization of the United States is a complicated one. Nevertheless, the major causes can be summarized briefly:

1. Steam, coal, and iron were basic ingredients of the new industrial system. The United States borrowed from Great Britain and adapted for its own needs the technology of steam power. By 1869, 52 per cent of the power used in American manufacturing was steam-generated. In transportation, the conversion to steam was quicker and more complete than in manufacturing, first with application to river traffic and then to the new railroads.

The steam revolution was fired by coal. With the opening of Pennsylvania's anthracite fields in the 1830s, inexpensive coal became available in large quantities. The metal-making and metalworking industries were among the first to take advantage of this new source of power. With an abundance of iron ore and coal, the United States was able to adopt new British techniques for transforming iron into steel. A process invented at about the same time by the Englishman, Henry Bessemer, and the American, William Kelly, was widely employed by the 1870s. It was largely replaced in the 1890s and 1900s by the more efficient open-hearth method. Under the leadership of steelmakers such as Andrew Carnegie, production mushroomed. By the late 1890s, one of the blast furnaces at Carnegie's huge J. Edgar Thompson works in Pittsburgh produced more steel than had the entire nation in 1879.

2. Expansion of the American railroad network was a vital stimulus to industrialization. By providing fast, regular, and relatively cheap transportation and communication, the railroads (and telegraph) laid the groundwork for a continental market network, which in turn made possible the mass production and distribution of goods. Railroads were also the first American enterprises to face the problems of large and complex business operations.

3. Technological innovations made possible the exploitation of abundant raw materials, the generation of power to process them, and the creation of transportation systems to move them. Throughout the nineteenth century, machines replaced more and more hand operations. Some of the most important innovations were those in the generation of power, in metal making, and in metalworking.

4. The unskilled and semiskilled labor needed to operate the new factories was available in abundance. An increasing flow of immigrants from Europe joined a stream of Americans moving from farms to towns and cities. The number of industrial wage earners increased from nearly 1,000,000 in 1860 to more than 5,000,000 in 1900.

5. Capital was generally abundant. Beginning in the 1850s, European investors purchased large quantities of American railroad securities. This infusion of capital helped to centralize the American capital market in New York and to create the modern securities business.

6. Government at all levels stimulated economic growth. Local, state, and federal governments subsidized private railroad construction, and federal improvement of rivers and harbors also helped to develop the transportation network. Tariffs protected American manufacturers from foreign competition; at the same time, regulation of industry remained minimal.

Railroads and the Beginnings of Big Business

Between 1860 and 1900, the American railroad system grew from about 30,000 miles of track to 200,000. In size and complexity, the railroads dwarfed other business institutions and the agencies of the federal government. In 1891, one railroad alone employed more workers than the largest federal agency. As late as the 1860s, American railroads were not sufficiently integrated to move goods over long distances without frequent reloading. But, by the 1880s, due to physical expansion and integration of the lines, goods could be moved across the continent without transshipment.

The growth of the railroad system was of two kinds—construction of new lines in the West and completion and integration of existing systems east of the Mississippi. In 1862, the federal government stimulated transcontinental railroad construction by chartering the Union Pacific Railroad to build westward from Omaha, and the Central Pacific Railroad to build eastward from Sacramento. The government subsidized construction through grants of land along the right-of-way and through long-term loans. Construction began in 1865; the last rail, held in place by a golden spike, was laid on May 10, 1869, when the two lines met near Ogden, Utah. Altogether, federal, state,

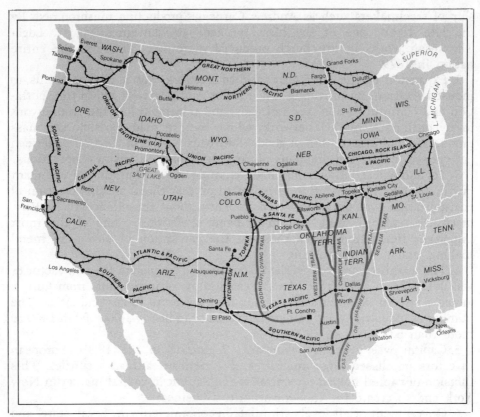

Railroads and Cattle Trails, 1850–1900

and local governments granted some 186,000,000 acres of land and over $600 million to western railroads. Wildcat financing, construction fraud, and the Panic of 1873 brought disaster to many of these enterprises. However, by 1900 six rail systems linked the West Coast with the Midwest and thus to connections with the eastern seaboard.

The development of railroad systems in the more settled regions of the country equaled in importance, if not in drama, the building of the transcontinentals. Integrated rail systems linked the eastern ports with the nation's heartland. Similar systems spread out from Chicago and St. Louis. In some cases, this expansion created duplication of services, and the available rail traffic could not support all the lines that had been built.

The growth of American railroads brought with it two sets of problems for their managers. First, how were they to operate such giant enterprises safely and efficiently? (Not the least of their problems was to keep the trains from running into each other on the single-track lines.) Second, with massive fixed costs, how were they to deal with the "ruinous" competition between duplicating lines? To deal with the first set of problems, railroad managers established the first modern system of business administration, which included (1) an organizational structure which integrated many operating units in one firm, (2) cost-accounting systems which enabled managers to measure precisely the unit cost of the services that they provided, and (3) a

Drawing of railroad building on the Great Plains by A. R. Waud.
Emerson observed that Americans took "to this little contrivance,
the railroad, as if it were the cradle in which they were born."
(Culver Pictures, Inc.)

hierarchy of salaried managers who came to dominate the railroads in place of the nominal owners. These methods of organizing economic activity have become so commonplace as to constitute a definition of the modern business firm. But before their development by the railroads in the 1850s, they simply did not exist.

Railroads in the South and East, faced with sharp competition for freight traffic in the 1870s, formed "pools," which were cartels designed to set rates among supposedly competing roads. Cooperating railroads pooled their profits or traffic in return for an agreed-upon share. But the pools were simply gentlemen's agreements, and, in the absence of enforceable sanctions, they failed to prevent secret rate cutting. By the mid-1880s, cooperation through pools had clearly failed to limit "cutthroat" competition, and more of the major lines turned to outright consolidation.

Until the 1890s, the efforts of the railroads to limit competition through cooperation or consolidation were not uniformly successful. However, these efforts, along with the railroads' influence on government at every level, evoked the wrath of shippers and reformers. Consequently, the railroads became the first industry to face demands for governmental regulation.

The Evolution of Modern Manufacturing Technology

The automobile assembly line has come to symbolize modern manufacturing. Innovations in automobile manufacturing early in the twentieth century marked a giant leap forward in the mass production of manufactured goods, but these innovations also rested on the evolution of manufacturing processes in the second half of the nineteenth century. By 1880, the giant mill and factory had already become a familiar part of the American landscape, but mass production, as symbolized by the automobile plant, was still in the future. Its full development would depend on the perfection and combination of four technological processes. The complete integration of all four of them at Henry Ford's automobile assembly plant in 1913 marked the beginning of a new industrial age.

1. Specialized machines were used in the individual steps of the manufacturing process. In key industries, machines gradually replaced many hand operations, even before the Civil War.

2. Interchangeable parts were used in assembling manufactured goods. Machine-made parts were not necessarily interchangeable with each other. In fact, before the late nineteenth century, most parts had to be fitted together by skilled craftsmen using files and other tools.

3. There was a continuous flow of goods in the manufacturing process. This innovation, introduced in the milling of grain in the eighteenth century, was adopted by slaughterhouses ("disassembly" plants for beef and pork) in the 1860s. By the 1870s and 1880s, continuous-flow techniques were only beginning to make their way into the metalworking industries.

4. There was centralized, or "scientific," management. As late as 1900, individual foremen still controlled production to a substantial degree. Beginning in the 1880s, several efficiency-minded engineers developed ways to centralize management of the industrial work place. The most influential of these innovators was Frederick W. Taylor. Taylor and his associates devised a plan of "scientific management," which included cost accounting, systematic purchasing, efficient plant design, and—most controversially—the use of time and motion studies to capture on paper the details of the work process and to determine the most expeditious methods to carry out the specialized tasks of factory work. These studies, coupled with wage scales based on output, were designed to increase the efficiency of workers. They also transferred actual control over the work place from foremen and workers to central managers. By the First World War, scientific management had become commonplace in American industry.

Combination and Consolidation in Big Business

Along with the increasing complexity and speed which technological innovation brought to American industry, there was a steady movement toward bigness and consolidation. There were obvious advantages of large size in many fields. Savings resulted when the various steps in the manufacturing of a product were combined. Greater size and concentration of capital also created advantages in competition for raw materials and exploitation of markets. There were other reasons for business concentration: high profits could be maintained by curtailing competition, and more stability could be brought into an industry than was possible with wide-open competition.

The railroad pools discussed above constituted one early effort to achieve centralized control over an industry. In the 1870s and 1880s, groups of companies developed a more tightly knit instrument of concentration known as the trust or trustee device. In most instances, the combinations gained dominion over one phase of an industry and thus achieved "horizontal" control. The trust was an unchartered "corporation" that held the stock of the combined companies in trust and managed the new combination through a single set of officers and board of directors. Later, journalists, politicians, and the public at large began to apply the name "trust" to all corporations which enjoyed near monopolistic control of an industry.

The most important of the trusts was the Standard Oil Company. Toward the close of the Civil War, a young commission merchant from Cleveland, John D. Rockefeller, saw the possibilities of the new oil industry, then centered in western Pennsylvania, and set out to become an oil refiner. At that point, over 300 companies were engaged in refining. By 1870, Rockefeller's Standard Oil Company of Ohio controlled more than 90 per cent of the nation's refining industry. Rockefeller achieved this preeminence by adopting careful managerial practices in a generally chaotic industry, by translating efficiency into lower prices, and by ruthlessly suppressing competitors. For a brief time, he possessed a particularly deadly weapon. As the greatest shipper of oil, he was able to force the oil-carrying railroads to charge Standard Oil a rate of 10 cents a barrel, and all other oil companies 35 cents a barrel. In addition, he compelled the railroads to give (rebate) to the Standard Oil Company 25 out of the 35 cents that they had charged its competitors.

The horizontal integration of industries through the trustee device proved to be a temporary phase in the development of modern business. The trust encountered legal difficulties, both as a violation of common-law doctrines against the restraint of trade and as the object of antimonopoly legislation by federal and state governments. *Vertical* integration of industries superseded horizontal integration. In vertical integration, one firm combined mass production and mass distribution and thus administered the flow of goods from raw material, to manufacture, to purchase by the consumer. The organizational structure most commonly used in the drive for vertical integration was the holding company, which allowed one corporation to hold stock in another and thus legally control it.

In the 1880s, vertically integrated firms gained dominance in a few industries, including meat-packing, tobacco, and oil. Rockefeller's Standard Oil became a New Jersey holding company and diversified from refining backward into production of crude oil and forward into distribution. The major depression which hit the country in 1893 slowed combination for a time, but a spurt of vertical integration began as the depression ended in the late 1890s.

None of the efforts at combination was more spectacular than the industrial giant which emerged in steel. By 1890, Andrew Carnegie dominated steel manufacturing and also controlled huge iron ore and coal deposits. By the end of the 1890s, Carnegie threatened to diversify into the production of finished steel goods, an event which would have touched off competitive warfare among the steel companies. At that point, J. Pierpont Morgan, head of the preeminent investment firm in the United States, offered to buy Carnegie's steel interests for nearly half a billion dollars. Carnegie accepted

John D. Rockefeller, a
ruthless fighter with a
passion for perfection.
This painting was
described by the artist
Deferraris as the
"intimate portrait of
Mr. Rockefeller." (Culver
Pictures, Inc.)

the offer and retired to a life of philanthropy. Morgan then combined
Carnegie's properties with several smaller firms to form the United States
Steel Corporation, which controlled 60 per cent of the steel industry of the
United States.

The role of Morgan and other bankers in reorganizing American corporations around the turn of the century led some observers to conclude that
bankers were replacing entrepreneurs as the dominant force in business.
Such a conclusion ignores the increasingly important role of the salaried
managers who actually operated the new firms. Beginning with the railroads,
a hierarchy of professional managers assumed control of American industry.
By the time of the First World War, this new breed of technically trained
managers had come to dominate even high-level policy in most major
corporations. With the ascendancy of the manager and the spread of huge,
vertically integrated corporations, the American economy no longer fitted
Adam Smith's classic description of a system moved by the "invisible hand"
of market forces. To a remarkable extent, those forces were replaced, in one
historian's phrase, by the "visible hand" of the corporate managers.

Business, Government, and the Public

Despite the radical departure from classical capitalism which characterized modern American business, the idea has persisted that the great economic expansion of the late nineteenth century was the exclusive work of heroic captains of industry, with no important role by government. There is just enough truth to this idea to give it the appearance of authenticity. Moreover, the popularity of social Darwinism—the application of Charles Darwin's theories of natural selection to civilized societies—seemed to indicate widespread support for complete laissez faire. Some businessmen discovered that this body of thought supported their belief that governmental interference in economic life was both dangerous and futile because it violated basic economic laws.

In fact, much of the economic development was the result of direct or indirect governmental encouragement. The building of a national railroad network could not have occurred so quickly without massive public assistance to the railroad companies. Liberal land policies and governmental support of silver prices spurred the development of the West. High tariffs stimulated certain industries such as steel, copper, and wool. Federal banking and monetary policies also stimulated the growth of a far-flung financial structure.

Even the Supreme Court played an important role by insisting that railroads and corporations had certain rights which the states had to respect. That tribunal, in Munn v. Illinois (1877), had declared that the right of the states to regulate business enterprise was virtually unlimited. But the court did an about-face in the Wabash case (1886) and related decisions. The court now declared that corporations were persons entitled to protection under the Fourteenth Amendment, and that states could not deprive them of property through regulation without due process of law. These decisions did not forbid the states to regulate railroads and corporations, but they did severely limit their right to do so.

The dominant philosophy of the period was not classical laissez faire. The governing doctrine was partnership between government and business enterprise. To be sure, the federal government did refrain from extensive regulation of business, but this was a deliberate policy with widespread support from people who believed that it would promote economic growth.

2. WORKERS IN INDUSTRIAL AMERICA

The New World of Work

The technological revolution was accompanied by profound changes in the kinds of work performed by Americans and in relationships among working people. At the time of the Civil War, most American workers were engaged in agriculture and perhaps half were self-employed. However, fifty years later, the typical worker was a wage-earning employee engaged in manufacturing or mining.

The new world of work carried with it a host of contradictions. The standard of living for many workers rose dramatically, yet the gap also widened between the "haves" and the "have-nots." A broad range of Americans embraced the idea that material advancement was open to all who were willing to work. Yet the creation of a permanent body of industrial wage earners brought into being a new sense of working-class solidarity. The roots of these contradictions are to be found in both the material conditions of work and in the work-related ideas and values which Americans shared.

The factory system spread unevenly, but relentlessly, across the American landscape in the late nineteenth century. Old ways of working and old ideas about work were pushed aside. The artisan gave way increasingly to the semiskilled machine tender, and the place of work shifted from the craftsman's home or shop to the factory. Increases in productivity, which accompanied the introduction of the factory system, were attributable not only to machinery but also to new work habits and work discipline. For artisans and farmers, work involved alternating periods of intense labor and idleness. This pattern of hard work mixed with recreation was a way of life for many people, and they resisted efforts to change it. But the dictates of factory and machine production required sobriety and, above all, steady attention to work over a fixed period of time. The factory bell, which summoned and dismissed the workers, symbolized the new order in which time replaced the specific task as the measure of work.

The craftsman's detailed knowledge of the processes of production had given him considerable control of the work place, even when he was an employee. But the routinization and division of labor, the perfection of machine tools, and the rise of professional management all eroded traditional patterns of control by workers and foremen. Resistance to this loss of control helped to stimulate the organization of skilled craftsmen in unions in the late nineteenth century.

The evidence is mixed about the well-being of workers in industrializing America. Real wages rose sharply between 1860 and 1890, and the living conditions of American workers were better than those of their European counterparts. However, there was also widespread poverty among industrial workers in some fields. Seasonal layoffs were a fact of life for most workers, and depressions caused widespread unemployment and wage reductions in 1873–1878, 1883–1885, and 1893–1897. Furthermore, safety standards were lax, and workers were presumed to be responsible when accidents occurred. The United States had one of the highest rates of industrial accidents in the world. Finally, living conditions for workers and their families were often grim. Modern conveniences such as public sewer and water systems were slow to penetrate the crowded neighborhoods of the working class, and few could afford the new labor-saving appliances for the home.

Historians often assert that, as manufacturing shifted from home to factory, women withdrew from income-producing work to manage the household. To the extent that such a withdrawal occurred, it was largely a middle-class phenomenon. In many working-class families, the income of the mother was essential for survival. In absolute terms, the number of women in industry actually increased in the late nineteenth century. In addition, a growing number of women worked in "white-collar" jobs such as retail sales and office work, but the largest number of women employed outside the home were in domestic or personal service.

The world of work and the world of family were not so separate for many nineteenth-century Americans as we might imagine. Home place and work place were usually not far distant before the rise of the suburbs. Furthermore, the family unit often served as a source of recruitment and job placement in the days before professionalized personnel management. Families, voluntary associations, and ethnic groups helped to create a supportive environment for industrial workers. The vitality of these institutions both sustained the individual and made more difficult the formation of a self-conscious working class.

In the latter part of the nineteenth century, traditional ideas about work collided with the new reality of factory production. The so-called Protestant work ethic had shaped middle-class thinking about work for generations. By the early nineteenth century, the work ethic in the United States had come to mean that individuals gained worth and freedom through constructive, self-directed toil. The corollary of this idea was that anyone who chose to work hard in America could get ahead.

In reality, American workers were losing their independent status. The very idea of a large permanent class of wage workers engaged in routine machine tending contradicted the American dream of upward mobility. People dealt with this contradiction in a variety of ways. Some simply continued to affirm the idea that hard work was both a virtue and a ticket to advancement. Others added a new twist: success required not only hard work but self-advertisement, aggressiveness, and, as in the case of the novels of Horatio Alger, a measure of luck.

The undermining of workers' independence and the creation of a permanent wage-earning class brought protests from many quarters. In the 1870s and 1880s, a variety of reformers called for the cooperative production and distribution of goods as an alternative to private ownership. Toward the end of the century, similar concerns led some Americans to embrace socialism. Although many of the first American socialists were disciples of Karl Marx, the brand of socialism which predominated in America owed more to Edward Bellamy than to Marx. Bellamy's novel, *Looking Backward* (1888), described the United States in the year 2000, by which time it had become a socialist utopia in which Christian ideals were practiced as well as preached. Bellamy and other non-Marxist radicals made socialism palatable enough to Americans for the Socialist party to become a major political force in the twentieth century.

The Beginnings of Organized Labor

Organized labor in the United States, like business enterprise, was largely local in character until after the Civil War. Local unions of workers in the same craft had existed from the earliest days of the republic. On the other hand, class consciousness developed very slowly among American industrial workers. At first, most of them refused to regard themselves as a separate class apart from the employers and consumers. Hence they concentrated less upon organization for collective bargaining than upon the generalized reform of society. During the 1850s, the first important organization of trade unions occurred primarily to improve wages and the conditions of employment.

Among these were the National Typographical Union and the International Union of Machinists and Blacksmiths.

Labor unions of all kinds increased fourfold during the Civil War and could claim a membership of 200,000 at its end. In 1866, this upsurge culminated in the National Labor Union (NLU), a loose confederation of trade unions, reform associations, labor parties, and even the Marxist International Workingmen's Association. At its peak in about 1869, it enrolled between 200,000 and 400,000—a substantial portion of the industrial work force.

The NLU was momentarily so successful that it attracted a variety of reform movements to its ranks. The reformers, many of whom were also trade unionists, advocated banking and monetary reform, the reconstitution of society through cooperatives, and even the abolition of industrial capitalism as it was then taking shape. The main purpose of the NLU, these reformers believed, was to help to achieve these goals by lobbying and by the education of the working classes. Despite its auspicious beginnings, the NLU began to decline in 1870. Disagreement over politics split the organization. The weakened NLU received a death blow from the depression of 1873–1878.

Extensive working-class organization next occurred in the mid-1880s, and this time the dominant organization was the Knights of Labor. It was first organized in 1869 as a secret society of Philadelphia garment cutters. The Knights survived the depression and reorganized in 1878 with the stated purpose of mobilizing skilled and unskilled workers into one big union for mutual protection. Under the leadership of Terence V. Powderly, the Knights reached a peak of about 700,000 members in 1886. Most persons who joined were wage earners, although the organization also attracted a substantial number of farmers and a small but influential group of self-employed craftsmen and professionals.

The Knights, like the NLU, were not prepared to accept industrial capitalism as a permanent state of affairs. But the Knights suffered the same internal conflict that had plagued the NLU—conflict between long-term, generalized reform and short-term benefits for union members. The Knights also came on the scene at a time of intense antiunion sentiment. The Knights of Labor collapsed as quickly as it had sprung up. By the early 1890s, it had shrunk to a fraction of its former strength.

The organization which would eventually succeed in permanently organizing large numbers of workers was the American Federation of Labor (AFL). It was formed in 1886 by Adolph Strasser and Samuel Gompers of the Cigar Makers' Union. Gompers, elected president of the AFL every year but one from 1886 until his death in 1924, had long opposed the general reform wing of the labor movement. The AFL, which consisted largely of workers in the skilled trades, refused to take an active role in politics during the early years of his leadership.

The AFL focused, instead, on higher wages, shorter hours, job security, the protection of women and children against exploitation and overwork, recognition of the legality of labor unions by legislatures and courts, and, above all, the right to bargain with employers, through strikes if need be. Since it focused on these bread-and-butter issues, the AFL conceded the permanence of the wage-labor system and cut the ties between trade unionism and intellectual and middle-class reformers.

At the turn of the century, neither the AFL's preeminent position within the labor movement nor its overwhelming commitment to business union-ism was self-evident. The craft unions which made up the AFL enrolled fewer than 5 per cent of all wage earners and had failed to make inroads among the semiskilled workers of the new mass-production industries. Furthermore, members of many constituent unions rejected Gompers' disavowal of working-class politics.

However, unlike the earlier national groups, the AFL survived, and by 1914 it spoke for a substantial proportion of the skilled workers in the United States. In the early years of the twentieth century, the AFL modified its stand on political activism. Unlike the general reformism of earlier labor politics, the AFL's political goals were narrowly focused on obtaining amendments to the Sherman Antitrust Act to exempt labor unions from that law's restraints.

The AFL's brand of bread-and-butter unionism did not completely domi-nate organized labor in the first years of the twentieth century. In 1905, a small group of socialists and labor radicals formed the Industrial Workers of the World (IWW). The "Wobblies," as they were called, rejected the AFL's conservative, craft-oriented approach and set out to organize the mass of unskilled workers in manufacturing, mining, and agriculture. The IWW never gained a mass following, but between 1905 and 1917 the headline-grabbing rhetoric of its militant leaders and their knack for appearing wherever violent strikes broke out, made the small, faction-ridden group appear to threaten public safety.

Violence in Labor-Management Relations

From the 1870s to the turn of the century and beyond, the industrializing process was accompanied by brutal conflict between workers and owners. It ranged from spontaneous and isolated outbursts to massive urban rioting, such as occurred during the railroad strike of 1877; pitched battles between workers and private armies employed by managers, such as took place during the strike against Andrew Carnegie's Homestead plant in 1892; and large-scale boycotts, such as happened during the Pullman strike of 1894.

The Pullman strike and boycott revealed the extent to which, by the 1890s, large corporations had both the will and the power to break strikes and unions. The Pullman Palace Car Company, manufacturer of railroad sleeping cars, cut wages for its workers five times within a year without lowering rents on company-owned houses. The new American Railway Union (ARU), led by Eugene V. Debs, supported the Pullman workers and launched a boycott against all trains which pulled Pullman cars. Rail traffic in the Midwest ground to a halt. With support from Attorney General Richard Olney, a former railroad lawyer, the railroads won a federal court injunction which forbade the ARU and Debs to interfere with the shipment of United States mail. When the boycott continued despite the injunction, President Grover Cleveland sent 2,000 troops to Chicago. When the troops arrived on July 4, Debs appealed for order, but some of the strikers ditched trains and looted and burned buildings. Soldiers killed twelve of the rioters. In effect, the Cleveland administration broke the strike, while the federal court in Chicago sent Debs to jail for violating its injunction. The experience converted Debs to socialism.

With very few exceptions, the outbreaks of violence were not the work of

The Homestead Strike, July 1892. Strikers at Carnegie's Homestead steel plant fired upon barges carrying 300 Pinkerton detectives. (Library of Congress)

organized terrorists or revolutionaries, nor were they necessarily touched off by ruthless businessmen eager to stifle the aspirations of labor. Yet violent confrontation between workers and managers was commonplace between the 1870s and the 1890s. Workers, faced with an adversary organized on a national scale and backed by massive resources, including, at times, the authority of government, took to the streets in a wave of violent outbursts. To many contemporary observers, these actions seemed to threaten the very social fabric of the republic.

3. THE SOUTH AND THE WEST IN THE AGE OF INDUSTRIALIZATION

The New South

Despite appeals for industrialization, the South's economy remained predominantly agricultural and its people overwhelmingly rural. The war swept away slavery, but not its companion, the plantation. Cotton plantations, which had formerly been operated by slaves working in gangs, were "divided" into small plots worked by families of former slaves, who now became sharecroppers for the plantation owners. The sharecropping system —based on a division of the crop between the owner and the tiller of the land—enabled plantation owners to maintain considerable economic and social control. The large number of former slaves who became enmeshed in the sharecropping system found that it left them facing a life of grinding poverty with little hope of material improvement.

The agricultural transformation which white small farmers faced began differently from that of the former slaves, but sometimes ended the same way. The small farmers had been less dependent than the planters on cash crops before the Civil War. Instead, they had concentrated on food crops for their own subsistence. But, after the war, many gambled on lifting themselves above bare subsistence through concentration on cotton. As cotton prices dropped in the 1880s, however, many small farmers lost their land and sank into the tenant class.

In the early 1880s, Henry W. Grady, editor of the Atlanta *Constitution*, told the story of a Georgia farmer who had been recently laid to rest. Even though the land around the cemetery was rich in natural resources, the burial clothes, coffin, coffin nails, and tombstone had been manufactured outside the South. "The South," remarked Grady, "didn't furnish a thing on earth for that funeral but the corpse and the hold in the ground." The point of Grady's story, and others like it, was that Southerners should pull themselves and their region out of poverty through industrialization.

In fact, manufacturing was not unknown in the Old South. Modest textile and iron factories had flourished for decades, and, during the Civil War, Southerners even established government-owned factories to arm the Confederacy. However, much of the South's manufacturing capacity and railroad network were destroyed during the war. Beginning around 1880, new cotton mills and tobacco and furniture factories sprang up, often backed by local capital. By the end of the century, advocates of an industrialized New South were citing all manner of statistics to show that their goal was being achieved. But, despite a substantial increase in the amount of manufactures, the South's share of the nation's total remained virtually unchanged from 1860 at about 10.5 per cent.

The New West

After the Civil War, the almost unexplored area between the midwestern prairies and the Pacific Coast offered obvious opportunities for development. In 1860, the frontier was an irregular line extending from western Minnesota to the Gulf of Mexico. Beyond lay an empire still largely uninhabited by Anglo-Americans except for settlements in New Mexico, Utah, and on the Pacific Coast.

It was an empire not only dazzling in size and scenic splendor but also immensely varied in soil and other natural resources. There were several different kinds of frontiers, not all of them agricultural. Beneath the soil lay some of the earth's greatest deposits of copper, petroleum, and other resources. These could be brought to the industrial centers of the East on the same trains that carried cattle and corn.

The Homestead Act and cheap land sales by the railroads spurred the settlement of the western part of the prairies between the Civil War and the early 1870s. Meanwhile, a new frontier—the Cattle Kingdom on the Great Plains—had come into being. It started in Texas just before the Civil War, when cowboys rounded up the numerous wild Texas longhorns and stockmen began to domesticate them. Texans rounded up a herd of some 26,000 in 1866 and drove them to rail terminals in Missouri and Kansas. These cattle, after fattening, were sold to packers and shippers for the eastern market.

Cattle raising and herding was a booming business from Texas northward into Canada during the 1870s and early 1880s. But a combination of severe winters, droughts, and low prices struck the cattlemen in the mid-1880s. Worse still for them, farmers and sheep raisers began to encroach upon the open range. Bitter feuds and range wars broke out as cattlemen fought against those who settled on the range. Meanwhile, the cowboy had become firmly embedded in American legend and song. At one point, at least, the legendary cowboy departs from reality. Unlike the movie and advertising versions, about one fourth of the real-life cowboys were black.

The Great Plains, which include most of the area in western Kansas, Nebraska, Oklahoma, and the Dakotas, are treeless, windswept, and subject to extremes of heat and cold. The soil is so tough that it breaks wooden or iron plowshares. Yet the pressure on the agricultural frontier was so great in the early 1870s that farmers began to move into this inhospitable region.

What really made agriculture possible on the Plains were the steel plow, barbed wire, and the windmill. The steel plow proved ideally suited to the hard soil of the Plains. Barbed wire, first produced about 1875, made an excellent substitute for wooden and stone fences. Windmills, which could pump water from great depths, came into general use in the 1870s.

An unusual amount of rainfall and relatively good prices for wheat and corn encouraged such rapid settlement that the Plains area underwent something of a boom in the 1870s and 1880s. Nebraska, for example, grew in population from 123,000 in 1870 to 1,063,000 in 1890. After he surveyed the results of the Census of 1890, the Superintendent of the Census wrote: "Up to and including 1880 the country had a frontier of settlement, but at present the unsettled area has been so broken into by isolated bodies of settlement that there can hardly be said to be a frontier line." As matters turned out, the announcement of the death of the frontier was somewhat premature. A frontier line beyond which there were virtually no white inhabitants was of course gone, but vast quantities of free or very cheap land remained.

Next to farming, mining was the most important industry of the New West. The California gold rush was only the first of many western rushes, which drew some 200,000 persons into the West between the 1850s and 1880. Large-scale mining began when gold was discovered in the Pike's Peak district of Colorado in 1858. Before the end of the Civil War, Colorado had already sent more than $10 million in gold to the United States mint. Nevada was probably even richer in mineral wealth. The Comstock Lode at Virginia City was yielding $20 million worth of silver annually by the early 1860s. Gold was discovered in the Black Hills of the Dakota Territory, which set off another rush. California, Colorado, and Nevada produced 90 per cent of the country's gold and 73.5 per cent of its silver in 1880. By that time, the West also produced most of the nation's copper and a growing proportion of its iron ore.

Assaults on Western Indian and Mexican-American Lands and Cultures

The advancing tides of cattlemen, farmers, and miners doomed the independence of the great Indian tribes which roamed the Plains and inhabited the mountains. Between 1862 and 1890, Indians and whites clashed in a series of bloody confrontations, most of them triggered by the steady encroachment of white settlement. The worst outbreak occurred in 1876. The Sioux, outraged by the movement of whites into the Black Hills area of Dakota, which had been set apart "forever" as part of the Sioux domain, left their reservation, and it required a long and bloody campaign by the army to drive them back. The largest battle occurred at the Little Big Horn River in what is now Montana on June 25, 1876. General George A. Custer and his entire force of 264 men were wiped out when Custer recklessly attacked a huge force of Sioux under Chief Sitting Bull. However, the campaign ended, as did all the others, with the defeat of the outgunned Indians.

Still, the Indians' final defeat was caused less by military conquest than by

Indian Reservations in the West, 1890

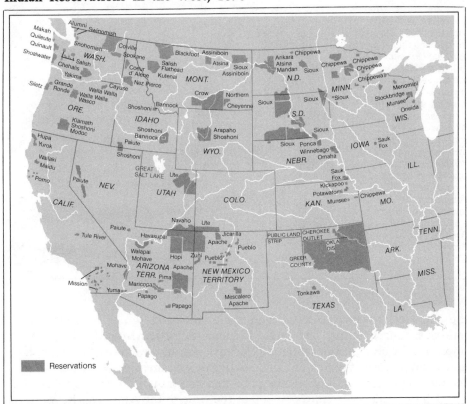

Reservations

Portrait of Red Cloud (c. 1822–1909), chief of the Oglala Sioux. A celebrated warrior who took eighty coups, Red Cloud was one of the few Indian leaders to score military victories against the U.S. Army. Asked to sign a treaty in 1865 to allow passage through Indian lands, Red Cloud refused. When forts were built along the trail, the Sioux and Cheyenne allies cut off supplies and forced the army to abandon all of the posts in the Powder River country by 1868. Red Cloud became an eminent and forceful statesman from the time of his first visit to Washington in 1870. Thereafter his life was spent in pursuit of peace and preservation of Indian values. If you wish to possess the whiteman's things, he cautioned his people, "you must begin anew and put away the wisdom of your fathers. You must lay up food and forget the hungry. When your house is built, your storeroom filled, then look around for a neighbor whom you can take advantage of and seize all he has." (Smithsonian Institutuion National Anthropological Archives, Bureau of American Ethnology Collection)

the relentless advance of European-style civilization, which brought with it railroads, fenced farms, and large, permanent settlements of whites. Most important, it brought the systematic destruction of the life-sustaining buffalo herds and diseases such as cholera, smallpox, and measles, which decimated the Indian population. The number of American Indians dwindled to a low of 220,000 in 1910, down from 600,000 at the time of the American Revolution.

Many of the surviving western Indians were herded into reservations and stripped of all but nominal tribal independence.

By the 1880s, humanitarian and religious concern over the plight of the Indians was gaining momentum in the East. Unfortunately, the plans of well-meaning reformers coincided with the persistent efforts of persons hungry for still more Indian land. Consequently, a series of governmental measures adopted in the 1880s almost eradicated Indian culture and tribal life. Missionaries and governmental agents pressed Indians to embrace Christianity and integrate into the American agricultural economy. In 1884, Congress actually authorized the suppression of Indian religions on the Sioux, Ute, and Shoshone reservations, and governmental agents worked to stamp out Indian languages and culture.

Reformers argued that, for their own benefit, Indians should forsake tribal living in favor of individual assimilation. Congress debated this issue for years; finally, in 1887, it passed the Dawes Severalty Act, which provided that tribal lands should be divided into family homesteads of 160 acres. Indians who accepted the homesteads would be given American citizenship. Ominously, the law provided that "surplus" tribal lands not allocated to Indians could be sold to whites. Before the allotment program was ended in 1934, Indians had lost 90,000,000 of the 138,000,000 acres which had comprised the reservations in 1887.

The loss of Indian land was tragically duplicated in the case of many Mexican Americans in the Southwest. The Treaty of Guadalupe Hidalgo, which ended the Mexican War in 1848, brought some 78,000 Mexican citizens under the American flag, supposedly with full rights of American

A migratory labor camp in the Salt River Valley, Arizona, in the 1890s. (Los Angeles County Musuem)

citizenship and protection for their land titles. In California, home of 11,000 of these new American citizens, a small Mexican elite *(Californios)* dominated both the land and the government. But with the discovery of gold in 1848 and the subsequent realization of California's agricultural riches, Anglo squatters began challenging the land titles of the *Californio* ranchers. Biased arbitration boards and even less objective vigilantes forced many Mexican Americans off their land. By 1880, they had lost their dominant position in landholding.

In Texas, where Mexican Americans had come under Anglo control following the revolution of 1836, relations between Anglo-American Protestants and Mexican-American Catholics were even more hostile than in California. In predominantly Mexican-American areas of southern Texas, land hunger triggered confrontations between the two groups. In Texas, as elsewhere in the Southwest, Mexican Americans resisted forcibly the takeover of their property, most often through guerrilla-style banditry.

Prior to 1900, most of the 300,000 Mexican Americans were descendants of people living in the Southwest before its annexation by the United States. By the turn of the century, loss of land, the breakup of traditional patterns of land tenure, and the curtailment of political and civil rights had reduced southwestern Mexican Americans to the status of a subservient underclass and had eroded their own cultural values, which, like those of the Indians, had stressed the solidarity of the community and the extended family.

SUGGESTED READINGS

Two general studies of the industrial era are John A. Garraty, *The New Commonwealth, 1877–1890* (1968), and Edward C. Kirkland, *Industry Comes of Age* (1961). Alfred D. Chandler, Jr., *The Visible Hand: The Managerial Revolution in American Business* (1977), assesses the development of modern business organizaion. George R. Taylor and Irene Neu, *The American Railroad Network, 1861–1890* (1956), and John F. Stover, *The Life and Decline of the American Railroad* (1970), are useful surveys.

On Carnegie and the steel industry, see Joseph F. Wall, *Andrew Carnegie* (1970). Conflicting views of Rockefeller are to be found in Allan Nevins, *Study in Power: John D. Rockefeller*, 2 vols. (1953), and Ralph W. Hidy and M. E. Hidy, *Pioneering in Big Business, 1882–1911* (1955). On technological innovation in general, see Nathan Rosenberg, *Technology and American Economic Growth* (1972).

Attitudes toward business and economic development are discussed in Sidney Fine, *Laissez Faire and the General Welfare State* (1964), and Daniel T. Rodgers, *The Work Ethic in Industrializing America, 1850–1920*

(1978). The problem of monopoly can be viewed in the writings of contemporary social critics cited in the text. Attempts at federal regulation of the railroads can be traced in Ari Hoogenboom and Olive Hoogenboom, *A History of the ICC* (1976).

On industrial workers, see Melvyn Dubofsky, *Industrialism and the American Worker, 1865–1920* (1975), and David Montgomery, *Beyond Equality* (1967). Edith Abbott, *Women in Industry* (1910), remains a valuable introduction. Two autobiographies worth consulting are Terence V. Powderly, *Thirty Years of Labor* (1889), and Samuel Gompers, *Seventy Years of Life and Labor*, 2 vols. (1925).

The standard account of the post-Reconstruction South remains C. Vann Woodward, *Origins of the New South, 1877–1913* (1951). In addition to the surveys of western history previously cited, see Howard R. Lamar, *The Far Southwest, 1846–1912* (1966). Fred A. Shannon, *The Farmer's Last Frontier, 1860–1897* (1945), is a good survey of the agricultural problems of the period, but it should be supplemented by Gilbert C. Fite, *The Farmer's Frontier, 1865–1900* (1966).

CHAPTER 19
NATIONAL POLITICS IN THE AGE OF INDUSTRIALIZATION

1. POLITICS IN THE GILDED AGE

The Hayes Administration

The period following Reconstruction has been called the Gilded Age, largely because of the crass materialism common to the new class of wealthy businessmen. Some historians have said that political leaders of the Gilded Age reflected the businessman's materialism, fought sham battles in the political arena, and showed little wisdom in helping to solve new social problems. These assertions are somewhat overdrawn. It is true that politicians failed to devise a constructive program to meet the problems caused by drastic social and economic change. But their failures were not due altogether to lack of effort or intelligence. Change simply came too fast. People with a political philosophy suited to the needs of an earlier, simpler society proved unable to answer the challenges of a new industrial age.

The first of these post-Reconstruction leaders, Rutherford B. Hayes, entered the White House without enthusiastic support, even within his own party. He had been nominated in 1876 only because the supporters of Grant and Blaine were hopelessly deadlocked. Democratic newspapers charged that he had stolen the election from Tilden, and the Democratic House of Representatives threatened to investigate his title to the presidency.

Hayes' most difficult problem in office was dealing with the rising popular demand for increased currency through the free coinage of silver. The Resumption

Rutherford B. Hayes, a temperate and cautious man, restored respectability and degnity to the presidency after the corruption of the Grant administration. Thoroughly uncomfortable in the high office, Hayes write in 1879: "I am heartily tires of this life of bondage, responsibility, and toil." (Library of Congress)

Act of 1875 made greenbacks redeemable in gold on January 1, 1879. The desire for a larger money supply led debtors and Westerners to demand a return to the free and unlimited coinage of silver.

By 1873, the price of silver had increased so much in relation to gold that silver miners preferred to sell their metal on the open market rather than to bring it to the mints for exchange at the official ratio. Few paid much attention, therefore, when Congress, in the Coinage Act of 1873, provided that the government should no longer buy and coin silver. But, by 1877, rising output of silver from the West had caused its price to drop. Mine owners demanded that the government take it all at the old ratio of sixteen to one. They called the demonetization of silver "the crime of 1873" and were joined in their demands by farmers and debtors. The latter now saw in silver a vehicle for the expansion of the money supply much more respectable than greenbacks.

Richard P. ("Silver Dick") Bland of Missouri thereupon introduced a bill into the House in December 1876 which provided for the unlimited coinage of silver at the ratio of sixteen to one. The Senate passed a version of his bill, modified by William B. Allison of Iowa, which stipulated that the Treasury should purchase and coin from $2 million to $4 million in silver a month. Approved by both houses in 1878 and passed over Hayes' veto, the Bland-Allison Act only partially satisfied the popular demand for a large money supply.

The other major issue confronting Hayes was reform of the civil service, that great army of officials and clerks who worked for the government. It had been the custom, especially since Andrew Jackson's day, to give these

This illustration from Frank Leslie's Illustrated Newspaper
(1877) shows office-seekers in the lobby of the White House
awaiting an interview with President Hayes. It was Hayes who
later advocated abolishment of the spoils system and encouraged
civil service reform. (Library of Congress)

positions to faithful party workers. Abolition of the "spoils system" was the
first great national reform movement of the postwar era. A large body of
thoughtful people, including influential editors, pleaded for modernization.
Under their pressure, Congress in 1871 authorized President Grant to
appoint a Civil Service Commission. But the commission could do little in
the face of opposition from the Stalwart faction of the Republican party.

Hayes' immediate task was to clean up the corruption left by the Grant
administration. The new President appointed the civil-service reformer, Carl
Schurz, as Secretary of the Interior and supported him in thoroughgoing
reforms in his department. He removed two leading Stalwarts, Chester A.
Arthur and Alonzo B. Cornell, from positions in the New York customs-
house. They had been using their office to build up Senator Roscoe
Conkling's state Republican machine. Although Hayes was unable to obtain
civil-service legislation from Congress, his efforts for reform aroused widespread interest and sympathy.

The Election of 1880 and the Triumph of Civil-Service Reform

Hayes had given the country an honest administration, which was more than
Americans had come to expect; but he had declared that he would not accept

a second term. Furthermore, his alienation from the Republican professionals would have made his renomination difficult, if not impossible, to accomplish. Thus the Republican field was wide open for other presidential hopefuls.

One was none other than former President Grant, who had returned in 1879 from a trip around the world. Another contender was James G. Blaine, senator from Maine. At the Republican national convention, Grant and Blaine ran neck and neck for thirty-five ballots. Then the deadlock was broken by the selection of a dark horse, James A. Garfield of Ohio. To appease the Stalwarts, the convention nominated Chester A. Arthur for Vice-President.

The campaign which followed was not notably exciting. The Democrats nominated General Winfield S. Hancock, a lackluster candidate, and the Democratic platform differed from the Republican only in that it demanded substantial reductions in the tariff. Furthermore, what had promised to be an important development—the entry into the presidential race of the Greenback-Labor party—turned out to be of minor consequence. In 1878, the new Greenback party had elected fourteen members of Congress. But the adoption of the Bland-Allison Act and substantial recovery from the Panic of 1873 deprived the Greenbackers of their issues and greatly reduced the potential vote for their presidential candidate, James B. Weaver.

The election of 1880, dull though it may have been, revealed four important facts about American national politics at this juncture. First, the issues of Reconstruction were dead, and most Americans had reverted to traditional voting habits. Second, Republicans and Democrats were almost evenly balanced. Garfield won the election but received a minority of the popular vote, and his plurality over Hancock was only about 40,000 out of the nearly 9,000,000 votes cast for both men. Third, the return of white Southerners to power in their states had resulted in the creation of a "Solid South" committed to the Democratic party. Fourth, Weaver's success in winning more than 300,000 votes revealed that agrarian discontent still survived, particularly in the Middle West.

The election of Garfield brought no peace to the faction-torn GOP. Stalwarts such as Conkling had done much to secure his election, but Garfield refused to fulfill the promises which, they claimed, he had made to them, during the campaign. The President appointed Conkling's chief rival, Blaine, as Secretary of State and removed the Collector of the Port of New York to make a place for one of Blaine's friends.

On July 2, 1881, Garfield was shot in the Washington railroad station by a demented office seeker, Charles J. Guiteau, who boasted, "I am a Stalwart and Arthur is President now." Garfield died on September 19. To friends of good government, "Chet" Arthur's elevation to the presidency seemed to be the worst thing that could have happened. They feared that this former companion of bosses and spoilsmen might wink at graft and corruption. Yet Arthur rose to the responsibilities of his office and gave the country a vigorous and efficient administration.

Arthur tried to prevent congressional raids on the Treasury by vetoing bills which appropriated huge sums for small harbors and unnavigable rivers. With congressional approval, he appointed a Tariff Commission in 1882 to investigate and recommend new rates. Congress reduced rates slightly in

1883 in response to its suggestions. Arthur also laid the foundation of the modern American navy by undertaking the construction of steel cruisers to replace rotting wooden ships. Finally, he signed the act that has been called the "Magna Carta of Civil Service Reform."

Garfield's assassination shocked the American people into support for a cleanup in the civil service. Arthur took up the cause with vigor, and Congress responded by approving the measure introduced by Senator George H. Pendleton of Ohio. It provided for a bipartisan Civil Service Commission to classify the grades of the civil service and a merit system to select candidates. The bill also forbade political assessments against federal employees. Both houses of Congress passed the bill by large majorities, and Arthur signed it on January 16, 1883. Arthur immediately put about 15,000 federal employees into the classified service and continued his program of reform. By 1900, the professionalization of the federal civil service was substantially complete.

The Democrats Return to Power

Arthur, unlike Hayes, was eager for renomination, but the Republican national convention nominated Blaine on the fourth ballot. The smoothness of Blaine's nomination was deceptive. A sizable group of independent Republicans, called Mugwumps, did not like Blaine's shady railroad deals or his opposition to civil-service reform. The Mugwumps had no candidate to put up against Blaine, but they invited the Democrats to nominate a candidate for whom citizens could vote without being ashamed of themselves.

The Democrats replied by nominating Grover Cleveland, governor of New York. Cleveland was a self-made man who had worked his way up to be elected mayor of Buffalo in 1881. His administration of the office was so honest, able, and courageous that it brought him the Democratic nomination for governor the next year. As governor, he was fearless in dealing with corrupt machine politicians.

The presidential campaign of 1884 was one of the bitterest political contests in American history. Blaine was pictured as a scoundrel who had enriched himself by accepting bribes from railroad promoters. Cleveland was called a drunkard and accused of having fathered an illegitimate child, a charge which he refused to deny, apparently because it was true.

The election on November 4 was so close that it turned on the key state of New York, which Cleveland narrowly won. The final returns gave 4,880,000 popular and 219 electoral votes to Cleveland and 4,850,000 popular and 182 electoral votes to Blaine.

Grover Cleveland was not a dynamic leader, but he compensated for his lack of forcefulness by his honesty and courage. He also was deeply devoted to political principles. On the other hand, Cleveland ended his career as one of the worst failures in American political history. He did not grow into a national leader concerned about the problems and welfare of all the people. He had absorbed his ideals from the upper middle class of the East—honesty in government but no governmental support for special groups, even the underprivileged. Cleveland was totally unable to respond when southern and western elements in his party demanded legislation to help farmers and

Grover Cleveland earned distinction as a President in his fight for tariff reform. He attacked high rates as "the vicious, inequitable, and illogical source of unnecessary taxation." (Library of Congress)

workers in the dismal 1890s. Here, as elsewhere, his rigid dogmatism prevented him from recognizing that politics usually runs on compromise.

During his first administration, Cleveland faced four great tasks. First, he had to demonstrate that the Democratic party, out of power since 1861, was capable of governing the country. Second, he had to preside over the return of Southerners to national councils, without raising the specter of southern domination. Third, he had to complete the work of civil-service reform begun by his predecessors. Fourth, he had to formulate a national program for the Democratic party. Cleveland attacked these problems vigorously, but with limited success.

Cleveland believed that the time had come to bury the hatreds of the Civil War. Moreover, as the leader of a party with its greatest strength in the South, he had no choice but to welcome Southerners back into "the house of their fathers." Hence Cleveland appointed two Southerners to his cabinet and one to the Supreme Court. For this policy of fairness to all sections, he was attacked as a friend of "rebels."

Cleveland wanted very much to extend the reform of the civil service. However, his party had been deprived of the spoils for a quarter of a century and thirsted for offices. Even so, Cleveland strongly supported the work of the Civil Service Commission.

Another problem was the burgeoning of expenditures for pensions to Union veterans, which had increased from $15 million in 1866 to $56 million in 1885. There was also an immense amount of fraud in the system. More than 700 private bills for pensions to individuals were passed in Cleveland's administration, and he insisted on examining each one of them. Personal inspection of those bills led him to veto 233 of them.

Cleveland wanted above all to reform the revenue system. Because of thriving foreign trade and the high protective tariff, surplus funds were piling up in the Treasury at the rate of about $100 million a year. Hence, the tariff was the point of Cleveland's attack. It was the largest source of the government's income, since there was, as yet, no income tax; it was, he claimed, an outright subsidy to manufacturers. Manufacturers replied that the high tariff made high wages possible. Cleveland insisted that it was more to the point that the high tariff made high prices possible. Not until July 1888 was Cleveland able to get the Mills bill for tariff reduction through the House of Representatives. However, the Republican Senate not only defeated the Mills bill but also adopted a new protective tariff bill of its own. This impasse between the two houses insured that the tariff would be the single major issue of the presidential campaign just ahead.

Ironically, Cleveland played very little part in the enactment of the one really consequential measure of his first term—the Interstate Commerce Act of 1887. The act was the result, first, of a growing popular demand for national regulation of the railroads. The failure of midwestern state legislation of the 1870s made it crystal clear that Congress alone was competent to deal with the problem. That conclusion was confirmed by the Supreme Court's decision in the Wabash case of 1886, which declared that state authorities had no jurisdiction over interstate rates and services. The Interstate Commerce Act was also the product of the desire of some railroad managers for an end to competitive practices which kept rates unstable and reduced profits.

Senator Shelby M. Cullom, Republican of Illinois and chairman of a special committee on railroads, led the movement for national legislation. The result of the committee's labor was the Interstate Commerce Act, approved on February 4, 1887. The measure created an Interstate Commerce Commission of five members to enforce the law. The act forbade rebates and other favors to powerful shippers and stipulated that freight rates should be charged in proportion to distance and should not be raised for short hauls on which no competition existed. It also outlawed pooling.

The huge majorities by which the Interstate Commerce bill was approved by both houses of Congress revealed that leaders in Washington were beginnning to recognize the problems of the new industrial age, but those comfortable margins also raised questions about just how radical the new departure was. This was the first act of Congress to attempt to regulate a major industry. It created the first of many federal commissions and agencies which have since been established to deal with economic questions raised by the nation's changing and expanding economy.

Harrison, the Antitrust Law, and the McKinley Tariff

In 1888, at the suggestion of the ailing Blaine, the Republicans nominated Benjamin Harrison of Indiana for President. Harrison was a former senator and a grandson of President William Henry Harrison. The Democrats renominated Cleveland. The campaign was waged almost wholly on the tariff issue. The Republicans concentrated their efforts on the two doubtful states of Indiana and New York, both of which had gone to Cleveland in 1884. These two states (the only ones which shifted their votes of four years earlier) were enough to give the victory to Harrison. Cleveland led in popular votes, however, by nearly 100,000.

Benjamin Harrison took a very limited view of the presidential function. The chief executive, he thought, should carry out laws that Congress might enact, not give leadership to public opinion or to the lawmakers on Capitol Hill. Much of the leadership of the government therefore fell to the forceful new Speaker of the House of Representatives, Thomas B. Reed of Maine. Reed was determined not to let the Democrats block the business of the House. The election of 1888 had given the Republicans narrow majorities in both houses of Congress. Tight party discipline enabled them to reverse some of Cleveland's policies and to enact new tariff legislation. In addition, bipartisan coalitions produced new laws to deal with two of the most important economic issues of the day.

Harrison and Congress were both bountiful toward veterans. Harrison's Commissioner of Pensions, "Corporal" James Tanner, welcomed applications and shouted, "God help the surplus!" Outlays for pensions increased from $81 million in 1889 to $135 million in 1891. This was a sum greater than the combined cost of the army and navy in any year of peace in the nineteenth century. The expenditures of the Fifty-first Congress totaled $1 billion. When the Democrats cried out against this "billion-dollar Congress," Reed replied that this was a "billion-dollar country."

The most important problem which the Harrison administration faced was an overwhelming public demand for federal legislation to curb monopoly. There was a rising public fear that trusts were stifling competition and overcharging for their products. Henry George had attacked the tremendous inequality of wealth in the United States in his influential *Progress and Poverty* in 1879. Henry Demarest Lloyd's "The Story of a Great Monopoly" appeared two years later in the *Atlantic Monthly*. It was a scathing exposure of the Standard Oil Company. Other investigations added to the alarm. Owners of small businesses cried out for protection against big business. In response, twenty-seven states and territories had outlawed trusts by 1890. But this did not quiet the public demand, since the problem was national in scope.

The Republican party was not eager to act against the trusts. However, popular agitation had reached such a high pitch by 1888 that both major parties incorporated antitrust planks in their platforms. In 1890, Congress adopted the Sherman Antitrust Act, one of the most important pieces of legislation in American history. It declared that "every contract, combination . . . or conspiracy in restraint of trade" was illegal. The language of the Sherman Act was sweeping, but the law remained a dead letter for the next dozen years, mainly because Harrison and his two successors did not enforce it.

But the McKinley Tariff Act, adopted in the same year as the Sherman Act, was legislation much more to the GOP's liking. In April 1890, William McKinley of Ohio, chairman of the House Ways and Means Committee, introduced a bill which increased duties on almost every import that competed with American products. McKinley boasted that his bill was "protective in every paragraph and American in every line and word."

Although the McKinley bill had fairly smooth sailing in the House, it was a different story when the measure reached the Senate. Senators from the West and South threatened to block passage of the bill if the Republicans did not alter their stand on legislation considered vital to the political interests of those regions. Republican senators from the Far West demanded something for silver before they would support the McKinley tariff. Next, southern senators wanted to head off a Republican attempt to protect black voters in the southern states. On July 2, 1890, the House of Representatives passed a federal election bill. It stipulated that supervisors from Washington should have the right to inspect and verify the votes cast in federal elections. When the southern senators joined the Westerners to block the McKinley bill, the Republicans dropped the federal election bill.

The deadlock continued because the western silver senators would not vote for the tariff until their demands for free coinage of silver had been satisfied. Despite adoption of the Bland-Allison Act of 1878, the price of the metal had steadily declined, largely because of immense production from the recently opened mines.

Although Republicans wanted very much to avoid free silver, they were even more eager to find the votes necessary to pass the McKinley bill. Therefore a compromise was reached which resulted in the Sherman Silver Purchase Act, approved July 4, 1890. It required the Treasury to purchase 4,500,000 ounces of silver a month at prevailing prices. In addition, the act provided for the issuance of a new currency—silver certificates—to pay for the silver purchased. The Sherman Silver Purchase Act was enough to win western votes for the McKinley tariff bill, and they insured its enactment.

Democrats had a heyday during the mid-term campaign of 1890. They pointed to the extravagance of the billion-dollar Congress and the "tyranny" of "Czar" Reed. Democrats had the most fun, however, attacking the McKinley tariff, which they predicted would cause prices to rise and wreck the American economy. The returns of the congressional elections in November 1890 were a landslide against the GOP. The Democrats controlled the House, 235 to eighty-eight, but the Republicans narrowly retained control of the Senate. The Congress was deadlocked again, and no significant legislation would be forthcoming during the next two years.

2. POLITICAL UPHEAVALS OF THE 1890s

The Agrarian Revolt

During the 1890s, two distinct but interrelated challenges to the prevailing party system sent shock waves through the American society. First, the decades-old struggle of farmers for economic and political well-being culminated in the formation of the Populist party. Second, the rough equilibrium which had existed between Democrats and Republicans for forty years collapsed in a realignment of the two-party system.

A storm was brewing in the South and West in the late 1880s. Farmers assembled to discuss common problems and the means to solve them. Their spokesmen charged that railroad managers, bankers, and businessmen had conspired to keep farmers' costs high and farm prices low. Farm leaders accused both parties of serving as agents of Wall Street.

A complex set of economic problems set off the agrarian revolt. Fundamentally, almost every sector of the economy was caught in a system of fierce international competition which drove prices steadily downward from about 1867 to 1897. Prices of American agricultural products fell close to and even below the cost of production.

Everywhere, farmers with debts found them difficult to pay. Westerners who had borrowed money to expand production were obliged in the subsequent era of declining prices to increase their indebtedness. In the South, the crop-lien system bound many farmers to an annual cycle of indebtedness. Merchants advanced supplies in return for a lien on the crop to be produced by the farmer. Annual interest rates under this system ran to 25 per cent or higher. Within the crop year, prices were further depressed by the seasonal glut on the market at harvest time.

In the West, even the weather seemed to conspire against farmers during this troubled period. Exceptionally abundant rain in the middle 1880s tempted farmers to move into the Great Plains. But the entire Plains area was plunged into depression and despair by droughts that began in the summer of 1886.

With some justification, farmers believed that state and federal officeholders had neglected them in favor of bankers, railroad promoters, and industrialists. Farmers, once economically self-sufficient, had now lost both economic independence and political power to the new business class.

The farmers' movement which culminated in the organization of the Populist party in 1892 owed a great intellectual debt to the greenback, antimonopoly, and cooperative traditions (see Chapters 17 and 18). As an institution, however, the Populist party sprang from a series of farmer organizations which began with the Patrons of Husbandry, commonly known as the Grange. The Grange was organized in 1867. As part of their program of self-help, the Grangers established cooperative stores and marketing agencies, which usually required cash payment for goods. This requirement limited access to farmers who were relatively well off. However, by 1875 the Grange claimed over 500,000 members.

The sharp decline of farm prices, which began with the Panic of 1873, coupled with discriminatory freight rates, led Grangers to demand governmental assistance. They entered politics both as an interest group within the major parties and as participants in splinter parties. Beginning in 1870, Grangers gained influence in several midwestern and southern state legislatures. They instituted state regulation of railroads and in other ways fostered the interests of farmers. The failure of many Grange cooperatives in the mid-1870s, coupled with internal dissension over political activism, led to a sharp decline in membership.

The successor to the Grange—the Farmers' Alliance, which swept across the southern and Plains states in the late 1880s—grew out of several community-based farm organizations in the Southwest, particularly one established in Texas in 1877. By 1890, the Texas-based Alliance's membership had grown to 1,500,000, mainly in the southern and Plains states. Membership in this, the so-called Southern Farmers' Alliance, was restricted to whites, but it maintained a loose affiliation with a parallel black organization.

The Farmers' Alliance, like the Grange and the Knights of Labor, was a secret fraternal organization. It brought isolated farm families together in neighborhood assemblies which functioned as a kind of community of the true believers. Here members could reaffirm their commitment to common values and translate them into specific programs.

The program which enabled the Alliance to mobilize farmers was one of economic cooperation. What made the new Alliance cooperatives different from most Granger ventures was that they attempted to pool the credit resources of members, and thus allowed cash-poor farmers and tenants to participate. Partially because of this feature, the Alliance attracted more of a cross section of rural communities than had the Grange. Despite some well-publicized successes, the Alliance's cooperatives could not overcome the harsh realities of the agricultural systems of credit and marketing. But the struggle against these systems raised the expectations of countless farmers, and the failure of the cooperatives radicalized many of them.

From its inception, the Farmers' Alliance was involved in politics as well as in cooperative enterprises. In 1886, the Texas Alliance adopted a platform of political demands which formed the ideological basis of Alliance and Populist activism. The demands included legal recognition of trade unions and producer cooperatives, governmental action to prevent monopolization of land by corporate syndicates, regulation of the railroads, and reform of the nation's banking and currency systems.

Alliancemen, like earlier reformers, faced a choice about how to achieve their demands. Should they work within the two major parties or form a new party? Grass-roots insurgency had cropped up throughout the rural South and West during the 1880s, but the Alliance at first largely avoided this approach. In the Plains states, farmers worked through the dominant Republican party, while in the South most pressed their demands upon the reigning Democratic party. However, in 1890, midwestern alliancemen, rebuffed by entrenched Republican politicians, formed independent state parties. Most southern white alliancemen still concentrated on forcing Democratic nominees to endorse the Alliance demands. Both strategies seemed to work in 1890, for, by one means or another, farm protesters captured several state governments, and some fifty congressmen elected that year were nominally committed to support the Alliance's demands.

However, events soon propelled many southern alliancemen toward insurgency in league with their western counterparts. The failure of many Alliance cooperatives in 1890–1891 convinced many persons that only governmental action could save the American farmer. Of particular importance for southern alliancemen was the organization's subtreasury plan, which became both an economic panacea and a political litmus test for the Alliance. The subtreasury plan called for the federal government to establish commodity storage facilities where farmers could store their nonperishable crops and receive, in return, legal-tender notes equal to 80 per cent of the value of the crops.

To many alliancemen, the subtreasury plan seemed able to achieve for farmers precisely the benefits which the cooperatives had been unable to deliver, and also to reform the nation's currency system. It would create a flexible currency (the legal-tender notes), which would expand to meet the increased seasonal demand for money at harvest time. It would also extend credit to farmers at low rates (2 per cent), based on the value of their stored crops.

To most professional politicians, the subtreasury plan was an unconstitutional departure from traditional economic policy and a direct threat to party loyalty. By demanding that politicians endorse the bill or face reprisal, the Alliance was planting the seeds of mass defection from the "party of the fathers." In the South, the result of this confrontation was a split in the Alliance. Many members balked at political insurgency, but a large section of the Alliance concluded that enactment of the demands could come only through a third party.

The first step came at a meeting in Cincinnati in May 1891, where farm leaders called for a national convention to meet in Omaha to form a new People's party. By the time that the Omaha convention was gaveled to order in July 1892, many southern alliancemen were prepared to join with western farmers in an act of political insurgency. The platform which they adopted was a reiteration of Alliance demands and reflected a vision of what the United States should be which was sharply at odds with the views of the two major parties. The Populists demanded free coinage of silver at sixteen to one, the subtreasury system, abolition of National Bank notes and issuance by the Treasury of abundant legal-tender currency, a graduated income tax, governmental ownership of railroads, return to the government of unused lands granted to the railroads, restriction of immigration, the eight-hour day for labor, postal savings banks, and the election of United States senators by popular vote.

The Populists planned to use the presidential election of 1892 to launch their party into national politics. The party named as its standard-bearer James B. Weaver, a former Union general and presidential candidate of the Greenback-Labor party in 1880. As his vice-presidential running mate, the Populists chose a former Confederate general, James G. Field of Virginia. Thus the People's party set out to unite the North and the South, blacks and whites, and the city and the countryside in a crusade to reshape American politics.

Grover Cleveland and the Perils of the Presidency

The party system which the Populists sought to overturn was dominated by Democrats and Republicans, as it had been since the 1860s. Despite the close balance between the two parties, support for each tended to cluster around certain regional and cultural poles. The regional segregation of the two parties was a legacy of the Civil War era. Republicans remained strongest in the Midwest and Northeast, where the GOP had begun. The Democratic party's strength lay with white Southerners and the immigrants and working classes of the northern cities. The regional identity of the two parties was so clear-cut that a handful of "swing" states almost always determined the outcome of presidential elections between 1880 and 1892.

In addition to these sectional cleavages, party loyalties also followed ethnic and religious lines. In the Midwest and Northeast, the Republican party continued to attract many old-stock evangelical Protestants. They tended to favor prohibition of alcoholic beverages and the rooting out of "un-American" cultures. In their minds, the business of government included the active promotion of morality and righteousness—as they defined those terms. In those same areas of the country, the Democratic party attracted many voters of recent immigrant stock. For them, the suppression of alcohol and threats to non-Protestant religions and immigrant cultures were denials of individual freedom.

The major parties were connected, though never completely, with sectional, religious, and ethnic subcultures, and, on occasion, with differing moral senses of what government's role in the society ought to be. Thus distinguishable political cultures—sets of values and ideas—underlay partisan politics. The strength and persistence of these conflicting political cultures help to explain both the intensity of political participation and the long-term stability of the two parties in the late nineteenth century.

This equilibrium of sectional and cultural politics was upset in the 1890s by Populism and by the economic traumas of industrialization and the commercialization of agriculture. The ups and downs of the international market system compounded these traumas. Both came to a climax during the grim depression which began in 1893. However, the breakup of the old party system actually began in 1892.

In 1892, the Republicans nominated the incumbent, Harrison. The Democrats named Grover Cleveland for the third successive time. Cleveland made his fight mainly against the McKinley Tariff Act, while Harrison defended protection as a boon to labor. Voters eager for a change not only elected Cleveland by a large plurality; they also returned Democratic majorities to both houses of Congress for the first time in over a decade.

Weaver polled slightly over 1,000,000 votes (the largest number for a new party since 1856) and won twenty-two electoral votes. However, in several western states the strong Populist showing was aided by "fusion" with the Democrats and by support from organized silver-mining interests. Even so, the Populist party had established itself as a force to be reckoned with in the South and the West. Moreover, it more than held its own in the mid-term congressional elections of 1894, when the Republicans once more regained control of the House.

Cleveland had the bad luck to be in the White House when a major depression hit the country. In fact, the financial panic which triggered the depression was touched off ten days before Cleveland took office and deepened into depression during the summer of 1893. By the end of the year, nearly 16,000 business firms had gone into bankruptcy, and farm prices had begun a new plunge. By 1895, almost 3,000,000 workers were unemployed. The Populists' direst predictions seemed to be coming true.

Cleveland struggled according to his lights to meet these challenges, but his policies alienated farmers and workers and disrupted his party. The country was suffering from a massive deflation, caused in part by rapid industrial expansion and an inelastic money supply. Instead of permitting expansion of the money supply, Cleveland fought to defend the gold standard at the cost of further deflation. Workers and the unemployed were in desperate need. Rather than responding to their plight, Cleveland used force to break strikes and demonstrations and would not listen to proposals for federal relief. Cleveland believed, incorrectly, that the depression had originated in a lack of confidence in the Treasury's ability to maintain the gold standard. The chief source of the drain on gold, he thought, was the Sherman Silver Purchase Act. BY 1893, the Treasury was purchasing about $50 million worth of silver a year; at the same time, bankers and others were redeeming their silver certificates in gold.

Cleveland asked Congress for immediate repeal of the Sherman Silver Purchase Act. After a bitter battle in the Senate, the act was repealed. Most Republicans voted for repeal and most Democrats voted against it, despite Cleveland's vigorous efforts on its behalf. This ended governmental purchase of silver and all hopes of Democratic unity.

Although repeal of the Sherman Silver Purchase Act stopped the flow of silver into the Treasury, it had not added to the diminished gold fund. Early in 1895, Cleveland invited J. P. Morgan to the White House and asked for his help. Morgan and his European banking associates agreed to furnish $62 million in gold in return for 4 per cent government bonds. Morgan made a profit of more than $6 million on the deal.

Cleveland's vigorous action on monetary policy contrasts with his lackluster efforts on behalf of another issue which he believed to be important —downward revision of the tariff. In December 1893, William L. Wilson of West Virginia, chairman of the House Ways and Means Committee, introduced a bill for the removal of duties on many raw materials and the reduction of duties on many manufactures. The Democratic House promptly passed the Wilson bill. However, Democratic senators added some 600 amendments to it. Even so, the Senate measure, which both houses approved as the Wilson-Gorman Tariff Act, reduced duties from an average of 49.5 per cent under the McKinley Act to 39.9 per cent. Finally, the Senate, at the

"Giving the Butt" by Frederic Remington, a Harper's Weekly correspondent, who was at the scene of what he called the "rape of the government." In this sketch of the Pullman strike, he illustrates how federal troops dealt with the strikers. (The Bettmann Archive)

insistence of Democratic agrarians, added a tax of 2 per cent on incomes of over $4,000 per year. Cleveland let the bill become law without his signature.

While Cleveland quarreled with his party leaders in the Senate, the country suffered through one of the worst winters in its history. One out of every six workers was unemployed. There were two dramatic confrontations between the federal government and the poor in the spring of 1894. One, involving the strike and boycott against the Pullman Palace Car Company, has already been discussed (see pp. 271). The other incident was the march of an "army" of about 500 unemployed men under Jacob S. Coxey, a Populist reformer, from Massillon, Ohio, to Washington. They went to support a bill to provide road-construction jobs for the unemployed. Coxey and his followers were met at the Capitol by a corps of policemen who arrested two marchers and then dispersed the rest with clubs. Thus Cleveland made clear his determination to deal sternly with demonstrations of protest, even peaceful ones.

By the end of 1894, it seemed as if Cleveland had set out to alienate all major groups in the country. He offended eastern industrialists by his attack on the tariff. He incensed agrarians by his defense of the gold standard and his deal with Morgan. He alienated organized labor by his suppression of the Pullman strike. Businessmen blamed him for the Panic of 1893. Democratic party leaders accused him of splitting his party and of causing a landslide victory for the Republicans in the mid-term election of 1894.

Three decisions by the Supreme Court in the spring of 1895 added to the discontent, particularly among farmers and laborers. The court, in a five-to-four decision in the Pollock *v.* Farmers' Loan and Trust Company, killed the income-tax provision of the Wilson-Gorman Tariff Act on the ground that it was a direct tax and thus had to be levied in proportion to population (Constitution, Article 1, Section 2, paragraph 3). A week later, the court, in the case of *In re* Debs, unanimously upheld the injunction under which Debs had been imprisoned at the time of the Pullman strike, on the ground that the ARU's boycott had been a violation of the Sherman Antitrust Act. By implication, all restraints of trade by labor unions fell under the purview of the courts. At the same time, the court, in United States *v.* E. C. Knight Company, declared that the Sherman Antitrust Act did not apply to combinations of manufacturing concerns, because manufacturing was a local activity, and thus gave the green light to further industrial combinations.

The Realignment of the Party System

Cleveland's Democratic party was a principal loser in the political upheaval of the mid-1890s. Among the Democrats who lost their seats in Congress during the Republican landslide of 1894 was a young lawyer from Nebraska, William Jennings Bryan. He had remarkable oratorical powers and an infectious moralistic enthusiasm. Between 1894 and 1896, Bryan became a focal point of anti-Cleveland sentiment within the Democratic party; conservative Democrats and Republicans thought that he was a dangerous demagogue and a radical. In fact, Bryan was radical only in comparison with the position of both major parties.

Like many Populists, Bryan believed that the eastern monied classes controlled the national government and used it to protect their own interests. He believed in some degree of inflation and advocated free coinage of silver to achieve it. Yet Bryan was not part of the great mass movement which produced the Populist party. Radical Populists distrusted and even feared him, because he seemed capable of persuading farmers that free silver was *the* panacea for their problems.

The new star on the Republican horizon, William McKinley, was in some respects similar to Bryan. Both had served in the House of Representatives, and McKinley had lost his seat in the Democratic landslide of 1890. Both men were devout evangelical Protestants. McKinley, like Bryan, courted the labor vote. Despite his good relations with industrial workers, McKinley was not threatening to big business. His efforts in Congress on behalf of protection won him much business support, and his position on the money question (he favored "international bimetalism") was close enough to an endorsement of the gold standard to satisfy most "goldbugs."

McKinley caught the eye of a would-be Republican kingmaker, Marcus Alonzo Hanna, an industrialist from Cleveland, Ohio. Hanna gave his time and money to the advancement of Ohio Republicans who sympathized with his ideas. He supported John Sherman for the presidential nomination in three conventions. Thereafter he acted as McKinley's political and economic benefactor.

Just as Bryan was a very different kind of Democrat from Grover Cleveland, so McKinley and Hanna were new kinds of Republicans. Although they were clearly supportive of big business, they were not stridently antiunion. And although McKinley was a devout Methodist and a supporter of prohibition, he rejected the militant defense of evangelical culture which had long been a hallmark of Republican politics.

The presidential campaign in which McKinley and Bryan first met was also a departure in national politics. The election of 1896 has been called the "Battle of the Standards," which means that it pitted free silver against the gold standard. Monetary policy did dominate the speechmaking, but the real issues ran deeper.

Hanna's careful work on behalf of McKinley enabled McKinley to secure the Republican nomination with ease. Meanwhile, Bryan had been rallying the agrarian forces to wrest control of the Democratic party from Cleveland. When the Democratic national convention opened in Chicago, the free-silver forces were in complete command. They adopted a platform which advocated the free coinage of silver. A motion praising the "honesty and courage" of President Cleveland was soundly defeated.

Bryan had come to the convention confident that he could win the party's nomination for President. He did so, due in part to an electrifying speech which he delivered during the debate on the platform. "We are fighting," he cried, "in the defense of our homes, our families, and posterity . . . . We will answer their demand for a gold standard by saying to them: You shall not press upon the brow of labor this crown of thorns, you shall not crucify mankind upon a cross of gold." A listless convention came to life as Bryan's speech progressed. At the end, his nomination was assured.

The Populists were in a painful dilemma because the Democrats had stolen their issue and nominated a candidate who at least sounded like a Populist. For some time, one faction had worked to soften the party's

William Jennings Bryan during the presidential campaign of 1896. He rallied the agrarian, silver forces behind him at the Democratic convention with these words: "You shall not press down upon the brow of labor this crown of thorns, you shall not crucify mankind upon a cross of gold." (The Bettmann Archive)

demands by concentrating on the free-silver issue. To them, the nomination of Bryan represented an opportunity rather than a dilemma. In the western states, Populist-Democratic fusion had provided such victories as the party had enjoyed, and extension of this principle to the national level seemed quite sensible to many Populists. On the other hand, southern and southwestern Populists did not want to be pushed back into the Democratic party. They strongly opposed soft-pedaling the more controversial planks of the Omaha platform.

The Populists met in St. Louis just two weeks after the Democrats had nominated Bryan in Chicago. After bitter debate they nominated Bryan for President by a narrow margin, but they then rejected Bryan's Democratic running mate in favor of Thomas E. Watson, the fiery Georgia Populist.

During the campaign, the Populist party virtually ceased to function as a national institution. The real battle was between Bryan, the Democrat (he never formally accepted the Populist nomination), and McKinley. Both men employed novel electioneering techniques which, in different ways, prefigured twentieth-century campaigning.

Bryan broke with tradition by campaigning personally and extensively for the office. He traveled throughout the country and made more than 600 speeches to an estimated 5,000,000 people. This was probably the largest audience that ever listened to a single voice before the invention of the radio. McKinley's campaign appeared to be more traditional, but in fact it also broke with past practice. McKinley stayed at home in Canton, Ohio, and received delegations on his front porch. But while McKinley stayed at home, Hanna raised huge sums of money for the first time during a presidential campaign. He collected millions of dollars from corporations and disbursed them to hire an army of campaign speakers and to flood the country with campaign literature.

The campaigning was thus intense to an unprecedented degree. Bryan's invectives against eastern business tycoons were matched by Republican charges that he was a demagogue. The very heavy turnout on November 3 showed how stirred the people had been. McKinley carried the Northeast, the Middle West, and several border states. Bryan's electoral votes came from the Solid South and from the West. The popular vote gave the Republicans a majority in a presidential election for the first time since 1868.

The presidential election of 1896 was one of the most significant in American history. It established the dominance of the Republican party, virtually reduced the Democrats to the status of a southern regional party, and killed the Populists. It marked the end, at least until the 1930s, of continuous efforts to win governmental support for an inflated currency. Furthermore, it indicated the emergence of the cities as a dominant force in national politics.

Some accounts suggest that the Republicans bribed and bullied their way to victory. Political chicanery did occur in 1896, but Republicans had no monopoly on corruption. Some industrial workers were intimidated into voting for McKinley, but this cannot account for the persistence of Republican support over the next thirty years. The fact is that, in 1896, the Republican party appealed to a broader constituency than either the Democrats or the Populists. The Republican party appealed to workers on the ground that Republican policies would bring them economic well-being; in addition, it modified its evangelical image to take into account the cultural pluralism of the American electorate.

In contrast, by the time that Bryan took control, the Democratic party had already been blamed for the worst depression in the nation's history. The free-silver crusade made little headway among urban workers, who feared substantial increases in the prices of consumer goods. Many urban workers were put off by Bryan's antiurban remarks, while many immigrants were suspicious of his evangelical style.

As for the Populists, they were the victims of voter fraud, internal divisions, and, above all, the limited constituency to which they appealed. The Populists had dreamed of uniting all producers under one banner of reform. However, the reform measures which they promoted in the 1880s and 1890s appealed to relatively few nonfarmers. The Populists did indeed help to revive old but dormant traditions of economic and political democracy in America. For a time, they seemed to offer a serious challenge to industrial capitalism. Their demise at the end of the nineteenth century would limit the range of political discourse in the twentieth.

SUGGESTED READINGS

The best general surveys of politics in this period are Morton Keller, *Affairs of State: Public Life in Late Nineteenth Century America* (1977) and Garraty, *The New Commonwealth,* already cited. See also David J. Rothman, *Politics and Power: The United States Senate, 1869–1901* (1966), and Robert D. Marcus, *Grand Old Party: Political Structure in the Gilded Age, 1880–1896* (1971). On civil-service reform, see Ari Hoogenboom, *Fighting the Spoilsmen* (1961). The classic works on American politics during the Gilded Age are Woodrow Wilson, *Congressional Government* (1885), and James Bryce, *The American Commonwealth,* 2 vols. (1895). Excellent studies of the Mugwump reformers are John G. Sproat, *"The Best Men,"* already cited, and Geoffrey Blodgett, *The Gentle Reformers: Massachusetts Democrats in the Cleveland Era* (1966).

Lawrence Goodwyn, *Democratic Promise: The Populist Moment in America* (1976), is now the standard history of Populism, but the older general study of the movement, John D. Hicks, *The Populist Revolt* (1931), remains useful. The farm cooperative movement which led to Populism is described in Robert C. McMath, Jr., *Populist Vanguard: A History of the Southern Farmers' Alliance* (1975), and Theodore Saloutos, *Farmer Movements in the South, 1865–1933* (1960).

The ethnocultural dimension of political conflict is discussed most extensively in Paul Kleppner, *The Third Electoral System, 1853–1892: Parties, Voters, and Political Cultures* (1979). The racial dimension of politics is discussed in J. Morgan Kousser, *The Shaping of Southern Politics: Suffrage Restriction and the Establishment of the One-Party South, 1880–1910* (1974).

George H. Knowles, *The Presidential Campaign and Election of 1892* (1942), also has useful information on the depression. The election of 1896 has been subjected to close scrutiny. In addition to the previously cited studies of Populism, see Stanley Jones, *The Presidential Election of 1896* (1964). See also H. Wayne Morgan, *William McKinley and His America* (1963); Lewis C. Gould, *The Presidency of William McKinley* (1980); and Paolo E. Coletta, *William Jennings Bryan,* 3 vols. (1964–1969).

CHAPTER 20
THE RISE OF THE UNITED STATES TO WORLD POWER

1. DIPLOMACY IN THE GILDED AGE

Foreign Policy at a Low Ebb

American foreign policy between Hayes' inauguration in 1877 and Arthur's retirement in 1885 was virtually nonexistent. The Secretaries of State during this period were capable, but the world scene was quiet. The above would suffice to dispose of this subject had it not been for James G. Blaine, who served as Secretary of State from March to December in 1881. Blaine was an energetic Secretary of State with an inventive mind and some understanding of the importance of foreign policy.

Blaine's greatest interest was Latin America, where he hoped to promote stability, stimulate trade, obtain naval bases, and encourage the construction of a canal across Central America. Soon after taking office, Blaine tried unsuccessfully to mediate both a border dispute between Mexico and Guatemala and a war between Chile and the allied forces of Bolivia and Peru. He later persuaded President Garfield to approve the calling of a Pan-American conference, but the meeting was canceled after Garfield's assassination.

Expanding Horizons, 1888 – 1893

James G. Blaine returned to the cabinet as Secretary of State in 1889. Great changes had occurred since his first frustrating tenure. The United States had emerged as a major industrial power. A modern navy was under way. Many Americans were beginning to believe that the United States should follow Europe in seeking new territories and markets. A whole new way of looking at the world and the role that the United States should play in it was coming into being. Thus Blaine found much wider support for aggressive foreign policies during his second tenure than during his first.

At a Pan-American conference, held in Washington in 1889, Blaine worked hard for a Pan-American customs union and arbitration treaty, but failed. However, he did persuade the delegates to create the Pan American Union to promote hemispheric unity and cooperation. Great international undertakings require many years for their realization. So it was with Blaine's projects for Pan-American cooperation. He laid the foundations for what would become a major regional organization.

Blaine was also interested in extending American influence in the Pacific. Blaine had earlier taken steps to keep Great Britain from controlling the Hawaiian Islands. Now he came into conflict with the German Chancellor, Otto von Bismarck, over control of the Samoan Islands. After that conflict had brought the two nations to the brink of armed hostilities, American, British, and German delegates met at Berlin in 1889 and agreed to a joint protectorate over the Samoan archipelago. Great Britain withdrew from Samoa in 1899, and the islands were divided between Germany and the United States. After the First World War, the German portion of the islands was awarded to New Zealand.

A more serious conflict with Chile almost led to war. That country was torn in 1891 by a civil war. The American minister to Chile tactlessly took sides in the struggle, and, worse still, supported the losers. On October 16, 1891, after the rebels had finally triumphed, Chileans attacked a party of American sailors on shore leave. They killed two of them and wounded eighteen others. The Chilean government refused to apologize. Prodded by jingoistic newspapers and politicians, President Harrison himself wrote the ultimatum which was delivered to the Chilean government over Blaine's signature on January 21, 1892. Harrison also sent a special message to Congress which almost invited a declaration of war. Fortunately, Chile's government had the good sense to yield to the overwhelming military force of the United States. It apologized and paid an indemnity of $75,000. It would be many years, however, before Latin Americans would listen again to announcements that the United States wanted friendlier relations with other nations in the hemisphere.

Foreign Affairs, 1893–1896

The Hawaiian Islands had long had a close relationship to the United States. American missionaries, merchants, and planters had been in the islands since the 1830s. In January 1893, a group of Americans, with the help of marines from U.S.S. *Boston*, deposed Queen Liliuokalani, established a government, and declared the islands a protectorate of the United States. A few days later, President Harrison sent a treaty of annexation to the Senate, but his term ended before the Senate could vote on it.

Cleveland immediately withdrew the Hawaiian treaty from the Senate and sent a special commissioner to Honolulu to investigate. The commissioner reported that the American minister to Hawaii had participated in the

Queen Liliuokalani,
last of the Hawaiian
monarchs, who tried
to free the islands of
American influence in
the government and was
forced to abdicate.
(Culver Pictures, Inc.)

revolution and had called in the marines. Cleveland offered to restore the Queen to her throne if she would promise to take no reprisals against the revolutionists. She replied that she would cut their heads off. An embarrassed Cleveland simply withdrew, and the revolutionary government had no difficulty in maintaining itself in power until Congress, in July 1898, annexed the Hawaiian Islands by joint resolution.

Ineptness and stubbornness now led Cleveland into a controversy with Great Britain which might easily have resulted in a useless and dreadful war. The dispute was triggered by a border conflict between Venezuela and British Guiana. At stake were 230,000 square miles of rich mineral land. In 1895, the United States became embroiled in the controversy and attempted to invoke the Monroe Doctrine in support of its right to force arbitration of the border dispute. When the British Prime Minister refused American offers of mediation, Congress authorized President Cleveland to act unilaterally and to set up an arbitration commission.

A wave of chauvinism swept the country, and there was loud talk of war. Then a sober second thought set in as Americans began to contemplate war with Great Britain over so trivial an issue. The British government was at this time involved in other difficulties in South Africa, Europe, and the Far East. It had no desire for a war with the United States. Thus the British government accepted the American offer of arbitration. The arbitral commission began its hearings in Paris in 1899. Its award, ironically, was generally favorable to Great Britain.

2. THE WAR WITH SPAIN

The Problem of Cuba

Cuba had been the object of American interest since the time of Thomas Jefferson. More recently, Americans had talked of intervention when Cubans revolted against Spanish rule between 1868 and 1878, but nothing came of it. The revolt that broke out on the island in 1895, however, was much more brutal, and the rebels made more skillful appeals to American humanitarianism. The immediate cause of the uprising was the Wilson-Gorman tariff of 1894, which destroyed the favored position enjoyed by Cuban sugar. Cuban exports to the United States fell precipitately, bringing terrible poverty to the island. Cuban nationalists took advantage of the dissatisfaction to organize a new revolt. Bands of guerrillas ambushed Spanish troops and destroyed property owned by loyalists and foreigners—especially the large sugar plantations.

In desperation, the Spanish sent their most forceful commander, Captain General Valeriano Weyler y Nicolau to Cuba. He organized a system of concentration camps into which the populations of whole villages were herded. There the ill, the young, and the old, especially, died by the thousands. American newspaper reporters, who wrote graphic descriptions of the camps, called Weyler "Butcher."

Americans had invested more than $50 million in the island, and trade between the United States and Cuba totaled nearly $100 million annually. American citizens with economic interests in Cuba naturally hoped that the United States Government would act to restore stability to the island, but they were far from certain that forcing the Spaniards out of Cuba would protect their interests. It was the rebels, after all, who were burning plantations.

Cuban refugees in the United States were much more single-minded. They not only collected money and bought guns for fellow revolutionaries in their homeland; they also spread very effective anti-Spanish propaganda. In addition, the New York *World* and *New York Journal,* owned by Joseph Pulitzer and William Randolph Hearst, respectively, engaged in a fierce battle for readers with the aid of lurid descriptions of alleged Spanish atrocities against the Cubans. These accounts strongly stimulated the growth of popular demands for action to drive the Spaniards from the Caribbean.

Pride in American power played a part in encouraging this stridency in foreign affairs. In addition, many of the rising generation of political leaders—men such as Theodore Roosevelt and Henry Cabot Lodge—were infected with a virulent strain of chauvinism; they also believed that war with Spain would toughen the national fiber. However, the revulsion that a growing number of Americans felt toward Spanish methods was the chief cause of American preoccupation with Cuba. American feelings against Spain ran so high early in 1896 that Congress adopted a resolution favoring recognition of Cuban belligerency. Even Cleveland, who had resisted all pressure for war with Spain, warned that the American government would not stand by idly if the slaughter in Cuba continued.

This was the situation which William McKinley inherited in March 1897. The new President, a well-meaning, deeply religious man, sincerely wanted to avoid war with Spain. He was accused of cowardice. Theodore Roosevelt said that McKinley had "no more backbone than a chocolate eclair." However, two incidents early in 1898 set off what would become an irresistible demand for war against Spain. One was the *New York Journal's* publication on February 9 of a private letter written by Dupuy de Lôme, the Spanish minister to the United States. In it, De Lôme denounced the United States and described McKinley as a "cheap politician" and "bidder for the admiration of the crowd." The Spanish government immediately accepted De Lôme's resignation and apologized for his indiscretion.

The second incident was much more damaging to Spanish-American relations. U.S.S. *Maine*, in Havana harbor on a "friendly" visit, was sunk by a tremendous explosion on February 15, with the loss of 260 lives. The American public was convinced that the battleship had been blown up on orders from Spanish officials. To this day no one knows who planted the mine, although the most likely culprits would seem to be either the Cuban rebels or else Spanish nationalists in Havana, whose rioting in protest against the softening of Spain's military policies had brought *Maine* into Havana harbor to protect Americans in the first place.

Neither McKinley nor the Spanish government wanted war. Nevertheless, Congress, on March 8, responded to the hysteria following the sinking of *Maine* by unanimously voting the President $50 million as "an emergency fund for national defense." On April 9, the Queen Regent of Spain yielded to the demands of the United States. She revoked the concentration policy and instructed her commander in Cuba to stop all hostilities. The American minister in Madrid immediately cabled that, if the Spanish government was given time, he was sure that Cuban independence could be arranged during the armistice. At this point, McKinley failed to back up his peaceful intentions with courageous actions. He had already written a message to Congress asking for authority to use the armed forces to end the fighting. McKinley did not tear up that message and write a new one. Instead, he simply added a paragraph which mentioned the concessions and sent the message to an angry Congress on April 11, 1898.

Both houses immediately adopted resolutions that recognized the independence of Cuba, demanded the immediate withdrawal of Spain from the island, and authorized the President to employ the armed forces to carry out the resolution. At the same time, Congress adopted a second resolution, introduced by Senator Henry M. Teller of Colorado, which declared that the United States did not intend to annex Cuba.

Naval and Military Operations

Thanks to the naval modernization begun fifteen years before, the American navy entered the conflict in peak condition. When war broke out, the Asiatic Squadron of four cruisers and two gunboats, under the command of Commodore George Dewey, steamed toward the Spanish colony of the Philippines, according to a prearranged plan. Dewey entered Manila Bay early on the morning of May 1 and attacked the decrepit Spanish fleet. By noon, every one of the Spanish ships was sunk or in flames, and the city of Manila was at the mercy of Dewey's guns. Then he awaited transports from San Francisco with troops for land operations against the city.

As Dewey's vessels approached Manila, a Spanish fleet, commanded by Admiral Pascual Cervera y Topete, sailed westward across the Atlantic from the Cape Verde Islands. Cervera's destination was unknown, and there was fear in the United States that he intended to bombard the unfortified cities of the Atlantic coast. The North Atlantic Squadron, under Rear Admiral William T. Sampson, was patrolling the coast of Cuba, but the Spanish fleet slipped undetected into the harbor of Santiago on May 19. There the small Spanish fleet was bottled up by a vastly superior squadron under Admiral Sampson.

Meanwhile, about 17,000 troops, under the command of Major General William R. Shafter, had sailed from Florida to Cuba. The most publicized unit of this army was the First Volunteer Cavalry Regiment, popularly known as the "Rough Riders." It was made up of cowboys, ranchers, Indians, and a number of graduates of eastern colleges. Colonel Leonard Wood commanded the Rough Riders, and Theodore Roosevelt resigned his post in the Navy Department to become their lieutenant colonel.

American troops stormed the fortified town of El Caney and San Juan Hill, just east of Santiago, on July 1. They won these strategic positions, but they were in a precarious situation. The men were clothed in winter uniforms and unused to the torrid heat. Moreover, illness had taken a far greater toll than the enemy's rifles. The army's food supply was so low that a number of officers joined in a petition of protest to Washington. General Shafter considered the withdrawal of his army from the heights above Santiago because he feared that his troops might be driven off by the guns of Cervera's fleet.

Then fortune smiled on the American cause. On Sunday morning, July 3, the Spanish fleet attempted to escape from Santiago. Cervera's ships steamed out of the harbor and started to run westward along the southern coast of Cuba. The American ships closed in on the Spaniards in a wild chase along the coast. The Spanish cruisers, one by one, disabled or in flames, turned and headed for the shore.

The enemy's fleet was completely destroyed—474 men were killed or wounded, and 1,750 were taken prisoner. A few days later, the Spaniards surrendered the city of Santiago and their entire army. The war in Cuba was over, and the American army prepared to subdue Puerto Rico, the sole remaining Spanish outpost in the new world.

The total loss of two fleets and an army caused Spain to sue for peace. The news stopped General Nelson A. Miles' advance against the Spanish forces in

After landing at Daiquiri, American troops are seen under
Spanish fire from San Juan Hill on July 1, 1898. Of the expeditionary
force sent to Cuba, reporter Richard Davis wrote: "It was a most
happy-go-lucky expedition, run with real American optimism and
readiness to take big chances, and with the spirit of a people who
recklessly trust that it will come out all right in the end. ..."
(Library of Congress)

Puerto Rico, but the Spanish governor immediately surrendered the island.
On August 13, an American army of some 11,000 men entered Manila and
raised the American flag over the governor's palace.

3. THE UNITED STATES BECOMES A COLONIAL POWER

Ending the War with Spain

The preliminary peace agreement provided that Spain should immediately
evacuate and renounce all claims to Cuba and cede Puerto Rico and Guam,
an island in the Pacific, to the United States. In addition, the United States
would occupy Manila, pending a final settlement.

When peace commissioners from the two countries met in Paris, the
Spaniards reminded the Americans that the war had been undertaken for the
liberation of Cuba, not the Philippines. They pointed out that Manila had
not been taken until the day *after* the preliminary peace treaty had been
signed. They claimed, therefore, that the Philippines should remain in their
country's possession.

Various considerations gradually caused McKinley to join in the demand that the whole of the Philippine archipelago be ceded to the United States. McKinley, and others, believed that it was the moral duty of Americans to teach good government to the Filipinos. Commercial interests were also putting pressure upon the administration to take the Philippines for use as an entrepôt for trade with China. Imperialists, such as Secretary of State John Hay, Lodge, and Roosevelt, argued that the United States should share in the spheres of influence that western European powers were rapidly establishing in the Far East. The Spanish commissioners resisted stubbornly. However, when the American commissioners made an offer of $20 million, Spain agreed to "sell" the islands to the United States.

Meanwhile, an ugly situation had been developing in the Philippines. The Filipinos had been in revolt against Spain at the same time as the Cubans. The Filipinos had declared their independence of Spain on June 12, 1898, and proclaimed a provisional Republic of the Philippines, with Emilio Aguinaldo, leader of the revolution, as President.

It was clear by early February 1899 that the United States meant to occupy the Philippines, much as the Spanish had. The Filipinos then prepared to renew the revolution against their new masters. Fighting broke out around

U.S. troops marching in formation through the streets of Manila during the Philippine Insurrection, 1899–1901. Many Filipinos soon realized that the Spanish-American War had only made them pawns of another colonial power. Fighting for independence broke out and continued for several years in guerrilla fashion until U.S. forces were able to "pacify" the Islands. It was not until 1946 that the Philippines achieved independence from the United States. (Brown Brothers)

Manila between Aguinaldo's insurgents and American troops on February 4, 1899. The Filipinos took to savage guerrilla warfare in the swamps and jungles, and the Americans retaliated in kind. American superior power prevailed in the end, but only at a terrible cost of human lives—1,000 Americans and tens of thousands of Filipinos. Aguinaldo was finally captured on March 23, 1901. Two months later he issued a proclamation which acknowledged American sovereignty over the islands, but it was not until April 1902 that the last rebel surrendered.

By a narrow two-thirds majority, the Senate consented, on February 6, 1899, to ratification of the Treaty of Paris. The United States was thus launched upon a course of overseas expansion. It had already annexed the Hawaiian Islands. The United States then added the smaller Pacific coaling islands of Guam, Wake, and Baker. It had undertaken responsibility for establishing an orderly government for Cuba. It had also adopted nearly 1,000,000 subjects in Puerto Rico. Finally, the United States had become the master of 8,000,000 people in the Philippines.

Many Americans, called antiimperialists, were distressed and angered by these developments. The use of brute force to impose American rule on peoples different in language, race, and customs, they argued, was no different from the imperialistic policies of European states that most Americans had loudly condemned. The battle was taken up at once by advocates of overseas expansion. Manufacturers and bankers were among those who wanted markets for surplus goods and the investment of surplus funds. Sympathetic, too, were many moralists like McKinley. They quoted the British poet, Rudyard Kipling, to argue that Americans had a sacred duty to "take up the white man's burden" and help to civilize the "backward" natives. A small group, which included Theodore Roosevelt and Captain Alfred T. Mahan of the navy, argued that the United States could never be a great power until it had acquired naval bases far from its own shores.

Americans had an opportunity to vote on imperialism in the election of 1900. The Republican national convention renominated McKinley by acclamation. Theodore Roosevelt, now a popular war hero, was drafted for the vice-presidency. Roosevelt had been elected governor of New York in 1898 and had proved himself to be both a natural vote-getter and a threat to the well-entrenched state Republican organization. Hence the effort by the New York politicians to shunt him into the vice-presidency. The Democrats unanimously renominated William Jennings Bryan. Although the Democratic platform remained faithful to free silver, it made imperialism the paramount issue of the campaign by demanding independence for the Philippines.

Antiimperialist spokesmen emphasized the evils of attempting to govern alien peoples against their wills. Support was given to their arguments by the Philippine insurrection, which was at its height during the summer of 1900. The Republicans angrily claimed to be the liberators, not the oppressors, of the Filipinos. It is impossible to know whether the voters endorsed overseas expansion in the election of 1900 or not. Most historians regard McKinley's reelection more as a repudiation of Bryan and free silver than as a mandate for imperialism. For better or worse, Americans were in the business of running a colonial empire.

Organizing an Empire

The United States Government, by the Teller Resolution, had obligated itself to turn the government of Cuba over to Cubans after the restoration of order. The military governor, General Leonard Wood, oversaw the repair of wartime destruction and the organization of an educational system. Through the brilliant work of Major Walter Reed of the Army Medical Corps, the mosquito which carried the yellow-fever virus was discovered and destroyed.

In the summer of 1900, General Wood ordered elections for a constitutional convention. Secretary of War Elihu Root demanded that the Cuban constitution recognize the special responsibilities of the United States in the island. The provisions which Root demanded would have limited Cuba's diplomatic and financial sovereignty, guaranteed United States control over coaling and naval stations on the island, and recognized the right of the United States to intervene when the Washington government thought it necessary to do so.

Cuban nationalists naturally objected. The Cuban constitutional convention therefore wrote a constitution patterned on that of the United States, but with no mention of the provisions demanded by Root. Thereupon, Senator Orville H. Platt of Connecticut wrote these provisions into the army appropriation bill of 1901. It authorized the President to withdraw American forces only after the Cubans had accepted Root's terms. The Cubans finally yielded and incorporated the Platt Amendment into their constitution. The American army withdrew from the island, and the Platt Amendment was embodied in a Cuban-American treaty in 1903. In the years that followed, the United States on several occasions intervened in Cuba under the provisions of the Platt Amendment. In all cases, the United States acted to protect upper- and middle-class Cubans against leaders of the lower classes.

The Foraker Act of 1900 gave Puerto Rico a status between that of a colony and that of a territory. It empowered the President of the United States to appoint a governor and a council of eleven, of whom five should be Puerto Ricans. A legislature of thirty-five members was to be elected by the citizens. The Jones Act of 1917 gave Puerto Rico full territorial status and American citizenship to her inhabitants.

Governance of the Philippines was the hardest test of American abilities at colonial administration. Nearly 8,000,000 people, 7,000 miles from American shores, had been turned over to the rule of the United States against their consent. The Spooner Amendment of 1901 gave the President of the United States absolute power over the Philippines. McKinley appointed William Howard Taft as governor of the islands. The Philippine Government Act, approved on July 1, 1902, provided for the faint beginnings of self-government. Elections held in 1907 resulted in the choice of an assembly of eighty-one members. About three fourths of these were supporters of Philippine independence. Meanwhile, ex-Governor Taft had won great popularity by his fair, friendly, and forward-looking administration.

Both the Republican and Democratic parties were committed to eventual independence for the Philippines during this period. President Woodrow Wilson was able partially to redeem these promises in the Jones Act of 1916. Although the act reserved ultimate sovereignty to the United States,

Filipinos were far along the road to full self-government by the end of the Wilson administration in 1921.

The Open Door in China

Victory over Spain and the acquisition of a colonial empire marked the end of American isolation, as many Americans realized. They became more conscious of events in Asia; and American manufacturers, merchants, and shippers dreamed once more of potentially enormous markets, particularly in China.

China had been badly defeated by Japan in a war in 1894–1895. The great powers then proceeded to carve China's territory into spheres of influence. The United States took the Philippines just at the time that the European nations and Japan seemed about to agree on a permanent division of China. The prospect of far eastern markets made Americans eager to preserve equal opportunities for trade in China. In addition, Americans already had begun extensive missionary work in China and desired to see her treated fairly. Finally, the British government, whose subjects had the biggest stake, urged the American government to join it to try to preserve equal economic opportunity in China.

On September 6, 1899, Secretary of State John Hay therefore circulated what is called the first Open Door note to the powers which were then busy dividing up China. It asked them not to interfere with the freedom of trade in Chinese ports. None of the governments which received Hay's note wished to appear more grasping than the rest. All but Russia answered by accepting the terms of the note on condition that all the other governments concurred. Hay, in a gigantic bluff, announced that all the powers had agreed to respect the Open Door in China. It was a futile effort to protect American merchants and investors in China without any commitment, or even threat, of force. It did not work. The powers continued systematically to close their spheres.

Meanwhile, the exploitation of China had aroused fierce anger among the masses of the Chinese people. Millions joined a semireligious patriotic society called the "Righteous Fists of Harmony" (abbreviated to "Boxers"). A determined army of Boxers besieged the Chinese capital of Peking in 1900, and some 400 persons, including members of the diplomatic corps and their families, took refuge in the British legation. The Boxers held them under continuous fire, killing sixty-five and wounding 135. Finally, an army of American, British, French, German, Russian, and Japanese troops captured the city of Peking. The imperial court fled, and the foreign troops plundered the great city.

Hay feared that the victors would take revenge by dividing China among themselves. Therefore, he addressed a second circular note to the powers involved on July 3, 1900. It announced that it was the purpose of the United States to preserve Chinese territorial and administrative integrity. This second Open Door note may have had some effect, because the powers did not even discuss a division of Chinese territory. Instead, they imposed an indemnity of $334 million upon the Chinese Empire. Half of the American share of $24 million sufficed to satisfy the claims of United States citizens, and the balance was returned to Peking.

Prosperity and the Death of McKinley

While these events were taking place abroad, the United States was entering a period of remarkable prosperity at home. Gold discoveries added new money to the stream of currency throughout the world and caused a mild inflation which began in 1897. Farmers began to pull themselves out of debt. Orders for industrial products picked up. In 1897, the Republican Congress tried to insure high profits for American manufacturers by passing the Dingley tariff, which increased rates to unprecedented levels. The Gold Standard Act of 1900 not only established gold as the single monetary standard; it also provided for the creation of more national banks in small towns.

It was no accident that American interest in new markets and foreign sources of raw materials grew with the development of big business. So long as Americans remained chiefly an agricultural people, their surplus crops had gone to feed the industrialized nations of Europe. But the rapid growth of manufacturing had brought a profound change. Now important sectors of American industry needed supplies of raw materials that were unobtainable

President McKinley and party at the U.S. Government Building at the Pan-American Exposition, 1901. This is the last known photograph of McKinley before he was struck down by an assassin's bullet the next day. (Culver Pictures, Inc.)

at home. The tropical countries could furnish such materials and, at the same time, their peoples could be educated to buy and use American manufactured goods. Increasingly, it worked out that way after 1900. American foreign trade and investment increased sharply thereafter.

Fortune seemed to smile on McKinley as he began his second term. The country had just given his administration a vote of confidence, and he left Washington with members of his cabinet at the end of April for a grand tour of the country. On September 5, 1901, McKinley spoke at the Pan-American Exposition at Buffalo, New York. The next day he was shot by a young anarchist named Leon Czolgosz, whose emotions had been aroused by attacks against "Czar McKinley" in sensational journals. After a week of suffering, McKinley died. He was the third American President to fall by an assassin's bullet.

SUGGESTED READINGS

Robert L. Beisner, *From the Old Diplomacy to the New, 1865–1900* (1975), is the best survey of the diplomatic history of the period. But see also Walter LeFeber, *The New Empire: An Interpretation of American Expansion, 1860–1898* (1963). These works of course deal with the war with Spain. More specialized but very significant are Ernest R. May, *Imperial Democracy* (1961), and Julius W. Pratt, *The Expansionists of 1898* (1964). On military and naval operations, see Frank Freidel, *The Splendid Little War* (1958), and R. S. West, Jr., *Admirals of the American Empire* (1948). Stuart C. Miller, *"Benevolent Assimilation": The American Conquest of the Philippines, 1899–1903* (1982), is definitive.

For expansionism in general, see Edmund Morris, *The Rise of Theodore Roosevelt* (1979), and William C. Widenor, *Henry Cabot Lodge and the Search for an American Foreign Policy* (1980). The mood of late nineteenth-century America can best be caught by reading two very influential books—Josiah Strong, *Our Country* (1885), and Alfred T. Mahan, *The Influence of Sea Power upon History* (1890).

On the antiimperialists, see E. Berkeley Tompkins, *Anti-Imperialism in the United States, 1890–1920* (1970), and Robert L. Beisner, *Twelve against Empire: The Anti-Imperialists, 1898–1900* (1968).

CHAPTER 21
THE AMERICAN PEOPLE AT THE END OF THE CENTURY

1. URBAN AMERICA

The Growth and Physical Transformation of the City

In the last decades of the nineteenth century, the urbanization of the United States began in earnest. Urbanization and immigration, along with industrialization itself, brought into focus the outlines of modern mass society.

At the turn of the century, more Americans lived outside of large towns and cities than in them; less than 14 per cent were foreign-born; and three out of four lived east of the Mississippi River. All that was about to change. For one thing, the westward movement was continuing apace, despite the "closing" of the frontier in 1890. Even more important was the migration of people from the country and small towns to the cities. By 1910, more than 46 per cent would live in cities and towns. Finally, immigration was not only increasing but was also changing profoundly in character. To a large extent, immigrants were settling permanently in America's cities—a new frontier which drew immigrants from the countryside and foreign shores with the promise of a better life.

Cities had long been the centers of American commercial, cultural, and political life. What was different about the last decades of the nineteenth century was the *rate* of urban growth, the expanded role of cities in the nation's economy, and the altered physical configurations of the cities themselves. In the last part of the nineteenth century, New York City more than doubled in size to 3,400,000. Chicago grew from less than 300,000 in 1870 to 2,700,000 in 1920. By 1920, the nation had twenty-five cities with populations over 250,000. Hundreds of smaller towns and cities, many of them created by the rail lines which crisscrossed the nation, were also an important part of the urban network.

Urban growth was almost entirely the result of industrial, financial, and commercial development. The railroad network made many of the large cities into the principal "nodes" of a vast national transportation and market system. Consequently, cities became the loci of manufacturing to a much larger extent than had been the case earlier.

While the size and economic function of cities was being altered, so, too, was their physical layout. For one thing, cities became easier to get around in, and thus constraints on urban size were lifted. Trolley systems, which were in common use by the end of the 1890s, freed urbanites from the old limits of the "walking city." Trolleys and interurban railroads made possible the appearance of a new species of American—the suburban commuter. Movement within cities was also facilitated during this era by the construction of steel suspension and truss bridges across rivers which often divided cities.

Not only were cities growing *outward,* but they were also growing *upward.* The development of high-quality steel was a crucial cause of this phenomenon. In the 1880s, a group of Chicago-based architects developed steel-framed high-rise buildings which were structurally capable of surpassing the maximum height of traditional masonry-walled buildings. The soaring height of the commercial skyscrapers reflected not only the technological breakthrough of steel-frame construction and the costliness of urban land but also the expanding scale of American commercial and industrial enterprise. The same was true of many new factories, which dwarfed older buildings in order to accommodate the increased scale of industrial production.

Increasingly, these giant industrial structures were located at the outer edge of the metropolis or even in "satellite cities" such as Pullman, Illinois, or Gary, Indiana, both built near Chicago in the late nineteenth century. Rapidly disappearing was the older urban pattern in which small commercial, manufacturing, and residential buildings were side by side. At the same time, residential areas were more and more segregated along class and ethnic lines. One could discern the now familiar radial pattern of residential segregation, with a decaying core inhabited by the poor, surrounded by rings where the more well-to-do lived.

The City and American Democracy

When Lincoln Steffens published a book on the government of American cities in 1904, he could find a no more accurate title than *The Shame of the Cities.* As Steffens described it, municipal administration everywhere was characterized by waste, inefficiency, and, above all, corruption.

City founders had deliberately diffused power among mayors, aldermen, and numerous boards, but in most cities the formal government was a mere facade. The real government was the "machine" headed by a boss and numerous lieutenants. They were usually not officeholders, but were in business for the profit that officeholding would yield from the sale of franchises for street railways and utilities and for protection against enforcement of all sorts of municipal regulations.

This bribery was the oil that lubricated the machines. The votes of immigrants often supplied their political power. The machines, with their political clubs and friendly societies, were the one great assimilating force in the large American cities in the late nineteenth century. Moreover, the machine maintained its political base by providing all kinds of social services for its constituents. These services were usually delivered by the same neighborhood functionaries who got out the vote on election day.

There were periodic campaigns to organize the "better" elements (usually the commercial elite) and to overthrow corrupt machines. But campaigns for municipal reform were sporadic and usually only temporarily successful before the end of the century. Many thoughtful Americans saw that the cities were beset by social and economic ills which threatened the very foundations of democratic society. But their perceptions of what the problems *were* varied sharply. Some persons were preoccupied with political corruption and individual vice (they usually meant drunkenness and prostitution), and some saw the cities as a potential battleground of class warfare. Others focused more on the quieter crises of overcrowding and inadequate medical care, sanitation, and fire protection. Out of this discovery of urban poverty would come a wide variety of humanitarian reform crusades, often linked to the campaigns to reform city governments.

Wash day in a tenement apartment, c. 1910. (The Bettmann Archive)

The Transformation of Community Life in Urban America

Until the middle of the nineteenth century, the lives of most Americans were rooted in a place, or series of places, within which networks of family, kin, and neighbor created a powerful sense of communal solidarity. The westward movement weakened the bonds of those social networks, but people often moved as families or neighborhood groups; and, even in the new settlements, the "voluntary communities" of church, benevolent societies, and fraternal orders had provided surrogates for community ties based on blood, marriage, and long association.

But the primacy of these "island communities" was fading by the 1870s, as railroads and telegraph lines strung together villages and towns into vast marketing networks, and burgeoning cities expanded the scale of urban life beyond the physical limits of the face-to-face community. At the same time, the "wholeness" of community life was splitting into specialized segments (work life vs. family life, for example), each with different and even conflicting values. More and more, Americans found themselves living in two worlds—the small, private world of family and community, and a larger, public world in which one's identity lay with an abstract group such as a profession, trade, or class.

However, these physical and cultural changes by no means spelled the end of face-to-face community life in America. On the contrary, the *transformation* of community life, which had begun before the Civil War, continued apace: social relations rooted in a particular locality became relatively less important than interlocal social networks. And even the most closely knit of all communities—the family—changed in response to the modernizing influences of urbanization and industrialization. In short, community life was not bulldozed out of existence by the forces of modernization. It was reformulated and forced into tense coexistence with impersonal, modern social relationships; but it did not collapse.

2. IMMIGRATION, ETHNICITY, AND ETHNIC CONFLICT

The "New" Immigration

Between 1860 and 1900, almost 14,000,000 immigrants came to the United States, and another 14,500,000 followed between 1900 and 1915. The most important fact of this huge movement was not its size, but the changing origin of the immigrants. A shift in the tide of immigration from northern Europe to southern and eastern Europe gained speed in the 1890s and early 1900s. In the first decade of the new century, nearly three quarters of all immigrants coming to the United States were from southern and eastern Europe, in particular, Italy, Russia, and the Austro-Hungarian Empire.

These "new" immigrants were not only pulled by the promise of a better life in the United States; they were also pushed by economic, social, and political pressures in parts of Europe which threatened traditional cultures and, for some, even life itself. For whatever reason they came, Europeans who came to the new world in 1900 found the voyage itself much easier than had been the case for earlier immigrants. Although immigrants were still typically crowded into steerage, they now had dramatically greater prospects

An Italian family arriving at Ellis Island in 1905 by Lewis Hine, the reformer-photographer who earned a fine reputation for his studies of immigrants. The story of American immigration contains motives that were "a mixture of yearning—for riches, for land, for change, for tranquility, for freedom, and for something not definable in words." (Collection of International Museum of Photography at George Eastman House)

of surviving the voyage, and the cost was low. In 1911, the fare from Naples to New York was as low as $15.

For the most part, the new immigrants were people of the land. For them, ties of family and village were vitally important. Except for the Jews, most of them were Roman Catholic or Eastern Orthodox in religion. Their cultural heritage was both a source of strength and a barrier to participation in the life of their adopted country.

Although most of them were of rural origin, the new immigrants flocked to the cities of America. The high cost of taking up land and the declining need for farm laborers blocked their access to the countryside. The cities, on the other hand, held out the hope of employment and of maintaining ties with their own people. Indeed, many had come because friends or relatives in the United States or agents of American companies had promised them jobs and paid their passage. Many who could not find jobs in manufacturing or construction eked out a living as street peddlers or domestic servants, or in similarly low-paying jobs. Even in industry, the jobs open to most immigrants were low paying.

Most of these immigrants came from communal societies in which kinship networks and the seasonal rhythms of village life had framed their very existence. Their experiences in adjusting to an urban world differed from place to place and from one group to another. However, in general, families survived the trauma of migration, and they retained many of their old-world functions in the new. Extended families, and even groups of families from the same village, clustered together in neighborhoods in American cities. This promoted social cohesion and economic security and made it easier to maintain ties with family and friends in the old country. Many immigrants also found a sense of identity in their new home through ethnic parishes, fraternal orders, and mutual benefit societies. Taken together, these various social institutions created remarkably cohesive cultural enclaves within the anonymity of American cities.

The economic fortunes of the new immigrants have to be discussed in the context of the immigrants' own cultural heritage, since definitions of "success" are by no means culture-free. Most of the new immigrants began on the bottom of the economic ladder. Some groups, particularly those which placed a premium on education, moved rather quickly into the middle class. In other groups, upward occupational mobility was valued less highly than the maintenance of stability within the ethnic community, and these groups tended more often to maintain working-class status.

The economic condition of the new immigrants should also be viewed within the overall context of affluence and poverty in urban-industrial America. At the end of the century, the gap between the haves and the have-nots continued to widen. In 1910, 1 per cent of the people owned 47 per cent of the national wealth and received 15 per cent of the annual income. In the days before income and inheritance taxes, a few individuals built unbelievable fortunes. For example, by 1900 John D. Rockefeller's income was about $100 million a year (a dollar in 1900 would be worth about four dollars today).

Things were different at the other end of the scale. As late as 1915, between one third and one half of all American workers in mining and manufacturing earned less than enough to buy the food, shelter, and clothing needed by their families. Conditions were even worse in some rural sections, particularly in the South. Everywhere, the lot of the very poor included drab surroundings, poor educational opportunities, exceptional health hazards, and shortened life expectancy.

The opportunity for poor people to move into the emerging middle class varied from place to place. For example, the rigid class and caste system of the rural South severely limited upward mobility. On the other hand, a sizable proportion of those who stayed in industrial communities for several years advanced from blue-collar to white-collar jobs. However, many of those who were left behind were unquestionably part of a floating underclass. Opportunities for economic advancement certainly existed at the turn of the century, but the pervasiveness of poverty did not change.

Racism and the Immigrants: Nativism and the Drive for Exclusion

The influx of immigrants, coupled with hard times, created severe social tensions in the United States at the turn of the century. It was neither the first nor the last outburst of nativism in the United States, but the coming of so many immigrants in such a short period seemed to raise insoluble problems. Because the new immigrants were very different in language and customs, many Americans wondered whether they could ever be assimilated into the mainstream of national life. The new immigrants were usually poor and often illiterate. Their self-contained ethnic communities were perceived by others as proof of their unwillingness to assimilate.

Some Protestants resented the fact that a high percentage of the new immigrants were Roman Catholics and Jews. Others were sure that they threatened the country with revolutionary upheavals. Many frightened Americans thought that the new immigrants were "racially" inferior. The popular view was reinforced by the prevailing scientific and scholarly thought of the day.

Such hostilities and fears provoked movements which were themselves alien to the most highly valued American traditions. The most powerful nativist group during this period was the American Protective Association, organized in 1887 to rally Americans for a fight against Catholicism. It grew with startling rapidity in the 1890s and stirred hostilities that would weaken the society for decades to come.

Many Americans who believed that there was an "immigrant problem" saw its solution in reducing the numbers coming to the United States. One method proposed was to require that immigrants be able to read and write. Congress adopted such a measure three times, only to have it vetoed by Presidents Cleveland, Taft, and Wilson. Finally, in 1917, Congress passed the literacy test over Wilson's veto. Other forms of restrictive legislation began in the 1880s. In 1882, Congress excluded Chinese immigrants, convicts, and the insane. Subsequent laws denied entry to certain "undesirable" types of individuals. The exclusionary legislation would culminate, as we shall see, in the National Origins Act of 1924.

Racism and Afro-Americans: Disfranchisement and Segregation

Despite the nominal equality afforded blacks by the Thirteenth, Fourteenth, and Fifteenth Amendments, the freedmen continually had to deal with racism similar to that which confronted the new immigrants. The presumption of black inferiority was widespread among white Americans throughout the nineteenth century. What was new at the end of the century was the institutionalization of racism. Southern states and localities legally disfranchised and segregated blacks, and the federal government and national public opinion tolerated those processes.

As late as 1880, a majority of adult black males voted in the presidential election in every southern state except two. However, in the next thirty years southern states and municipalities passed ordinances which, without violating the letter of the Fifteenth Amendment, effectively disfranchised almost all southern blacks. Property requirements and cumulative poll taxes excluded many of the poor. Literacy and "understanding" tests screened out those who could not read, and many of those who could. Along with these and other legal restrictions, outright terrorism was again used, as in the Reconstruction era, to prevent blacks from voting.

In 1890, Congress failed to enact an election bill (see p. 287) which would have instituted federal supervision of elections in the South. In 1898, in the case of Williams v. Mississippi, the Supreme Court upheld the constitutionality of that state's thoroughgoing system of disfranchisement.

Why did the holders of political power in the South, who had not attempted to prevent black voting altogether at the end of Reconstruction, do so at the end of the century? Some historians have linked disfranchisement with Populism; they say that white Populists, who had tried and failed to establish an effective biracial coalition, revealed their underlying racism by leading the movement for disfranchisement. However, the same laws which removed most blacks from politics also sharply reduced voting among poor whites. The most thorough study of disfranchisement in the South concludes that it was engineered not by the Populists, but by their archenemies, the conservative Democrats, who wished to stamp out political opposition among both blacks and poor whites.

At the same time, southern states and cities enacted segregation ordinances which separated blacks and whites in schools, restaurants, hotels, theaters, railway cars, and even courtrooms. South Carolina went so far as to provide separate Bibles to administer oaths to black witnesses. Some degree of racial segregation had long existed, in the North as well as in the South. But these new ordinances made segregation virtually universal in the South and backed it with the full force of the law.

Again, the federal judiciary chose to overlook the obvious affront to constitutional safeguards which legal segregation represented. In 1883, the Supreme Court struck down the Civil Rights Act of 1875, which had prohibited the segregation of public facilities. In the case of Plessy v. Ferguson (1896), the court established the doctrine of "separate but equal" and held that, so long as "equal" facilities were provided for blacks and whites, they need not be integrated. For over half a century, this principle governed civil-rights cases. Neither in Plessy v. Ferguson nor in most subsequent cases did the court examine closely the actual conditions which were alleged to be equal.

Legal segregation and disfranchisement were accompanied by an upsurge of racial violence. In 1900 and 1901, 214 blacks were lynched in the United States. Mobs in Atlanta attacked blacks and black-owned property in 1906. Armed Democrats in Wilmington, North Carolina, in 1898 overthrew the duly elected Republican government. These repressive acts occurred within a climate of popular and scholarly opinion which found them at least tolerable and sometimes even justifiable. Only a few white Americans in either the North or the South possessed both the courage and the detachment from their own culture to protest.

Black Americans resisted as best they could, but for the most part the forms of their resistance resembled those practiced by their forebears under slavery. A few fled to the West or the North. Others employed the day-to-day resistance of the field hand. Others, even after the turn of the century, risked life and property to protest openly against segregation.

Among the educated elite a few, such as William Monroe Trotter of Boston, still clung to the dream of full equality. Others, such as Bishop Henry M. Turner, despaired of American justice and urged Afro-Americans to return to Africa. However, the strategy which won the broadest support was that of Booker T. Washington, the former slave who founded Tuskegee

Institute in Alabama. Washington publicly urged blacks to defer hopes of political and social equality and to concentrate on economic self-improvement. Privately, even secretly, Washington consulted with Presidents and leaders of business on matters relating to blacks. With strong support from wealthy white philanthropists, Washington exerted a powerful influence over the press, the pulpit, and the classroom in black America until his death in 1915.

Militant blacks denounced Washington as a self-serving accommodationist (see pp. 326). Washington's preeminence owned much to the support of prominent whites who found his rhetoric reassuring. But his strategy was double-edged. He called for temporary acquiescence in a bad, but virtually intractable, situation. At the same time, he nurtured the cultural pride and interior resourcefulness which had sustained Afro-Americans during the long night of slavery.

3. CULTURAL CHANGE IN THE AGE OF INDUSTRIALIZATION

Old and New Currents of Social Reform

Throughout most of the nineteenth century, genteel and middle-class reformers had proposed all kinds of cures for the ills of American society. The great wave of reform which began early in the century had been optimistic about the prospects of reforming individuals (and thus society) by moral suasion (see pp. 201–204, 211).

However, the optimistic individualism of the antebellum reformers did not fare so well in the age of urbanization, industrialization, and massive immigration. The temperance crusade gave way to a tight-lipped prohibitionism. The asylum movement was conceded to be a failure before the end of the century. And even large elements of the abolitionist army could not see beyond emancipation to the structural barriers which confronted freedmen. Perhaps the women's movement most nearly retained its antebellum vitality and imagination, although even here the concentration on suffrage caused a narrowing of the movement's objectives.

The new breed of social reformers who emerged in the 1890s retained some of the religious fervor and optimistic individualism of their predecessors. However, social reformers of the 1890s looked at the structural and environmental ills of the cities and of modern industry in different ways. In addition, they began to adopt tactics quite unlike the once-for-all plans so common in the mid-nineteenth century.

By the end of the century, religious organizations and a new group of professional social workers were addressing themselves to problems of the urban poor. Protestant churches, influenced by an earlier movement in Great Britain, began to awaken to the challenges to Christian ethics raised by slums, poverty, disease, and human exploitation. This new perspective came to be known as the Social Gospel, and its most eloquent spokesmen included the Baptist minister Walter Rauschenbusch. In his words, the Social Gospel was the "application of the teachings of Jesus and the total message of the Christian salvation to society, economic life, and social institutions . . . as well as to individuals." The Roman Catholic Church, which had been operating in urban slums since the massive Irish immigration of the 1850s, redoubled its ministrations to the poor. Moreover, Pope Leo XIII's encyclical of 1891, *Rerum Novarum*, put the Catholic Church squarely behind the movement for social justice.

Ministers and priests were in the vanguard of efforts to improve life in city slums. A separate class of social workers followed closely on their trail. Not only did they minister to the needs of the poor, but they also made intensive surveys of labor conditions, the causes of poverty and crime, and the means of alleviating social distress. One group of the social workers made a major contribution through the founding of settlement houses as social-service centers in the heart of the slums (see p. 328).

The professionalization of social work (one of the few professions open to women at the time) was part of the larger trend toward professionalization in America. Whether in medicine, law, education, engineering, or a host of other occupations, these new college-trained professionals believed that knowledge and skill, not merely wealth and social standing, held the key to power in modern America—and also to the resolution of social ills. At the turn of the century, to a much greater extent than would later be the case, professional men and women believed that social reform *was* humanly possible and that the responsibility for its achievement was theirs. Economic and social problems, as well as the physical problem of urban overcrowding, could be attacked rationally—"scientifically"—by experts. Their persistent application of scientific and bureaucratic methods would, they believed, bring results where less "practical" approaches had failed.

Educational Innovations

The emergence of modern professionalism at the end of the nineteenth century was a consequence of important changes in American higher education. The antebellum colleges were intended to provide a general education rather than to prepare individuals for a particular occupation (with the exception of training for the ministry). Beginning in the 1870s, major changes began to occur in college curricula and in the purposes of higher education. Harvard led the way in broadening the classical curriculum, raising academic standards, and identifying university training more explicitly with the professions. The Johns Hopkins University, founded in 1876, brought to the United States the model of the German graduate and research institution. Equally important was the proliferation of state-supported colleges of agriculture and engineering. These land-grant colleges were committed to broadening the social base and academic content of higher education. These developments had important consequences for higher education. The older professions and many newer ones, such as engineering and business management, became more dependent on the university. One could no longer "read" law or medicine or learn engineering in the shop. In turn, practicing professionals, organized into national associations, had considerable influence over curricula related to their fields.

The transformation of the classical college into the modern university also affected the growing public-school systems. Widespread university training of high quality presupposed a broad network of high schools with similarly

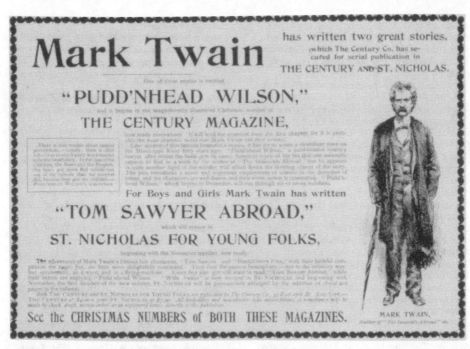

An advertisement for two stories by Mark Twain, "Pudd 'nhead
Wilson" and "Tom Sawyer Abroad." Convinced that Twain's
literature documented an entire epoch in American history,
playwright George Bernard Shaw once wrote to him: "The future
historian of America will find your works as indispensable to
him as a French historian finds the political tracts of Voltaire." (The
Bettmann Archive)

rigorous standards and a uniform curriculum. In many parts of the country,
particularly in rural areas, high schools were either nonexistent or substan-
dard, and the content of their curricula varied widely. Colleges and
universities led the fight for higher standards and a uniform curriculum. The
high schools thus formed a link in the educational chain that was being
forged at the end of the century, one between the new universities and the
expanding elementary school system, which was just then being organized
into a graded curriculum. At the turn of the century, the outline of our
modern educational system had taken shape, but the structure was far from
complete.

SUGGESTED READINGS

Three general studies which interpret social change at the end of the nineteenth century are Robert H. Wiebe, *The Search for
Order, 1887–1920* (1967); Samuel P. Hays,
The Response to Industrialism, 1885–1914
(1957); and Alan Tractenberg, *The Incorporation of America: Culture and Society in the
Gilded Age* (1982).

Sam B. Warner, Jr., *The Urban Wilder-
ness: A History of the American City* (1972),
provides a good description of American
cities, while Arthur M. Schlesinger, Sr., *The
Rise of the City, 1878–1898* (1933), remains useful.

A number of recent works focus on social and occupational mobility and family

structure in late nineteenth-century cities. Among them are Stephan Thernstrom and Richard Sennett, eds., *Nineteenth Century Cities: Essays in the New Urban History* (1969); Michael Frisch, *Town into City: Springfield, Massachusetts, and the Meaning of Community, 1840–1880* (1972); and Clyde Griffen and Sally Griffen, *Natives and Newcomers: The Ordering of Opportunity in Mid-Nineteenth Century Poughkeepsie* (1977). A thoughtful discussion of the changing meaning of community is found in Thomas Bender, *Community and Social Change in America* (1978).

A pioneering study of the immigrant experience in America, Oscar Handlin, *The Uprooted* (1951), has been subjected to serious criticism by later works, which have focused on immigrants in particular cities. Among these are Josef Barton, *Peasants and Strangers: Italians, Rumanians, and Slovaks in an American City, 1890–1950* (1975), and Thomas Kessner, *The Golden Door: Italian and Jewish Immigrant Mobility* (1977). James Stuart Olson, *The Ethnic Dimension in American History* (1979), is a useful survey but see also Alan M. Kraut, *The Huddled Masses: The Immigrant in American Society, 1880–1921* (1982). John Higham, *Strangers in the Land: Patterns of Nativism, 1860–1925* (1955), remains the standard treatment of that subject.

Robert H. Bremner, *From the Depths* (1956), is a fine introduction to the problems of poverty and slums. Among contemporary comments on those problems, see especially Jacob Riis, *How the Other Half Lives* (1890), and Jane Addams, *Twenty Years at Hull-House* (1890). The most profound

contemporary criticism of corruption in city government is Lincoln Steffens, *The Shame of the Cities* (1904).

The role of religious organizations in dealing with social problems of urban-industrial America is discussed in Henry F. May, *Protestant Churches and Industrial America* (1949), and Aaron I. Abell, *American Catholicism and Social Action: A Search for Social Justice, 1865–1950* (1960).

The rise of legal segregation is discussed in a classic study, C. Vann Woodward, *The Strange Career of Jim Crow* (3rd ed., 1974), although some of its conclusions are challenged in Joel Williamson, *After Slavery: The Negro in South Carolina during Reconstruction, 1861–1877* (1965). The standard account of disfranchisement is J. Morgan Kousser, *The Shaping of Southern Politics: Suffrage Restriction and the Establishment of the One-Party South, 1880–1910* (1974). Booker T. Washington's career is examined in Louis R. Harlan, *Booker T. Washington: The Making of a Black Leader, 1856–1901* (1972) and *Booker T. Washington: The Wizard of Tuskegee, 1901–1915* (1983).

Useful information on public education is found in Lawrence A. Cremin, *The Transformation of the School: Progressivism in American Education, 1876–1957* (1961). On higher education, see especially Lawrence R. Veysey, *The Emergence of the American University* (1965). On art and architecture, see Lewis Mumford, *The Brown Decades: A Study of the Arts in America, 1865–1895* (1931), and John E. Burchard and Albert Bush-Brown, *The Architecture of America* (1961).

CHAPTER 22
PROGRESSIVISM
AND THE ERA OF
THEODORE ROOSEVELT

1. THE PROGRESSIVE MOVEMENT

Background of Revolt

When Theodore Roosevelt succeeded McKinley in 1901, the United States was already in the first stages of the political eruption that historians call the progressive movement. In essence, progressivism was the response of Americans to the problems raised by industrialization and urbanization. The most disturbing of these problems were the breakdown of democratic government; the spread of poverty and crime in the large cities; the exploitation of workers, especially women and children; and, above all, the emergence of great economic interests—railroads, large corporations, and banking empires—that had the power to affect the destinies of the people and yet remained beyond popular control.

In fact, progressivism was an aggregation of many movements for social, economic, and political reform. These movements were enormously varied and sometimes mutually antagonistic, and this fact sometimes causes confusion in historical understanding. Progressivism's roots lay deep in American traditions, but it had its immediate origins in a series of disconnected movements for reform and reconstruction during the 1890s.

1. The most obvious was Populism. Although the Populists failed to win national power, their propaganda publicized widespread distress at the same time that it succeeded in reviving the concept of governmental action to insure the people's economic well-being.

2. The intensification of human distress during the 1890s dramatized for many urban Americans the wide contrast between the privileged position of the well-to-do and the plight of the poor. Although the depression that began in 1893 was much less severe in the United States than the economic catastrophe of the 1930s, the suffering connected with the depression of the 1890s stimulated the two movements that furnished much of the moral zeal for progressivism—the Social Gospel and the movement for social justice.

3. Americans in the 1890s were further agitated by a growing literature of exposure, including Henry George's *Progress and Poverty* (1879); Edward Bellamy's utopian socialist novel, *Looking Backward* (1888); and Henry Demarest Lloyd's indictment of the Standard Oil Trust, *Wealth against Commonwealth* (1894). Soon mass circulation magazines, such as *McClure's, Everybody's,* and the *American Magazine,* and muckrakers, such as Lincoln Steffens, Ida M. Tarbell, and Ray Stannard Baker, were exploring every dark corner of American life.

4. By the 1890s, social scientists were beginning to challenge the philosophical foundations of the laissez-faire state and the cluster of ideas associated with it. Leaders of this revolt were young economists, such as Richard T. Ely and Thorstein Veblen, and sociologists, such as Lester F. Ward and Edward A. Ross. Their ranks swelled in the early 1900s. Herbert Croly (*The Promise of American Life,* 1909), Walter Weyl (*The New Democracy,* 1912), and Walter Lippmann (*Preface to Politics,* 1913) worked out a sophisticated justification for the welfare state.

5. Progressivism became largely an urban, middle-class movement after 1900. Three profoundly important things happened to the urban middle classes in the 1890s and early 1900s. First, they grew so rapidly in numbers that they were able to wield the balance of political power in many sections of the country. Second, influential segments of these classes, molded by their specialized training, insisted on rationality and efficient administration in public affairs. Finally, they were deeply affected by the exposures of corruption and accounts of economic distress. By the late 1890s, they were building up a full head of steam of moral indignation.

The Municipal Reform Movement

The crusade for municipal reform marked the beginning of progressivism as a *political* movement. It began sporadically in the early 1890s and became a widespread revolt about 1896–1897. Hazen S. Pingree, elected mayor of Detroit in 1889, led the way by battling and subduing that city's trolley, gas, and telephone companies. Similar movements sprang up in other cities. The most successful municipal reformer of this era was Tom L. Johnson of Cleveland, elected mayor of that city in 1901. Johnson gained a national reputation for his fight against the Cleveland street railways. But he made his greatest contributions by streamlining the Cleveland city government and by proving that it could be efficient even while greatly expanding its services.

Municipal reformers fought corrupt city officials. In addition, they all fought for efficient government, fair taxation, regulation of public utilities, and better education and expanded social services for the poor. In order to achieve these goals, progressives in the cities joined hands with other groups to obtain new machinery which would assure popular control of political processes. These campaigns were carried out on the state level, and will be discussed in connection with the progressive movement in the states.

At the municipal level, progressives implemented two new forms of government. The first—the commission form—was instituted in Galveston, Texas, in 1900, after a tidal wave inundated the city, and the mayor and alderman proved unable to cope with the emergency. Government of the city was vested in five commissioners, elected, after 1903, by the people. The commission form spread rapidly to other cities, particularly after the Iowa legislature, in 1907, adopted a more elaborate version of the Texas model. Each commissioner was responsible for a single administrative department such as finance, public health, or public works. By 1914, some 400 municipalities, chiefly medium-sized cities, had adopted the commission form.

Between 1908 and 1912, progressives refined a new idea—government by an expert city manager appointed by and responsible to a popularly elected city council. The city-manager plan, first adopted in its complete form by Dayton, Ohio, in 1913, spread rapidly. More than 300 cities had adopted it by 1923.

The accomplishments of the municipal crusaders were substantial. Cities not only were being governed more honestly and efficiently, but they were also beginning to grapple with economic and social problems. Moreover, a whole new class of professional municipal administrators was in training throughout the country. The city, while far from the bright hope of American democracy, was no longer its nemesis.

The Struggle for Self-Government in the States

At the turn of the century, there were state political machines, just like city machines, which governed behind the facade of the formal structure. And, as in the cities, they came under fire from progressives. The progressive revolt in the states was the product of earlier reform movements, both urban and rural. In the South and the West, agrarian radicalism gave way to progressivism after 1896, as urban spokesmen took leadership in the fight against railroad and corporate dominance. The Middle West was swept by a series of spectacular state revolts from about 1900 to 1908, under the leadership of Republicans such as Robert M. La Follette of Wisconsin and Albert B. Cummins of Iowa.

State progressive movements in the East were more often the culmination of earlier municipal movements. Woodrow Wilson's election as governor of New Jersey in 1910 was the culmination of a movement begun largely by Republican progressives. Politics was equally convulsed on the West Coast by the successful campaigns of reformers such as William S. U'Ren in Oregon and Hiram W. Johnson in California.

In the struggle to make institutions of government more susceptible to public control, new forms had to be found to help to restore democracy. One such device was the direct primary, in which the people themselves, rather than a coterie of politicians in caucuses and conventions, would nominate the party candidates. By 1916, only three states still used the convention system for nominations. Progressives also obtained the direct election of United States senators by the people instead of by the state legislatures. The demand for the direct election of senators had originated with the Populists and had been pursued by muckraking journalists. Despite the resistance of the United States Senate, state after state adopted the plan of permitting the voters to indicate their choice of a senatorial candidate in primary elections. After a scandal in the Illinois senatorial election, the Senate finally yielded in 1912 and approved the Seventeenth Amendment for the direct election of senators. Another democratic innovation—the presidential preferential primary—was first adopted by Oregon in 1910; a dozen states used it in 1912.

Finally, progressives championed measures to be used in the event that governments became irresponsible even under the new representative forms. The *initiative* enabled voters to initiate and submit legislation to the general electorate. The *referendum* enabled voters to repeal bills enacted by the legislature. Some twenty-one states had adopted the initiative and referendum by 1915. A further safeguard was the *recall,* which enabled voters to unseat unpopular or dishonest officials.

Progressives must be judged not so much by the institutional changes which they wrought, but on a basis of what they did with the political power which they won. Their achievement in modernizing the administrative structures of government was impressive in itself. Even more impressive were their accomplishments in social and economic reform. By 1914, every state but one had established minimum age limits for child labor. By 1917, some thirty-nine states had attempted to protect women workers by limiting the numbers of hours that they might work. The Supreme Court, in Muller v. Oregon, in 1908 upheld the constitutionality of this legislation. Between 1912 and 1923, fifteen states established some form of minimum wage for women. In the latter year, the Supreme Court declared all such laws unconstitutional. Between 1911 and 1916, thirty states established accident insurance systems for industrial workers. By 1917, two thirds of the states, many of them in the South and West, had prohibited the manufacture and sale of intoxicating beverages. Although many Americans did not consider prohibition either progressive or a reform, the leaders of the movement were sincerely trying to improve the quality of American life. Most states that did not have them by the beginning of the progressive era established railroad and public-utility commissions to regulate rates and services. So effective had state regulation become by 1914 that the railroad managers were then begging Congress to save them from harsh controls by state commissions.

Progressives, despite their concern for vital democratic government, generally ignored the plight of the one tenth of Americans who were black. They remained economically submerged, socially ostracized, and, in the South, disfranchised as well. Faint glimmerings of hope did appear for black Americans. A small group of black intellectuals, led by W. E. B. Du Bois, organized the Niagara Movement in 1905 to work for the advancement of blacks. But Du Bois' movement became mired in controversy with those who looked to Booker T. Washington as the chief spokesman of black Americans.

It was largely to protest against Washington's program of accommodation that a group of black and white educators, editors, clergymen, and social workers organized the National Association for the Advancement of Colored People (NAACP) in 1909, the year after a race riot in Springfield, Illinois. The NAACP kept the American democratic conscience alive, in part through its journal, the *Crisis,* which Du Bois edited; but the NAACP represented only a tiny minority even as late as the First World War. In addition, a group of

Theodore Roosevelt speaking at a meeting of the National Negro Business League with Booker T. Washington on his left. Because of his belief that "the agitation of questions of social equality is the extremest folly," Washington's conservative and submissive doctrine was later rejected as "Uncle Tomism." (Culver Pictures, Inc.)

black and white social workers and philanthropists organized the National Urban League in New York in 1911. It worked to find jobs for blacks and to improve their living standards in the large northern cities.

Blacks continued to struggle for education and reduced their illiteracy rate from 44.5 per cent in 1900 to 22.9 per cent in 1920. But their social condition actually worsened as racism and segregation spread throughout the North. As we have seen, the political and social condition of southern blacks had deteriorated earlier in the aftermath of the agrarian revolt. Lynching continued in the twentieth century to be an important means to control or intimidate blacks. More than 1,100 of them fell victims to lynch mobs between 1900 and 1914. Few progressive leaders acted as though the terrible plight of black Americans was a problem that ought seriously to concern them.

Women and the Progressive Movement

Much of the generative power of progressivism came from one of the most remarkable generations of women in American history. Middle-class women began to go in larger numbers to college, particularly to the women's colleges which were founded during the last four decades of the nineteenth century. The number of women graduating from college annually increased from 2,500 in 1890 to 8,500 in 1910.

Susan Brownell Anthony, born into a large Quaker family in 1820, fought for woman suffrage and other major reforms throughout her life. She died fourteen years before ratification of what was known as the Susan B. Anthony amendment, but she is fully credited with the groundbreaking work that made its passage possible. (Historical Pictures Service, Inc., Chicago)

A few brave women fought their way into graduate and professional schools, but they were rare exceptions. Many went into elementary and secondary school teaching. A large number of the graduates were filled with a zeal for social service and reform. Of this latter group, some established settlement houses—social centers built in the midst of urban slums that provided day-care services for children, classes for immigrants, and a wide variety of social services. To mention only two, Jane Addams founded Hull-House in Chicago in 1889 and became in the eyes of many persons the greatest woman of her generation. Lillian D. Wald founded the Henry Street Settlement in New York in 1895. Numerous women went into the new profession of social work. Others, such as Frances Willard, led the fight against the saloon. Still others worked for child-labor legislation and the regulation of the hours and wages of women and helped to organize female workers in the garment industry. Margaret Drier Robins and Mary McDowell were the driving forces in the National Women's Trade Union League, founded in 1903. These are only a few representatives of thousands of women who were in the forefront of the movement for social justice.

The movement for woman suffrage, begun so bravely at the Seneca Falls convention of July 1848 (see pp. 204), did not prosper as the Victorian period,

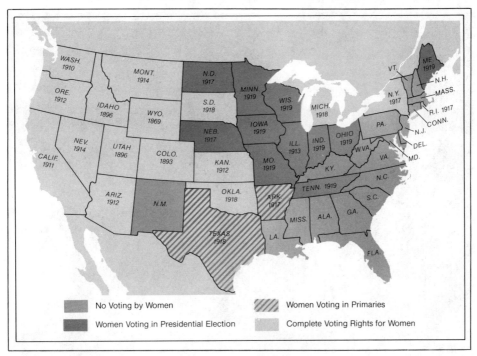

Woman Suffrage before 1920

with its emphasis on male supremacy, wore on. Elizabeth Cady Stanton and a younger recruit, Susan Brownell Anthony, organized the National Woman Suffrage Association in 1869; it was reorganized in 1890 as the National American Woman Suffrage Association (NAWSA). But woman suffrage reformers met abuse and ridicule, from women as well as men. The real momentum of the campaign had to await the emergence of the new middle-class generation of women about whom we have just written. By 1900, only Wyoming, Colorado, Idaho, and Utah had granted the suffrage to women.

After 1900, the NAWSA, under the leadership of Carrie Chapman Catt and Dr. Anna Howard Shaw, turned from propaganda work to political action. By 1914, seven more states had given the vote to women, and Illinois permitted women to vote in presidential elections. But resistance remained formidable, particularly in the South and the East. In 1915, four northeastern states rejected woman suffrage. Moreover, the ranks of women reformers divided when a militant group, led by Alice Paul, broke away from the NAWSA in 1914 and formed the Congressional Union (later the National Woman's party).

The Progressive party platform of 1912 contained a plank vaguely favoring woman suffrage; the Democrats and Republicans were silent on the issue that year. But Catt and Shaw began to bombard Woodrow Wilson with petitions once he was in the White House. Wilson at first refused to take a position. Then he wrote a plank for the Democratic platform of 1916 which recommended that the *states* initiate woman suffrage.

Beginning in 1916, Wilson became a leading advocate of woman suffrage

Carrie Chapman Catt, chosen by Susan B. Anthony as her immediate successor to the presidency of the National Woman Suffrage Association, called for the establishment of a League of Women Voters in 1919 in states where suffrage had already been won. She also collaborated with Jane Addams in founding the Women's Peace Party in 1915. (National Archives)

and worked in cooperation with Catt and Shaw. In 1918, prodded in part by the picketing and hunger strikes of members of the National Woman's party, he pressed to secure congressional approval of a woman-suffrage amendment. He even took the unprecedented step of appearing before the Senate to appeal for its passage. Wilson worked as hard for ratification as he had for congressional approval of what was now the Nineteenth Amendment. It was due to his influence that Tennessee ratified the amendment on August 21, 1919, and made it a part of the Constitution. It was officially declared ratified five days later.

The Nineteenth Amendment marked the beginning, not the culmination, of the fight for equality for women. But that amendment was the necessary beginning and the cornerstone of what would eventually become a powerful movement to recognize the human rights of more than one half of the American people.

Socialism and the Spread of Labor Unrest

The spectacular growth of socialism after 1900 dramatized the extent of discontent in America. After a period of conflict between ideological factions, less radical socialists, led by Morris Hillquit of New York, Victor Berger of Milwaukee, and Eugene V. Debs joined hands to launch the Socialist Party of America in 1901.

The new party was still torn by dissension. On one side were doctrinaire Marxists and radical labor leaders such as William D. Haywood of the Industrial Workers of the World (IWW). On the other side stood moderates such as Hillquit and Berger, who advocated using democratic processes to achieve a limited socialistic economy. The moderates triumphed, at least temporarily, and the party's increasing commitment to democratic gradualism attracted to its ranks a large number of clergymen, writers, and others who believed that thoroughgoing reform was impossible through the major parties. By 1912, Socialist mayors held office in Milwaukee, Schenectady, and Berkeley, California. In the presidential election of 1912, the Socialist candidate, Debs, won 900,000 votes.

Moderate, or reform, socialistic ideas had a greater impact upon progressivism than the record of socialist political accomplishment would indicate. For one thing, socialism had a strong impact upon the leading American social scientists, particularly the economists, and upon the Social Gospel leaders, the chief propounder of which, Walter Rauschenbusch, was a socialist. For a second thing, the American people were not so wedded to the idea of private ownership that they were unwilling to undertake public ownership whenever they concluded that the latter would furnish essential services more efficiently and more cheaply than private companies. In 1917, 2,318 cities owned their own central electrical power stations, nearly half the number that used the services of private companies. During the progressive era, various municipalities operated their own streetcar lines, fuel yards, and even banks.

The prevalence of labor unrest, particularly among unskilled and exploited workers, was a further sign of social ferment. Violence, even open warfare, was connected with ongoing efforts to organize the mass of industrial workers. The worst episode was the so-called Ludlow Massacre in Colorado, when National Guard troops attacked a miners' tent colony in 1914 and accidentally killed eleven women and two children.

The most eloquent and revolutionary voice of labor discontent was the IWW, which worked largely among western lumbermen and miners. In the East, it organized unskilled workers, especially in the textile industry. The IWW seemed to be gaining strength just before the First World War, in spite of its advocacy of violence.

The most important challenge to progressive leaders during this era, in addition to the plight of blacks, was the struggle for economic justice by millions of impoverished workers. Progressives were divided in their responses. Most urban middle-class progressives remained unsympathetic, but they supported measures such as those for minimum wages and workmen's compensation in the hope that these measures would prevent the spread of labor radicalism. Others, particularly leaders of the social-justice movement, warned that American democracy could not survive if a large element of workers felt powerless to shape their own destinies. These progressives asserted that the government should encourage unionization and collective bargaining.

A meeting of the militant Industrial Workers of the World (IWW) in 1908 in New York. Its members, called "Wobblies," denounced the capitalist system and attempted to organize all workers into one industrial union. (Culver Pictures, Inc.)

2. THEODORE ROOSEVELT TAKES COMMAND

Roosevelt and Big Business

Theodore Roosevelt, only forty-three years old when elevated to the presidency by an assassin's bullet, was born in New York in 1858 into a wealthy and aristocratic family. After graduation from Harvard, Roosevelt spent two years on a ranch in North Dakota to rebuild his health. He broke with family tradition and decided to make politics his profession. He served in the New York state legislature and as president of the Police Board of New York City. McKinley appointed Roosevelt as Assistant Secretary of the Navy, but he soon resigned to help organize the Rough Riders. With the help of publicity about his battlefield exploits, Roosevelt won election as governor of New York in 1898. Then he was nominated for the vice-presidency in 1900 at the insistence of the New York Republican boss, Thomas C. Platt, who was eager to speed Roosevelt's exit from the state.

Dynamic energy is the key to understanding Roosevelt's character from boyhood onward. The variety of his interests, activities, and accomplishments was incredible. He was a distinguished amateur historian and naturalist and an accomplished explorer and big-game hunter. Although born to wealth, he chose his friends from all walks of life: cowboys, ambassadors, labor leaders, senators, clergymen, and prize fighters shared his company.

Roosevelt aggressively revived the presidency and made it an effective instrument of national leadership. In the process, he showed contempt for those whom he called "malefactors of great wealth" and for exploiters of human and natural resources. Hence, even though fundamentally conservative, Roosevelt responded to the rising demand for reform.

Roosevelt found obstacles strewn in the path toward reform. Influential business interests had constructed an organization within the Republican party, known as the Old Guard, which could not be toppled by mere bugle blasts. Unable to destroy the Old Guard, Roosevelt decided to work with it; meanwhile he would undermine its power and gain personal control of the GOP.

At the same time, Roosevelt was responsive to public alarm about the rapid spread of industrial consolidation. Roosevelt had a fairly sophisticated understanding of the economic causes for the concentration movement. He never opposed giant corporations simply because of their size. Rather, he tended to apply subjective moral standards to differentiate between "good" corporations and "bad" ones. But he strongly opposed monopoly in industry, and he believed that great corporations should be subjected to considerable regulation.

In February 1902, Roosevelt instructed the Attorney General to bring suit under the Sherman Act for the dissolution of the Northern Securities Company, a holding company which J. P. Morgan had recently formed to control the Northern Pacific and Great Northern railroads. A federal court ordered dissolution of the Northern Securities Company in 1903, and the Supreme Court upheld the decision by a five-to-four vote in 1904.

The government's action in this case symbolized the beginning of a vigorous antitrust crusade. Roosevelt activated the Sherman Act against industrial corporations, beginning with a suit against the so-called Beef Trust. Suits followed against, among others, the Standard Oil Company in 1907 and the American Tobacco Company in 1908. The Supreme Court supported the government in every case; it even went so far in the oil and tobacco cases in 1911 as to reverse the Knight decision (see p. 293) and to rule that the Sherman Act did outlaw monopolies in manufacturing.

Meanwhile, in 1903, Roosevelt demanded enactment of a bill to create a Bureau of Corporations empowered to investigate all business practices. Immense opposition developed from big business interests, but Roosevelt prevailed by appealing over the head of Congress to public opinion.

Roosevelt again asserted his leadership dramatically in the same year that he opened his antitrust crusade. Anthracite coal miners in Pennsylvania began a strike on May 14, 1902. John Mitchell, president of the United Mine Workers, tried in vain to persuade the mine operators to hear the workers' grievances. As the strike dragged on, coal prices rose from $5 to $30 a ton for those fortunate enough to find any. Roosevelt found the situation intolerable and decided to intervene. The President summoned Mitchell and the mine operators to the White House. Let the miners go back to work at once, he demanded. Meanwhile, he would appoint an arbitral commission to recommend a settlement. Mitchell accepted the plan, but the operators refused.

To the strong-willed, "imperial" President, the operators' refusal was nothing less than defiance of *his* authority and the national interest. He issued secret orders to move 10,000 troops into the anthracite region, seize the mines, and operate them for the government. The operators then accepted his plan of mediation on the condition that Roosevelt would not name a labor leader to the arbitral commission. Roosevelt coolly named a former railway union official to the commission as a "sociologist." The miners returned to work in October, and a short time later the arbitral commission essentially ruled in their favor. But the significance of the affair went far beyond the miners' immediate gains. For the first time, the federal government had intervened in a labor dispute without automatically taking the side of management.

The Big Stick in Diplomacy

The young President increasingly took part in world affairs with the same vigor which he showed in domestic policies, and he justified his actions with what he said was an old African proverb: "Speak softly and carry a big stick, and you will go far." Roosevelt carried a big stick, but he did not always speak softly during his first years as President.

Americans had long dreamed of uniting the Atlantic and Pacific oceans by an interoceanic canal. A French company obtained from Colombia in 1878 the right to dig a canal across the Colombian province of Panama. But disease and engineering obstacles dashed their hopes, and the company abandoned work.

The war with Spain revived American interest in connecting the two oceans. Also, the development of the West Coast, anticipation of a large far eastern trade, and acquisition of distant Pacific colonies highlighted the economic and strategic needs. Therefore Congress created an Isthmian Canal Commission and directed it to investigate the comparative advantages of routes through Nicaragua and Panama.

One diplomatic obstacle blocked the way—the Clayton-Bulwer Treaty of 1850, by which Great Britain and the United States had promised not to build a canal without the other's participation. The British government abandoned its rights under the treaty in the first Hay-Pauncefote Treaty (1900) on condition that the United States should never fortify the canal. The Senate refused to accept the condition, and the British, in the second Hay-Pauncefote Treaty (1901), withdrew their objection to fortification.

Roosevelt and the canal commission favored a Nicaraguan route, but, when agents of the New Panama Canal Company (which owned the rights of the old French company) cut their price from $109 million to $40 million, Roosevelt and the commission thought that this was a good bargain. In June 1902, Congress authorized use of the Panamanian route, provided that the President could obtain a right-of-way from Colombia.

Secretary Hay concluded a treaty with the Colombian chargé, Tomás Herrán, on January 22, 1903. The United States agreed to pay Colombia $10 million at once and an annual sum of $250,000. In return, Colombia leased to the United States forever a strip of land six miles wide across the Isthmus of Panama. The Colombian government rejected the treaty, chiefly because the rights of the French company would expire within a year, and Colombia could then demand payment to herself of the $40 million. Roosevelt was infuriated. It was, he said, as if "a road agent had tried to hold up a man." An angry President made plans to seize the isthmus by force.

He did not have to. Panamanian leaders, financed by Philippe Bunau-Varilla, agent of the New Panama Canal Company in the United States, set plans in motion for a revolution. Roosevelt and Secretary of State Hay knew about the plot and at least indirectly supported it. The revolution took place in Panama City on schedule on November 3, 1903. To prevent it, 400 Colombian troops had been landed at Colón, on the Atlantic side of the isthmus. But U.S.S. *Nashville* had, quite providentially, arrived at Colón on the preceding day. Its commander, under instructions from Washington, landed troops and forbade the Colombian general to march his troops across the isthmus.

The United States recognized the independence of Panama on November 6. Bunau-Varilla, a French citizen, hastened to Washington as Panamanian minister to the United States. On November 18, he signed with Secretary Hay a duplicate of the Hay-Herrán Treaty—except that the strip of land was widened to ten miles, and the United States obtained the right to intervene at any time in order to protect Panama City and Colón. The Senate enthusiastically approved the Hay-Bunau-Varilla Treaty, but Americans gradually developed a guilty conscience about the affair, and a committee of the House of Representatives in 1912 virtually accused Roosevelt of wrongdoing. He never seemed to have any regrets, but in 1911 he acknowledged: "I took the Canal Zone and let Congress debate, and while the debate goes on the Canal does also."

The first ship passed through the canal on January 7, 1914. It soon proved a tremendous boon to world trade, as well as a vital link in American national security. Whether the good accomplished justified the United States Government's aggression against Colombia remains doubtful.

In 1903, Roosevelt became embroiled in a controversy with Germany over Venezuela's nonpayment of debts to that country (Germany had bombarded a Venezuelan fort in reprisal). The issue was finally adjudicated by the Hague Tribunal, a world agency created in 1899. In its ruling the Hague Tribunal awarded first claim on Venezuela's debt payments to Germany, Britain, and Italy—the very countries which had used force to attempt to collect the debts. The ruling, therefore, seemed to suggest that the application of military force was the surest guarantee of collection of debts against Latin American countries. Roosevelt agreed that European creditors were due payment of just debts, but he believed that the American people would not tolerate armed intervention by a European power in Latin America.

In 1904, American sensitivity over armed European intervention in Latin America, plus concern for the defense of the Panama Canal, led Roosevelt to announce a new policy, soon called the Roosevelt Corollary to the Monroe Doctrine. The Monroe Doctrine, Roosevelt stated, prohibited European use of force in the new world. Since the United States forbade European nations to intervene, it would itself take action to guarantee that Latin American nations paid their debts. The Roosevelt Corollary was based on bad history: no one had ever before suggested that the Monroe Doctrine forbade temporary European interventions. Nor was it clear that the United States possessed any right, other than that derived from superior military power, to collect the debts of Latin American countries and supervise their payments.

Roosevelt and Conservation

Theodore Roosevelt came to the presidency with a concern for the conservation of America's enormous but dwindling natural resources. His education as a conservationist was advanced by his friend and favorite White House boxing partner, Gifford Pinchot, chief of the Forestry Service. With aid from

Pinchot and others, Roosevelt took up the work of conservation in a program with four main objectives. First, national forests should be enlarged, protected, and carefully exploited in order to guarantee that their yield would be perpetual. Second, irrigation projects should be launched to reclaim arid lands. Third, internal waterways should be improved and extended. Fourth, state governments should cooperate with the national government in conservation programs.

Congress, in 1891, had given the President power to withdraw public lands from sale and homesteading and establish them as forest reserves. However, the total combined area of lands reserved before 1901 was less than 50,000,000 acres. Roosevelt added 148,000,000 acres, plus additional millions in mineral lands and waterpower sites.

Moreover, a new era of federal participation in irrigation began with the adoption of the National Reclamation, or Newlands, Act of 1902. It awarded the proceeds from the sale of public lands in sixteen western states to finance irrigation projects. The acreage of irrigated land, less than 1,000,000 in 1880, had increased to more than 20,000,000 by 1920. Arid lands, formerly worth only a cent or two an acre for grazing, became worth hundreds of dollars an acre for agriculture. Fruits and vegetables came to eastern markets from Arizona and California farms which, a few years earlier, had been sandy wastes. Almost 10 per cent of the population of Mexico crossed the border and provided the labor which made this transformation possible.

The White House, Roosevelt said, was a "bully pulpit," and he used it to arouse public support for his policies. He used the "bully pulpit" with particular success in his campaign for conservation. The high point of that campaign was the Conservation Conference which he summoned to the White House in May 1908. The East Room was crowded with governors, members of the cabinet and of the Supreme Court, congressmen, influential businessmen, labor leaders, and delegates from conservation organizations. The Conference resulted in the appointment of national and state conservation commissions. Moreover, private citizens organized a National Conservation Association in 1909, which soon became one of the most powerful special-interest groups in the United States.

President in His Own Right

Four Vice-Presidents had succeeded to the presidency during the nineteenth century, but none had been able to win nomination for a full presidential term. Big business interests eagerly sought Roosevelt's retirement in 1904, but he had so completely mastered the GOP organizations and so mesmerized the rank and file of Republican voters that even the Old Guard could not possibly have prevented his nomination.

The Democrats hoped to capitalize on conservative opposition to Roosevelt and nominated a colorless nonentity, Judge Alton B. Parker of New York. A dull campaign followed. It was enlivened only by Parker's charge that Roosevelt had blackmailed Wall Street into financing his campaign. Roosevelt blackmailed no one, but J. P. Morgan and other men of wealth did contribute generously to the Republican war chest. In the end, the voters gave Roosevelt the largest popular majority awarded a presidential candidate to that time.

Roosevelt was stunned by the size of his popular mandate, but he quickly grasped the significance of his victory. Progressivism and insurgency were sweeping the country. Roosevelt responded by taking leadership of the nationwide reform movement. Great corporations, railroads, and financial institutions had to submit to public control, Roosevelt warned. The people particularly demanded effective control of railroads, and he would see to it that this control was obtained. When Congress assembled in December 1905, Roosevelt demanded a new railroad-regulation law, pure-food and drug legislation, and other reforms. The fight for railroad legislation was long and hard, but Roosevelt won his essential objectives in the Hepburn Act, which he signed on June 29, 1906. The act tightened the provisions against rebating and gave the ICC power to reduce unreasonable rates on the complaint of shippers, subject to the review of federal courts. The Hepburn Act, in short, gave the ICC effective power for the first time in its history.

Roosevelt won passage of three other reform measures. A Meat Inspection Act gave federal officials authority to see that all meat shipped in interstate commerce came from healthy animals and was packed under sanitary conditions. It was passed soon after the publication of Upton Sinclair's novel, *The Jungle*, a socialist exposé of the meat-packing industry. The Food and Drug Act forbade the manufacture and sale of adulterated or poisonous foods, drugs, and liquors. Finally, the Employers' Liability Act of 1906 established a system of accident insurance for workers in the District of Columbia and on interstate railroads.

A sharp decline on the New York Stock Exchange began in March 1907. It led to business failures and runs on banks which caused a dangerous financial stringency. For a brief period, Roosevelt relaxed his reform energies. Indeed, during the worst of the panic he permitted the United States Steel Corporation to purchase a large competitor in the South, the Tennessee Coal and Iron Company, in violation of the Sherman Antitrust Act.

Business confidence and prosperity returned rapidly in 1908, and Roosevelt resumed his drive for reform. He obtained little legislation from Congress during his last year in office, but, in a series of messages, he advocated income and estate taxes, reduction of the tariff, and more effective governmental control of business.

Hindsight makes it clear that Roosevelt was not the radical that his critics charged. He believed in the free-enterprise system, but he wanted to make it work for the benefit of all people, not just the privileged few. To him must go the credit for giving voice to popular demands for reform and for the first successful leadership of the progressive movement on the national level.

Imperial Diplomacy

Theodore Roosevelt was a more tactful and restrained diplomatist during his second term. This new style was first revealed when Roosevelt mediated the Russo-Japanese War. Japan had gone to war with Russia in 1904 to block Russian expansion into Korea and Manchuria. The Japanese were victorious by 1905, but they were also financially exhausted, and the Japanese government appealed to the American President in April 1905 to mediate the conflict. Roosevelt earlier had supported the Japanese, but he refused to intercede until the Japanese had agreed to respect the Open Door and to return Manchuria to China. The Japanese finally consented, and, in August 1905, Roosevelt invited Japanese and Russian delegates to a peace conference in Portsmouth, New Hampshire. For his part in ending this conflict, Roosevelt was awarded the Nobel Peace Prize.

Roosevelt's efforts to establish good relations with Japan hit a snag in 1906. Japanese laborers had been coming into California at the rate of about 1,000 a year since the 1890s—to the consternation of many Californians. The San Francisco school board, in the autumn of 1906, required the segregation of all Oriental school children. It was an open insult to a proud and hitherto friendly people. Roosevelt persuaded the school board to revoke the segregation order. In return, the State Department negotiated a "Gentlemen's Agreement" with the Japanese government—an informal understanding that the Tokyo government would issue no more passports to workers who intended to go to the continental United States.

Meanwhile, an even more dangerous situation had been developing in Europe. The German government deeply resented France's expanding control over Morocco, which endangered German commercial interests. The Germans demanded an international conference to protect the open door in Morocco. The French refused, and war seemed certain. Then the German Emperor appealed to Roosevelt, who reluctantly supported him. The French yielded, and a conference of the major powers, including the United States, met in Algeciras, in southern Spain, in early 1906. The conference reached an agreement that averted war but did not prevent the French from closing the open door in Morocco. German leaders then realized that they could obtain world power commensurate with their nation's wealth and military might only by force of arms. Thus, the Moroccan controversy helped to bring on the First World War.

As a sign of America's emergence as a world power, Roosevelt decided in the summer of 1907 to send the American battle fleet around the world. A fleet of twenty-eight vessels steamed out of Hampton Roads, Virginia, on December 16, 1907. The officers and men were received warmly at every port of call, and nowhere was there greater friendliness than at Yokohama and Tokyo. As he looked back over his administration a few years later, Roosevelt concluded that sending the fleet on its fourteen-month, 46,000-mile voyage had been his most important contribution to the cause of peace. He exaggerated, but one fact was clear in 1909: the American navy was an efficient and highly mobile striking force—a power to be reckoned with in the councils of the world.

3. REPUBLICAN TROUBLES UNDER TAFT

Roosevelt Dictates His Successor

After his election in 1904, Roosevelt had announced that he would not be a candidate again in 1908, and he kept his pledge. Roosevelt would have preferred to choose as his successor his Secretary of State, Elihu Root. Root's career as an attorney for major business firms, however, eliminated him as a candidate. Roosevelt finally turned to his Secretary of War, William Howard Taft, who was nominated on the first ballot by the Republican national convention.

The Democrats turned again to Bryan. The "Great Commoner" made his

William Howard Taft campaigning for the presidency in 1908. A large, good-natured man, Taft had little interest in politics and once wrote: "Politics, when I am in it, makes me sick." His basic conservatism, complacency, and lack of vigor made him a weak and ineffective President amid the fervor and conflict of the progressive era. (United Press International)

campaign largely on the tariff and trust issues, but he also frankly appealed for labor support by promising unions relief from injunctions. Gompers and the AFL departed from their policy of nonpartisanship and entered the campaign for Bryan. Taft won the election handily, but Democratic governors were elected in several states which went for Taft. More significant was the increase in Republican insurgency in the Middle West. The midwestern progressive group in Congress, heretofore a small minority, would be a powerful force in the Sixty-first Congress.

Taft as President

William Howard Taft, born in Cincinnati in 1857, had enjoyed a distinguished career in public service since the 1880s. A fine lawyer and administrator, Taft was also the largest man, physically, ever to sit in the presidential chair. In a quiet period of political life, Taft would have been a successful President. Unhappily for this man who wanted only to do well, the country simmered in political revolt, and the Republican party was split between the rising insurgents and the Old Guard. Had Roosevelt been in

Taft's place, he probably could have kept the GOP together. Taft was not only unable to keep peace within his party; he also contributed to its disruption. The new President thought himself to be a progressive, and in many ways he was. He believed in tariff and tax reform, and he carried on Roosevelt's conservation and antitrust policies.

Taft ran into grave difficulties for several reasons. He was slow-moving, put off problems until it was too late, and gave the appearance of laziness. Several failures could have been avoided if he had only given decisive leadership to his party in Congress. Taft's judicial temperament also inhibited his progressivism. He had grave doubts about the legality of many advanced progressive measures. Finally, Taft disliked and distrusted the new insurgent leaders in his own party. He inevitably drifted toward the political attitudes of his conservative friends.

The Republican platform of 1908 pledged the new administration to revise the highly protective Dingley Tariff Act of 1897. The cost of living had increased some 40 per cent between 1897 and 1909, and most people had assumed, incorrectly, that high tariff rates were responsible for the increase. Taft called Congress into special session in March 1909 for the purpose of lowering the tariff. An administration bill, introduced by Representative Sereno E. Payne of New York, passed the House of Representatives by a large majority. However, the Senate Finance Committee, headed by Senator Nelson W. Aldrich of Rhode Island, reported the Payne bill to the Senate with 847 amendments, more than 600 of which increased rates. A wave of indignation swept the country, particularly after a group of insurgent Republican senators took leadership in the fight against the Aldrich bill. Their efforts failed, and the measure, now known as the Payne-Aldrich bill, passed both houses and was signed by Taft.

In a speech in September 1909, Taft foolishly called the Payne-Aldrich Act the best tariff measure which the Republican party had ever passed. However, angry public opinion disagreed. Even Republican newspapers published fiery editorials about the tariff "betrayal," and insurgent Republican leaders wondered whether Taft had deserted to the Old Guard.

The so-called Ballinger affair, which followed immediately after the tariff fight, widened the breach between Taft and the progressives. An investigator in the Interior Department told Gifford Pinchot that Richard A. Ballinger, Secretary of the Interior, was showing favoritism to a private syndicate which sought to develop coal properties in Alaska. Pinchot urged the investigator to go directly to the President. He did so, but Taft accepted Ballinger's explanation and dismissed the investigator. Then Pinchot entered the controversy publicly with accusations against Ballinger; Taft at once dismissed Pinchot. A congressional committee later cleared Ballinger of wrongdoing, but the committee's investigation revealed that the secretary was openly antagonistic to conservation.

Taft was convinced early in 1910 that the insurgents planned to prevent his renomination. The President therefore joined with leaders of the Old Guard in a nationwide campaign to defeat the insurgents in the mid-term Republican primaries. But the flames of insurgency continued to rage, and the administration's candidates went down to defeat everywhere. By the summer of 1910, Republican insurgents were talking about organizing a new party if Taft won renomination in 1912.

Unlike his predecessor, Taft had neither the will nor the ability to play a leading role in world affairs. The most important new departure under Taft was "dollar diplomacy." Taft and his Secretary of State, Philander C. Knox, desired above all to increase American security and influence in the Caribbean; and this they attempted to do by persuading American bankers to displace European creditors in that region. Taft defended his policies on humanitarian and economic grounds. However, implementing "dollar diplomacy" led, among other things, to American participation in a civil war in Nicaragua and the victory of the conservative party of that country. Equally ill-fated was the Washington government's proposal in 1909 to internationalize the railroads of Manchuria. This move drove Russia and Japan together in order to ward off American influence.

Repudiation of Taft

The revolt against the administration reached its first culmination in the mid-term elections of 1910. Repudiation of the Taft policies seemed inevitable, so great was public indignation against them. Taft tried to make peace with the midwestern insurgents, but to no avail. He blundered again by alienating Theodore Roosevelt.

Actually, that alienation had begun much earlier. Roosevelt, after Taft's inauguration, departed for Africa to hunt lions. He then made a triumphal tour through Europe. But he also followed events at home with a careful eye. He returned to New York on June 18, 1910, convinced that Taft's betrayal of his policies had made a division in the Republican party inevitable. Roosevelt was still eager to heal party wounds, but Taft rebuffed his efforts at mediation. Roosevelt then set out upon a speaking tour in which he expounded his now fully matured advanced progressivism—the New Nationalism. He advocated strict regulation of large corporations, publicity of campaign funds, income and estate taxes, workmen's compensation laws, protective legislation for women and children in industry, and all the measures for reform of political institutions which progressives were championing.

Roosevelt's eloquent articulation of an advanced progressive program only emphasized the wide gulf between the insurgents and the Taft administration. It also contributed to the emphatic repudiation of Taft and the Old Guard which occurred in November 1910. The Democrats won control of the House of Representatives for the first time since 1892. Old Guard strength in the Senate was so greatly reduced that a coalition of Democrats and progressive Republicans won control of that body. Moreover, Democrats elected twenty-six governors, including governors in several traditionally Republican states. The progressive movement was profoundly affecting American politics.

SUGGESTED READINGS

Among the useful general works on the progressive era are Wiebe, *The Search for Order*, and Hays, *The Response to Industrialism*, both previously cited; John W. Chambers III, *The Tyranny of Change* (1980); Robert M. Crunden, *Ministers of Reform: The Progressives' Achievement* (1982); and Arthur S. Link and Richard L. McCormick, *Progressivism (1983). Wiebe, *Businessmen and Reform* (1962), and Gabriel Kolko, *The Triumph of Conservatism* (1963), emphasize the role which businessmen played, although the latter book is badly flawed. See also Fine, *Laissez Faire and the General Welfare State*, already cited; Eric F. Goldman, *Rendezvous with Destiny* (1953); John D. Buenker, *Urban Liberalism and Progressive Reform* (1973); and James T. Timberlake, *Prohibition and the Progressive Movement* (1963).

Most of the works mentioned on reform movements in Suggested Readings for Chapter 19 are relevant here. The best work on the muckrakers is David M. Chalmers, *The Social and Political Ideas of the Muckrakers* (1964), but there is no substitute for the writings of the muckrakers themselves, particularly Lincoln Steffens, *The Shame of the Cities* (1904), and *The Struggle for Self-Government* (1906).

The best state study on progressivism is David P. Thelen, *The New Citizenship: Origins of Progressivism in Wisconsin, 1885–1900* (1972). Other good local and state studies are David C. Hammack, *Power and Society: Greater New York at the Turn of the Century* (1982); Ransom E. Noble, Jr., *New Jersey Progressivism before Wilson* (1946); George E. Mowry, *The California Progressives* (1951); Richard L. McCormick, *From Realignment to Reform: Political Change in New York State, 1893–1910* (1981); and, more generally, Martin J. Schiesl, *The Politics of Efficiency: Municipal Administration and Reform in America, 1880–1920* (1977).

Robert H. Bremner, *From the Depths: The Discovery of Poverty in the United States* (1956), is the best general study of the movement for social justice. Allen F. Davis, *Spearheads for Reform: The Social Settlements and the Progressive Movement* (1967), is also excellent. A broad and important study is James T. Patterson, *America's Struggle against Poverty 1900–1980* (1981). For the contributions of women, see John C. Farrell, *Beloved Lady* (1967), on Jane Addams, and Josephine C. Goldmark, *Impatient Crusader: Florence Kelley's Life Story* (1953). Some of the most important works on the

subject of women's rights are Eleanor Flexner, *Century of Struggle: The Woman's Rights Movement in the United States* (1975); Aileen S. Kraditor, *The Ideas of the Woman Suffrage Movement, 1890–1920* (1965); and Anne F. Scott, *The Southern Lady: From Pedestal to Politics, 1830–1930* (1971).

For socialism and left-wing unionism during the progressive era, see Nick Salvatore, *Eugene V. Debs, Citizen and Socialist* (1982); David A. Shannon, *The Socialist Party of America: A History* (1955); John P. Diggins, *The American Left in the Twentieth Century* (1973); and Melvyn Dubofsky, *We Shall Be All: A History of the Industrial Workers of the World* (1969).

The best introduction to the national politics of this period is George E. Mowry, *The Era of Theodore Roosevelt* (1958) and *Theodore Roosevelt and the Progressive Movement* (1947). Elmo P. Richardson, *The Politics of Conservation . . . 1897–1913* (1962); Sidney Ratner, *Taxation and Democracy in America* (1967); and Hans Thorelli, *The Federal Antitrust Policy* (1954), are the standard works on these subjects.

The biographical literature on the political leaders of this period is quite rich. William H. Harbaugh, *The Life and Times of Theodore Roosevelt* (1963), is the best one-volume biography, but see also Morris, *The Rise of Theodore Roosevelt,* already cited, and John M. Blum, *The Republican Roosevelt* (1954). Henry F. Pringle, *The Life and Times of William Howard Taft,* 2 vols. (1938), is uncritical. Richard W. Leopold, *Elihu Root and the Conservative Tradition* (1954); Merlo J. Pusey, *Charles Evans Hughes,* 2 vols. (1951); John A. Garraty, *Henry Cabot Lodge* (1953); and Widenor, *Henry Cabot Lodge,* cited earlier, are all excellent biographies of Republican leaders.

For the diplomacy of the Roosevelt and Taft administrations, see Howard K. Beale, *Theodore Roosevelt and the Rise of America to World Power* (1961), and Walter V. and Marie V. Scholes, *The Foreign Policies of the Taft Administration* (1970).

CHAPTER 23
WOODROW WILSON
AND THE TRIUMPH OF
PROGRESSIVISM

1. REVOLT AT HIGH TIDE, 1910–1912

The Fight for Control of the GOP

Republican insurgents did not wait long after the elections of 1910 to organize a fight for control of their party. In January 1911, their leaders formed the National Republican Progressive League, and soon thereafter a conference of 300 progressives, most of them Republicans, endorsed Senator Robert La Follette for President. The great enigma in the Republican situation was Theodore Roosevelt. Republican progressives pressed him to enter the race against Taft. They admired La Follette, but they knew that only Roosevelt could unseat an incumbent President. Roosevelt hated the thought of a personal battle against Taft, and he did not want to destroy the Republican unity so essential to victory in 1912.

Roosevelt finally yielded to the pleadings of his friends, mainly because he was convinced that Taft's renomination would wreck the GOP and lead to Democratic victory in 1912. The battle that ensued within the Republican party was one of the bitterest in the history of American politics. Roosevelt and his followers fought with incredible vigor. Taft's friends replied with personal attacks that soon brought the campaign to a very low level. In the end, the mass of Republican voters rallied to the man who remained their hero. Roosevelt won smashing victories in the states which had presidential primaries, even defeating Taft in his home state of Ohio.

Yet the issue was still very much in doubt at the

end of the Republican preconvention campaign. Roosevelt had barely missed winning a majority of the delegates. Taft had collected about one third, most of them controlled by conservative state Republican machines. The outcone depended on the decision over 254 contested delegates. Taft and the Old Guard controlled the Republican National Committee. Its credentials committee awarded nineteen of the contested delegates to Roosevelt and 235 to Taft—just enough to insure Taft a majority.

Roosevelt was convinced that the bosses had stolen the nomination. Immediately after the convention, he agreed to accept nomination on a third-party ticket. The rebels returned to Chicago, organized the Progressive party, and nominated Roosevelt and Governor Hiram W. Johnson of California to head their ticket. The delegates sang "Onward Christian Soldiers" and listened, enraptured, as Roosevelt announced that they stood at Armageddon and battled for the Lord.

The Emergence of Woodrow Wilson

It seemed obvious after the election of 1910 that, with new leadership, the Democratic party could win the presidency in 1912. When Bryan announced that he would not be a candidate, party leadership and a chance for the highest office were open, and an all-out struggle for control followed.

Woodrow Wilson had made a brilliant campaign for the governorship of New Jersey in 1910. Then he had pushed a series of important reform laws through the state legislature in 1911. Bold and aggressive, he was rapidly transforming himself into a true progressive—and a leading contender for the Democratic presidential nomination. Wilson began an exhaustive campaign for that nomination in the spring of 1911. He was so successful that, by the end of the year, victory seemed certain.

Opposition developed suddenly in the candidacy of Champ Clark of Missouri, Speaker of the House of Representatives. He was a disciple of Bryan who had served without distinction in the House since the 1890s. Wilson campaigned widely, but would make no promises to conservative state organizations. Clark remained in Washington and lined up the support of many state leaders and of William Randolph Hearst, the demagogic publisher, who was powerful in the Democratic party. To make matters worse for Wilson, Representative Oscar W. Underwood of Alabama also entered the contest. Underwood drew off support in the South which, otherwise, probably would have gone to Wilson.

The Wilson cause seemed hopeless when the Democrats assembled in their national convention on June 25, 1912. Clark won a majority, but not the two thirds needed for nomination, on the tenth ballot. Bryan switched his vote from Clark to Wilson on the fourteenth ballot. Finally, Underwood's supporters threw their votes to Wilson, and the nomination went to the New Jersey governor on the forty-sixth ballot.

The New Freedom versus the New Nationalism

Taft made almost no effort to campaign and was never in the running. The Socialist candidate, Debs, made a hard fight and had some impact, but he never had a chance. However, in Roosevelt and Wilson the people had candidates of superb intelligence, great capacity for leadership, and boldness of vision. Both men called themselves progressives, but important differences separated them. The campaign revealed, for the first time, a deep cleavage in national progressivism.

The Democratic platform of 1912 approved most of the then widely supported measures for political and economic reform. But on the great issue of 1912—how far the federal government should go to promote human welfare—the Democratic platform was vague. Indeed, its silence on specific social and economic welfare legislation indicated that the party still adhered to its traditional state-rights doctrines and a general policy of modified laissez faire on the federal level.

Wilson, following his party's platform, began by highlighting the tariff issue. But this drew little response. While he searched for a more dramatic issue, Wilson met Louis D. Brandeis of Boston, a prominent foe of big business. Brandeis persuaded Wilson that the most important national problem was the destruction of monopoly. Wilson developed the program which he called the New Freedom. He would unleash American economic energies through the destruction of special privileges and the preservation of competition in the business world. And he would accomplish this great goal by reducing the tariff, reforming the banking and currency system, and

The Election of 1912

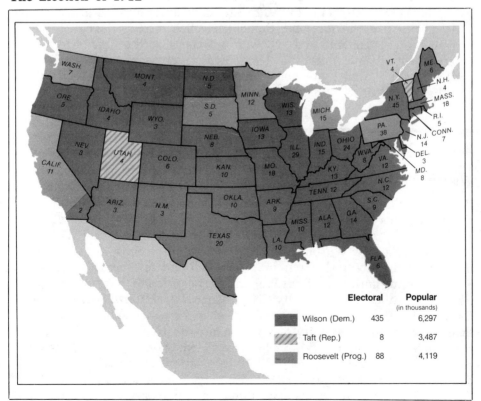

	Electoral	Popular (in thousands)
Wilson (Dem.)	435	6,297
Taft (Rep.)	8	3,487
Roosevelt (Prog.)	88	4,119

strengthening the Sherman Act. Thus he would renew the individualism that had made the United States rich and powerful.

Theodore Roosevelt responded with what he called the New Nationalism, a program which expressed advanced American political and socioeconomic thinking in a remarkable way. It included all the various proposals then advanced for the reform of political institutions and practices. It embodied, moreover, Roosevelt's more recent thinking about the most effective way to deal with big business. Great corporations were here to stay, Roosevelt asserted, and they should be subjected to sweeping regulation by a federal trade commission. Finally, the New Nationalism demanded graduated federal income and estate taxes, a national child-labor law, and other measures to protect the exploited. The Progressive platform laid down the guidelines for federal policies for at least a generation.

The debate between Wilson and Roosevelt only emphasized the wide ideological gulf between the New Freedom and the New Nationalism. Wilson charged that the New Nationalism would end in the acceptance of monopoly by the federal government and the enslavement of the American people by a paternalistic government dominated by great economic interests. Roosevelt replied that the New Freedom was oblivious to the great social and economic challenges of the time. The New Freedom, he declared contemptuously, was really the old economic freedom to cut your neighbor's throat.

Wilson and the Democrats swept the country on election day in 1912. Wilson carried forty states and received more electoral votes (435) than any previous presidential contender. The Democrats also won control of the Sixty-third Congress and elected governors in three fifths of the states which had gubernatorial elections in 1912. But the election returns also provided Wilson with material for sober thought. He had received less than 42 per cent of the popular vote and had won only because the Republicans were divided and because Roosevelt had failed to unite progressives of both parties. Perhaps even more unsettling was the spectacular increase in the Socialist presidential vote to nearly 900,000.

2. THE NEW FREEDOM

Woodrow Wilson and the Progressive Movement

Woodrow Wilson carried on the work which Roosevelt had begun in laying the foundations for the modern political economy of the United States and in reconstructing the presidency into the powerful office which it is today.

Thomas Woodrow Wilson was born in Staunton, Virginia, in 1856, the son of a distinguished Presbyterian minister. Wilson grew up in Georgia and South Carolina during the Civil War and Reconstruction, but from his youth he was an American nationalist. He attended Davidson College in North Carolina and then Princeton University, where he was graduated in 1879. He studied law at the University of Virginia and practiced for a year in Atlanta. He then went to the newly founded Johns Hopkins University for graduate work in history, political science, and economics, and received the Ph.D. degree from that institution in 1886. He taught, successively, at Bryn Mawr College, Wesleyan University, and Princeton University between 1885 and

Woodrow Wilson as president of Princeton University is shown here with Andrew Carnegie to his left at commencement exercises. Carnegie had recently become a Princeton benefactor. (Brown Brothers)

1902. He was elected president of Princeton in 1902 and soon earned a national reputation as a pioneer in the field of higher education.

The obsession of Wilson during all of his adult life was the study of how leadership could make democracy work more effectively. He believed for many years that the chief defect of the American constitutional system was the division of responsibility between Congress and the President. That division, he thought, made responsible leadership impossible. His remedy was an adaptation of the British cabinet system, which concentrates all responsibility in a ministry answerable directly to the legislature. However, the War with Spain and, particularly, Roosevelt's revitalization of the presidential office caused Wilson to view the presidency in a new light. The President, Wilson wrote, "is . . . the political leader of the nation, or has it in his choice to be. The nation as a whole has chosen him, and is conscious that it has no other political spokesman. . . . If he rightly interprets the national thought and boldly insists upon it, he is irresistible."

Wilson himself literally transformed the presidency. He was a strong-willed activist who took control of his party in Congress and became, in effect, its prime minister. He originated legislation, saw it through to passage, and, if necessary, used public opinion as a club over Congress. Although a latecomer to the ranks of progressivism, Wilson made his greatest domestic contribution by bringing the national progressive movement to its first full flowering.

Wilson and the Triumph of Tariff Reform

The first item on Wilson's legislative agenda was tariff reform, specifically, revision of the Payne-Aldrich Act. On the very day that he was inaugurated,

Wilson called Congress into special session. When it met, he went in person to deliver a brief and forceful address. It was the first time since John Adams that a President had addressed a joint session of Congress. Thus, at the very beginning of his administration, Wilson asserted his leadership in legislation.

The administration's bill, drafted under Wilson's supervision by Oscar W. Underwood, fulfilled all of the Democratic party's promises of tariff reduction. It also included a provision for a slight income tax, which ranged from 1 to 4 per cent. The measure easily passed the House. Then, as had so often happened before, lobbyists descended on Washington to put pressure on the Senate Finance Committee, which would consider the Underwood bill. Wilson struck out boldly in a public statement which denounced the lobbyists who, he said, infested Washington. Wilson, moreover, put such heavy personal pressure on wavering Democratic senators that all but two of them fell into line. The bill that the Finance Committee reported and the Senate approved actually *reduced* the Underwood bill's rates and *increased* the maximum income tax to 7 per cent. Both houses approved this version, and Wilson signed the bill on October 3, 1913.

The First World War broke out before the effects of the new rates could be felt significantly, but the Underwood-Simmons Act had an enormous political significance. Wilson's victory in his first test fastened his control over the Democratic forces in Congress and won the confidence of people still skeptical about the Democratic party's ability to fulfill its campaign promises.

The Federal Reserve Act

Wilson went to the Capitol again on June 23, 1913, to demand thoroughgoing banking and currency reform. Everyone agreed that the banking structure and currency systems were inadequate for the needs of the American economy in the twentieth century. The Panic of 1907 had revealed two major flaws—the absence of a central bank to mobilize reserves in emergencies and a currency based upon inflexible supplies of gold and the bonded indebtedness of the United States, rather than upon the real wealth of the nation.

Most bankers wanted a reserve system and money supply controlled by private banks, similar to a plan proposed by Senator Aldrich in 1912. On the other hand, Bryan and his followers, particularly Senator Robert L. Owen of Oklahoma, chairman of the Senate Banking Committee, wanted total public control of the reserve bank (or banks) and exclusive governmental issue of currency. Carter Glass of Virginia, chairman of the Banking Committee of the House of Representatives, however, demanded a decentralized reserve system under private control.

Wilson himself made the final decisions about the banking and currency measure called the federal reserve bill. A decentralized system of Federal Reserve Banks, to be owned and largely controlled by private banks, would mobilize reserves and perform other central banking functions. These Federal Reserve Banks would issue a new currency—Federal Reserve notes—based on gold and commercial and agricultural paper, in accordance with fluctuating needs. Moreover, Federal Reserve notes would be obligations of the United States Government. A Federal Reserve Board, composed entirely of presidential appointees, would be the "capstone" of the system. It would mobilize and shift banking reserves from one section of the country when needed, set interest rates, and, in general, determine the money supply of the country. Glass introduced the federal reserve bill on September 9, and the House quickly approved it by a huge majority. The fight in the Senate, in contrast, was long and harrowing on account of the frantic opposition of certain big-city banking interests. But Wilson would not yield on any major points, and the bill was passed as he wanted it on December 23.

The Federal Reserve Act was the crowning domestic achievement of his administration. The Federal Reserve system, with twelve regional banks united by the Federal Reserve Board, went into operation in 1914. It was a success from the outset, and, soon, the very bankers who had condemned the bill were its strongest supporters. As a result of the collapse of the American banking system in the early 1930s, the Federal Reserve Board was reorganized and its powers enlarged. But our present-day banking and currency structures remain essentially those established by the Wilsonian legislation.

A New Solution for the Trust Problem

The last major item on the New Freedom schedule was legislation to strengthen the Sherman Antitrust Act. Many conservatives, including former President Taft, asserted that there was no need for new legislation in view of the Supreme Court's recent clarification of the Sherman Act in the Standard Oil and American Tobacco Company decisions. Advanced progressives such as Roosevelt demanded a powerful federal trade commission with comprehensive control over business.

Wilson came out firmly on the side of those who wanted merely to strengthen the Sherman Act. The original administration program consisted of three measures: first, an antitrust bill, sponsored by Representative Henry D. Clayton of Alabama, which contained severe provisions against interlocking directorates and practices used to suppress competition; second, a bill introduced by Representative James H. Covington of Maryland, which established an interstate trade commission, but one with no regulatory authority; and third, a railway-securities bill, sponsored by Representative Sam Rayburn of Texas, which gave the ICC authority over the issuance of new securities by railroads. The House approved all three bills on June 5, 1914.

House approval only intensified the public furor. Businessmen were up in arms against the draconian features of the Clayton bill. Meanwhile, a close friend of Brandeis, Representative Raymond B. Stevens of New Hampshire, had introduced a bill to establish a strong federal trade commission. At Brandeis' urging, Wilson shifted ground, took up the Stevens bill, and made it the cornerstone of his antitrust program. Wilson signed the Federal Trade Commission Act on September 26, 1914.

Meanwhile, Wilson and his lieutenants had rewritten the Clayton bill. They softened somewhat its severest provisions. Even so, the measure which Wilson signed on October 15, 1913, greatly strengthened the antitrust powers of the government; moreover, it made businessmen, personally, criminally liable for infractions. In addition, the Clayton Act explicitly declared that labor unions and farm organizations were not, per se, conspiracies in restraint of trade.

The adoption of the Federal Trade Commission Act signaled an important new departure in antitrust policy. The federal government now had an agency—the Federal Trade Commission—whose business it was to protect competition and deter would-be monopolists before they had crushed competitors. The bill's adoption also demonstrated an important shift in Wilson's philosophy. He had adopted much of the program for control of corporations which he had condemned when it was advanced by Theodore Roosevelt during the campaign of 1912. Wilson was soon to demonstrate flexibility in other areas of domestic and foreign policy as well.

3. THE NEW FREEDOM ABROAD

New Freedom Diplomacy

Wilson, of course, had had no practical training in diplomacy before 1913. However, his long study of history and international relations prepared him well for that task. He made some mistakes at the beginning. However, he quickly learned not only the skills of diplomacy but also how to use power wisely and with restraint. By 1916, his was a major voice in world affairs.

Wilson was, in many respects, the pivot of democratic foreign policy of the twentieth century. He was the first effective decolonizer among statesmen of the twentieth century. The Jones Act of 1916, which Wilson sponsored, gave self-government and promised early independence to the Philippine Islands. His mandate system, embodied in the covenant of the League of Nations, promised eventual independence to many of the former German and Turkish colonies.

Wilson also used the power of the United States to protect weak nations against aggression by stronger powers. He was also the most effective champion of self-determination—that is, of the right of peoples with a common language, culture, and history to govern themselves—in the history of the United States. Wilson believed strongly in a world united by trade and commerce, but he believed even more strongly that it was morally wrong for rich powers to exploit underdeveloped countries and colonies. Finally, Wilson was an ardent champion of peace and world unity. He hated war and the use of force in international relations, although he did have to use force himself. He was also the chief architect of the League of Nations.

Wilson appointed William Jennings Bryan as his Secretary of State. Bryan and Wilson, although formerly political antagonists, shared common assumptions about the proper goals of foreign policy. They embarked upon various programs to further peace, restore the integrity of the United States in the eyes of the world, and advance the cause of human rights.

With Wilson's blessing, Bryan negotiated conciliation (not arbitration) treaties with thirty nations. These provided for a "cooling-off" period and an investigation of disputes before nations in controversy could resort to war. Whether the treaties did much good is doubtful, but they were evidence of the dedication of the administration to the cause of world peace.

The administration tried to make amends for Roosevelt's aggression against Colombia in a treaty signed in 1914. The United States expressed "sincere regret" that anything should have happened to mar good relations between the two countries and agreed to pay Colombia $25 million for the

*Formal portrait of Woodrow Wilson, a masterful politician and an
inspiring leader, who added strength and power to the presidency.
While in office he made imaginative and aggressive use of power,
and felt that "we have grown more and more inclined to look to the
President as the unifying force of our complex system, the leader
of both his party and his nation." (Princeton University)*

loss of Panama. Roosevelt's friends in the Senate prevented ratification of the
treaty. But in 1921, after Roosevelt's death, a Republican Senate approved the
treaty—with the expression of "sincere regret" omitted.

Wilson withdrew American bankers from an international group formed to lend money to China because he believed, correctly, that the loan agreement was a blatant instrument of "dollar diplomacy." He also recognized the new Republic of China of 1913, without insistence upon the concessions that the other great powers had laid down as the price of recognition. Furthermore, in 1915, when Japan tried to make China a virtual protectorate by imposing twenty-one "demands" upon her, Wilson intervened so strongly in China's behalf that the Japanese withdrew the "demands" which would have gravely impaired Chinese sovereignty.

Missionary Diplomacy in the Caribbean

The results of Wilson's and Bryan's policies in certain Caribbean and Central American republics reveal that good intentions do not always produce anticipated results. Wilson and Bryan carried on active diplomacy in the Caribbean region partly because of their concern to protect the Panama Canal. Hence the Wilson administration continued to support the conservative government of Nicaragua which Secretary Knox had helped to install.

But the main objectives of the Wilson-Bryan policies in Latin America were maintenance of the peace of the western hemisphere and the development of orderly, democratic governments. Wilson and Bryan were, in their own view, missionaries of democracy, who sincerely hoped to help Latin American peoples to develop stable, representative governments.

With these objectives in mind, Wilson and Bryan became entangled in the Dominican Republic and Haiti, where revolutions recurred between 1913 and 1915. Wilson and Bryan were drawn into the quagmire of local politics. When their efforts failed to restore order, they used force. American marines and sailors occupied Port-au-Prince, the capital of Haiti, in 1915, and established a puppet government. American forces seized Santo Domingo, the capital of the Dominican Republic, in 1916. They proceeded to govern the country themselves when they were unable to form a stable puppet regime. Both Haiti and the Dominican Republic were forced to become protectorates of the United States under treaties like the "Platt Amendment."

American control did bring material benefits to these Caribbean nations. Sanitation, roads, schools, and hospitals were improved. More orderly political conditions attracted American and other foreign capital to develop such resources as sugar, fruit, and coffee. Yet this experiment in "missionary diplomacy" did not succeed in the long run. Neither in the Dominican Republic, nor in Haiti, nor in Nicaragua did American administrators establish a legacy of effective self-government. Once American forces were withdrawn in the 1920s, military dictators again seized power.

Wilson and the Mexican Revolution

The acid test of Wilson's sincerity about advancing human rights abroad was the nagging problem of Mexico, where the first authentic socioeconomic revolution of the twentieth century broke out in 1911. The United States was vitally concerned not only because Mexico was its nearest southern neighbor but also because Americans had invested nearly $1 billion in

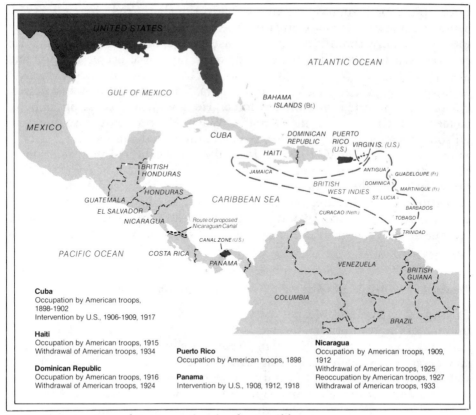

Cuba
Occupation by American troops, 1898-1902
Intervention by U.S., 1906-1909, 1917

Haiti
Occupation by American troops, 1915
Withdrawal of American troops, 1934

Dominican Republic
Occupation by American troops, 1916
Withdrawal of American troops, 1924

Puerto Rico
Occupation by American troops, 1898

Panama
Intervention by U.S., 1908, 1912, 1918

Nicaragua
Occupation by American troops, 1909, 1912
Withdrawal of American troops, 1925
Reoccupation by American troops, 1927
Withdrawal of American troops, 1933

United States Armed Intervention in the Caribbean

Mexican properties. As the revolution became more violent, there were threats to these property interests and to Americans living in Mexico.

The revolution began hopefully when the middle-class reformer, Francisco I. Madero, ousted the aged Mexican dictator, Porfirio Díaz, and was elected President in 1911. In February 1913, General Victoriano Huerta proclaimed himself to be President and had Madero murdered. Huerta promised to accord full protection to foreign property, and most of the major powers hastened to recognize his government. Business interests put great pressure on Wilson to grant recognition as soon as he entered the White House. But the new President hesitated; he said privately that he would not recognize a "government of butchers."

Wilson announced in mid-June 1913 that he would seek to mediate between Huerta's regime and the followers of Madero, called Constitutionalists, who had begun the revolution anew under Venustiano Carranza. Mexico should have early elections, and Huerta should not be a candidate for the presidency.

Huerta, encouraged by the British government (British subjects had large oil interests in Mexico), replied with the establishment of a military dictatorship. Wilson then went into action with grim determination. First, he compelled the British to withdraw support for Huerta. Second, Wilson threw his moral support to the Constitutionalists and, in early 1914, permitted them to purchase arms in the United States. By this time, Wilson was emotionally committed to the cause of the Mexican Revolution. He believed that it represented the struggle of an oppressed people for land and liberty.

However, by the spring of 1914, Huerta was consolidating his power. Wilson now resorted to military force. He found an excuse in a petty incident which occurred in Tampico. When Huerta refused to yield to Wilson's extreme demands, Wilson sent marines and sailors into Veracruz and seized the port on April 22, 1914. Wilson had expected the operation to be bloodless. However, fighting broke out, and there were heavy casualties, particularly on the Mexican side. Wilson quickly accepted an offer of mediation of the dispute. But all through the mediation, Wilson insisted upon the triumph of the revolution. Huerta, greatly weakened by the loss of revenue from Veracruz and hard pressed by the Constitutionalists, fled to Spain in July 1914.

Toward the Brink of War with Mexico and Back Again

Carranza's entry into Mexico City on August 20 seemed to mark the triumph of the revolution. However, even worse difficulties were brewing at that very time. Francisco (Pancho) Villa, Carranza's most colorful general, now began a new revolt. Civil war raged for another year. Carranza emerged as the head of the more democratic, modernizing forces; Villa, as leader of the wild and corrupt elements. But Villa shrewdly appealed for American support by promising to protect American property interests in Mexico. The State Department actually made plans for American military intervention in order to assure the victory of Villa's army. But Wilson had learned his lesson at Veracruz; he would not intervene in any way. After Carranza had dealt Villa several crushing defeats, Wilson extended *de facto* recognition to the Carranza regime in October 1915.

Mexican-American relations improved during the following months. Then Villa, in order to provoke war between the United States and the Carranza regime, swooped down on the border town of Columbus, New Mexico, on March 9, 1916; he burned the town and killed nineteen inhabitants. Wilson sent a punitive expedition, under General John J. Pershing, into Mexican territory to apprehend Villa. By April, Pershing had advanced 300 miles below the border. Fighting broke out between Carranza's forces and American troops on April 12, 1916. This led Carranza to demand the immediate withdrawal of Pershing's command from Mexican soil. The American government replied in a stinging rebuke, and Wilson mobilized most of the National Guard and sent it to the Mexican border. Another sharp engagement between Mexican and American troops occurred on June 21. Without waiting for an accurate report, Wilson assumed—incorrectly—that the Mexicans were responsible. He drafted a message which requested authority from Congress to occupy northern Mexico.

Both nations recoiled from the thought of war just as it seemed inevitable. A joint high commission was appointed to try to settle Mexican-American differences. The commission failed because Wilson would not yield to Carranza's demand for immediate withdrawal of all American troops. However, once Carranza had succeeded in decimating Villa's forces, Wilson withdrew Pershing in January 1917. Wilson also accorded full diplomatic recognition to Carranza's new constitutional regime in April 1917.

Wilson made many mistakes in his relations with Mexico. Most particularly, he tried, at least at first, to impose his own solution upon Mexico, and he permitted Pershing to go too far and stay too long. But Wilson was a sincere friend of the Mexican Revolution. He prevented Huerta from consolidating his regime with European support, and he helped the Constitutionalists to overthrow the dictator. He never permitted American interests with property in Mexico to swerve him from support of the revolution. Along with Carranza, Wilson preserved the peace until Mexican-American friendship could be built on solid foundations.

4. THE TRIUMPH OF THE NEW NATIONALISM

Wilson and the Dilemma of National Progressivism

The great dilemma of national progressivism was the question of how far the federal government should go to promote economic security and social welfare. More cautious progressives adhered to the type of program which Wilson had advocated in 1912 and argued that the federal government should never favor one class or classes. Advanced progressives and spokesmen for workers and farmers replied that the national government should help to correct the injustices, which it had helped to create, by giving special protection to the disadvantaged and exploited. Labor unions wanted exemption from prosecution under antitrust laws. Farmers wanted the federal government to subsidize long-term loans to them. Labor leaders and many social workers demanded the restriction of immigration. Social-justice advocates pressed for federal child-labor legislation and a new workmen's compensation act for federal employees.

Wilson resisted or did not support these demands during the first two years of his administration. He endorsed a federally chartered system of rural credits, but he threatened to veto a bill which provided for the federal operation and subsidy of the system. In 1915, Wilson vetoed a bill for the restriction of immigration by the imposition of a literacy test. The bill was passed over his veto in 1917. Wilson refused to fight for passage of a child-labor bill, on the ground that it was unconstitutional, even after the House approved it by a huge majority in 1914. Wilson even permitted his Secretary of the Treasury and Postmaster General to institute a limited segregation of black and white employees in their departments in 1913. This action provoked such a storm of protest that it was substantially reversed in 1914.

The first clear sign that Wilson was beginning to doubt that a limited progressivism would either satisfy public opinion or meet the problems of the modern age came when he accepted the proposal for a strong Federal Trade Commission. His switch revealed that, in the future, he might not adhere rigidly to the ideology of the New Freedom.

The Triumph of the New Nationalism

Wilson became a convert to the New Nationalism in 1916. The longer he served as President, the more he became convinced that the federal government had to take leadership in social and economic reform. Moreover, by the summer of 1914, the Mexican Revolution and the Colorado coal strike had considerably radicalized him. Also, he knew that he faced defeat in the coming presidential election unless he came out wholeheartedly for advanced reform. The Progressive party had virtually disintegrated by the early months of 1916. Wilson knew that the only hope for Democratic success lay in attracting the support of Roosevelt's followers. The Democratic party would have to be rebuilt from a southern party with northern and western allies into a great national party with strength among the urban middle classes and working people.

Wilson signaled his new departure by appointing Brandeis, perhaps the foremost champion of social-justice measures in the country, to the Supreme Court in January 1916. Next, Wilson came out in support of the same rural credits bill which he had earlier threatened to veto. It was adopted in July 1916 and established twelve Federal Land Banks. At the same time, Wilson pushed the federal child-labor and workmen's compensation bills through Congress. The former forbade shipment in interstate commerce of goods manufactured in whole or in part by children. It marked the first effort by Congress to regulate conditions of labor *within the states* by use of its control over interstate commerce. As such, it was the forerunner of all such legislation in the 1930s and afterward. Again, Wilson had forced passage of legislation that he had earlier refused to support.

To avert a nationwide railroad strike, Wilson, in September 1916, persuaded Congress to adopt the Adamson Act, which established the eight-hour day as the standard for workers on interstate railroads. Finally, Wilson signed a tax bill which greatly increased the income tax and imposed a new federal estate tax and taxes on excess profits, corporation income, and munitions manufacturers. It marked the triumph of Populist tax policy and was the first serious effort in American history to effect some redistribution of wealth through taxation.

SUGGESTED READINGS

The basic source for Wilson and his era is Arthur S. Link, David W. Hirst, John E. Little *et al.*, eds., *The Papers of Woodrow Wilson,* 43 vols. to date (1966-). The only general works on the Wilson era are Arthur S. Link, *Woodrow Wilson and the Progressive Era* (1954), and Frederick L. Paxson, *The American Democracy and the World War,* 3 vols. (1936–1948). The richest literature on Wilson's first administration is in the form of biographies. Arthur S. Link, *Wilson,* 5 vols. (1947–1965), covers Wilson's early career and first administration in detail. Arthur Walworth, *Woodrow Wilson,* 2 vols. (1958), is a good personal biography, but Edwin A. Weinstein, *Woodrow Wilson: A Medical and Psychological Biography* (1981), is full of new and significant insights, while John M. Mulder, *Woodrow Wilson: The Years of Preparation* (1978), is a fine intellectual biography. See also Charles Seymour, ed., *The Intimate Papers of Colonel*

House, 4 vols (1926–1928); John M. Blum, *Joe Tumulty and the Wilson Era* (1951); Paolo E. Coletta, *William Jennings Bryan: Progressive Politician and Moral Statesman, 1909–1915* (1969); and Richard Lowitt, *George W. Norris: The Persistence of a Progressive* (1971).

The second, third, fourth, and fifth volumes of Link's biography cover Wilson's Caribbean, Mexican, Latin American, and far eastern policies from 1913 to 1917 in detail. However, the following specialized works are helpful: Kenneth J. Grieb, *The United States and Huerta* (1969), and Robert E. Quirk, *An Affair of Honor: Woodrow Wilson and the Occupation of Veracruz* (1962). Finally, the essays in Arthur S. Link, ed., *Woodrow Wilson and a Revolutionary World, 1913-1921* (1982), reflect the newest research on such subjects as Wilson as a diplomatist and his most important foreign policies.

CHAPTER 24
THE UNITED STATES AND
THE FIRST WORLD WAR

1. THE STRUGGLE FOR NE'

The Crisis of Europe

The First World War destroy'
an empires, terribly wea¹
political foundations of
leashed forces that wo'
stability for decades
great events are a)
less, that conflic
and markets }
tial for gene
armed car
compos'
the ot'
Ger
ir

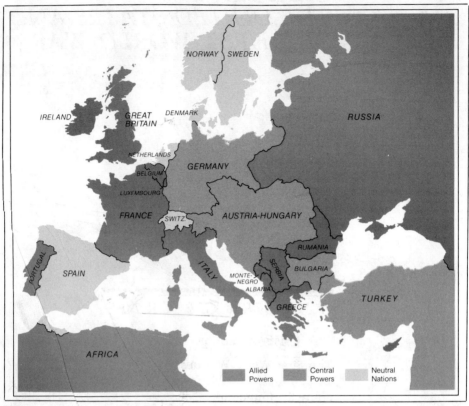

European Alliances in World War I

moved them into positions according to long-standing war plans. As the Russians prepared to march against Austria-Hungary, Germany struck first and declared war on Russia. This involved Russia's ally, France. Germany sent her armies across Belgium in order to strike a fatal blow at France before the massive Russian army could move on Germany's eastern flank. Since England was committed to defend the neutrality of Belgium, Parliament declared war on Germany on August 4. The system of alliances was now operating almost automatically. Bulgaria and Turkey joined Germany and Austria-Hungary—the Central Powers; Japan and Italy were lured to the side of the Entente—or Allies—by promises of territory.

The Establishment of American Neutrality

Probably a majority of Americans were pro-Allied in sentiment. However, the Germans also had many defenders among the large German-American and Irish-American communities. Americans in general, whomever they blamed for the onset of the war, were determined to avoid entanglement if at all possible. In light of this determination and Wilson's own passion for peace, the President issued a proclamation of neutrality and appealed to his fellow citizens to be "neutral in fact as well as in name."

Neutrality was easier to announce than to achieve. The Wilson administration resisted demands by German Americans and others for an arms embargo, because such an embargo would have denied to the British the access to American markets that their dominant sea power gave them. The administration did at first discourage American loans to the belligerents, but it reversed that policy when the British and French governments sought to float a public loan in the United States during the summer of 1915.

The British were determined to use their great fleet to cut off the flow of materials from the United States to the Central Powers. Wilson and his administration were equally determined to preserve as much freedom of trade as possible for Americans. On the matter of shipment to Germany of munitions and articles destined for military use, there was no difference between the British and American governments. But there were innumerable controversies over articles that *might* be used by armed forces and goods destined for use by civilians. Controversies occurred also over certain British blockade policies. The American government protested, but Anglo-American differences over the blockade were never acute, at least not before 1916.

The Germans decided in early 1915 to challenge British control of the seas by using the submarine. The German Admiralty announced on February 4, 1915, that all enemy vessels would be torpedoed without warning in a broad area around the British Isles, and that even neutral vessels would not be safe. Wilson responded that the United States would hold Germany to a "strict accountability" for illegal destruction of *American* ships and lives. The German government retreated temporarily from its threat against American ships.

Much more complex and difficult questions were involved when the Germans sank Allied ships on which Americans were traveling, and especially when these ships were armed. Wilson did not desire to deprive the Germans of the advantage that came from their use of the submarines, and he evolved his policies in response to particular situations.

On May 7, 1915, a German submarine sank the great British liner *Lusitania*, without warning, in the Irish Sea. Nearly 1,200 persons, including 124 American citizens, perished. Wilson appealed to the German government to abandon its attacks against *unarmed* passenger liners. The Berlin government responded evasively or negatively to each note from Washington. When another British liner, *Arabic,* was sunk with the loss of American lives, Wilson said that he would break diplomatic relations if Germany did not stop sinking unarmed passenger ships. The Germans had no alternative but to yield.

One result of the *Lusitania* crisis was the loss of Bryan as Secretary of State. He resigned on June 8, 1915, rather than sign the second *Lusitania* note to Germany, because he thought that it was not conciliatory enough. Bryan's successor was Robert Lansing, former Counselor of the State Department.

The Preparedness Campaign

The *Lusitania* and *Arabic* crises accelerated the expansion of America's armed forces. The Army Reorganization Act of June 1916 greatly expanded the National Guard and brought it under strict federal control. The act also provided for large increases in the regular army. Congress followed with authorization for huge increases in the navy. A month later, Congress also created a United States Shipping Board to build, purchase, or lease merchant ships. Wilson rounded out his preparedness program by appointing a Council of National Defense to advise the administration on problems of economic mobilization, if war should come.

One by-product of the increased concern for national security was the purchase of the Danish West Indies, or the Virgin Islands. Wilson pursued this objective in 1915 after he was warned that Germany might absorb Denmark, and with it the Virgin Islands, if she won the war. A treaty signed in August 1916 provided for the transfer of the islands to the United States for $25 million.

Wilson's First Peace Moves

Wilson offered American mediation to the belligerents immediately after the outbreak of hostilities. A short time later, he tried to prevent Japan's entrance on the Allied side. Despite failure in these first overtures, Wilson sent his close friend and confidential adviser, Colonel Edward M. House, to Europe in the early months of 1915 to explore further the possibilities of American mediation.

After the *Lusitania* and *Arabic* crises, the British Foreign Secretary, Sir Edward Grey, indicated that his government might be willing to discuss peace terms. Wilson sent House back to London to propose that the American President should call a peace conference and would probably enter the war if Germany refused the call. House made it very clear that Wilson had in mind a peace of reconciliation accompanied by substantial disarmament and the establishment of a league of nations. Grey initialed an agreement (known as the House-Grey Memorandum) which embodied the Wilson-House plan on February 22, 1916, but the Foreign Secretary stipulated that the British and French governments would decide when the plan was to be implemented.

The Sussex Crisis and Wilson's Efforts to Mediate

Late in 1915, the Allies began to arm both cargo and passenger ships. The Germans argued that it would be very dangerous for submarine commanders to surface their frail craft in order to demand that armed merchant ships stop and submit to search. Lansing, on January 18, 1916, proposed to the Allied governments that they disarm their merchantmen in return for a pledge by the Germans that they would not sink ships without warning. This proposal enraged the British leaders. Wilson thereupon withdrew the proposal and announced that the United States Government would defend the right of Americans to travel on ships which were armed *defensively*. Wilson's announcement set off a rebellion in the House of Representatives which threatened to take control of foreign policy out of his hands. A resolution was introduced to forbid Americans to travel on armed foreign ships. Wilson finally blocked the resolution, although only by reassuring Congress that he did not intend to go to war if the Germans sank a ship that had acted aggressively toward an attacking submarine.

The controversy with Germany soon escalated, when a German U-boat torpedoed the unarmed French ship, *Sussex*, on March 24 with heavy loss of life. Americans were aboard, but none died. In the belief that the British were eager to implement the House-Grey Memorandum, Wilson warned the German government that the United States would break diplomatic relations if German submarines did not cease their attacks against merchantmen without warning. The German leaders capitulated, but they threatened to resume unrestricted submarine warfare if the British continued to violate international law in their blockade practices.

Wilson lost no time in trying to put the House-Grey Memorandum into operation. He announced that the United States was prepared to join a postwar league of nations, and he pressed the British government to accept American mediation under the House-Grey Memorandum. But the British had never taken the memorandum seriously, and they declined to submit to American mediation.

This convinced Wilson that the British were fighting for unworthy objectives. A series of events in 1916 confirmed Wilson's suspicions and caused him and many Americans to turn sharply against the Allies. Anti-British feelings ran so high, in fact, that Congress authorized the President to take retaliatory measures against the British in certain circumstances.

The Campaign and Election of 1916

With the American presidential election approaching, the Republicans faced a cruel dilemma. They had to nominate a candidate acceptable to factions now divided on foreign as well as domestic policy. The Republican convention solved the problem by nominating Charles Evans Hughes, Associate Justice of the Supreme Court. As governor of New York from 1906 to 1910, Hughes had been a strong progressive, yet he had retained the respect of conservatives. As a member of the Supreme Court since 1910, he had said not a word about foreign policy. There never was any doubt that the Democrats would renominate Wilson. The big surprises of the Democratic convention were the demonstrations for peace that followed every reference to Wilson's success in keeping the country out of war. Indeed, "He kept us out of war" was written into the Democratic platform as the slogan of the party.

Hughes stumped the country and denounced the administration for its alleged bungling diplomacy and inefficiency. He said that he stood for the "firm and unflinching maintenance of all the rights of American citizens on land and sea." But when asked what he would do if elected, he fell silent. Wilson conducted a "front-porch" campaign from his summer home in New Jersey. Wilson implied that the Republicans would take the country into war. Moreover, he frankly said that the Democrats had taken over the Progressive platform of 1912 and enacted most of it into law. When Hughes denounced the Adamson Act, Wilson replied that the eight-hour day should be the standard for *all* American workers. Labor and farm leaders, social-justice champions, and many former Progressives and Socialists responded by moving into Wilson's camp. The two great streams of progressivism were now united, at least temporarily, in the Democratic party.

Even so, the election proved to be the closest since 1876. Before midnight of election day it was clear that Hughes had carried virtually all the eastern states, plus key midwestern states. But Wilson's prospects grew brighter as returns began to come in from the West. Wilson carried California by a slim margin, and therewith the election.

Toward the Brink

By the end of the campaign, Wilson was convinced that, while the American people ardently desired to avoid war, the European rivals were so intensifying the war on the seas that it might become impossible to avoid entanglement. On December 18, 1916, Wilson sent a moving appeal to all the belligerents; he asked that they state the terms upon which they would be willing to conclude a settlement. The Germans returned an evasive reply to Washington. The Allies announced sweeping terms which could be achieved only by military victory. Wilson, undisturbed, opened secret negotiations with the British and German governments for a peace conference.

While he waited for replies from Berlin and London, Wilson appeared before the Senate on January 22, 1917. There he explained the conditions on which the United States would "give its formal and solemn adherence to a league of peace." The present war had to be ended first, he announced, by terms which would create a peace worth guaranteeing. First of all, it had to be "a peace without victory." Wilson went on to list what he thought should be the terms: limitation of armaments, freedom of the seas, self-determination for peoples under alien domination, and security against aggression for nations great and small.

The British government appeared to be ready to negotiate, but the German government replied by announcing that submarines would begin unrestricted operations on February 1. They would sink *all* ships without warning, but would permit a limited number of American passenger ships to sail without danger. The German Chancellor, in a confidential message to Wilson, also divulged some of the German peace terms and begged Wilson to continue his efforts for peace.

Wilson broke diplomatic relations with the German Empire on February 3, mainly as a protest against the new German submarine decree. But Wilson made it clear that he would not go to war merely because the Germans sank Allied ships. However, two events soon pushed him nearer to the brink of war. One was the disclosure by the British of a telegram from the German Foreign Secretary, Arthur Zimmermann, to the German minister in Mexico. Zimmermann invited Mexico to attack the United States in the event of war between the United States and Germany. In return, Germany would restore to Mexico her "lost provinces" in the American Southwest. The other event was the near paralysis of American foreign trade that occurred when American shipowners refused to send their unarmed vessels into the blockaded area.

Wilson responded on February 26 by asking Congress for authority to arm American merchant ships. Strong opposition to the proposal developed in the House, whereupon the President gave the Zimmermann telegram to the newspapers. It aroused such anger across the nation that the House of Representatives approved an armed-ship bill at once. However, in the Senate the measure met the stubborn resistance of about a dozen men, headed by La Follette. They prevented the bill's passage until the mandatory adjournment of Congress on March 4. Wilson bitterly criticized what he called this "little group of willful men, representing no opinion but their own." On March 9, the President invoked the authority of an old piracy statute and instructed the Navy Department to arm merchant vessels.

The Decision for War

Wilson still wanted desperately to avoid belligerency. He had no illusions about Allied war objectives; they were, he knew, punitive. He realized, too, that participation in a total war would cause grave damage to democracy at home. Nevertheless, he was drawn to a decision for war, for the following reasons:

1. The Zimmermann telegram had caused Wilson to lose all faith in the German government. He believed that it proved that the military leaders were the true masters of Germany.

2. Wilson concluded that armed neutrality could not protect American maritime rights against the German challenge.

3. Wilson was heartened by news of the Russian Revolution on March 15. It would be easier, Wilson thought, to make a lasting peace with a democratic Russian government involved at the peace conference.

4. German submarines on March 16 sank three American merchantmen, one with the heavy loss of American lives.

5. Most important, Wilson was convinced that Europe could not endure its agony much longer. The war was in its final stages, and American belligerency would hasten its end. Moreover, Wilson knew that he would have much greater influence at the peace conference as a belligerent leader than as a neutral outsider.

Thus Wilson, on the evening of April 2, 1917, went before a joint session of Congress to ask it to recognize that a state of war existed between the United States and the German Empire. On that same evening, resolutions to that effect were introduced into both houses of Congress. The Senate adopted the resolution on April 4. The House followed on April 6, and the President signed it on the same day. For the first time in their history, Americans were about to enter, militarily, upon the European stage.

2. THE AMERICAN PEOPLE AT WAR

The American Military and Naval Contributions

Most Americans, including Wilson, believed initially that their contributions would be limited to naval cooperation and credit and supplies. However, British and French officials made it clear that American soldiers were desperately needed. In response, Wilson obtained quick approval by Congress of a Selective Service Act to raise a huge national army. Eventually some 4,000,000 men and women entered military service.

As supreme commander of the American Expeditionary Force, Wilson appointed General John J. Pershing. A series of events emphasized the desperate need for massive American reinforcements. In November 1917, the Bolsheviks seized control of the Russian government and sued for an armistice with the Germans. As a consequence, forty German divisions were transferred to the western front. There, in March 1918, the Germans began a great offensive to break the Allied lines and capture both the Channel ports and Paris before the Americans could intervene in force. The Germans conquered 3,000 square miles of territory, but they failed to achieve their main objectives.

The American navy was fully mobilized when war came. At this time it seemed that German U-boats might well succeed in starving the British into surrender. All available destroyers steamed to British waters to help the British navy to convoy merchantmen. This convoy system, introduced largely at Wilson's insistence, turned the tide against the submarines in the last months of 1917.

Some 112,000 Americans sacrificed their lives for the Allied-American victory, as compared to 1,700,000 Russians, 1,385,300 Frenchmen, and 900,000 Britons. But the American contribution proved decisive against what might have otherwise been an irresistible German assault. American troops participated heavily in the land fighting at the height of the second Battle of the Marne, first in capturing the heavily fortified town of Cantigny and then in helping the French to stop the Germans at Château-Thierry on the Marne River. By mid-July, the German drive had been checked. Marshal Ferdinand Foch, the Supreme Allied Commander, then began a counteroffensive. The American army in France, now more than 1,000,000 strong, participated significantly in this drive which brought the war to an end on November 11, 1918.

Mobilizing for Total War at Home

The government's efforts at economic mobilization during the First World War went through two stages. In the first stage, the administration relied mainly on both coercion and voluntary efforts. During the second stage, after about December 1917, the administration established sweeping control over every important phase of economic life.

Farmers and housewives were mobilized by the Food Administration, headed by Herbert Hoover. Hoover's effort to increase production was hampered by bad weather, but his system of indirect rationing and voluntary reduction in home consumption of food was quite successful.

When war came, many American railroads were in a rundown condition. Wilson took over the railroads on December 26, 1917, and named Secretary of the Treasury William G. McAdoo as Director-General. McAdoo abolished competition, pooled terminals and rolling stock, poured $500 million into improvements, and created an efficient nationwide railway system. The government also moved to build a "bridge of ships" to western Europe. The Shipping Board seized eighty-seven German ships in American ports and commandeered some 3,000,000 tons of merchant ships in process of construction. In addition, the Shipping Board's Emergency Fleet Corporation built ninety-four shipways designed to construct some 15,000,000 tons of new ships. However, these shipways had turned out only 500,000 tons of ships when the war ended.

All of the aforementioned efforts would have been in vain without a smoothly functioning and highly coordinated production of materials for the armed forces. Early efforts to achieve industrial mobilization through the voluntary cooperation of businessmen and industrialists nearly collapsed in the face of a wild scramble for supplies. Wilson, on March 4, 1918, gave sweeping new powers to the War Industries Board. Bernard M. Baruch, new head of the board, soon brought order out of chaos, mainly by controlling prices and the allocation of scarce raw materials such as steel. By the spring of 1918, the great American industrial machine had been tightly harnessed for a victory effort.

Organized labor rallied to the war effort, and the AFL agreed not to engage in strikes during the war. But strikes occurred nevertheless. Hence Wilson established a National War Labor Board in April 1918 to arbitrate labor disputes. Labor was held to its promise not to strike; but employers were forbidden to discharge workers for union activities. As a consequence, total union membership grew from 2,722,000 in 1916 to 4,046,000 in 1919. As a result of high wages and overtime payments, most workers actually were in a better economic position at the end of the war than at the beginning.

The direct costs of the war to the American people by 1920 were about $33.5 billion. Arguments raged over the amounts to be raised by loans and by taxation. Progressives and socialists demanded that the entire cost be met by taxation, particularly upon the rich. Spokesmen for the wealthy replied that most of the costs should be raised by borrowing. Congress imposed heavy excess profits taxes and increased maximum income and estate taxes. As a result, those persons most able to pay were saddled with the burdens of the costs of the war.

Public Opinion, Anti-German Hysteria, and Civil Liberties

"Once lead this people into war," Woodrow Wilson said just before the United States entered the conflict, "and they'll forget there ever was such a thing as tolerance." Wilson's doleful prophecy came true, and his own administration contributed to a nationwide hysteria. Wilson created the Committee on Public Information, headed by the journalist George Creel, to generate public enthusiasm for the war effort. Such an agency was necessary, Wilson believed, because the American people at the outset were still bitterly divided over the wisdom of fighting Germany.

The IWW and the Socialist party openly opposed participation in the war. No government engaged in fighting a modern total war has been willing to tolerate open opposition to its war effort. Congress responded during the First World War with the Espionage Act of 1917. It provided heavy punishment for any persons who willfully helped the enemy, engaged in espionage, or obstructed the draft.

Hysteria mounted as prosecutions were announced, particularly when the government arrested and tried most of the leaders (including Eugene V. Debs) of the Socialist party and the IWW. Fear of internal subversion reached such a height that Congress, in the spring of 1918, adopted a Sedition Act similar to the Sedition Act of 1798 (see pp. 126–127). The act of 1918 empowered the federal government to punish persons guilty of disloyal, profane, or abusive language about the American flag, form of government, or uniform.

The Supreme Court upheld the Espionage and Sedition Acts since they were based on the government's inherent wartime powers. Justice Oliver

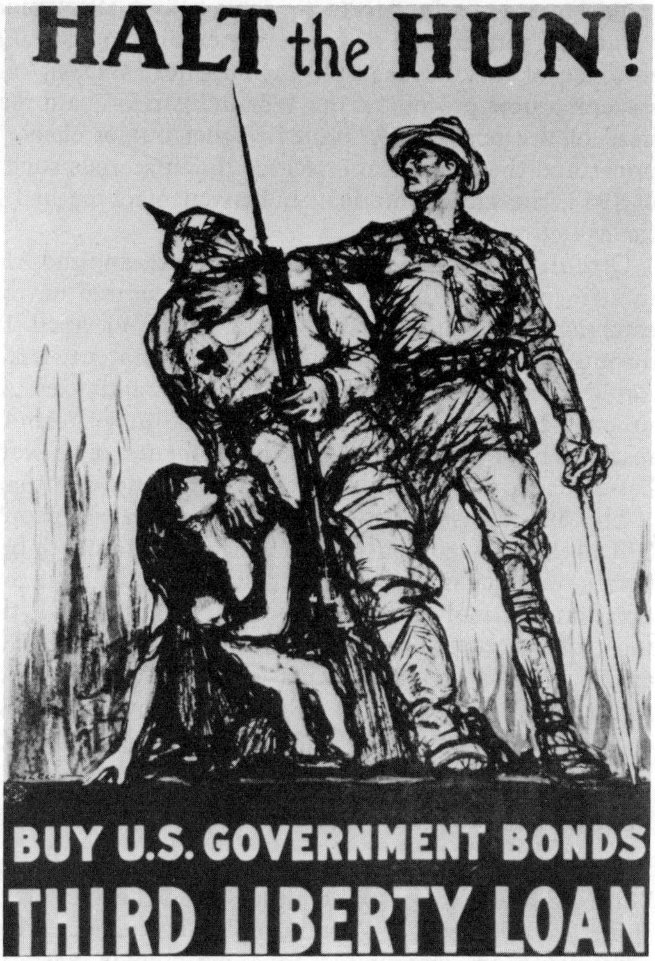
HALT the HUN!
BUY U.S. GOVERNMENT BONDS
THIRD LIBERTY LOAN

A Liberty Bond poster during the First World War. Highly successful advertisements to buy bonds, such as this one, helped to finance a major portion of the war. They appealed to patriotism, and were often printed in several languages to reach the immigrants. (Historical Pictures Service, Inc., Chicago)

Wendell Holmes, in Schenck *v.* the United States (1919), upheld the Espionage Act on the ground that the government had a right to protect itself against internal threats to its security. The court, in Abrams *v.* the United States (1919), gave the government *carte blanche* to move against seditionists even after the war had ended.

3. THE VERSAILLES TREATY, THE LEAGUE OF NATIONS, AND A SEPARATE PEACE

Wilson Proclaims a War for the Liberation of Mankind

Woodrow Wilson attempted to rally the people of the western world in a movement for a peace settlement which would remove the causes of future conflicts and establish machinery to preserve peace. He carefully dissociated himself from Allied war aims, and he waited for some move from Germany and Austria-Hungary to open peace negotiations. Wilson announced his program to the world in his Fourteen Points Address to Congress on January 8, 1918. He summarized his objectives in a series of general points, which included "open covenants, openly arrived at," freedom of the seas, general disarmament, removal of artificial barriers to international trade, an impartial settlement of colonial claims, and the establishment of a league of nations. Two points—the restoration of Belgium and self-determination for Russia—were, Wilson said, indispensable to a just settlement. Other points were desirable but presumably negotiable.

The Fourteen Points Address was much more than an avowal of peace aims. It was western democracy's statement in its first debate with international communism. The Bolshevik leaders, Lenin and Trotsky, had appealed to a peace-hungry world for a universal class war to destroy western capitalism. Wilson appealed for peace in order to give modern western civilization a second chance.

Wilson's hopes for immediate peace discussions were cut short by the second Marne offensive and by Germany's strengthened position in the East. The war, Wilson now believed, had to be fought to the bitter end. But, even while the fighting intensified, Wilson refused to yield to motives of hatred and revenge. On the contrary, in July and September 1918, he set forth his liberal war aims more clearly than ever before.

The Armistice and the Paris Peace Conference

A series of events in the summer and autumn of 1918 gravely impaired Wilson's opportunities to establish a new world order. The first of these events was the Allied decision to intervene in the civil war which then raged in Russia between the Bolsheviks and various conservative groups. The second was the sudden collapse of the Imperial German Government in late October. Wilson wanted German participation in the coming peace conference. The Germans appealed to Wilson for an armistice based on the Fourteen Points, but the German Emperor, William II, abdicated and fled to Holland, and German morale had collapsed by the time that the Armistice was signed in November. Germany was completely at the mercy of the Allies, and Wilson had lost a crucial bargaining weapon.

The third event was a diminution of Wilson's position as the spokesman of the American people. At the end of a hotly contested congressional campaign, Wilson appealed for the election of a Democratic Congress. He declared that world opinion would interpret a Republican victory as the repudiation of his leadership by the American people. For reasons largely unrelated to the peace settlement, voters elected Republican majorities in both houses of Congress in November. As Wilson had predicted, his leadership was seriously undermined.

Wilson, nevertheless, proceeded with preparations for the peace conference scheduled to meet in Paris in January 1919. He decided to go in person to Paris as head of the American delegation. But he failed to name any prominent Republicans to accompany him. This would have serious repercussions when a Republican-dominated Senate would review Wilson's handiwork at Paris.

In spite of these handicaps. Wilson, accompanied by a large body of experts, went to Europe in late December 1918 determined to fight for a just

The "Big Four" at Wilson's Paris home during the peace
conference at Versailles: Mr. Lloyd George, Signor Orlando,
M. Clemenceau, and President Wilson. Regarding the peace
conferences, Lloyd George later told Parliament: "I am doubtful
whether any body of men with a difficult task have worked under
greater difficulties . . ." (U.S. Signal Corps Photo, courtesy of
Historical Pictures Service, Inc., Chicago)

peace. Wilson visited Paris, London, Rome, and other places before the
conference opened; everywhere he was hailed as a great world leader.

It was a different story when the conference opened in Paris. No
representatives from the defeated powers or Russia were present. Wilson
stood alone against the Allied leaders—Prime Minister David Lloyd George
of Great Britain, Premier Georges Clemenceau of France, and Prime Minister
Vittorio Orlando of Italy. These statesmen were determined to divide the
territories of the vanquished and to make Germany pay the costs of the war.

Wilson fought throughout the conference for the achievement of the
Fourteen Points. He made compromises, such as to permit the Allies to
acquire all former German colonies. Also, the peace treaty imposed a huge
bill for war damages upon Germany. But Wilson won many more of his
Fourteen Points than he lost. Belgium was restored, Alsace-Lorraine returned
to France. The former subject peoples of the Austro-Hungarian Empire won
independence. An independent Poland was established. In addition, Wilson
would have nothing further to do with the futile Allied plans to intervene
militarily in the Russian civil war. And Wilson, by dramatically threatening

to leave the conference, prevented the French from annexing German territory west of the Rhine.

Wilson's greatest victory, however, was the establishment of the League of Nations. Many leaders, particularly Clemenceau, regarded it with indifference. At Wilson's insistence, a commission was named to draft the covenant of the League. The most important provisions of the covenant concerned the reduction of armaments, guarantees of security for all member nations, arbitration of disputes, and measures to be taken against nations which went to war in violation of the covenant. Article X, which Wilson called the heart of the agreement, read in part: "The members of the League undertake to respect and preserve as against external aggression the territorial integrity and existing political independence of all the members of the League."

The treaty was completed and presented to the German envoys in early May. The Germans protested strongly against the violations of the Fourteen Points, but they were in no position to renew hostilities, and the treaty was signed in the Versailles Palace on June 28, 1919.

The Fight for the Treaty

There were early signs that Wilson would encounter strong opposition in the Senate if he insisted upon incorporating the covenant of the League of Nations into the Versailles Treaty. Henry Cabot Lodge of Massachusetts, the Republican leader in the Senate, responded to Wilson's endorsement of the League with a statement signed by more than one third of the senators; he declared that the upper house would never approve the treaty with the covenant in its present form. Consequently, Wilson obtained all of the changes that his critics demanded through additional negotiations with the Allies.

Wilson, immediately after his return to the United States in July 1919, presented the Versailles Treaty to the Senate. A few newspapers were already raising cries of alarm against what they called an entangling alliance. A small group of isolationist senators, called "bitter enders," had announced that they would fight to the bitter end to prevent ratification. But Wilson was confident that the overwhelming majority of Americans was on his side.

Wilson did not know it, but Lodge, now chairman of the Foreign Relations Committee, had decided to kill the treaty if he possibly could. At first, Lodge did not dare openly to oppose the treaty; hence, he used delaying tactics in order to give its opponents time to mobilize and get their message to the country. Wilson knew that the treaty was in danger, and he decided to go to the country in order to rally support. He set out from Washington on September 3, traveled more than 8,000 miles, and spoke to large and enthusiastic audiences all the way to the Pacific Coast and back to Colorado. The speeches took a heavy toll of Wilson's limited physical reserves. He collapsed after an address at Pueblo, Colorado, on September 25. His doctor canceled the rest of Wilson's speeches, but a few days later—on October 2—Wilson suffered a massive stroke which paralyzed his left side.

Meanwhile, on September 10, Lodge had reported the treaty to the Senate with a number of reservations. Most were unimportant, but the senator's second reservation stated that the United States assumed no obligations under Article X of the covenant and would not commit its armed forces to

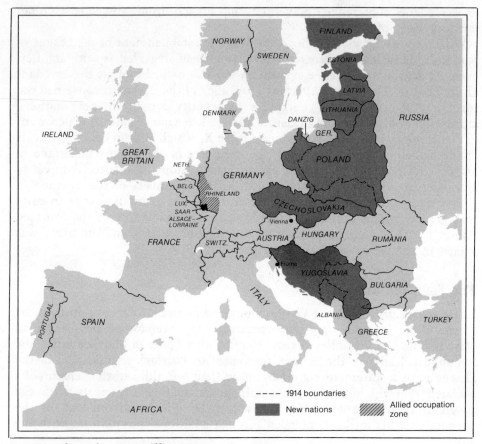

Europe after the Versailles Treaty

uphold the covenant unless Congress so provided. Wilson absolutely refused to accept the second Lodge reservation on the ground that it nullified the treaty. Hence, when the treaty came up for a vote in the Senate on November 19, most Democrats joined the "bitter enders" to defeat the Lodge reservations. On a second vote, the Republicans and "bitter enders" combined to defeat approval without the reservations.

Wilson stood firm. He announced that the presidential election of 1920 should be a "great and solemn referendum" on the League of Nations. When the treaty came up for a vote a second time on March 19, 1920, Wilson again instructed Democratic senators to oppose approval with the Lodge reservations. Enough of them did so to defeat approval.

Wilson has been accused of killing his own child—the League of Nations. It is certainly true that he prevented the Senate's approval on the final vote. He believed that the question of the character of American participation in the League was so fundamental that it could not be compromised. In addition, although Wilson's illness had not weakened his ordinary mental processes, it had gravely affected his temperament and ability to make decisions. Finally, Wilson was so isolated in the White House that he was out of touch both with the situation on Capitol Hill and with public opinion.

Whatever the reasons, the treaty was doomed. Congress adopted a resolution which declared the war with Germany at an end. This Wilson vetoed on May 27 as "an ineffaceable stain on the gallantry and honor of the United States." The United States remained technically at war with Germany until July 2, 1921, when Wilson's successor approved a resolution for a separate peace.

4. THE AFTERMATH OF WAR

Demobilization

The signing of the Armistice occurred so unexpectedly that it caught the American government without any plans for a smooth transition to a peacetime economy. War agencies were quickly dismantled. More than two thirds of the American Expeditionary Force had returned home before the Versailles Treaty was signed.

One of the many domestic problems that the government faced was what to do with the railroads. Labor unions urged the government to purchase them and give railroad workers a share in their management and profits. Wilson laid the problem before Congress, which responded with the Esch-Cummins Transportation Act of 1920. It rejected governmental ownership, but it vastly enlarged the powers of the Interstate Commerce Commission.

Meanwhile, the nation had embarked on an ambitious effort at social reform—nationwide prohibition of the manufacture and sale of intoxicating beverages. The long campaign against Demon Rum picked up strength from progressives who were eager to cleanse society of vice, from businessmen attracted to the idea of sober workers, and from conservatives who feared violence from the poor. A prohibition amendment, the Eighteenth, was submitted to the states in 1917 and ratified in January 1919.

Economic Distress and Social Upheaval

The administration was powerless to cope with perhaps the most urgent domestic problem—a spiraling inflation in prices caused by a wild scramble of businessmen and industrialists for goods and raw materials. The cost of living rose to 77 per cent above the prewar level in 1919 and to 105 per cent in 1920.

The most dramatic repercussion of this inflation was an epidemic of strikes in 1919. All told, they involved 4,000,000 workers. The strikes of 1919 began in November, when 435,000 bituminous coal miners laid down their tools. Attorney General A. Mitchell Palmer broke this strike by obtaining an injunction from a federal judge which ordered the miners back to work on the ground that the strike violated the wartime Lever Act, which was still, technically, in effect. Another strike—in Boston—seemed to lend credence to the widespread popular fear that the country was in the midst of a dangerous social upheaval. The police commissioner of Boston suspended nineteen policemen for organizing a union affiliated with the AFL. Thereupon, 90 per cent of the police force walked out. For two or three days, lawlessness threatened to engulf the city. Then Governor Calvin Coolidge mobilized the National Guard and backed the police commissioner's refusal to reinstate the striking policemen.

The churning events of 1919 included an outbreak of hysteria against

Communists. The hysteria began in earnest during February 1919, when workers in Seattle staged a general strike. A crude scheme to assassinate prominent Americans was uncovered in April; then a bomb blew off the front of Attorney General Palmer's home in June. Americans, disconcerted by the wartime excitement, rocketing prices, gigantic strikes, revolutions abroad, and now talk of revolt at home, feared that they lived on the brink of catastrophe. When radical Socialists announced their intention to promote a proletarian revolution, otherwise sane Americans believed that this tiny band threatened the national government.

Public alarm was so great that the Labor Department rounded up 249 Russian Communists in November and shipped them to Russia. The popular excitement also affected Attorney General Palmer, who was eager for the Democratic presidential nomination. First, Palmer set the Justice Department's Bureau of Investigation to work to infiltrate and investigate Communist groups. J. Edgar Hoover of that bureau reported that revolution was imminent.

Palmer organized a great federal dragnet to ferret out all alien Communists. On January 2, 1920, federal agents swooped down upon Communist headquarters all over the country and arrested well over 6,000 persons—American citizens as well as aliens—most without proper warrants. They were hustled off to jails and detention centers, where many were held for weeks without the rights of bond or counsel. Eventually only 556 of them were deported as Communist aliens.

In the early spring of 1920, public fear subsided rapidly. Prices fell sharply, strikes virtually ceased, the Communist tide in Europe receded, and the bombing and riots in the United States ended. Palmer warned of a great Red uprising on May Day, 1920. When it did not occur, the Attorney General became the laughingstock of the country.

American blacks were among the chief victims of the turbulence which followed the Armistice. The drop in immigration in 1914 had created such a scarcity of unskilled labor in industrial centers that several hundred thousand blacks left the South to take advantage of employment opportunities. They had to crowd into slum areas and at once aroused the hatred of white unskilled workers. Race relations deteriorated during the war—ironically, because some 400,000 blacks served in the armed services. White Southerners, particularly, feared that Negro veterans would return home to demand some measure of equality. Lynchings increased from thirty-four in 1917 to more than seventy in 1919.

A terrible race riot took place in East St. Louis in 1917, and succeedingly worse ones occurred in Washington, Chicago, and other places in 1919. All told, twenty-five riots left hundreds dead. The most significant fact about these riots was that blacks, determined to protect their families, fought back bravely.

The Campaign and Election of 1920

The country had regained a large measure of its sanity by the early months of 1920, when the presidential campaign began. The leading contenders for the Democratic nomination were Wilson's son-in-law, William G. McAdoo, Attorney General Palmer, and Governor James M. Cox of Ohio. Cox won the nomination at the convention in San Francisco and chose for his running mate Franklin D. Roosevelt of New York.

The Republican struggle narrowed to an evenly matched contest between General Leonard Wood and Governor Frank O. Lowden of Illinois. Deadlock between the Wood and Lowden delegates resulted in the nomination of Senator Warren G. Harding of Ohio. Governor Coolidge, hero of the Boston police strike, was nominated for the vice-presidency.

Cox and Roosevelt promised President Wilson that they would continue the fight for the League of Nations. They fulfilled their promise in a strenuous campaign. But they never had a chance because the coalition that had put Wilson back in office in 1916 was in shambles. Harding conducted a low-keyed campaign full of soothing but meaningless generalities. Not until the end of the campaign did Harding make it clear that he opposed American membership in the League.

The victory of Harding was the most smashing electoral triumph since the election of James Monroe in 1820. The landslide also carried large Republican majorities into both houses of Congress. The outcome, as one Democrat sadly described it, was a political earthquake, but the election was neither a mandate on the League of Nations nor a struggle between progressives and conservatives. Harding won a huge majority because he was able to add a large number of discontented voters to the ordinary Republican majority.

SUGGESTED READINGS

Link *et al.*, *The Papers of Woodrow Wilson,* and Link, *Wilson,* Vols. 3-5, both already cited, cover the period of neutrality and American entrance into the war in most detail. Link covers the same period in brief form in *Woodrow Wilson and Progressive Era,* already cited, and all of Wilson's foreign policies in *Woodrow Wilson: Revolution, War, and Peace* (1979). Among the general studies, the best are Charles Seymour, *American Neutrality, 1914–1917* (1935), and Ernest R. May, *The World War and American Isolation* (1959). John Milton Cooper, Jr., *The Vanity of Power: American Isolationism and the First World War* (1969), presents good analyses of the reactions of the American people to the war in Europe.

For the American home front, 1917–1918, see especially David M. Kennedy, *Over Here: The First World War and American Society* (1980); Seward W. Livermore, *Politics Is Adjourned: Woodrow Wilson and the War Congress* (1966); and Stephen Vaughn, *Holding Fast the Inner Lines: Democracy, Nationalism, and the Committee on Public Information* (1980). H. C. Peterson and Gilbert C. Fite, *Opponents of War, 1917–1918* (1957), relates the suppression of civil liberties during the war period.

The best account of American military participation is in Frank E. Vandiver, *Black Jack: The Life and Times of John J. Pershing,* 2 vols. (1977), but see also David F. Trask, *The United States in the Supreme War Council* (1961). We now have an impressive literature on American diplomacy, 1917–1918: W. B. Fowler, *British-American Relations, 1917–1918* (1969); Arno J. Mayer, *Political Origins of the New Diplomacy, 1917–1918* (1959); Betty Miller Unterberger, *America's Siberian Expedition* (1956); and Carl P. Parrini, *Heir to Empire: United States Economic Diplomacy, 1916–1923* (1969).

For the early American movement for a league of nations, see Ruhl J. Bartlett, *The League to Enforce Peace* (1944). The best one-volume book on the Paris Peace Conference is Inga Floto, *Colonel House in Paris* (1980). Also important is N. Gordon Levin, Jr., *Woodrow Wilson and World Politics: America's Response to War and Revolution* (1968). The best accounts of the fight over the Versailles Treaty are Denna F. Fleming, *The United States and the League of Nations* (1932), and Ralph Stone, *The Irreconcilables: The Fight against the League of Nations* (1970).

There is a growing literature on demobilization and the immediate postwar period. William E. Leuchtenburg, *The Perils of Prosperity, 1914–1932* (1958); and Preston W. Slosson, *The Great Crusade and After* (1930), are good introductions. Elliott M. Rudwick, *Race Riot at East St. Louis* (1964), and William M. Tuttle, Jr., *Race Riot: Chicago in the Red Summer of 1919* (1970), are both classics. For the Red Scare, see Robert K. Murray, *Red Scare: A Study in National Hysteria* (1955); and Stanley Coben, *A. Mitchell Palmer: Politician* (1963).

The standard work on the presidential campaign of 1920 is Wesley M. Bagby, Jr., *The Road to Normalcy: The Presidential Campaign and Election of 1920* (1962).

CHAPTER 25
THE UNITED STATES
IN THE 1920s

1. PROSPERITY DECADE

A Population on the Move

During the 1920s, the movement of Americans from the countryside to the cities and suburbs continued at an unprecedented rate. By 1930, 69,000,000 Americans lived in cities, compared to less than 54,000,000 in rural areas. The five largest cities grew more than 50 per cent during the 1920s, and most of their suburbs—with the aid of automobile transportation—grew even more rapidly. The traditional movement westward continued, and California became the prime beneficiary. Los Angeles absorbed much of the westward migration and spread horizontally into fragmented sections of single-family homes connected largely by automotive arteries and telephone wires.

The "New Economic Era"

The postwar economic boom and price inflation ended abruptly in mid-1920. As has happened so often in American history, excessive optimism and speculation collapsed, to be followed by a sharp recession and declining prices. Recovery was achieved by 1923, and in the following six years spectacular growth occurred in some of the most visible sectors of the economy. By 1927, businessmen were prophesying a "new economic era" of permanent prosperity and a higher standard of living for everyone.

On the whole, the American people *did* make mighty strides on economic fronts between 1919 and 1929. Per capita income increased significantly during the decade. This income, however, went largely to the wealthiest 5 or 10 per cent of Americans and to skilled workers, and most Americans remained near or below the level of subsistence. Farmers suffered most from the postwar recession and never fully recovered before the Great Depression.

At the same time, manufacturing industries increased their output by 60 per cent during the postwar decade, and the construction industry prospered as never before as cities grew, suburbs spread, and roads were built. Financial resources grew apace with the output of goods and services, and the United States became the world's leading banker. Western European nations incurred enormous debts during the war, while the supply of capital in America multiplied in the long, prosperous period from 1900 to 1929. In 1914, Americans owed Europeans a net debt of nearly $4 billion. Only five years later, Europeans owed Americans and the American government nearly $13 billion. At the same time, the dollar displaced the pound as the chief medium of international exchange.

The Technological Revolution and the Rise of New Industries

One of the main reasons for the American economic advance of the 1920s was a revolution in technology. Innovations helped to spawn new industries which, in turn, greatly stimulated the entire economy. The technological revolutions occurred largely because scientists and industrialists set out intentionally to develop new products and methods of production which would increase productivity, or output per man hour. American universities gave advanced training to huge numbers of scientists and engineers and thus made possible impressive industrial research laboratories.

The new school of industrial-efficiency experts, begun by Frederick W. Taylor (see p. 264), had a growing impact. Between 1899 and 1909, industrial productivity had increased by only 7 per cent; however, between 1919 and 1929, it rose by 40 per cent. Several industries which had been in their infancy just before the First World War grew lustily during the 1920s. They not only stimulated the economy but also helped profoundly to change American life.

Europeans had developed the first gasoline-powered automobile in the 1880s. It was not until 1892–1893 that Charles and Frank Duryea and Henry Ford produced the first workable American models. Only 4,000 automobiles were produced in the United States in 1900. Large-scale production began when Henry Ford instituted the assembly line and started to manufacture the rugged Model T at a cheap price. Automobile production grew to nearly 5,000,000 units in 1929.

Automobile drivers needed hard-surface roads, gasoline, garages for maintenance, and other products and services. According to one estimate, the automobile industry in 1929 gave employment, directly or indirectly, to nearly 4,000,000 persons. Through skillful use of advertising and design, manufacturers began to sell a commodity which was much more than simple transportation. By the mid-1920s, automobile manufacturers were merchandising comfort, power, luxury, and sex appeal.

The electric-power industry grew from insignificance in 1900 into America's second most important economic interest by 1929. Sixty-eight per cent of American homes were electrified by 1929. The increase in the sale of power was accompanied by the growing manufacture of electric turbines, motors, and home appliances. Radio transmitters and receivers had been invented before the First World War, but their production on a large scale and the consequent development of a nationwide broadcasting industry did not occur until the 1920s. By 1929, more than 10,000,000 families owned sets.

The story of the rise of the motion-picture industry is as dramatic as the saga of the automobile. Thomas A. Edison invented the first motion-picture camera in 1896. Both technological progress and the development of the motion picture as an art form continued steadily thereafter. By 1930, more than 23,000 motion-picture theaters were operating throughout the country.

Motion-picture production eventually concentrated in Los Angeles, where the weather was conducive to year-round outdoor photography. A galaxy of great directors, actors, and actresses became a new species of American folk heroes. Although situation comedies, westerns, and crime thrillers flourished, the motion-picture industry was based even more firmly on a frank exploitation of sexual themes. Conventional sexual mores were broken by the dramatic heroes and heroines until a self-imposed censorship stopped, temporarily at least, the tendency toward blatant sexuality.

Charlie Chaplin and Jackie Coogan in The Kid, *1921. By the middle of the 1920s, immense movie theaters sprang up in all major cities, and millions of adoring fans flocked weekly to see their heroes — comedian Charlie Chaplin, the "it" girl, Clara Bow, and the glamorous Rudolph Valentino — on the screen. The motion-picture industry heralded a new moral code and helped to standardize American habits. Since 90 percent of all films were made in the United States, motion pictures carried American speech and a rather distorted view of American culture around the world. The main themes, continuously repeated in predictable patterns, were sex, crime, broad comedy, and romantic adventure. (United Press International)*

Orville and Wilbur Wright and their "flying machine" at Kitty Hawk, North Carolina, December 17, 1903. In the first flight, by Orville, the craft remained aloft for 12 seconds and covered about 120 feet. Of the four flights made that day, Wilbur's flight of 59 seconds over a distance of 852 feet was the longest. (Library of Congress)

The most spectacular technological development during the 1920s was the growth of air transportation. Although the first successful flight in a heavier-than-air machine had been made by Wilbur and Orville Wright at Kitty Hawk, North Carolina, in 1903, aviation made little progress in the United States until the First World War. Air routes for mail, passengers, and cargo developed rapidly in the postwar decade, especially after the introduction of the Ford trimotor plane in the late 1920s. In that decade, aviation heroes gave a tremendous stimulus to public interest in flying. The entire world was thrilled in 1927 by the solo flight of a young American pilot, Charles A. Lindbergh. The "Lone Eagle" landed his monoplane, *The Spirit of St. Louis*, at Le Bourget Airport near Paris after a nonstop flight of thirty-three hours from New York.

Big Business and the Decline of Organized Labor

The movement toward consolidation in American industry proceeded during the first three decades of the twentieth century, in spite of antitrust laws and prosecutions. By 1929, the 200 largest corporations controlled 49 per cent of all corporate wealth. Most major industries by 1929 were characterized by oligopoly, or control of production by a few large producers. These few producers, however, often fought keenly among themselves, especially when major distributors—such as grocery chains and mail-order houses—could play one off against another.

The managerial revolution in American industry continued during this period (see pp. 262, 266). By 1929, most industries were run by professionally trained managers who did not own the industries which they controlled. A growing class of executives and managers operated corporations in trust for owners interested only in profits and dividends.

Organized labor suffered heavy losses in spite of full employment and a shortage of skilled labor. The powerful railroad brotherhoods held their own, but membership in AFL unions declined from more than 4,000,000 in 1919 to 2,770,000 in 1929. A number of factors caused this decline. Employers had been frightened by the labor troubles of 1919. Many of them set out to alleviate labor discontent by instituting welfare programs of their own, including profit-sharing and group-insurance programs. Employers also encouraged their workers to form unions under the company's sponsorship. Many employers engaged in "open shop" drives to root out unions which already existed. Furthermore, the AFL itself increasingly came under the control of conservative trade unionists who had little interest in organizing workers in mass-production industries.

2. SOCIAL TENSIONS OF THE 1920s

The "Revolution in Morals"

Many Americans believed that, during the 1920s, the country was experiencing a widespread rebellion against traditional morality, religion, and patterns of family authority. Significant changes in social life did occur, but the word "revolution" is too strong a description for most of them.

The most important long-run shift took place in the appearance and status of women. Women cut their hair short, wore short skirts, and began to smoke, drink, and discuss with men hitherto tabooed matters. These changes were part of a long-term rebellion against Victorian sexual standards. Women went to work in increasing numbers in the rapidly expanding services and professions (they constituted nearly one fourth of the nonfarm work force in 1930), and some were able, therefore, to support themselves. Better economic opportunities also brought increasing independence within the family. However, the improvements for women during the 1920s were less drastic than contemporaries believed. Within recent immigrant groups and among the poor, they may not have occurred to any great extent.

Young people also were allegedly in rebellion. To be sure, they did reject older forms of dance in favor of the fast fox-trot and the Charleston, and the minority who drank to excess and lived what was considered a bohemian life attracted much wider attention. There is only slight and inconclusive evidence, however, that the moral standards of young people changed dramatically during the 1920s.

Crusades against Evolution and Demon Rum

One symptom of the reaction against rapid social change in the 1920s was a crusade to forbid the teaching of evolution in schools, colleges, and universities. The Darwinian hypothesis had caused some conflict between science and religion in the 1860s and 1870s, but theologians and urban churchmen had largely accepted the evolutionary hypothesis by 1900. This was not true of "fundamentalist" Christians, particularly in the rural South and Southwest. They deeply abhorred not only the evolutionary concept but also criticism of the Bible in any form.

"Fundamentalist" fears might only have simmered had it not been for William Jennings Bryan. The "Great Commoner" opened a crusade in 1921 for the adoption of antievolution laws. Tennessee, Mississippi, and Arkansas adopted statutes which forbade the teaching of evolution in public institutions.

In 1925, John T. Scopes, a young biology teacher in Dayton, Tennessee, decided to test the act just passed by his state's legislature. He was arrested and tried. Bryan joined the prosecution, while the American Civil Liberties Union sent the famed trial lawyer, Clarence Darrow, to defend Scopes. The so-called "monkey trial" degenerated into a verbal battle in which Darrow ridiculed Bryan for his beliefs in the literal truth of the Bible. Scopes received a light fine which was later revoked. The antievolution crusade fizzled and sputtered almost to an end by 1928. However, antievolution laws remained in the statute books.

As the 1920s began, another form of reaction against social change was in

Dumping beer into Lake Michigan in 1919. Prohibition, called the "noble experiment" by Herbert Hoover, gave rise to massive violation of the law through the "bootlegger," the "speakeasy," and gangsterism. (United Press International)

its ascendancy. No experiment in recent American history stirred higher hopes than prohibition. At a victory celebration in 1920, Bryan announced that the liquor issue finally rested as dead as slavery. He proved to be a very poor prophet in this matter. Passage of the prohibition amendment did not prevent millions of Americans from continuing to drink alcoholic beverages. Illegal distillers, smugglers, and brewers soon encountered no difficulty in keeping up with the demand. Speakeasies (illegal saloons) flourished in the cities, and bootleggers did a booming business. Urban populations, and often their policemen and elected officials, cooperated in what amounted to guerrilla warfare against federal prohibition enforcement agencies.

One result of prohibition was the stimulus which it gave to the growth of professional criminal gangs in large cities. The most infamous of these gangs, virtually a private army in Chicago led by Al Capone, did a $60 million business in liquor alone by 1927. Except for the gangsters, who had a vested interest in its continuation, most urban Americans favored repeal of the Eighteenth Amendment. Prohibition became one of the leading political issues of the 1920s—further evidence of the struggle between those Americans who adhered to traditional nineteenth-century values and their cultural and political enemies.

Immigrants arriving at Ellis Island. The narrowness and provincialism of Americans who had developed a dislike and distrust of foreigners became evident in the 1920s when quotas reduced sharply immigration from eastern and southern Europe and from Asia. (United Press International)

A black family, just arrived in Chicago from the South, during the World War I migration. (Reprinted from Allan H. Spear, Black Chicago: The Making of a Negro Ghetto, 1890–1920, by permission of the University of Chicago Press, 1967.)

Nativism, the Rise of the Ku Klux Klan, and the Black Nationalist Response

One aftermath of the Red Scare of 1919–1920 was a large residue of nativism. This nativism also was a manifestation of the resentment of native white Protestant Americans against the rising dominance of the cities, increasingly the home of blacks and non-Protestant immigrants. Among the consequences of nativism in the 1920s was an increase in anti-Semitism and anti-Catholicism. Hostility to blacks, Hispanics, and Orientals never had decreased appreciably.

The Knights of the Ku Klux Klan was revived by William J. Simmons in Atlanta in 1915. After 1920, it moved rapidly throughout the Southwest, Middle West, and the Pacific Coast area. At its peak in 1925, it probably had 5,000,000 members and was a powerful force in the politics of a score of states. The Klan's leadership was openly anti-Negro, anti-Catholic, and anti-Jewish. The Klan also fed upon and encouraged the suspicion of rural and small-town America against the "alien" cities which supposedly were corrupting American life. In some areas, the Klan dedicated itself more firmly to opposition to sexual permissiveness and alcoholic indulgence than to defense of racial and religious ideals.

Partially as a result of the increase in racism between 1890 and the 1920s, black Americans developed (and rediscovered) ideas which promoted withdrawal from white society into their own cultural, social, and economic enclaves. Such ideas were articulated by Marcus Garvey, already the leading black nationalist leader in the West Indies and Central America. When he arrived in the United States in 1916, Garvey merely intended to win recruits for his Jamaican-based Universal Negro Improvement Association (UNIA). After the race riots of 1919, however, Garvey won so many converts that he moved his headquarters to Harlem. A minimum of 100,000 blacks (Garvey

Marcus Garvey, 1922.
(United Press
International Photo)

claimed millions) joined the American UNIA. Many more attended meetings, subscribed to Garvey's newspaper, the *Negro World*, and bought stock in UNIA enterprises. Garvey's widespread appeal owed much to his plans to increase black strength everywhere by freeing Africa from white domination and to his concept of black economic self-help. We will never know how powerful Garvey and his UNIA might have become, since he was prosecuted for mail fraud only a few years after his rise to leadership and was convicted and deported.

3. THE MATURING OF AMERICAN CULTURE

School and Church in the Urban Age

The history of American intellectual life in the 1920s has long been written in terms of the invectives of its severest critics—a group of writers who belonged to what Gertrude Stein called the "lost generation." Their indictment of the quality of American civilization was reasonably accurate, but its very persuasiveness tended to obscure cultural progress in areas which some of these writers failed to notice.

The American people made greater educational advances during the 1920s than in any earlier decade in their history. The total expenditures on schools doubled, and illiteracy declined from 6 per cent to 4.3 per cent. Two accomplishments of the 1920s stand out especially. One was the construction of a public high-school system which enabled almost every American child to obtain some secondary education. High-school enrollment doubled during the decade. The second noteworthy accomplishment was a tremendous expansion of American colleges and universities and an enrichment of their curricula. College students increased in number from 598,000 in 1920 to more than 1,000,000 in 1930. At the same time, graduate and professional schools reached such a level of excellence that Americans were largely freed from dependence upon European universities for advanced training.

On the other hand, critics of American mass education complained, accurately, that, despite the opportunity open to most citizens for learning, standards in general remained low. Visitors from Europe commented that sports stadiums and social clubs appeared to be the most important places in colleges, insofar as most students were concerned.

Meanwhile, American churches grew in membership faster than the population as a whole. There is no measurable evidence that the alleged revolution in morals undermined the religious faith of most Americans during the 1920s. On the contrary, some evidence suggests that religious faith may have increased. A poll taken in 1927 of 250,000 newspaper readers and 36,000 college students indicated that they were even more certain about their faith than their parents were.

The Flowering of American Literature and Music

American writers during the 1920s produced a literature of artistic excellence unrivaled in American history. Americans, even in the dull midwestern small towns satirized by Sinclair Lewis, responded to books such as Lewis' Main Street with efforts at self-improvement which resembled earlier responses to disclosures by muckraking journalists. Among the other fine writers of the period, F. Scott Fitzgerald wrote elegantly about the hollow lives of the eastern and midwestern upper classes. William Faulkner began a series of penetrating novels about the decayed society of his native Mississippi. Thomas Wolfe published his first and greatest novel in 1929, Look Homeward, Angel. The most important literary trends of the 1920s were full development of the naturalistic school in the novels of Ernest Hemingway, John Dos Passos, Theodore Dreiser, and Sherwood Anderson, and the burgeoning of a school of first-rate dramatists. Eugene O'Neill was the towering figure among this latter group, but a number of lesser playwrights such as Maxwell Anderson also enlivened the American stage. Three novelists—Lewis, Faulkner, and Hemingway—and one dramatist, O'Neill, all began their significant work in the decade and later won Nobel prizes for literature.

During the 1920s, a group of writers in Harlem consciously attempted to create a black literature. Among the more successful of these authors, along with W. E. B. Du Bois, were the young poets, Langston Hughes, Countee

William E. Burghardt
Du Bois, 1868 – 1963,
black educational
leader and writer. (Library
of Congress)

Cullen, and Claude McKay. James Weldon Johnson worked with both poetry and the novel and wrote essays, songs, and history as well. Jean Toomer's mystical celebration of black culture in his novel-poem, *Cane*, may have been the greatest single literary contribution of this group.

America's original contributions to the world of music before the First World War had been limited largely to various kinds of folk music, although black ragtime gave a hint of great innovations to come. The American tradition in popular music grew apace with the work of many composers such as Cole Porter, Jerome Kern, George Gershwin, and Irving Berlin. The most important development in this field was the beginning of a native American musical form—jazz—a highly sophisticated form based largely on African traditions. Jazz began among black musicians in New Orleans, moved up the Mississippi Valley, and reached Chicago about 1916. It spread rapidly through the country and the world in the 1920s.

4. THE REPUBLICAN RESTORATION

Ebb Tide of Progressivism

All superficial signs point to a rejection of progressivism during the 1920s. Both of Woodrow Wilson's successors were conservative Republicans who believed that the encouragement of business was the government's first duty. They also packed federal regulatory agencies with men friendly to the industries which they regulated. Moreover, the Supreme Court wrecked two of progressivism's most notable achievements. In Hammer v. Dagenhart (1918) and Bailey v. Drexel Furniture Company (1922), the court nullified the Child Labor Acts of 1916 and 1919. The court went a step further in Adkins v. Children's Hospital (1923) and outlawed all state attempts to set minimum wages for women workers.

Actually the political developments of the 1920s were more complex than the foregoing generalizations would imply. Although progressivism as a force in national politics was at ebb tide, the progressive *movement* not only survived but also expanded its objectives in the 1920s.

Progressivism was gravely weakened by the desertion of some intellectuals who were disenchanted with democracy because of such popular movements as the prohibition and antievolution crusades. A more important cause of the decline of progressivism was the widespread defection of the urban middle classes. Many were tired of successive calls to reform the nation and the world; but they were also caught up in a great technological revolution, and they thought that they were building a new civilization. It was to be a civilization based upon a whole new set of business values—mass production and consumption, full employment, and welfare capitalism. With such bright prospects, it was no wonder that the groups who constituted the urban middle classes lost interest in reform.

Progressivism had succeeded only when its forces captured a great national party. In the 1920s, the movement was unable to find an acceptable political vehicle. During the presidential primaries of 1920, the Republican progressives, Hiram W. Johnson, Frank Lowden, and Leonard Wood, won almost all the contested states. However, at the convention, they refused to compromise, and Warren G. Harding, whom they had all easily defeated in Republican primaries, was nominated by a deadlocked convention. Real control of the GOP remained in the hands of the eastern and midwestern industrial, financial, and oil interests, as it had since 1910.

There was always the hope of a third party. Numerous progressive groups came together under Senator Robert M. La Follette's leadership in 1924. But these progressives soon discovered the historical weaknesses of third-party movements in the United States. However, the fact that La Follette won about 17 per cent of the total vote in the presidential election of 1924 in spite of insuperable handicaps indicated the potential strength of a progressive candidate.

The Democratic party remained the only vehicle through which progres-

"The essence of the progressive movement, as I see it, lies in its struggle to uphold the fundamental principles of representative government . . ." These are the words of Robert M. La Follette of Wisconsin, one of the most militant of the progressives, who was called "Battling Bob" for his crusading methods in politics.

sives might work. However, that party lacked leadership and was so torn by internal conflicts that it literally ceased to be a national political force.

Nevertheless, progressives from both parties were still strong enough to dominate Congress during most of the 1920s. However, they were so divided among themselves as partisans that they could not unite to capture the national government, as they had done in 1912 and 1916.

The Travesty of Warren G. Harding

The history of the presidency has proved that a man of average mental equipment can do well in the office if he has the desire to be a strong leader and possesses integrity and reasonably good judgment. Unfortunately, Warren Gamaliel Harding had barely average intelligence, no desire to be a strong President, and abundant defects of character. As President, he carried on much stock speculation and devoted a great deal of time to drinking and playing cards with his associates. He was physically lazy, morally undisciplined, and had a positive dislike of mental effort. Harding as President simply refused to give leadership to the nation. Fortunately, several of his cabinet members, particularly Secretary of State Charles Evans Hughes, Secretary of Commerce Herbert Hoover, and Secretary of Agriculture Henry C. Wallace, were able to carry on constructive policies.

President Harding
makes a recording in the
early days of his
administration. (Library
of Congress)

Harding's own appointees and his personal cronies, called the "Ohio Gang," left a different legacy. The leader of the group was Harding's old intimate from Ohio and the new Attorney General, Harry M. Daugherty. He had already earned a reputation as a corrupt politician and lobbyist. Harding's devotion to these friends led to tragedy for both himself and the nation. With the possible exception of the Grant and Nixon administrations, the American government has never been so disgraced as it was during the two short years of Harding's tenure.

Thomas W. Miller, Alien Property Custodian, accepted a bribe, for which he was sentenced to eighteen months in a federal penitentiary. Charles R. Forbes stole an uncounted amount of money as head of the Veteran's Bureau before he was caught and sent to prison. "Jess" Smith, an intimate of Daugherty, collected and distributed graft from persons who broke the prohibition and tax laws and who wished to buy immunity from prosecution or presidential pardons. When Harding ordered him back to Ohio, Smith committed suicide in the apartment which he shared with Daugherty. The Attorney General was tried in 1927 on charges of bribery, but the indictment was dismissed after a jury twice failed to agree on a verdict.

The most sensational scandal of the Harding administration was an attempted theft of governmental oil reserves. The government had set aside, for use by the navy, oil reserves at Elk Hills, California, and Teapot Dome, Wyoming. The government later decided to lease the lands to private operators who would supply the navy with fuel oil.

A group of wealthy oil men, including Harry F. Sinclair of New York and Edward L. Doheny of Los Angeles, exercised an influence in the Republican party which rivaled that of the senatorial clique which represented big business interests. Secretary of the Interior Albert B. Fall leased Teapot Dome to Sinclair and Elk Hills to Doheny. Not long afterward, Fall's private fortunes, which had been in a bad way, began to show spectacular improvement. A special Senate committee, headed by Thomas J. Walsh of Montana, began an investigation into these matters in the autumn of 1923. It subsequently revealed that Fall had accepted a "loan" of $100,000 from Doheny while the lease of Elk Hills was under negotiation and, also, that Sinclair had given Fall over $300,000 and a herd of cattle while the lease for Teapot Dome was being concluded.

Sinclair and Doheny were tried for conspiracy and bribery in 1926. They were acquitted, although Sinclair had to spend a term in jail for attempted bribery of jurors in his case. Fall, who had fled to Europe, was brought home and tried for conspiracy to defraud the government in 1929. He was convicted, fined $100,000, and sentenced to a year in jail.

Harding set out on a transcontinental tour in late June 1923. He was deeply depressed. He feared disgrace and political doom because he already knew about Forbes' corruption and suspected that Fall was also guilty of fraud. Harding barely completed a speech in Vancouver before he collapsed. When he reached San Francisco, his condition became worse and he died suddenly on August 2, 1923. Death came none too soon to release Harding from his troubles. Americans mourned for the distinguished President whom they thought Harding had been. However, it was not long before the truth about the scandals emerged and Harding's personal misbehavior was exposed to full view.

Calvin Coolidge and the Politics of Prosperity

The news of Harding's death arrived at the Coolidge farmhouse in Plymouth, Vermont, where Vice-President Calvin Coolidge was spending his vacation. Unlike his predecessor, the new President was no handsome, genial fellow surrounded by cronies. Coolidge was a Puritan Yankee—plain and austere. He placed honesty, thrift, and individualism at the top of his list of virtues. Coolidge was born in Vermont on July 4, 1872, and moved to Massachusetts as a young man. He was elected governor of that state in 1918. The Boston police strike of 1919 had made him a national hero and boosted him into the vice-presidency.

Scrupulously honest himself, Coolidge systematically cleaned up the mess left by Harding. He discharged Daugherty and appointed Harlan F. Stone, dean of the Columbia University Law School, as Attorney General. Coolidge gave Stone and the Justice Department full support in further investigations and prosecutions.

Coolidge was heir to the Hamiltonian tradition of close relations between government, business, and finance. "The business of America is business," he said. Coolidge did not share Theodore Roosevelt's and Wilson's faith in governmental participation in economic and social affairs. He believed simply in low taxes, encouragement of business enterprise, and as little governmental interference as possible. When progressive groups in Congress adopted legislation in the reform tradition, Coolidge relentlessly vetoed their bills.

Midwestern insurgent Republicans had dominated Congress during Harding's tenure, and, in 1922, discontent was so strong that the Democrats narrowly missed winning both houses of Congress. By 1924, a new progressive revolt seemed to impend. The Republican national convention ignored the danger signals and nominated Coolidge for the presidency on a conservative platform.

It was a rare opportunity for the Democrats to rally agrarian and labor discontent into a new progressive coalition. However, the Democrats seemed more intent upon fighting each other than conservative Republicans. At their convention, northern big-city Democrats battled southern and rural Democrats over resolutions which condemned the Ku Klux Klan and called for repeal of the Eighteenth Amendment. These conflicts came to a head in the struggle over the presidential nomination. The chief contenders were Governor Alfred E. Smith of New York and former Secretary of the Treasury William G. McAdoo. Smith was a Roman Catholic, a "wet" on prohibition, and a chieftain of the Tammany organization; McAdoo had the support of southern and western farmers, drys, and most Protestant Democrats (including Klansmen). Smith and McAdoo fought it out for 103 ballots, until the convention in desperation turned to John W. Davis. Davis, although a distinguished lawyer, was allied with great New York banking and industrial interests and was incapable of leading any kind of revolt.

Convinced that both major parties were hopelessly reactionary, a group of progressives and labor leaders formed a new Progressive party and nominated Senator Robert M. La Follette. Their platform demanded nationalization of railroads, public development of hydroelectric facilities, and the right of Congress to override decisions of the Supreme Court. The campaign that ensued was enlivened only by La Follette's strenuous but ill-fated attempt to reach the country with his message. On election day, Coolidge ran up a popular vote far larger than the combined total of Davis and La Follette.

Domestic Issues of the 1920s

The next four years were prosperous, but there was little peace in Washington. Republicans held a majority of seats in Congress, but the controlling force on Capitol Hill was a coalition of midwestern Republicans and southern Democrats. The major struggles of these four years were between this reform coalition and the conservative Coolidge administration.

There were three major groups in Congress during this decade: midwestern insurgent Republicans (the so-called Farm Bloc); southern Democrats, who often cooperated with the Farm Bloc; and conservative Republicans and Democrats, mainly from urban areas. Since none of these groups had a majority, legislation could be achieved only by coalition. A fourth group represented northern urban workers and included recent immigrants and black migrants from the South. Senator Robert F. Wagner and Representative Fiorello La Guardia, both of New York, were the leaders of this increasingly powerful interest group. By the 1930s—perhaps by 1928—it constituted one of the major forces in American politics.

The Farm Bloc and administration Republicans combined in 1922 to pass the Fordney-McCumber Tariff Act. It greatly increased duties on farm products and helped new industries such as chemicals, but it provided only moderate increases for most industrial products.

Tax legislation was a different story. All through the 1920s, the chief objective of the business interests and of Secretary of the Treasury Andrew W. Mellon was drastic reduction of the high wartime taxes. A midwestern-southern Democratic coalition blocked Mellon's plan for five years. Mellon finally had his way in the Revenue Acts of 1926 and 1928, which cut the maximum surtax on incomes from 40 to 20 per cent and slashed the estate tax in half.

Congress defied the administration by adopting bonus measures for veterans. These bonuses were to recompense the men who had served in the armed forces at low pay during the First World War. Harding and Coolidge vetoed bonus bills, but in 1924 Congress passed one over Coolidge's veto.

The most important domestic problem of the 1920s was the agricultural depression. Although agricultural prices recovered somewhat in 1923, farmers operated at a net loss throughout most of the 1920s. Wartime demand had pushed farm prices up, and this caused farmers to increase acreage and to purchase land and machinery at high prices. Once the war was over, commodity prices declined sharply. On the other hand, the prices which farmers paid for essential items increased 30 per cent between 1919 and 1929. Mounting local taxes and interest charges increased the farmers' burden of debt. Finally, technological advances added to surpluses which were already smothering farmers.

Agrarian distress in the 1920s set off the same kind of demands for governmental relief as it had produced in the late nineteenth century. But the farmers had now learned how to wield political power effectively. In 1921, congressmen from the midwestern states formed the Farm Bloc to fight for the relief of agriculture. During the Harding administration, they won tariff protection for farm products, pushed through bills which prohibited certain kinds of speculation in grains, and established a new federal system of rural credit. Taken together, the farm bills of 1921-1923 completed the program begun by the Wilson administration and provided farmers with generous credit at low interest rates.

The main problem after 1923 was how to prevent farm surpluses from depressing prices at home. George N. Peek and Hugh S. Johnson, midwestern farm machinery manufacturers, proposed that the federal government should in effect guarantee minimum prices for agricultural products sold at home. Under their plan, federal agencies would purchase all major staples produced for the market at stipulated prices and would thus set a floor under them. These agencies would also sell the surplus on the world market and would then recoup their losses on products sold abroad by levying fees against the farmers at home.

The Peek-Johnson plan was embodied in a bill first introduced in Congress in 1924 by Charles L. McNary of Oregon and Gilbert N. Haugen of Iowa. The original McNary-Haugen bill applied only to midwestern farm products and failed in the House. However, the Midwesterners won southern allies in

1926 by including cotton, tobacco, and rice in the proposal. The midwestern-southern coalition pushed a new McNary-Haugen bill through Congress in 1927 and 1928, only to have it vetoed by Coolidge on both occasions. The McNary-Haugen bill, though never put into operation, signified that the best organized political group (farmers) had accepted the proposition that it was the federal government's duty to protect the economic security of all classes—and particularly of depressed groups.

One of the longest battles of the 1920s revolved around the disposition of two nitrate plants and the Wilson Dam and hydroelectric facility at Muscle Shoals on the Tennessee River in northern Alabama. The federal government had constructed them during the war in order to free the country from dependence on imported nitrates. Before this struggle ended, it had become the focus of a nationwide controversy over public development, ownership, or regulation of the entire electric-power industry.

One of the first acts of the Harding administration was to announce that it would lease the entire facility to any responsible private company which would complete the dams and guarantee a fair return to the government. Henry Ford offered to buy it; he promised to produce nitrates for cheap fertilizers and to build a gigantic industrial complex in the Tennessee Valley.

Congress, in 1924, would have authorized the lease of the Muscle Shoals facilities to Ford had it not been for the efforts of Senator George W. Norris of Nebraska. As early as 1922, the senator had begun to dream of a great federal agency which would build and operate a network of dams throughout the valley for flood control and the production of inexpensive electric power. With strong southern support, Norris pushed a bill through Congress in 1928 to create a corporation to operate Wilson Dam and the nitrate plants. The lines between the champions of public power and the defenders of the private utilities were now clearly drawn. Coolidge naturally gave the Muscle Shoals bill a pocket veto. In 1931, his successor, Herbert Hoover, vetoed a second such bill and denounced governmental operation of power facilities as socialistic. However, as we shall see, Norris had lost only two battles, not the war.

Congress, in several measures in the 1920s, effected a revolution in American public policies by decreeing an end to the centuries-old tradition of virtually free and unlimited immigration to the United States. Equally significant was the fact that this change was effected with little partisan controversy or struggle between conservatives and progressives. The country had come—temporarily, at least—to a fairly solid consensus on the subject, although different motivations contributed to this consensus. Labor leaders, social workers, and most progressives had, by 1921, come to favor outright exclusion of immigrants, at least those from southern and eastern Europe.

The catalyst for this change was the fear in 1919 and 1920 that millions of poor and homeless Europeans were preparing to move to the United States. The postwar Red Scare intensified this fear of an uncontrollable inundation. The National Origins Act of 1924 was severe enough to please all but the most extreme exclusionists. The measure abrogated the Gentlemen's Agreement with Japan by prohibiting the immigration of all Orientals. The act also limited the number of European immigrants to 2 per cent of the foreign-born, according to the Census of 1890—taken before the influx of southern and eastern European immigrants. The act also stipulated that, after July 1, 1927,

Senator George W. Norris, who had been at odds with both President Coolidge and President Hoover over private ownership and operation of public power, eagerly went on a coast to coast speaking tour on behalf of a new presidential candidate, Governor Roosevelt. Roosevelt had supported Norris and the progressives during the 1920s against the power trust which Norris called "the greatest monopolistic corporation that has been organized for private greed." (Wide World Photos)

only 150,000 immigrants should be admitted annually. The new system was put into effect in 1929. President Hoover drastically reduced the quotas in 1931, largely in response to high unemployment, and the total net immigration for the decade of the 1930s was only 69,000.

5. THE UNITED STATES AND WORLD AFFAIRS IN THE 1920s

The Washington Conference

The great majority of Americans were disillusioned by the results of their intervention in the First World War and were determined to avoid obligations which might draw them into some future war. Yet a powerful and wealthy nation cannot remain isolated merely by wanting to be left alone. The United States was a great power in the 1920s, with economic and political interests around the world. Therefore, it was impossible for the Harding and Coolidge administrations to withdraw completely from world affairs.

Harding started rather blithely on his way in foreign policy by announcing in his inaugural, "We do not mean to be entangled." His Secretary of State,

Charles Evans Hughes, refused for several months to answer communications from the League of Nations. Harding and Hughes knew, however, that the United States in 1921 was on the brink of an intense naval race with Great Britain and Japan. Moreover, relations with Japan had become embittered by diplomatic and naval controversies.

Few Americans wanted a naval race, much less a war, with Japan. Senator William E. Borah of Idaho therefore proposed that the President invite Great Britain and Japan to discuss naval disarmament. Congress approved the Borah resolution by overwhelming majorities. The British government, burdened by debt, was also eager for disarmament talks. Harding sent invitations, not only to Great Britain and Japan, but also to France, Italy, China, the Netherlands, Belgium, and Portugal.

Delegates from these eight countries and the United States met at Washington on November 12, 1921. Hughes startled the delegates by proposing a ten-year "holiday" in the construction of battleships. A number of large warships already built or under construction should be scrapped. The United States, Hughes went on, was ready to scrap thirty ships. Great Britain should scrap nineteen, and Japan, seventeen ships. This would amount to a total reduction in the navies of the three major naval powers of about 2,000,000 tons and leave the ratio in capital ships at five for Great Britain, five for the United States, and three for Japan. Thus, the United States and its former mother country would continue to rule the world's oceans and military supply routes, but at a lesser expense than before. The Japanese gained tangible recognition as the "great power" in the Pacific.

Negotiations proceeded smoothly, in spite of some difficulties in persuading France and Italy to accept inferior tonnages. In fact, Hughes seized the opportunity offered by the cooperation of Great Britain and Japan to conclude a comprehensive series of treaties relating not only to naval construction and tonnage but to the Far East as well. These treaties ratified Hughes' proposal relating to large warships, nullified the Anglo-Japanese Alliance of 1902, bound the signatories to respect one another's possessions in the Pacific region, and guaranteed the integrity of China and the preservation of the commercial Open Door in that country. A final treaty prohibited the use of submarines as commerce destroyers in wartime and outlawed the use of poisonous gases.

The Senate approved the treaties, but with an important reservation. It said that the United States had assumed "no commitment to armed forces, no alliance, no obligation to join in any defense." It was one of the clearest statements on record of American determination to cooperate in promoting world peace—but to assume no obligations to defend that peace.

The Washington Conference was the first successful disarmament conference in modern history. The Five-Power Treaty (which established the 5:5:3 ratio in capital ships) was a compromise, in which each nation gave up something. Through these mutual concessions, nevertheless, the conference stopped the naval race in capital ships and provided a political understanding which helped to preserve peace in the Orient for a decade. It was the chief accomplishment of the Harding administration.

It would have been well if congressmen and senators had remembered that international understanding is a two-way street. On the one side, Japanese friendship for the United States was already warm as a result of the negotiations in Washington and American aid to Japan following a great earthquake in 1923. On the other side, Congress, in the National Origins Act of 1924, abrogated the Gentlemen's Agreement which had governed immigration from Japan since 1907. Worse still, Congress prohibited Oriental immigration in words that were humiliating to the Japanese. Congress' action, and Coolidge's reluctant approval of it, destroyed all the progress which Hughes and the liberal Japanese leaders had made since 1921 in restoring cordial relations between their two countries.

War Debts and Reparations

The necessity to resolve the most vexing economic legacy of the war—the huge burden of war debts and reparations—gave additional proof that it was impossible for the American government to withdraw into blissful isolation. The burden of intergovernmental debts was a great cancer on the body of the international economy. The British government had loaned some $4 billion to seventeen nations during the war. The Allied governments had borrowed more than $10 billion from the United States during and just after the war. In addition, the Allied governments had imposed on Germany a reparations bill of $33 billion in 1921. This turned out to be a very precarious international financial situation.

The Allies proposed a mutual cancellation of Allied intergovernmental debts on the ground that they had been incurred in a common struggle against Germany. The Harding and Coolidge administrations insisted that the former Allies pay their debts to the United States in full. Long-term funding agreements were eventually negotiated with Great Britain, France, and Italy. But developments soon proved that Allied debt payments depended unofficially upon German reparation payments, and that the latter depended upon the flow of American capital to Germany.

The entire structure of intergovernmental payments broke down temporarily when the German government defaulted on reparations payments in 1922. A special committee headed by two American bankers worked out a settlement which provided for an American gold loan to Germany and a scaling down of that nation's payments. In 1929, a new committee further reduced the German reparations debt to $2 billion, but the structure of intergovernmental payments collapsed when depression struck the world economy after 1929. The former Allies then abandoned the effort to collect reparations from Germany, defaulted on their own debts to the United States, and embarked upon policies of economic nationalism which aggravated the worldwide depression by disrupting almost all trade and financial exchange.

The Pursuit of Peace

Events abroad, particularly after settlement of the Franco-German dispute over reparations, greatly encouraged hopes that the world had entered a new era in the pursuit of world peace. American political leaders, for the most part, were not inclined to stand idly by when international relations seemed to be moving in new channels. The United States Government slowly established cordial relations with the League of Nations and participated in numerous League conferences. But the American venture into world affairs in the 1920s was both cautious and naive because it was based on the assumption that the United States could play a leading role in the pursuit of peace without carrying commensurate responsibility.

Leadership without responsibility was also the assumption of the most spectacular peace movement of the 1920s. This was the campaign to outlaw war, which American peace groups and isolationists supported. It culminated in the Pact of Paris, or Kellogg-Briand Treaty (so named because Secretary of State Frank B. Kellogg and French Foreign Minister Aristide Briand were its chief negotiators). The treaty was signed on August 27, 1928, by representatives of all the great powers except Russia, which later signed it.

The Pact of Paris was certainly a pious affirmation of good intentions, but it provided no penalties against nations which resorted to force. The treaty contained enough loopholes to satisfy any major nation. It did not prevent Japan from seizing Manchuria in 1931, or Italy from invading Ethiopia in 1935, or Germany and Russia from devouring Poland in 1939.

The Beginnings of a Good Neighbor Policy

The removal of any threat to American hemispheric supremacy in the 1920s permitted leaders in Washington to view developments in the Caribbean and Central America with less concern. First evidence that a more relaxed policy

President Coolidge signing the antiwar treaty, the Kellogg-Briand Pact, on January 17, 1929, after it had been overwhelmingly endorsed by the Senate. Just before Secretary of State Kellogg went to Paris to sign the agreement, the President clearly expressed the enthusiasm of the nation for it: "It holds a greater hope for peaceful relations than was ever before given to the world."

might be in the making came when Hughes permitted the people of the Dominican Republic, which had been administered by an American military government since 1916, to form a constitutional regime. Hughes withdrew American troops in 1924.

Hughes, in 1925, also withdrew a force of marines which had been stationed in Nicaragua since 1909. However, when civil war broke out soon afterward, Coolidge sent back the marines to maintain an unpopular, pro-American regime. This set off such violent criticism among antiimperialists in the United States that Coolidge hastily sent Henry L. Stimson, former Secretary of War, to mediate between the warring factions. As peace returned to Nicaragua from 1931 to 1933, American troops were withdrawn. However, they left a family dynasty in control of Nicaragua, which ruled corruptly and violently, with the aid of American arms, until 1979.

Dealing with small Caribbean and Central American republics was easy compared to the difficulties of following wise policies toward the larger and more sensitive population of Mexico. Americans had invested about $1 billion in Mexican enterprises. Leaders of the Mexican Revolution had adopted a constitution in 1917, Article XXVII of which vested ownership of all oil and mineral resources in the Mexican people. All went reasonably well between the United States and Mexico so long as the Mexican government did not try to implement Article XXVII.

A strong nationalist, Plutarco Elías Calles, came to power in 1924. Two years later, the Mexican Congress passed laws for the enforcement of Article XXVII. Calles also embarked upon a bloody persecution of the Roman Catholic Church which inflamed sentiment in the United States.

Coolidge and Kellogg, who had succeeded Hughes, reacted violently. They accused Calles of violating international law (a dubious interpretation) and also (unjustly) of establishing a Bolshevik-controlled regime. However, tempers cooled on both sides once the new American ambassador, Dwight W. Morrow, arrived in Mexico City in 1927. Through tact, understanding of Mexican nationalism, and demonstrations of sympathy for Mexican ambitions, Morrow won a new agreement on American-owned oil fields and persuaded Calles to halt his campaign against the Roman Catholic Church.

Meanwhile, the State Department had also retreated from the Roosevelt Corollary to the Monroe Doctrine. The United States was not yet ready to abandon the alleged right to intervene when it thought that its vital interests were at stake. However, the State Department admitted that intervention in the affairs of other countries could not be justified by appealing to the Monroe Doctrine. Coolidge's successor, Herbert Hoover, refused to intervene in Latin America during his tenure from 1929 to 1933. Thus the way was prepared for what would be called the Good Neighbor policy of nonintervention and cooperation under Hoover's successor, Franklin D. Roosevelt.

SUGGESTED READINGS

A lively romp through the 1920s is Frederick Lewis Allen, *Only Yesterday* (1931). Leuchtenburg, *The Perils of Prosperity*, already cited, is an equally readable and a much more careful study. George Soule, *Prosperity Decade: From War to Depression, 1917–1929* (1947), is a good economic history. Useful information on the institutions of business will be found in Thomas C. Cochran, *The American Business System: A Historical*

Perspective, 1900–1955 (1957). Siegfried Giedion, *Mechanization Takes Command: A Contribution to Anonymous History* (1948), traces the growth of industrial technology. For a detailed account of the decade's most famous industrialist, see Allan Nevins and F. E. Hill, *Ford: The Times, the Man, and the Company* (1954) and *Ford: Expansion and Challenge* (1957). Labor and poverty in the twenties are examined in Irving Bernstein, *The Lean Years* (1960).

On intellectual currents, Edmund Wilson, *The Shores of Light* (1952) and *The American Earthquake* (1958), provide a good introduction. Among many fine literary portraits are Mark Schorer, *Sinclair Lewis* (1961); Joseph L. Blotner, *Faulkner*, 2 vols. (1974); H. D. Piper, *F. Scott Fitzgerald: A Critical Portrait* (1965); and Carlos Baker, *Hemingway: The Writer as Artist* (1956) and *Ernest Hemingway: A Life Story* (1969).

Norman F. Furniss, *The Fundamentalist Controversy, 1918–1931* (1954), is a detailed account of that movement. Ray Ginger, *Six Days or Forever?* (1958), is the best description of the Scopes trial. David M. Chalmers, *Hooded Americanism: The First Century of the Ku Klux Klan* (1965), is especially good on the twenties, but it should be supplemented by Kenneth T. Jackson, *The Ku Klux Klan in the City, 1915–1930* (1967), and Charles C. Alexander, *The Ku Klux Klan in the Southwest* (1965). On prohibition, Andrew Sinclair, *The Era of Excess* (1962), is readable and enjoyable. More theoretical works about the meaning of prohibition are Joseph Gusfield, *Symbolic Crusade: Status Politics and the American Temperance Movement* (1963), and Norman H. Clark, *Deliver Us from Evil: An Interpretation of American Prohibition* (1976).

On the Harlem Renaissance, see Nathan I. Huggins, *Harlem Renaissance* (1971). The best biography of Garvey is E. David Cronon, *Black Moses: The Story of Marcus Garvey* (1955).

Arthur M. Schlesinger, Jr., *The Crisis of*

the *Old Order* (1957), is a lucid interpretation of politics in the decade. Two major problems of the period can be studied in Theodore Saloutos and Johns D. Hicks, *Agricultural Discontent in the Middle West, 1900–1939* (1951), and Randolph E. Paul, *Taxation in the United States* (1954). For a classic history of the South during this period, see George B. Tindall, *The Emergence of the New South, 1913–1945* (1967).

Andrew Sinclair attempts to redeem some part of Harding's reputation in *The Available Man* (1965). Robert K. Murray's *The Harding Era* (1968), although based on more original research than Sinclair's book, is an even less persuasive defense. Francis Russell arouses sympathy for Harding somewhat more successfully in *The Shadow of Blooming Grove* (1968). J. Chalmers Vinson, *The Parchment Peace* (1950), is a good study of the Washington Conference. Dexter Perkins, *Charles Evans Hughes and American Democratic Statesmanship* (1953), is exceptionally good. Calvin Coolidge is the subject of William A. White's entertaining *A Puritan in Babylon* (1938). A more sympathetic and more penetrating biography is Donald R. McCoy, *Calvin Coolidge: The Quiet President* (1967).

Kenneth C. MacKay, *The Progressive Movement of 1924* (1947), is a detailed analysis. For a revisionist view of La Follette's candidacy, see James Weinstein, *The Decline of Socialism in America, 1912–1925* (1967). The reorientation of the Democratic party is analyzed in David Burner, *The Politics of Provincialism: The Democratic Party in Transition, 1918–1932* (1968).

Several good biographies illuminate this period. Among them are Frank Freidel, *Franklin Roosevelt: The Ordeal* (1954); Matthew and Hannah Josephson, *Al Smith: Hero of the Cities* (1969); William H. Harbaugh, *Lawyer's Lawyer: The Life of John W. Davis* (1973); and Richard Lowitt, *George W. Norris: The Persistence of a Progressive* (1971).

CHAPTER 26
THE GREAT DEPRESSION
AND THE NEW DEAL

1. HERBERT HOOVER AND THE GREAT DEPRESSION

Hoover and the American Dream

On August 2, 1927, President Coolidge announced: "I do not choose to run for President in 1928." Coolidge would have welcomed a draft, but Republicans were delighted to release him from the burdens of office. They demanded the nomination of Herbert Hoover, Secretary of Commerce, who enjoyed a reputation for vigor and moderate progressivism. The Republican national convention nominated Hoover on the first ballot. The Democratic party was still deeply divided. However, Alfred E. Smith was the only Democrat of national stature available in 1928, and, with the support of northern and western delegates, the New Yorker won the nomination easily.

Hoover made only half a dozen speeches and emphasized the general prosperity under Republican rule and promised its continuance. As he put it in his acceptance speech: "We in America today are nearer to the final triumph over poverty than ever before in the history of any land." Moreover, Hoover made it plain that he rejected proposals such as the McNary-Haugen bill, federal operation of power projects, and legislation favoring organized labor.

Smith had a long record as a defender of civil rights and as a champion of progressive legislation. However, instead of trying to rally Americans to a new progressive coalition, he campaigned on the two issues of prohibition and religious toleration. He attacked prohibition, which Hoover had defended as an "experiment noble in intent." Smith was goaded into discussion of the religious issue because of numerous charges that he, a Roman Catholic, would move the Vatican to Washington and turn the government over to the Pope.

Few observers were surprised when Hoover won. He carried forty states and broke the Solid South. Yet there were signs of profound changes in American national politics. No longer could the Democrats go into a presidential campaign assured of solid southern support. Of even greater significance for the future, Smith—the hero of the urban Democracy—made the Democratic party indisputably the party of the non-Protestant masses in the great cities. He loosened black ties to the party of Lincoln by winning about half of the black vote in the northern cities. Finally, Smith ran far better in the midwestern farm states than any Democrat since Woodrow Wilson.

The man whom Americans had chosen to lead the way to permanent prosperity symbolized the American tradition of success through hard work. Herbert Clark Hoover was born on a small farm in Iowa on August 10, 1874. He was orphaned at the age of ten and later worked his way through Stanford University. He accumulated a large fortune as a mining engineer and mine owner. Hoover directed the Belgian Relief Commission in the First World War. When his country entered the war in 1917, he became Food Administra-

Calvin Coolidge and Herbert Hoover on March 4, 1929, en route to Hoover's inauguration where the new President expressed his confidence in the nation: "I have no fears for the future of our country. It is bright with hope." (Wide World Photos)

tor. As Secretary of Commerce under Harding and Coolidge, Hoover extended into peacetime the cooperation between government and industry which had been carried on by the War Industries Board and the Food Administration. He used industrial trade associations to exchange information and thereby promote standardization and reduce costs.

Hoover had never run for elective office or engaged in partisan politics. His lack of political experience, particularly in getting on with persons of opposing views, would place a heavy burden on Hoover once the political tide turned against him. Still, the presence in the White House of a successful businessman in 1929 seemed fitting.

Soon after his inauguration, Hoover called Congress into special session to consider agricultural relief. Farm leaders still insisted on something like the McNary-Haugen plan, but the new President would not accept any such thing. Hoover's alternative—the Agricultural Marketing bill—created a Federal Farm Board and gave it a revolving fund of $500 million to enable agricultural cooperatives to build warehouses and sell crops in an orderly way. However, farm-state senators added a provision which authorized the Federal Farm Board indirectly to purchase farm products in order to stabilize prices.

Hoover also urged Congress to give farmers additional tariff protection. The tariff bill presented by Representative Willis C. Hawley not only increased duties on agricultural products, it also included some 925 increases in the rates on manufactured goods. Senator Reed Smoot of Utah pushed the measure through the upper house in May 1930 in spite of growing public opposition. One thousand members of the American Economic Association signed a petition which begged Hoover to veto the Hawley-Smoot bill. What the world needed, they asserted, was freer trade, not economic nationalism.

Hoover not only signed the Hawley-Smoot bill but also, long afterward, argued that it had had no significant effect on world trade. From a statistical point of view, he was probably correct. However, the Hawley-Smoot Act gave European countries an excuse for sharply increasing their own tariff rates. The British, for example, adopted protection in 1932 in retaliation against American tariff policies.

Hoover appointed a Commission on Law Observance and Enforcement, headed by former Attorney General George W. Wickersham, to assess prohibition. The Wickersham Commission reported in January 1931 what everyone knew: enforcement of the Eighteenth Amendment had simply collapsed because of widespread opposition. The report was the death knell of prohibition. Congress, with a sigh of relief, approved the Twenty-first Amendment in February 1933. It repealed the Eighteenth Amendment and forbade the shipment of alcoholic beverages into dry states.

The Great Depression

Even in prosperous times, not all sectors of the American economy advance evenly; weaknesses always exist, and it is easy to discover them—years later. In 1929, the prospects for residential construction were adversely affected by demographic changes and rising construction costs. Farmers were in trouble because of the agricultural depression already discussed. This dried up markets for consumer goods in farm areas, and it weakened banks with loans outstanding to farmers. Over 70 per cent of the American people lived at or below the Labor Department's estimate of a decent living standard. These people, who lacked savings, would be vulnerable to any economic adversity, and so, too, would the manufacturers and retailers who served them.

The economy was endangered also by a rickety system of international debts and by the inflexibility of the gold standard upon which international trade was based. Some other alleged causes of the depression, such as the poor structure of the banking system, abuse of credit, and dishonesty within the business community, were probably no worse in 1929 than in most earlier periods of American history.

The most dramatic cause of the depression was the collapse of the stock market in the autumn of 1929. Between 1925 and 1929, stock prices rose about 300 per cent. By 1929, more than 1,000,000 American stock buyers were bidding up the prices of shares much faster than corporate profits increased. This process could not continue indefinitely.

In one terrible month, which started on October 23, 1929, prices on the New York Stock Exchange fell about $26 billion, and prices dropped for two and a half more years. The loss of $26 billion in less than a month and of more than $35 billion in a year, on the New York Stock Exchange alone, takes on added meaning when compared to the American gross national product (GNP = the total of all goods and services produced), which was slightly over $100 billion in 1929.

The depression passed through two distinct stages. The first, which lasted from the autumn of 1929 to the summer of 1931, might be called a severe recession. By the last quarter of 1930, for example, industrial production was only 26 per cent below its peak level of 1929. The second stage was the severe depression which set in during the summer of 1931 and lasted until 1935 or 1936. This second stage was related not only to domestic events but also to depressions in Germany, Austria, and Great Britain which were induced primarily by a sharp decline in American investment and purchasing abroad.

Some of the dimensions of the awful economic catastrophe that befell the American people can be seen by examining the statistical progress of the depression from 1929 to 1933. National income declined from $87.8 billion to $40.2 billion. More than 100,000 businesses failed. The number of unemployed, already at 7,000,000 in the autumn of 1931, swelled to about 14,000,000 in the early months of 1933.

The personal trauma of the Great Depression was horrendous. Two or three million people moved from cities back to the country in the hope of scratching out a living from the soil. Family tensions multiplied as mothers and fathers lost their jobs and relatives doubled up in houses and apartments. The number of marriages plummeted, as did the birthrate. People suffered and some died from malnutrition and lack of clothing, fuel, or medical care. Despair came to millions who wanted work but could not find it. Hardest hit were blacks, women workers, and recent immigrants in the large cities.

One of the most significant long-term impacts of the depression was the change that it brought in attitudes toward business and government. Loss of confidence in the nation's business leadership was almost complete by 1933. Mistrust increased after several congressional investigations revealed the extent to which bankers had misused depositors' funds and manipulated the stock market during the 1920s. Gradually, the great majority of Americans began to look to the federal government for protection. The stage was set first in 1930, when private charities ran out of money. Persons in distress

Jobless men sitting on a park bench, 1930. Photo by Lewis Hine. (Collection of International Museum of Photography at George Eastman House)

Right: A young man out of work, Washington D.C., 1938 (Library of Congress)

Destitute pea pickers in California: a mother of seven children, age thirty-two, February 1936. (Library of Congress)

then turned to city and state relief agencies, which in turn collapsed during 1931 and 1932. In the mid-1930s, a majority of Americans finally concluded that the federal government should provide jobs for the unemployed whenever private business proved unable to do so.

Although remarkably few people seemed to lose confidence in the capitalistic system altogether, the conviction spread that American capitalism had to change drastically. The old system of relatively unregulated free enterprise had to give way to a new system of governmental planning to assure the successful functioning of the economy.

There were some eruptions of disorder as the depression spread. Unemployed persons rioted in Dearborn, Michigan, and a number of hunger marches took place. Throughout the Middle West, farmers threatened to shoot bank and insurance agents who attempted to foreclose on farm mortgages. In Le Mars, Iowa, a large crowd of enraged farmers dragged a foreclosing judge from the bench and beat him into unconsciousness.

Some officials in the Hoover administration feared that serious disorder would result from the descent of the so-called Bonus Expeditionary Force upon Washington in the spring of 1932. About 12,000 to 15,000 veterans built a shantytown just outside Washington. They demanded immediate payment of the soldiers' bonus. A riot occurred on July 28, and two persons were killed. Hoover promptly called upon the army to maintain order.

National Guardsmen, armed with machine guns, are called in to
keep peace in Le Mars, Iowa, as irate farmers protest the foreclosures
of mortgages on their homes. The Guard was called in following
an attack on a judge. (United Press International Photo)

General Douglas MacArthur led an armored force that burned down the
shantytown and dispersed its residents with tear gas.

Hoover and the Crisis

The old myth about President Hoover fiddling while the country burned has
long been discredited. He labored tirelessly to prevent economic disintegra-
tion. Moreover, he acted upon his belief in the fundamental goodness of his
fellowmen and in the power of democracy to correct social and economic
injustices. Yet Hoover was a prisoner of his own ideology; he was unable to
consider seriously new remedies to meet an unforeseen catastrophe. While
the United States suffered from severe deflation, Hoover followed deflation-
ary policies that only aggravated the condition. The nation might have been
set on the road to prosperity by a large increase in the money supply,
substantial relief and public-works programs, and encouragement of private
investment. But to the embattled President, these programs were economic
heresy. Increasingly, leaders in Congress and the country pressed for
monetary inflation and a huge relief program. But Hoover insisted that the
only thing which would bring recovery was confidence in the soundness of
the dollar and in the integrity of the government.

During the first stage of the crisis (1929–1931) Hoover tried to mobilize a

Unemployed ex-soldiers heaving bricks and stones at
Washington, D.C., police in an unsuccessful effort to keep
themselves from being evicted from the city in 1932. They and
other unemployed veterans had marched to Washington as part of
the approximately 15,000-man "Bonus Expeditionary Force," to
demand immediate payment of certificates entitling World War I
veterans to bonus payments for their military service; the
certificates were not scheduled to fall due until 1945. President
Hoover called in troops to clear the marchers from Federal
property. In 1936 an act of Congress made it possible for veterans to
exchange their certificates for cashable bonds. (Wide World
Photos)

great national voluntary effort. He won from business and labor leaders
promises to maintain normal operations without severe wage reductions or
strikes. At the same time, he called upon mayors and governors to increase
expenditures for public works, and the Federal Farm Board went actively into
the market to maintain farm prices.

For a time it seemed that the nation would get through the slump without
major difficulties. But a storm of unprecedented magnitude broke over the
world in the summer of 1931. It followed the breakdown of the world
economy occasioned by the financial crisis in Europe. The withdrawal of
about $1.5 billion of foreign-owned gold from American banks, plus the
dumping of securities on the New York Stock Exchange and large losses
abroad by American banks, exacerbated the crisis in the United States.

Hoover still hoped for miracles through voluntary efforts, but the strain on
private resources was too great, and he reluctantly set to work to devise a
federal program for recovery. Hoover's chief antidepression weapon was the
Reconstruction Finance Corporation (RFC), chartered by Congress in January

Hooverville on the Seattle Washington Waterfront, 1933. (Wide World Photos)

1932, with potential capital of $2 billion. It went to work to save banks, railroads, and other financial institutions. The RFC earmarked no funds for small businesses or consumers, but it did protect most of the nation's large banks from failure. The Glass-Steagall Act of 1932 permitted Federal Reserve Banks to expand the currency. A Federal Home Loan Bank Act made capital available to building and loan associations, while the capital of Federal Land Banks was also increased. These measures helped to save the financial structure from total collapse in 1932.

Meanwhile, efforts on the agricultural front were less successful. The Federal Farm Board was powerless to maintain prices after they dropped sharply on world markets in the summer of 1931. The board confessed its impotence in 1932 and urged Congress to limit production. Meanwhile, millions of Americans had gone hungry, and thousands of persons starved or died from diseases associated with malnutrition because they could not pay for food.

Fierce struggles took place in Washington during 1932 over relief and monetary policies. Progressives and inflationists in Congress demanded immediate payment of the veteran's bonus and the adoption of a federal relief program. Hoover retained enough support in Congress to block these proposals. On relief, however, he did compromise by authorizing the RFC to lend an inadequate $300 million to the states to tide the unemployed over the winter. An additional $1.5 billion went to the states for public works such as airports, bridges, and tunnels.

Change of Command

The Great Depression was one of those profound internal upheavals that have fundamentally changed political alignments on several occasions in American history. Hoover had coasted into the presidency by claiming that the Republican business leadership had brought permanent prosperity to the country. As the depression deepened, Americans lost confidence in a leader who had so closely identified himself with the business classes.

The loss of confidence moved at about the same speed as the depression itself. The mid-term election of 1930 returned the first Democratic Congress since 1916, but the results constituted no landslide. The Democrats controlled both houses by bare majorities. Extensive loss of confidence in Hoover and in the Republican party did not begin until the autumn of 1931. The conviction then grew that Hoover was more interested in saving banks, railroads, and corporations than he was in saving people. Hoover became the object not merely of popular dislike but also of contempt.

Democratic presidential fever rose rapidly as it became obvious that almost any Democrat probably would win in 1932. The decisive struggle for party leadership was between former Governor Alfred E. Smith and Governor Franklin Delano Roosevelt of New York. Smith had the support of the Tammany organization in New York and of Democratic organizations in other eastern states. However, the odds were heavily against him. Enemies resented his stand against prohibition and his emphasis upon the religious issue in 1928. Smith's possibilities were imperiled most of all because the Democratic party now had another leader—Franklin D. Roosevelt. Roosevelt had fought his way back from a severe attack of polio in 1921. Meanwhile, he had maintained his political connections without engaging in the controversies which disrupted the Democratic party during the 1920s.

In 1928, Roosevelt was narrowly elected governor of New York in the face of the Hoover landslide. He won reelection in 1930 by the largest majority ever given a gubernatorial candidate in the history of New York. This victory made Roosevelt the leading contender for the Democratic presidential nomination in 1932. So successful were his managers that, by the early months of 1932, the Democratic preconvention contest had become a struggle of Roosevelt against the field.

When the Democratic national convention opened in Chicago, Roosevelt had a majority of the delegates, but not the two-thirds majority necessary for nomination. The deadlock was broken on the fourth ballot, when John Nance Garner of Texas, Speaker of the House of Representatives, threw his support to Roosevelt in return for the vice-presidential nomination. Roosevelt disagreed with the conservative Garner on almost every major issue, but the vice-presidency seemed a small price to pay for almost certain election as President.

Roosevelt promised a "New Deal" for the American people if they sent him to the White House, but neither his acceptance speech nor the Democratic platform gave any promise of fundamental changes in federal policies. The platform promised to *cut* federal expenditures by 25 per cent and to balance the budget. Meanwhile, the Republicans, who could not bring themselves to repudiate a sitting President, gloomily renominated Hoover. The Republican platform promised economy, defense of the gold standard, and reform of the banking system.

Governor Franklin D. Roosevelt of New York, Democratic presidential nominee, outlines his plan for farm relief while campaigning in Topeka, Kansas. In the election of 1932, Roosevelt carried most of the agricultural West and South. (Wide World Photos)

Both Hoover and Roosevelt campaigned strenuously, but the contest was an unequal one. Actually, the two men said much the same things, but they *sounded* very different. While Hoover talked mournfully about his battles to stem the depression, Roosevelt exuded confidence in his ability to make things come out right, quickly. Moreover, Roosevelt hit hard at Hoover's alleged callousness about the suffering of the poor and promised that he would do anything to keep people from starving. His active, nationwide campaign convinced voters that Roosevelt was fit for the burdens of the presidency and undoubtedly increased his margin of victory. Roosevelt won nearly 23,000,000 popular and 472 electoral votes. Democrats also elected large majorities in both houses of Congress.

The final session of the Seventy-second Congress from December 1932 to March 1933 proved to be the last for "lame ducks." These were members who had been defeated for reelection in November but continued to make laws in the three months still left before their successors took office. The Twentieth Amendment, ratified in January 1933, provided that the Congress elected in November should begin its session on the third of the following January, and that the President should be inaugurated on January 20 instead of March 4.

2. LAUNCHING THE NEW DEAL

Franklin D. Roosevelt and the Flowering of the Progressive Movement

An exciting era in American history began when Franklin D. Roosevelt took the oath of office on March 4, 1933. It commenced with a special session of Congress, which in one hundred days laid the framework of a New Deal aimed to combat the depression. It ended with the victory of the United States and its allies over dictatorships which had all but enslaved the peoples of Europe and Asia.

Franklin Roosevelt was born in Hyde Park, New York, in 1882. He received a proper patrician education at Groton and Harvard without revealing special promise. After a brief practice of law, Roosevelt entered politics as an anti-Tammany Democrat. He won election to the New York State Senate in 1910. President Wilson appointed him Assistant Secretary of the Navy in 1913. The rising young politician made peace with the Tammany organization, and he received the Democratic vice-presidential nomination in 1920.

While Herbert Hoover was trapped by his political and economic ideology, Franklin Roosevelt possessed virtually no ideology. This open-mindedness

Hoover shaking hands with his successor, Franklin D. Roosevelt, just prior to the President-elect's inauguration. In his inaugural address, Roosevelt promised the American people: "This great nation will endure as it has endured, will revive and prosper. So, first of all, let me assert my firm belief that the only thing we have to fear is fear itself." (Wide World Photos)

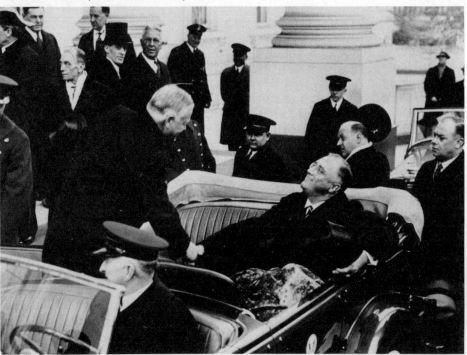

—some have called it lack of principle—made him willing and even eager to experiment. Furthermore, Roosevelt, like his fifth cousin and uncle-in-law, Theodore, believed that government should play a leading role in the American economy and society.

Roosevelt, like his two great teachers—Theodore Roosevelt and Woodrow Wilson—believed in a strong President who spoke for all people, coordinated various departments of the government, and directed foreign affairs. Roosevelt also developed a keen understanding of public opinion. He usually gave irresistible leadership to his party in Congress, precisely because he succeeded so well in interpreting the trends in public opinion. He also established direct communication with the people through addresses, press conferences, and the radio talks which he called "fireside chats."

Roosevelt possessed faults, of course. He was deficient as an administrator, and his lack of any consistent guide to policies led him to place unmerited faith in experimentation for its own sake. Nevertheless, Roosevelt revitalized the progressive movement. He revived faith in democracy and restructured the political economy of the United States so that the government could achieve the main goals of the progressive movement: protection for the underprivileged and a minimum of economic security for all people.

Prelude to the New Deal

The policies of the Roosevelt administration were shaped by the unique economic situation when Roosevelt was inaugurated. The history of the next eight years would have been very different if the worst economic catastrophe in the history of the nation—the banking panic of early 1933—had not made drastic action necessary.

The panic was the product of a chain reaction of fear. One contributing factor was the widespread suspicion that Roosevelt, in spite of his campaign assurances, would abolish the gold standard and inflate the currency. During the week of January 18, 1933, thousands of Americans withdrew bank deposits, purchased gold or tangible property, and sent their money abroad. Bank after bank was forced to close. Governors began to declare bank holidays—that is, they closed the banks in their states to stop the withdrawals. By March 3, general closings had occurred in twenty-three states. On March 4, the remainder of the governors followed suit.

All banks were thus closed as Roosevelt took the presidential oath. The economic life of the country was grinding to a halt. In accepting the nomination for President, Roosevelt had declared, "I pledge myself to a New Deal for the American people." Now, on March 4, he pledged himself to a dynamic program of action for the general welfare. Calling for faith and courage, he exclaimed: "This great nation will endure as it has endured, will revive and prosper. So, first of all, let me assert my firm belief that the only thing we have to fear is fear itself."

No President ever entered the office who faced such immense and complex problems as Roosevelt, but none before could call upon so many competent advisers as he could. In planning his early program, Roosevelt turned especially to Professors Raymond Moley, Adolf A. Berle, Jr., and Rexford G. Tugwell of Columbia University—the original "Brain Trust." Later, important advisers included Harry L. Hopkins, a former social worker, and

Professor Felix Frankfurter of the Harvard Law School, whom Roosevelt appointed to the Supreme Court.

Several members of the cabinet also helped to shape Roosevelt's policies. Secretary of State Cordell Hull obtained substantial freedom in making foreign policy. Secretary of the Interior Harold L. Ickes revived the old conservation crusade. Secretary of Agriculture Henry A. Wallace carried on the work which his father had done as Secretary of Agriculture under Harding and Coolidge. Secretary of Labor Frances Perkins, the first woman to hold a cabinet seat, was influential in shaping labor policies and in planning for economic security.

The most striking characteristics of the group around Roosevelt were creativity and variety—within a certain range. Roosevelt's advisers included Republicans and Democrats, conservatives and progressives, but very few could reasonably be called radical.

3. THE FIRST NEW DEAL

The Concept of Two New Deals

Some scholars have suggested that there were in fact two New Deals, or two separate stages in legislative policies. According to this interpretation, the first New Deal operated during 1933 and 1934. It was based upon a coalition of all classes united behind Roosevelt to fight the depression. During this period, the administration worked on the assumption that recovery could be achieved quickly, mainly by the continuation and expansion of Hoover's policies.

Legislative and administrative action would strengthen the banking and securities industries, but such activities would be aimed at making privately owned financial institutions more secure in the future. The dollar would be devalued in order to bring prices up to a normal level, but there would be no large-scale deficit spending. Business and industry would be given a relatively free hand to effect recovery under federal supervision. Labor would be given new protections, but mainly through federal action for minimum wages and maximum hours. As for relief, all that was needed was to increase assistance to the states and to stimulate the construction industry with federal public works. Finally, agriculture would be put on its feet by restricting output through production controls.

Parts of this program worked. However, according to the "two New Deals" interpretation, the first New Deal was in trouble by the middle of 1934. Recovery did not occur as planned. The first New Deal had failed to improve the lot of workers, old people, tenant farmers, and the unemployed. Roosevelt's coalition came apart in 1934 when the business classes deserted him.

The first New Deal came to an end in the elections of 1934, according to this scenario, when the voters sent a huge Democratic majority to Congress. The new members were responsive to organized labor, the elderly, the unemployed, and impoverished farmers. Roosevelt veered leftward and set about to launch a second New Deal to satisfy the demands of the new left-of-center coalition.

The "two New Deals" interpretation contains some major deficiencies. It gives the impression that the two phases were largely separated. Actually, the legislation of 1935 – 1938 was to a considerable extent a natural outgrowth of earlier programs. The "two New Deals" interpretation also implies that Roosevelt, the master politician, deliberately tailored the entire second New Deal program to retain the support of segments of his new coalition. In many cases the coalition pushed him, rather than the other way around. Finally, this interpretation incorrectly implies that the first New Deal was conservative, the second, progressive. Yet despite these shortcomings, this interpretation provides helpful guidelines through the complexities of the Roosevelt era.

Financial Reinforcement and Reform

Roosevelt issued an order on March 6 which kept all banks in the country closed for a four-day period. Then he called Congress into an extra session on March 9. On that same day, both houses passed the administration's Emergency Banking bill. It approved Roosevelt's actions and authorized the Secretary of the Treasury to investigate the condition of all banks. The Secretary could permit them to reopen for business at his discretion. By midsummer, banks holding 94 per cent of all deposits were again in business with additional help from the RFC.

Congress followed by adopting the second Glass-Steagall Act, which increased the Federal Reserve Board's control over credit, required commercial banks to divorce themselves from their investment affiliates, and established the Federal Deposit Insurance Corporation (FDIC). The FDIC initially insured deposits in member banks up to $5,000. To save embattled homeowners, Congress established the Home Owners Loan Corporation (HOLC). During the next three years, the HOLC lent more than $3 billion to 1,000,000 homeowners. There was considerable sentiment in Congress and the country for governmental ownership of banks and other financial institutions. Roosevelt spurned all such suggestions and restored and actually strengthened private ownership in the financial field.

As in banking, swift action was required to meet the problem of deflation. Purchasing power, prices, and exports had dropped sharply, and debtors found it increasingly difficult to meet their obligations. If the administration devalued the currency, inflationists argued, wages, prices, purchasing power, and exports would all rise, and it would be easier to pay debts. Then trade of all kinds could proceed at a more normal pace.

Roosevelt turned a deaf ear to inflationists, who demanded the printing of billions in paper money, and adopted a more cautious course. On March 6, 1933, he took the country off the domestic gold standard, in the expectation that the dollar would fall precipitately in value. By October, domestic prices had risen by 19 per cent. This was not enough inflation to restore the price level of 1926, and Roosevelt took additional steps to devalue the dollar.

The experiment in devaluation failed almost completely. Prices rose slightly as a result of Roosevelt's first steps in 1933, but they did not rise significantly in 1934. Roosevelt put so much trust in the simple device of dollar devaluation that he intentionally wrecked all hopes of achieving international economic cooperation toward monetary stabilization at the World Economic Conference, which met in London in June 1933.

Meanwhile, Congress moved to protect the public from fraud in the

Disappointed depositors in front of a New York bank. Following the national bank holiday, other members of the Federal Reserve System opened their doors again, but this bank had remained closed. (United Press International Photo)

purchase and sale of securities: first, through a Truth-in-Securities Act in 1933, and then with the Securities Exchange Act of 1934, which created the Securities and Exchange Commission (SEC). It was given power to regulate stock exchanges and to bring action against persons engaged in fraud.

Two important measures completed the New Deal's efforts at financial reform. The first was the Banking Act of 1935—the only fundamental revision of the Federal Reserve Act since its adoption in 1913. It concentrated immense power in the Board of Governors of the Federal Reserve system. The new board had complete control over interest rates, reserve requirements, and the open-market operations of the Federal Reserve Banks. The second measure was the Holding Company Act of 1935, the outcome of a long fight by Roosevelt to break up electric-power holding companies which had pyramided company upon company. The Holding Company Act, adopted over the bitter resistance of the utilities companies, compelled the dissolution of large holding companies, but it permitted small holding companies to survive.

Farm Relief and Recovery

The condition of American farmers had fallen to a desperate state by the early months of 1933. The new administration first acted to consolidate and expand farm credit programs. Such measures did not strike at the root of the problem—production in excess of consumption—which depressed prices. This problem was addressed through the Agricultural Adjustment Act of May 1933. The act sought to raise the real income of farmers to the level of 1909–1914, when farm prices were near parity, or equality, with prices of manufactured goods. The measure aimed to limit production of major crops by various devices. For example, the Department of Agriculture persuaded cotton growers to plow under about 30 per cent of their growing crop. The Agricultural Adjustment Administration (AAA) bought over 6,000,000 pigs and slaughtered them. For reducing output, farmers received governmental payments which were financed by a processing tax on the industries which handled raw agricultural products.

A severe drought in the Middle West and Southwest cooperated with the AAA to reduce farm production. When cotton and tobacco farmers poured fertilizer on reduced acres and produced large crops in 1933, Congress imposed direct production controls on both staples in 1934. Altogether, governmental credit assistance, the AAA, bad weather, and international economic recovery raised net farm income 250 per cent between 1932 and 1935. Moreover, parity for agriculture was nearly achieved. To be sure, the AAA program contained major deficiencies. For example, it benefited mainly large farmers and planters and largely ignored tenant farmers and sharecroppers. However, the AAA saved many American farm owners from bankruptcy.

An Experiment in Industrial Recovery

Industry was also in a desperate situation in 1933. Millions of men and women, who with their families made up fully a third of the population, were out of work. Roosevelt initially had no specific solution for industry. But he and his advisers hastily sought an alternative to drastic plans backed by organized labor. They worked one out in conference with the United States Chamber of Commerce in the form of the National Industrial Recovery Act (NIRA), approved in June 1933.

This measure created the National Recovery Administration (NRA), headed by Hugh S. Johnson, to establish code authorities for various industries. These groups, composed of representatives of industry, government, unions, and consumers, were empowered to prepare codes (reminiscent of those established by Hoover's Commerce Department, to set production goals and determine fair prices for their industries. In addition, they were directed to eliminate child labor and establish minimum wages and maximum hours for workers. Section 7a of the bill affirmed labor's right to organize and bargain collectively. The bill also appropriated $3.3 billion

Apple sellers on New York's 42nd Street. (Brown Brothers)

for a Public Works Administration (PWA) under Harold L. Ickes to stimulate the construction industry.

The code authorities prepared codes covering every phase of trade and industry. Large corporations gained disproportionate influence within the authorities and set standards, wages, and prices which best suited their interests. Hundreds of codes contained provisions for lower wages for females than for males who did the same work. Code makers rationalized this disparity by claiming that most women workers represented a second family income.

Bitter opposition to the NRA soon developed. Small businessmen were in revolt by the spring of 1934 because, they said, the code authorities were dominated by big business. Section 7a was widely disregarded. When the NRA attempted to discipline code violators, the courts became jammed with cases, and enforcement broke down completely. Meanwhile, Ickes, fearful of wasting government funds, spent virtually none of the PWA's $3.3 billion to fuel consumption under the NRA. Therefore, prices increased, but few consumers received new jobs at sufficiently high incomes to buy the higher priced goods.

The NRA was the only peacetime effort at national industrial planning. It wiped out child labor in industry and eliminated most sweatshops. However, the NRA probably *impeded* recovery. It and other early New Deal policies assumed that the country was suffering from overproduction and that the

A policeman attempts to maintain order as 15,000 women turn out to apply for six Civil Service charwoman jobs, October 12, 1938. (United Press International Photo)

government must limit output to actual need. In fact, the United States was suffering from severe underconsumption in 1933 because of unemployment and the decline in wages. The country needed most of all a vast injection of purchasing power.

Relief under the First New Deal

Roosevelt was personally responsible for the Civilian Conservation Corps (CCC), which enrolled 300,000 young men in camps throughout the country and engaged in reforestation and other work. Aside from the CCC, all the relief programs of the first New Deal continued policies begun by Hoover. The Federal Housing Authority, established in 1934 to provide credit for home repairs and new housing, continued a Hoover policy. The Federal Emergency Relief Act (FERA) of May 12, 1933, appropriated $500 million for assistance to the unemployed through the states.

A sharp increase in industrial production and employment took place during the summer of 1933, but industry slumped again in the autumn. As winter approached, Roosevelt created the Civil Works Administration (CWA)

These young men, photographed at a CCC camp in Wisconsin, fought forest fires and cleared brush and trees. The camps, started by the Civilian Conservation Corps in 1933, took men off the bread lines during the time of economic depression and provided healthy, outdoor jobs for thousands. (Wide World Photos)

to provide temporary jobs for some 4,000,000 unemployed. In 1934, Roosevelt returned to the policy of providing relief assistance to the states through the FERA.

Regional Resources Development

Roosevelt, an ardent conservationist, gave personal leadership to a movement for federal development of regional multipurpose projects. These promoted flood control, river navigation, irrigation, and the production of hydroelectric power. Roosevelt obtained congressional approval for the development of the Tennessee Valley and for the completion of the Boulder Dam on the Colorado River in Arizona and the Bonneville and Grand Coulee dams on the Columbia River.

Congress created the Tennessee Valley Authority (TVA) in the spring of 1933 and directed that agency to improve the navigation of the Tennessee River, to provide for flood control, and to provide for the overall development of the region. The TVA built twenty new dams and improved five old ones and achieved a system of flood control and an inland waterway stretching from the Ohio River into the heart of the Appalachians. The authority gradually established a monopoly on the production and sale of electric power in the entire Tennessee Valley. The TVA transformed a chronically impoverished area into one of the more heavily industrialized and wealthier sections of the nation.

4. THE SECOND NEW DEAL

Launching the Second New Deal

Discontent destroyed the first New Deal coalition and divided the country just before the mid-term election of 1934. The business classes generally turned against the administration; they charged that Roosevelt was coddling labor and spending the Treasury into bankruptcy. Roosevelt simultaneously felt the wrath of demagogues and radicals who accused him of being a tool of Wall Street. Among these critics were Senator Huey P. Long of Louisiana, who proposed to divide the national wealth and give every family a $2,500 annual income. In addition, there were Father Charles E. Coughlin, a priest from Detroit with fascist tendencies and a large radio audience, and Dr. Francis E. Townsend of California, who organized a national movement for federal pensions of $200 a month to every person over sixty. Signs that these and other demagogues were stirring the discontent of small farmers, the unemployed, and the aged disturbed Roosevelt more than the revolt of the conservatives. A poll conducted by the Democratic National Committee revealed that, if Long ran as an independent candidate in 1936, he could take three to four million votes from Roosevelt.

Perhaps fortunately for the moderate President, the revolt of the conservatives coalesced the lower classes and part of the middle class into a solid New Deal front. In the congressional election of 1934, the Democrats increased their large majorities in both houses. However, among this majority there now sat many who viewed Roosevelt's attempts to aid workers as inadequate. Roosevelt boldly assumed leadership of the new left-of-center coalition that had come into being and jettisoned much of the first New Deal. He demanded that the federal government assume direct responsibility for the economic security of the masses of the people.

The spearhead of the second New Deal was the $5 billion-work-relief program, the Works Progress Administration (WPA). Director Harry Hopkins immediately began to provide jobs for unemployed and needy workers. Between 1935 and 1941, the WPA employed a monthly average of 2,112,000 persons.

Signs that the Supreme Court might call a halt to social-welfare legislation appeared even before the launching of the second New Deal. In January 1935, the court nullified one section of the NIRA. On May 6, the court, in a five-to-four decision, nullified the Railroad Retirement Act of 1934 in language that seemed to doom any general social-security legislation. The court delivered its heaviest blow on May 27 in a decision in A. L. A. Schechter Corporation *v.* the United States. The justices unanimously nullified the NIRA.

New Laws for Old

The Schechter decision plunged the administration into considerable confusion. Roosevelt quickly recovered his balance and decided to proceed at full steam with his program, in spite of the court. Senator Robert F. Wagner had been working almost single-handedly on a National Labor Relations bill.

Roosevelt had opposed the Wagner bill on the grounds that it was better to protect labor through the NRA. After the election of 1934 and the Schechter decision, however, Roosevelt took up the Wagner bill and helped to push it through Congress.

The National Labor Relations Act (NLRA) was the most important labor legislation in American history. It strengthened Section 7a of the NIRA, outlawed a number of so-called unfair practices by employers, and established the National Labor Relations Board (NLRB). The NLRB was empowered to prevent "unfair" employment practices, to hold collective-bargaining elections when a certain number of workers petitioned for one, and to compel employers to bargain with unions once a majority of the workers had voted to join one.

Congress passed a number of other history-making laws in the summer of 1935. The Revenue Act, or wealth tax bill, increased the surtax on incomes to its highest level, and the federal estate tax to a maximum of 70 per cent. The measure was a direct assault on concentrated wealth. The most far-reaching law adopted in the summer of 1935 was the Social Security Act. It marked the beginning, on a national scale, of the kind of system to protect economic security which European nations had possessed for half a century. The Social Security Act was divided into three main parts. First, it provided a federal system of insurance against poverty in old age, to be financed by a compulsory old-age insurance fund, contributed to by employers and employees alike. Second, the act established a system of state-operated unemployment insurance and levied a 3 per cent tax on payrolls to fund it. Finally, the act provided financial assistance to the states for a variety of welfare programs. The federal government, for example, provided assistance for needy children, the physically handicapped, and widows with dependent children. The Social Security Act provided no coverage for agricultural workers, domestic servants, public employees, and professional people. Roosevelt and the authors of the measure acknowledged that it was experimental and inadequate, but they knew that the Social Security system would be enlarged in the future.

The Campaign and Election of 1936

Republicans turned their backs on Hoover in 1936 and nominated the progressive governor of Kansas, Alfred M. Landon. The Democrats renominated Roosevelt by acclamation. They also repealed the rule which required a two-thirds vote for the presidential nomination. Roosevelt's acceptance speech amounted to a declaration of war against "economic royalists." The Socialists again nominated Norman Thomas, as they had in 1932. A new party appeared under the banner of the Union for Social Justice. It consisted of the followers of Dr. Townsend and Father Coughlin and the heirs of Senator Long, who had been assassinated in 1935. Without Long, however, the Union party could not mount a real threat.

Landon made a game fight, but he was an inept campaigner. Moreover, he suffered from two other handicaps: first, he was reduced to endorsing the basic legislation of the New Deal and claiming that he would carry it out better than Roosevelt; second, recovery was in progress during the summer of 1936, and the upswing obviously did not help Landon's campaign.

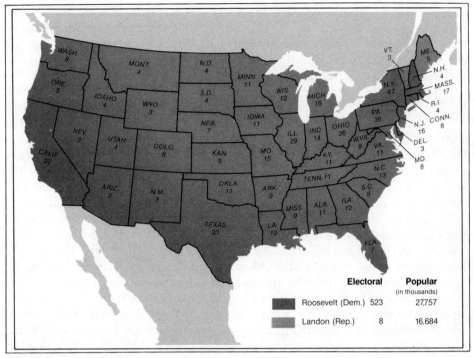

	Electoral	Popular
		(in thousands)
Roosevelt (Dem.)	523	27,757
Landon (Rep.)	8	16,684

The Election of 1936

Roosevelt was at his best as a campaigner in 1936. He stumped the country and appealed frankly for the support of the common people. When the votes were counted, Roosevelt had carried every state except Maine and Vermont, with 523 electoral votes to eight for Landon. The landslide also reduced the Republicans to a corporal's guard of eighty-nine in the House and twenty-one in the Senate. A great majority of the voters had given a mandate for the continuation of the New Deal. Analysts discovered other developments in the returns: organized labor had played a significant part in the Democratic victory, while an overwhelming majority of blacks had voted for a Democratic presidential candidate for the first time. Also, white ethnic groups, who still formed a majority of the urban poor, voted almost completely for Roosevelt.

The Constitutional Crisis

It was extremely doubtful at the end of 1936 whether Roosevelt could carry out his mandate, for a bare majority of the Supreme Court had almost paralyzed the ability of Congress and the President to deal with economic problems. The essential issue in 1936 was whether Congress could use its taxing power and its power over interstate commerce to control economic activities that had traditionally been defined as intrastate. The conservative majority of the Supreme Court gave its answer in two key decisions in 1936. United States *v.* Butler nullified the Agricultural Adjustment Act on the ground that the production of foodstuffs was local in character; and Carter *v.*

Carter Coal Company nullified the Coal Conservation Act on the ground that the mining of coal was a local activity. Furthermore, in Morehead *v. New York ex rel.* Tipaldo, the justices denied that the states could regulate the hours, wages, and conditions of labor, because such regulation violated the freedom of contract guaranteed by the Fourteenth Amendment.

Progressives in both parties demanded that the Supreme Court be curbed. Roosevelt virtually declared war on the Supreme Court's conservative majority soon after his reelection. In February 1937, he sent to Congress the draft of a bill for the reorganization of the federal judiciary. It authorized the President to appoint up to fifty new judges when incumbents failed to retire upon reaching the age of seventy. Six of these judges might be added to the Supreme Court. Roosevelt justified his proposal mainly on the ground that insufficient and infirm judicial personnel had caused intolerable delays.

For the first time, Roosevelt had blundered in both strategy and timing. He had grossly underestimated the power of the tradition of the separation of powers, and he had failed to be frank with Congress and the people. Progressives joined conservatives in attacking the judicial reorganization bill as an attempt to destroy the independence of the judicial branch.

The Supreme Court itself ended the quarrel, and with it, Roosevelt's court plan. While the controversy raged, the case of West Coast Hotel *v.* Parrish, which involved the constitutionality of state minimum-wage laws, came before the court. The court not only reversed the Tipaldo decision; it also left room for any reasonable state regulation of wages, hours, and working conditions. Two weeks later, in an even more important case—National Labor Relations Board *v.* Jones and Laughlin Steel Corporation, the justices said that the Wagner Act of 1935 was constitutional because Congress' power over interstate commerce was absolute and extended to every economic activity which affected the manufacture of goods.

Roosevelt had lost the battle and won the war. He accepted a watered-down bill which instituted the procedural reforms which he had requested but did not provide for the appointment of new federal judges and Supreme Court justices. Retirements from 1937 onward enabled Roosevelt to fill the Supreme Court with men closer to his own philosophy. The court subsequently upheld the constitutionality of every important New Deal measure.

The Rise of the CIO

The New Deal effected a near revolution in American labor relations. The profound changes were not, of course, all of Roosevelt's making. In 1934 and 1935, a group within the AFL, led by John L. Lewis, president of the United Mine Workers, and Sidney Hillman and David Dubinsky, presidents of the garment workers' unions, demanded that the AFL organize such industries as steel, automobiles, and rubber. A majority of the leaders of the AFL were still hostile to the very concept of industrial unionism. Lewis and his colleagues, rebuffed by the AFL in 1935, formed the Committee for Industrial Organization. It became the separate, independent Congress of Industrial Organizations (CIO) in 1937.

The Committee for Industrial Organization in 1936 launched a campaign to organize the steel industry, the citadel of antiunionism. It won this crucial struggle in 1937 and turned next to the automobile industry. In some of

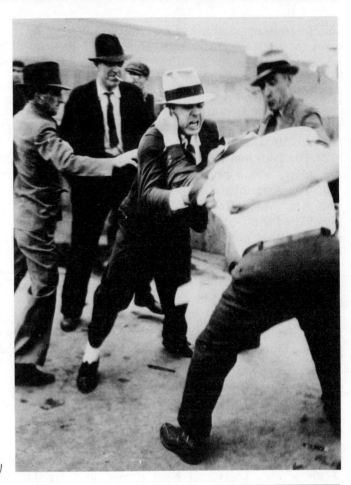

A CIO organizer being
beaten at the Ford plant
in Dearborn, Michigan,
May 26, 1937. (United
Press International Photo)

these fights for recognition, unions used sit-down strikes—that is, they
refused to leave factories until managers agreed to negotiate. Despite
opposition to its tactics—even from Roosevelt—the CIO by 1941 had
organized virtually every mass-production industry in the nation and had
about 5,000,000 members, surpassing in size the AFL. The support of the
NLRB played a crucial role in labor's success. This powerful new labor
movement became an indispensable source of political power for the second
New Deal.

Completing the Second New Deal

Roosevelt, in 1937, called for new legislation to benefit the "one third of a
nation ill-housed, ill-clad, ill-nourished." The New Deal legislation of 1937–
1938 provided the first large-scale effort to help the "invisible" people near
the bottom of the nation's economic structure. After the fight over the
judicial reorganization bill, Roosevelt drew his congressional forces together
and won most of the measures which he said were essential for completion
of his program. A sharp recession occurred in early 1938—the result of the

administration's slashing of expenditures in 1937 at the same time that new taxes for Social Security were collected. Industrial output fell 33 per cent, while unemployment again rose rapidly. Congressmen with nervous eyes on the impending mid-term election suddenly became eager to renew the spending programs.

1. The Farm Tenancy Act of 1937 established the Farm Security Administration. It provided assistance to tenants and migratory farm workers who had benefited hardly at all from the AAA.

2. The National Housing Act of 1937 created the United States Housing Authority, which began the first serious war on urban slums.

3. The Agricultural Adjustment Act of 1938 replaced the Soil Conservation Act, which Congress had adopted in 1936 after the Supreme Court invalidated the first AAA. The second AAA continued payments to farmers and permitted producers of the major staples to limit production by two-thirds votes.

4. The Fair Labor Standards Act of 1938 established a minimum wage of twenty-five cents an hour, to be increased to forty cents, and limited hours of labor to forty a week.

5. A frightened Congress made some $3 billion available to the WPA, launched a huge public-works program in cooperation with the states, and greatly expanded the lending power of the federal credit agencies.

5. THE PASSING OF THE NEW DEAL

The New Deal Comes to an End

The forward motion of the New Deal slowed between 1938 and 1939. Most of Roosevelt's ideas had been turned into legislation by then. It would remain for the next generation to expand progressive objectives to include urban revitalization, medical insurance, and full civil rights for blacks.

By 1939, the majority of Americans were apparently eager for a breathing spell. During the summer of 1938, Roosevelt set out to prevent the renomination of several Democratic congressmen and senators who opposed some of the administration's measures. With a single exception, his efforts backfired. What is more, the Republicans gained seats in both houses in the mid-term election of 1938. By joining with Democratic conservatives, they now had the power to prevent further enactment of New Deal legislation. Finally, Roosevelt was trying to build congressional support for a strong policy of resistance to Nazi Germany's aggressions. In order to accomplish this end, Roosevelt had to avoid alienating conservative southern Democrats, who were the most consistent internationalists in Congress.

The New Deal in Retrospect

The New Deal tried to achieve economic recovery as well as extensive economic and social reform. Even now it is difficult to say whether the Roosevelt administration achieved its first objective. A large measure of recovery did occur, yet substantial unemployment remained until 1941.

What has been the lasting significance of the New Deal?

1. The New Deal effected sweeping administrative and regulatory reforms. Theodore Roosevelt and Woodrow Wilson had laid the foundations for a modern regulatory and welfare state, but Franklin D. Roosevelt completed the superstructure of that state. Following generations have modified but not fundamentally altered the edifice which he created.

2. At the same time, the New Deal greatly strengthened the system of free-enterprise capitalism. To be sure, New Deal legislation put many restraints upon business and finance in order to guarantee that they would be socially responsible. But, while it subjected private economic institutions to new regulations, the New Deal left most important economic decisions to individuals and groups of individuals. The New Deal also gave to hitherto submerged groups such as farmers and workers a profound stake in the successful operation of the new economy.

3. The New Deal restored faith in democracy at a time when democracy seemed on the verge of extinction almost everywhere else in the world.

4. Roosevelt helped to revive confidence in the human spirit itself by his own example of overcoming a catastrophic illness and continuing to fight for the principles in which he believed.

SUGGESTED READINGS

For the election of 1928, see Allan J. Lichtman, *Prejudice and the Old Politics: The Presidential Election of 1928* (1979). The best accounts of the Hoover administration are found in Harris G. Warren, *Herbert Hoover and the Great Depression* (1959), and Albert U. Romasco, *The Poverty of Abundance* (1965). The administration is defended in David Burner, *Herbert Hoover* (1979), and in Herbert Hoover, *Memoirs: The Great Depression, 1929 – 1941* (1952). For correction at a crucial point in history, see Eliot A. Rosen, *Hoover, Roosevelt, and the Brains Trust* (1977), and Jordan A. Schwartz, *The Interregnum of Despair: Hoover, Congress, and the Depression* (1970).

John K. Galbraith, *The Great Crash* (1955), is a popular account of that tragedy. Thomas Wilson, *Fluctuations in Income and Employment* (1948), and Milton Friedman and Anna J. Schwartz, *The Great Contraction, 1929 – 1933* (1965), treat the depression from quite different economic perspectives. The impact of the depression on American society is vividly portrayed in David A. Shannon, ed., *The Great Depression* (1960), and Caroline Bird, *The Invisible Scar* (1966). Frank Freidel, *Franklin D. Roosevelt: The Triumph* (1956), and *Franklin D. Roosevelt: Launching the New Deal* (1973); Jame McGregor Burns, *Roosevelt: The Lion and the Fox* (1956); William E. Leuchtenburg, *Franklin D. Roosevelt and the New Deal* (1963); and Arthur M. Schlesinger, Jr., *The Coming of the New Deal* (1959) and *The Politics of Upheaval* (1960), all offer comprehensive treatments. The only good one-volume biogra-

phy of Roosevelt is Nathan Miller, *FDR: An Intimate History* (1983), but see also Joseph P. Lash, *Eleanor and Franklin* (1971). For more negative views of Roosevelt, see Edgar E. Robinson, *The Roosevelt Leadership, 1932 – 1945* (1955). For another thoughtful criticism, see Paul Conkin, *The New Deal* (1975).

Biographies and memoirs constitute a significant part of the literature of the New Deal period. Robert E. Sherwood, *Roosevelt and Hopkins* (rev. ed., 1950); J. Joseph Huthmacher, *Senator Robert F. Wagner and the Rise of Urban Liberalism* (1968); T. Harry Williams, *Huey Long* (1969); and John M. Blum, *From the Morgenthau Diaries* (1959, 1960), are illuminating. Some of the memoirs and personal accounts which ought to be consulted are Frances Perkins, *The Roosevelt I Knew* (1946); *The Secret Diary of Harold L. Ickes,* 3 vols. (1953 – 1954); and Eleanor Roosevelt's indispensable *This I Remember* (1949). Less sympathetic accounts are Raymond Moley, *After Seven Years* (1939) and *The First New Deal* (1966).

For economic policies and their effects, see Broadus Mitchell, *Depression Decade* (1947), and Kenneth D. Roose, *Economics of Recession and Revival* (1954). A subtly humorous and keen analysis is Thurman Arnold, *The Folklore of Capitalism* (1937). Ellis W. Hawley, *The New Deal and the Problem of Monopoly* (1966), is a good treatment, as is David E. Lilienthal, *The T.V.A.* (rev. ed., 1953). New Deal agricultural policy is discussed in Christiana M. Campbell, *The Farm Bureaus: A Study of the Making of National Farm Policy, 1933 – 1940* (1962);

Richard S. Kirkendall, *Social Scientists and Farm Politics in the Age of Roosevelt* (1966); and Gilbert C. Fite, *George M. Peek and the Fight for Farm Parity* (1954). Leonard Baker, *Back to Back: The Duel between FDR and the Supreme Court* (1967), is the most comprehensive account of that subject.

Incisive essays on social history can be found in Isabel Leighton, *The Aspirin Age* (1949). David A. Shannon, *The Socialist Party of America* (1955), and Daniel Bell, *Marxian Socialism in the United States* (1967), are good studies of the left. Huey P. Long, *Every Man a King* (1933), is fascinating, but see also T. Harry Williams' excellent biography of Long, already cited, and Alan Brinkley, *Voices of Protest: Huey Long, Father Coughlin, and the Great Depression* (1982).

The conservative reaction to the New Deal is discussed in George Wolfskill, *The Revolt of Conservatives* (1962), and James T. Patterson, *Congressional Conservatism and the New Deal* (1967). The New Deal's comparative neglect of black Americans is examined in Raymond Wolters, *Negroes and the Great Depression* (1970). For a more positive view, see Nancy J. Weiss, *Farewell to the Party of Lincoln: Black Politics in the Age of FDR* (1983).

CHAPTER 27
THE UNITED STATES AND THE SECOND WORLD WAR

1. A DECADE OF TURMOIL

Japanese Expansion

Depression, hunger, and domestic violence assaulted the peoples of Europe and the Far East at the same time as they did people in the United States. Many nations gave way to political or military leaders who promised economic security in exchange for liberties. Half the governments in Latin America, for example, toppled during the early 1930s without elections. During this worldwide chaos, several major industrial powers, including Japan and Germany, fell into the hands of groups which envisioned economic salvation and national aggrandizement through conquest. In their efforts to achieve their objectives through violence, they plunged the world into a decade of turmoil.

The first critical challenge to peace occurred in 1931, when Japan wrested Manchuria from China. Manchuria had been Japan's most important area for investment since the 1890s. Fear that China's new leader, Chiang Kai-shek, would reassert control prompted the leaders of the Japanese Kwantung Army in Manchuria to defy their home government and attack Chinese forces on September 18, 1931. Civilians in the Japanese cabinet could not control the army, and Japanese troops occupied all of Manchuria. The liberal government in Tokyo gave way in December to a coalition of military officers and imperialistic politicians.

The League of Nations could have responded forcefully, but only if the two great naval powers, the United States and Great Britain, had been willing to defend the League covenant. Neither was prepared to do so. While they condemned Japan, a majority of American political leaders opposed risking war to force the Japanese to obey the covenant. Nevertheless, in January 1932, Secretary of State Stimson warned that the United States would not recognize any territorial changes brought about in the Far East by force. The League of Nations endorsed the Stimson policy, but appeared helpless to act when Japan created a puppet state in Manchuria and withdrew from the League.

The Collapse of European Stability

After the international economic collapse of 1931, leaders in Europe and the United States tried last-ditch efforts to save the Versailles system. Clearly, one part of the Paris settlement—war debts and reparations—could not be salvaged. In 1932, the western European governments agreed in effect to cancel Germany's reparations debt. The following year, all governments which owed war debts to the United States, except Finland, defaulted. In the same year, leaders of western Europe tried to reestablish world trade at the London Economic Conference. President Roosevelt prevented agreement on the first step, monetary stabilization. It cannot be said, therefore, that the United States, either under Hoover or under Roosevelt in his first year in office, gave any leadership in reconstruction of the world economy.

During the next six years, Adolf Hitler and the Italian dictator, Benito Mussolini, destroyed both the Versailles treaty system and the League of Nations. Hitler made the first move in 1935, when he denounced the treaty's provisions for German disarmament and began a military buildup. Then Mussolini attacked Ethiopia. The League of Nations condemned this aggression, but Britain and France prevented effective retaliation by the League. Cheered on by Hitler and Mussolini, Spanish army leaders headed by General Francisco Franco in 1936 launched a civil war to destroy the liberal government in Madrid. Powerful industrialists and landowners supported Franco, whose army had destroyed the Spanish Republic by 1939.

In 1936, Hitler sent his armies into the demilitarized German Rhineland, and in 1938 he occupied Austria. At the same time, he concluded a military alliance with Italy and Japan. Later in 1938, Hitler threatened to invade Czechoslovakia when that country refused to hand over to Germany its Sudetenland, which contained more than 3,000,000 inhabitants of German ancestry. Neither Great Britain nor France was willing to go to war and save the Czech Republic. Instead, Prime Minister Neville Chamberlain of Great Britain and Premier Edouard Daladier of France met Hitler and Mussolini at Munich on September 28, 1938, and agreed to the dismemberment of Czechoslovakia. The British Prime Minister called this agreement a guarantee of "peace in our time."

Great Britain and France could have stopped Mussolini and Hitler in their tracks at any time before 1938. However, these democracies were unwilling to run even a slight risk of war. Both had been bled white by the First World War. The British and French leaders were, moreover, so afraid of communism that they did not look altogether with disfavor upon the rise of the militantly anti-Communist Nazi regime.

*Prime Minister Neville Chamberlain grasping the hand of
Chancellor Adolf Hitler as a gesture of friendship between England
and Germany after the Munich Conference in 1938. Chamberlain
returned home confident that he had preserved "peace in our time."
(Wide World Photos)*

Most Americans abhorred Hitler, especially for his brutal persecution of
German Jews. But Americans assumed that, if it came to war, the British
navy and the French army would make short work of Hitler and Mussolini.
The United States, they believed, could safely avoid entanglement in another
terrible European war.

Other developments strengthened this view. First, Americans were ob-
sessed with recovery and reconstruction of their own institutions. Second,
many believed that, in Hitler and Mussolini, the former Allies had got what
they deserved for their vindictiveness at the Paris Peace Conference. Third,
an investigation led by Senator Gerald P. Nye of North Dakota confirmed
millions of Americans in their belief that bankers and munitions makers had
manipulated the country into the First World War. Finally, a peace movement flourished in the United States. Pacifism swept through the churches
and college campuses. Movies and plays embellished the theme that war was
a grand illusion.

Congress in 1935 and 1936 prohibited the shipment of arms to Italy or
Ethiopia, or to either side in the Spanish Civil War, and refused to
distinguish between military aggressors and governments which defended
themselves. A more comprehensive Neutrality Act of 1937 prohibited the

shipment of arms or munitions, or the extension of loans, to *any* belligerents. The policies which allegedly had drawn the United States into the First World War thus would not be repeated.

Although Roosevelt and Hull worked to modify neutrality legislation so as to give the President more discretion in its application, the politically astute Roosevelt signed the bills and carried out their provisions. On one occasion, Roosevelt sent up a trial balloon to see whether public opinion was changing. In a speech in October 1937, he said that the time had come for peace-loving nations to quarantine aggressors. Negative reactions made it clear that Americans were, if anything, more strongly isolationist than before.

The Japanese army on July 7, 1937, began a full-scale war to seize the northern provinces of China. The League of Nations convened a conference to consider what should be done, but the conference was doomed before it began. Neither Great Britain nor the United States was eager to take strong action against Japan. In these circumstances the conference could issue only a harmless statement. The Japanese air force replied on December 12, 1937, by bombing U.S.S. *Panay*, a gunboat, and three American oil tankers in the Yangtze River. The reaction of most Americans was to demand that their government withdraw its small military and naval forces from China.

The Good Neighbor Policy

Secretary Hull believed profoundly that the United States should take leadership in reconstructing the world economy through currency stabilization and liberal trade policies. Economic nationalists overshadowed Hull during the first months of the Roosevelt administration, but he was able to take the lead once the President, late in 1933, had decided on stabilization. Hull persuaded Congress to adopt the Reciprocal Trade Agreements Act in June 1934. It authorized the President to negotiate trade agreements, which would lower or raise the Hawley-Smoot rates by as much as 50 per cent. By 1940, Hull had concluded agreements with twenty-one nations. However, while the depression lasted, Roosevelt refused to consider agreements on goods which competed with those produced by American farmers and factories.

Hopes of stimulating trade with Russia played a major role in the administration's decision to extend diplomatic recognition to the Soviet Union. Russia appeared to American businessmen as one area where goods, especially factory and agricultural machinery, could be sold in large quantities. Roosevelt extended recognition on November 16, 1933. However, hopes for flourishing Russian-American trade did not materialize until Germany attacked Russia in 1941.

Economic motivation also prompted the United States to end its colonial rule in the Philippines. American sugar and tobacco producers disliked the low tariffs on those crops grown in the Philippines. If the Filipinos obtained independence, the tariffs could be raised. In 1933, Congress adopted an act which forced independence upon the Philippines after ten years. The Filipinos asked for dominion status instead. However, the agricultural and business competitors of the Filipinos won their way with passage of the Philippine Independence Act in 1934.

President Roosevelt completed the retreat from intervention and occupation in Latin America already begun by his predecessors. Roosevelt sincerely believed that mutual respect and cooperation should replace the unilateral domination of the United States. At the same time, Roosevelt and Hull kept in mind the national self-interest. They believed that the United States would desperately need friends in the western hemisphere if the old world succumbed to war.

Roosevelt withdrew American marines from Haiti and surrendered treaty rights to interfere in the internal affairs of the Dominican Republic, Haiti, Panama, and Cuba. At the same time, Hull took leadership at Pan-American conferences in building a new system of mutual understanding and collective security.

The Good Neighbor policy reaped large dividends in Latin American cooperation when war broke out in Europe in 1939. In 1940, Hull won unanimous approval of a warning that an attack on any American nation would be considered to be an attack on all of them. Once the United States had entered the war, all Latin American states, except Argentina and Chile, at once broke relations with, or declared war upon, the Axis nations.

The climax of Roosevelt's and Hull's long efforts to build a new inter-American system was the Act of Chapultepec, adopted at Mexico City on March 3, 1945. This treaty completed the transformation of the Monroe Doctrine by declaring that any attack upon one American state would be met by the combined force of all of them.

Certain policies by the Mexican government put the Good Neighbor policy to the acid test. Beginning in 1934, Mexico began to expropriate American-owned estates. Then, in 1938, Mexican President Lázaro Cárdenas announced that the Mexican government would expropriate all foreign oil properties, valued at $459 million. Although compensation was promised, it was clear that Mexico could not pay even a small fraction of what the oil companies demanded. The British government protested in such a manner as to cause the Mexican government to break diplomatic relations with London. But Roosevelt, Hull, and the American ambassador to Mexico, Josephus Daniels, entered into negotiations which led to settlement of land and oil claims. Thus the Roosevelt administration won some degree of friendship from the Mexican people and gained a valuable ally during the Second World War.

The Second World War, 1939–1941

Adolf Hitler set out upon a collision course in March 1939 by invading the remnants of the Czech Republic. The British and French hastened to conclude defense treaties with Poland, next on Hitler's list of victims. On August 23, 1939, the Soviet Union concluded a nonaggression pact with the German government which gave western Poland to Germany, while Russia might occupy Estonia, Latvia, eastern Poland, Bessarabia, and Lithuania.

Hitler invaded Poland on September 1, 1939. Britain and France declared war on Germany two days later. Josef Stalin's armies invaded Poland on September 17, and that helpless nation was partitioned between Germany and Russia. Europeans had turned upon each other again, just twenty-five years after the outbreak of the "war to end wars."

In mid-1939, Roosevelt begged Congress either to repeal the arms embargo

The Second World War

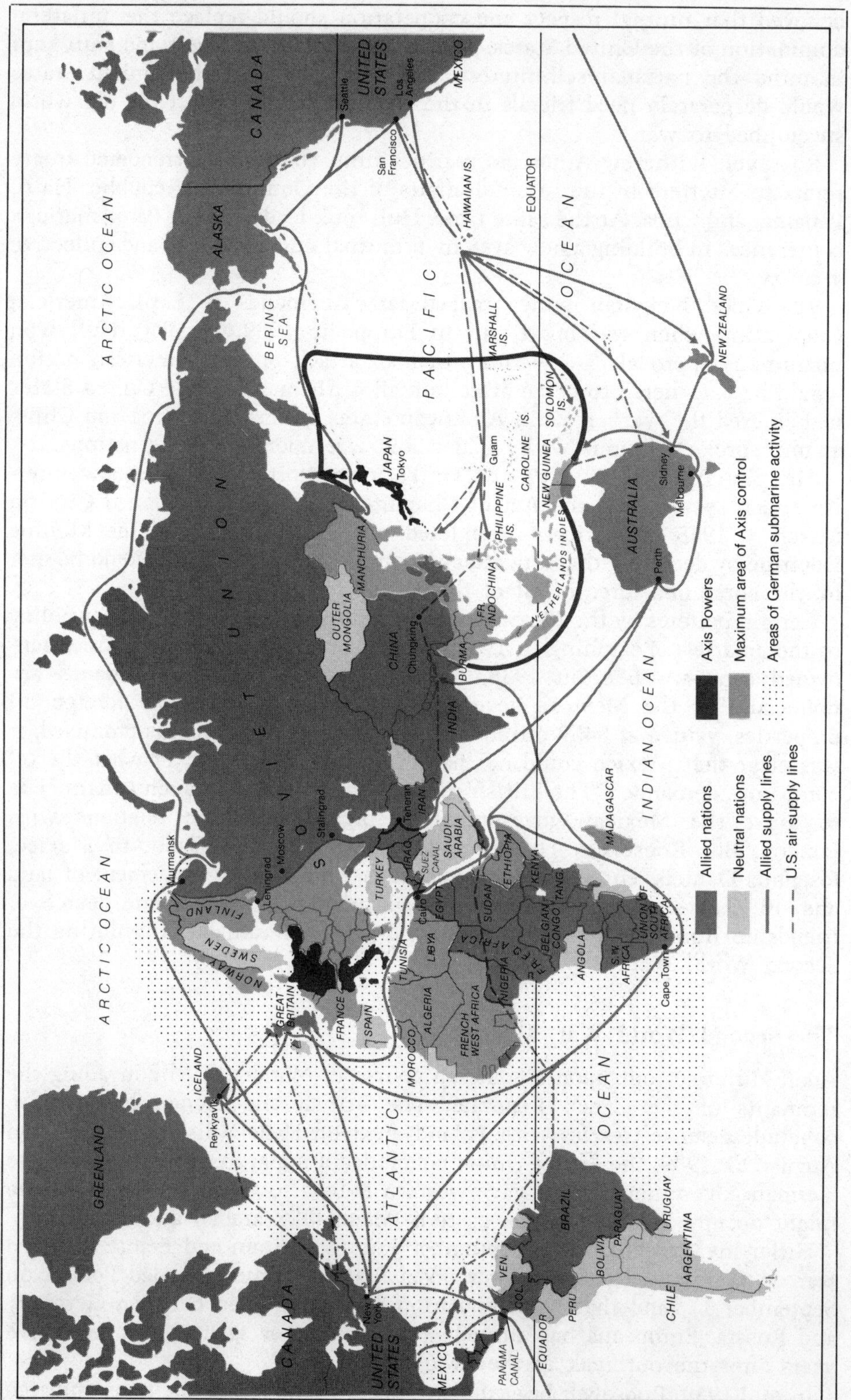

ARCTIC OCEAN
ATLANTIC OCEAN
PACIFIC OCEAN
INDIAN OCEAN
BERING SEA
EQUATOR
CANADA
ALASKA
UNITED STATES
MEXICO
Seattle
San Francisco
Los Angeles
HAWAIIAN IS.
MARSHALL IS.
SOLOMON IS.
CAROLINE IS.
Guam
NEW ZEALAND
JAPAN
Tokyo
S O V I E T U N I O N
Murmansk
Leningrad
Moscow
Stalingrad
Teheran
IRAN
IRAQ
TURKEY
SAUDI ARABIA
SUEZ CANAL
Cairo
EGYPT
LIBYA
TUNISIA
ALGERIA
MOROCCO
FRENCH WEST AFRICA
NIGERIA
SUDAN
ETHIOPIA
KENYA
TANG.
BELGIAN CONGO
ANGOLA
S.W. AFRICA
UNION OF SOUTH AFRICA
Cape Town
MADAGASCAR
FINLAND
SWEDEN
NORWAY
GREAT BRITAIN
FRANCE
SPAIN
ICELAND
Reykjavik
GREENLAND
OUTER MONGOLIA
MANCHURIA
CHINA
Chungking
INDIA
BURMA
FR. INDOCHINA
PHILIPPINE IS.
NETHERLANDS INDIES
NEW GUINEA
AUSTRALIA
Perth
Sidney
Melbourne
New York
PANAMA CANAL
COL.
VEN.
ECUADOR
PERU
BRAZIL
BOLIVIA
PARAGUAY
URUGUAY
CHILE
ARGENTINA
Allied nations
Neutral nations
Allied supply lines
U.S. air supply lines
Axis Powers
Maximum area of Axis control
Areas of German submarine activity

or else to permit the European democracies to purchase war supplies for cash. Both houses refused to act. Once war had broken out in Europe, Roosevelt again asked Congress to amend the Neutrality Act to permit Allied purchases of arms in the United States. There were still loud protests, but Roosevelt now had broad bipartisan support. After sharp debate, the Senate and House voted to repeal the embargo and also to impose new restrictions on American shipping. Roosevelt signed the repeal measure on November 4, 1939.

Americans reacted angrily when Russia invaded Finland in November. To the west, quiet reigned as the German and French armies faced each other in their fortified Siegfried and Maginot lines. Americans continued to view events in Europe with detachment. They felt secure in the belief that the Royal Navy and the French army would crush Germany once large-scale fighting broke out.

Hitler launched a *blitzkrieg*, or lightning war, on April 10, 1940, and invaded and overran Denmark, Norway, Holland, Belgium, Luxembourg, and France. Paris fell on June 16. Southern France—one third of the nation—was left to the rump government of the aged Marshal Henri-Philippe Pétain, who agreed to act as the symbol of partial French independence. Pétain, a fervent anti-Communist, evidently wished for true cooperation with Germany in its war against the Soviet Union, an attitude which enjoyed wide popularity in France.

Neville Chamberlain resigned as Prime Minister of Great Britain and was succeeded by Winston Churchill. Churchill's main weapons for the defense of the realm consisted of swift fighter planes and iron courage, for the British army of over 335,000 men, miraculously evacuated from Dunkirk, France, had returned home without armor and heavy equipment. Churchill promised his people nothing but "blood, toil, tears, and sweat"—and ultimate victory.

In reply, Hitler sent a vast fleet of bombers against London and other British cities. Fortunately for the British, the Germans did not have enough vessels available to carry their vastly superior army across the English Channel for a direct amphibious assault. Mussolini entered the war as France was collapsing; he thus extended the hostilities to the Mediterranean and Africa. Then Hitler unexpectedly turned to the Balkans, made satellites out of Rumania and Bulgaria, and conquered Yugoslavia and Greece.

The great majority of Americans who loathed Hitler remained divided over the wise course for the United States. The noninterventionists favored arming for defense, but declared that the United States could not save western Europe and should not waste its resources in an attempt to do so. In opposition stood the so-called internationalists, who believed that a Europe dominated by Hitler would threaten American security. The bitter debate—and the war in Europe—would clarify American opinion. By July 1940, 69 per cent of the persons queried in a public opinion poll at last replied that they thought that a German victory would imperil the United States.

The prime mover in this change in public opinion was Roosevelt himself. He cast political caution aside and led the movement to rally Americans to the perils of a Nazi victory. A month before the fall of France, he called for a vast expansion of defense expenditures. In September, Roosevelt transferred fifty destroyers to Britain to enable the Royal Navy to convoy merchantmen and hunt down German submarines. In return, the United States received the use of eight naval bases ranging from Newfoundland to British Guiana.

The most important—and controversial—part of Roosevelt's defense program was a selective-service bill. It passed both houses of Congress in September by large majorities.

Politics continued also, because 1940 was a presidential election year, but not politics of the usual sort. The Republicans nominated Wendell L. Willkie, president of a major utilities company, a former Democrat, and an ardent proponent of aid to Great Britain. Roosevelt almost certainly had decided to run for a third term long before the preconvention campaign began. Although party leaders would have preferred another candidate, they had to go along with the renomination. Roosevelt then forced the nomination of the sometimes radical Secretary of Agriculture, Henry A. Wallace, as his running mate.

Willkie was the first dynamic Republican candidate since Theodore

Franklin Delano Roosevelt in what was said to be his favorite portrait. He served longer than any U.S. President and led the country out of the depression and to victory in World War II. Shaping the office to himself, he greatly enlarged the powers of the presidency. (Historical Pictures Service, Inc., Chicago)

Roosevelt. He tried to capitalize upon the strong tradition against a third term, but he was handicapped by his substantial agreement with Roosevelt's domestic and foreign policies. Faced with defeat, Willkie suddenly shifted gears in October and began to attack Roosevelt for allegedly leading the country into war. Roosevelt replied that he would not send American boys into any "foreign" wars. In the election of November 5, 1940, Willkie polled 45 per cent of the popular vote, but only eighty-two electoral votes to Roosevelt's 449.

Roosevelt left for a Caribbean cruise soon after his election. On December 9, 1940, a seaplane delivered a letter from Churchill to the President. Great Britain was approaching a crisis, Churchill explained, because she had spent almost all her available dollars for supplies in the United States. Moreover, Britain desperately needed American help in keeping the North Atlantic supply lanes open against German submarines.

Roosevelt devised a solution which he announced on December 17. Because Great Britain was fighting America's fight, Roosevelt declared, the United States would lend or lease to her the supplies necessary for victory over the common foe. The lend-lease bill, introduced into Congress on January 9, 1941, received full and frank debate. Passage of the measure would mean nothing less than American commitment to the defeat of Germany. The Senate approved the lend-lease bill by a vote of sixty to thirty-one; the House, by a vote of 317 to seventy-one. Roosevelt signed the Lend-Lease Act at once and recommended an appropriation of $7 billion.

Roosevelt still wanted to avoid full-scale military participation, but he intended to assure Germany's defeat, no matter what the risks. Above all, he was determined that lend-lease supplies should get through to Britain. Consequently, during the spring and early summer, he seized ninety-two ships in American ports which belonged to German, Italian, French, Dutch, and Norwegian owners; froze German and Italian assets in the United States; occupied the Danish islands of Greenland and Iceland; and extended the American "neutrality" patrol to the mid-Atlantic. When German armies invaded Russia on June 21, 1941, the President assured Russian leaders that they would receive lend-lease assistance.

In August 1941, Roosevelt and Churchill met and agreed upon a declaration known as the Atlantic Charter. It called for the restoration of self-government to peoples oppressed by dictators. It also demanded equal access to raw materials for all nations, freedom of the seas, a peace with justice, and relief from the crushing burden of armaments.

Now that American naval vessels in fact convoyed British ships to Iceland, armed conflict was inevitable. A German submarine unsuccessfully attacked the destroyer Greer on September 4. On October 17, the destroyer Kearny was hit, with the loss of eleven lives. Then, on October 31, a German submarine sank the destroyer Reuben James with the loss of half her crew.

Roosevelt instituted an undeclared naval war with Germany by ordering American naval vessels to "shoot on sight" any submarines which appeared in waters west of Iceland. In November 1941, Congress authorized American merchantmen to arm and to sail through war zones to British ports. Congress renewed the Selective Service Act in August. The United States thus became a full member of a new alliance in every respect except a declaration of war against the common enemy.

2. THE ATTACK ON PEARL HARBOR UNITES THE NATION

The Road to Pearl Harbor

By late 1941, it probably remained only a question of *when,* not *whether,* full-scale fighting would break out with Germany. As events turned out, the United States was plunged into war, not by any incident in the North Atlantic, but by the action of Japan.

Even though the Japanese continued their aggression against China and occupied northern Indochina in 1940, the United States followed a restrained policy toward Tokyo out of fear that too much pressure might cause Japan to attack elsewhere. Roosevelt, however, issued a sharp warning on July 26, 1939, by renouncing the Japanese-American Commercial Treaty of 1911. The American government could now halt trade between the two countries within six months. Such action would cut off Japan from its major source of scrap iron, oil, and other materials necessary for war.

In September, the Japanese, German, and Italian governments concluded the Triple, or Axis, Alliance, which appeared to be aimed directly at the United States. Moreover, leaders of the Japanese government made it clear that, in spite of the risk of war with the United States, they meant to establish what they called a Greater East Asia Co-Prosperity Sphere, which meant, essentially, Japanese dominance over the entire Far East.

Japanese military leaders and their political allies hoped to take advantage of German victories in Europe and seize the relatively unprotected French, British, and Dutch possessions in Asia and to end successfully their costly war with China. In order to seal off supply lines to China and provide bases for possible future expansion southward, the Japanese occupied bases in French Indochina. In response, Roosevelt and Hull froze Japanese assets in the United States in July 1941 and clamped an embargo on the export to Japan of oil, steel, aviation gasoline, and other materials.

Authorities in Tokyo were now in a desperate dilemma. Half their supplies of oil, iron, and steel came from the United States. Japanese diplomats turned to Washington in hope of finding some compromise arrangement. Japanese-American negotiations dragged on into the autumn of 1941. The Japanese offered many concessions, but the more they conceded, the harder Secretary Hull turned the vise in the mistaken belief that the Japanese had to cave in. In the final analysis, the one sticking point was China. The Japanese demanded that the United States stop all aid to Chiang Kai-shek. Hull not only refused to abandon the Chinese but also insisted that the Japanese withdraw from China at once. The Japanese were faced with the alternative of either enormous blows to their new empire or war. They reluctantly chose the latter course.

On the morning of Sunday, December 7, 1941, Japanese bombers struck the American naval and air bases at Pearl Harbor and elsewhere in the Hawaiian Islands. Their rain of destruction surprised American leaders, despite warnings that a Japanese attack might be imminent. Roosevelt and Hull, among others, had refused to believe that a Japanese carrier flotilla could reach Pearl Harbor. Therefore, they neglected to keep naval and army commanders in Hawaii up to date on events.

Altogether, the Japanese sank or disabled nineteen ships, including eight

Magazine of U.S.S. Shaw exploding during the Japanese raid on Pearl Harbor, December 7, 1941. In this spectacular view, the destroyer had just been struck by a wave of bombers that blew off her bow and sunk the dock. Yet the damage was so slight from the bridge to the stern that Shaw was rebuilt and later rejoined the fleet. (United Press International)

battleships; in addition, they destroyed 120 planes and killed more than 2,300 men. The Japanese also blasted bases in the Philippines, Guam, Midway, British Hong Kong, and the Malay Peninsula. The American air force in the Philippines suffered near annihilation when its planes were caught on the ground, even though commanders in the area were aware of the earlier attack on Pearl Harbor. This negligence almost defies rational explanation. It does seem, however, that American political and military leaders simply underestimated the military capabilities of the Japanese. It was the most devastating military disaster that the United States had ever suffered.

Roosevelt appeared before Congress on December 8, 1941, to ask for a declaration of war against Japan. It was voted with but one dissenting voice. Three days later, Germany and Italy honored their agreement with Japan and declared war on the United States.

Uniting for Victory

In the Second World War, the American people were called upon to fight two major wars on two far-flung fronts at the same time. Never had Americans been so united as they were between 1941 and 1945. Their leaders did not proclaim a second crusade to make the world safe for democracy. It was, they said, rather a fight for the survival of American institutions. Leaders in Washington went about the job at hand with relentless determination to finish it as quickly as possible.

At Roosevelt's instructions, the army apprehended all inhabitants of Japanese ancestry, citizens and noncitizens alike, on the West Coast, although no evidence existed to show that they were disloyal. Nevertheless, the army transferred them to makeshift camps in the interior. The evidence is unmistakable that Caucasian Californians took advantage of the panic after Pearl Harbor to persuade federal authorities to "settle" the Japanese-American "problem" once and for all. Thousands of Californians of Japanese ancestry lost their homes, farms, and other businesses, and most of their possessions.

Young men rushed to recruiting stations after Pearl Harbor, but the main task of raising an army and navy fell upon the Selective Service. All told, it registered some 31,000,000 men, of whom nearly 10,000,000 were inducted into service. A total of more than 15,000,000 men and women (including volunteers) served before the end of the war. It was by far the largest mobilization of manpower in American history, but it was not exceptional compared to the mobilization of 22,000,000 in the Soviet Union and 17,000,000 in Germany.

American casualties numbered 253,573 dead and 651,042 wounded. However, these figures were remarkably low considering the numbers involved. For this fact, American fighting men could thank recent medical advances such as penicillin and the use of blood for transfusions.

Industrial mobilization went through several stages, just as it had done during the First World War. After the failure of early efforts to gain control of raw materials, Roosevelt, in October 1942, established the Office of Economic Stabilization, with former Supreme Court Justice James F. Byrnes at its head. Byrnes imposed priorities which assured the flow of raw materials to war industries. In May 1943, Roosevelt made Byrnes head of the new Office of War Mobilization, with near dictatorial authority over the entire economy.

To deal with the potential problem of runaway inflation, Roosevelt established an Office of Price Administration (OPA) in April 1941. After the OPA received statutory enforcement powers in 1942, the OPA and the Office of Economic Stabilization held the line against increases in wages and farm prices. The cost of living increased less than 1.5 per cent between 1943 and 1945, despite the scarcity of consumer goods and the huge increase in the number of Americans employed and in their incomes.

The growing demands of war industries pushed domestic civilian employment up from 46,500,000 in 1940 to 53,000,000 in 1945, despite the induction of millions of men into the military. The United States went to war in 1941 with about 7,000,000 unemployed workers. They were quickly absorbed into the labor force. Women who might otherwise have remained at home constituted another huge pool of workers which was tapped to fill wartime needs.

The main task in the mobilization of labor was to see that strikes did not slow down the war economy. The War Labor Board established guidelines for wages, hours, and collective bargaining. Employers, workers, and unions cooperated with an unprecedented show of unity. Under the protection of the War Labor Board, union membership grew to nearly 15,000,000 by 1945. The *real* weekly earnings of persons engaged in manufacturing increased by 70 per cent from 1941 to 1945.

The Second World War was a dividing line in the history of race relations in the United States. Segregation still prevailed throughout the South, but blacks acquired a new sense of participation in national affairs from the knowledge that 1,000,000 of their number were serving in the armed forces. Resentment continued, however, against policies which kept black soldiers in segregated units.

Blacks benefited greatly from the expanded opportunities which came with wartime full employment. Black demands for jobs and the dire need for labor combined to cause Roosevelt, on June 25, 1941, to issue Executive Order 8802 which forbade discrimination in defense hiring on account of color. However, it had taken the threat of a gigantic march by blacks on Washington, issued by A. Philip Randolph, head of the Brotherhood of Sleeping-car Porters, to cause Roosevelt to act. Roosevelt, at the same time, established the Fair Employment Practices Committee (FEPC) to investigate charges of economic discrimination on account of race. By the beginning of 1945, nearly 2,000,000 blacks were at work in war plants.

Stimulated by governmental credit, wartime demand, and effective organization, American factories turned out 275,000 military aircraft, 75,000 tanks, and 650,000 pieces of artillery. American shipyards built 55,239,000 tons of merchant shipping. Some idea of the dimension of the achievement on the home front can be seen in the fact that the total value of all goods and services in the United States increased about 75 per cent between 1939 and 1945.

Furthermore, American scientists, organized under the Office of Scientific Research and Development, matched their German counterparts, who enjoyed a lengthy head start, in devising weapons which might have been decisive in the war. American scientists developed highly effective radar with British assistance. Proximity fuses detonated explosives just as they reached their targets. Rockets increased enormously the firepower of planes, ships, and tanks, although German research went even further in this area. The German program to develop an atomic bomb came nowhere near matching American success, or the war might have had an entirely different ending.

Federal expenditures totaled a little more than $321 billion from 1941 to 1945. This sum was ten times as large as expenditures during the First World War. The government met 59 per cent of these costs by borrowing. As a result, the gross national debt increased from $49 billion in 1941 to $259 billion at the end of hostilities. The American people, already faced with greatly increased taxes in a bill passed in September 1941, accepted a new Revenue Act in October 1942 which more than doubled the tax burden and paid for 41 per cent of the cost of the war.

3. FIGHTING A WAR ON TWO FRONTS

The African and Italian Campaigns

The first massive operation in which American forces played a leading role was the campaign to drive the Italians and Germans from North Africa and to break their stranglehold on the Mediterranean supply line. On November 8, 1942, a huge Anglo-American force landed on the northwestern coast of Africa. The campaign was directed by General Dwight D. Eisenhower, new American commander in the European theater of operations. It had been planned by Roosevelt and Churchill to aid the Russians by diverting German troops from their crucial campaign against Stalingrad.

The German and Vichy French forces were taken by surprise. Within three days, the Anglo-American armies had gained the whole of French North Africa up to the border of Tunisia. They succeeded in bottling up the Germans in Tunisia while General Sir Bernard Montgomery and the British Eighth Army moved in from the east. Tunis was captured on May 7, 1943, after a bitter struggle, and the Axis threat to the Mediterranean was ended. Allied ships could now move from Gibraltar to the Suez Canal. In the meantime, Soviet armies had captured an entire German army at Stalingrad and raised the siege of Leningrad.

From Africa, the Anglo-American forces launched an attack on Italy.

World War II in Europe and North Africa

General George S. Patton's American Seventh Army and General Montgomery's Eighth Army invaded Sicily on July 10, 1943, and captured the island on August 17 after bitter fighting. Meanwhile, the Italian Fascist Grand Council deposed Mussolini on July 25. Mussolini was arrested but was rescued by German paratroopers, who took him to Lake Como in northern Italy.

Allied armies landed on the toe of the Italian peninsula on September 3, 1943, and made their way slowly northward against desperate resistance by the Germans. The Italian government, on September 3, 1943, signed a secret armistice. Nevertheless, the American and British armies in Italy endured a grueling test against the heavily reinforced Germans. The Allied armies finally entered Rome on June 4, 1944. The Germans hung on doggedly to the northern part of Italy until the war's end.

From Disaster to Victory in the Pacific

During the six months after the attack on Pearl Harbor, the Japanese engulfed more than 1,000,000 square miles in the Pacific Ocean. They captured the Philippines, Thailand, Burma, the Malay Peninsula, Singapore, New Guinea, and the Dutch East Indies. In addition, they occupied hundreds of islands from which they hoped to capture Australia and New Zealand. It was several months before the United States could bring sufficient military and naval strength to the Pacific to try even to stop the onrushing Japanese.

Two huge naval-air battles turned the tide. In the Battle of the Coral Sea, southeast of New Guinea, fought on May 7–8, 1942, planes from the American carriers *Lexington* and *Yorktown* repulsed a large Japanese armada on its way to attack Australia. Soon afterward, the Japanese sent a large invasion force against Midway, an outpost of the Hawaiian Islands. American experts had broken the Japanese military code, and the fleet under Admiral Chester Nimitz was waiting when the Japanese warships neared Midway on June 3. American carrier planes sank four of the enemy's finest carriers, a heavy cruiser, and three destroyers. The battle dealt a death blow to Japanese naval aviation.

American land operations began on August 7, 1942, when marines went ashore on Guadalcanal in the Solomon Islands. Then there began a two-year struggle to regain other islands, including Tarawa, Guam, and Iwo Jima, which the Japanese had heavily fortified and defended with extraordinary courage. American losses were extremely high. An even more furious battle followed when American forces attacked the island of Okinawa, only 350 miles south of Japan itself, in April 1945. When the battle ended on June 21, American naval and air forces were within easy striking distance of the Japanese homeland. By this time, the Japanese fleet had been almost totally destroyed. Japanese merchant ships were being sunk at so fast a pace that Japan faced starvation in the near future.

To Americans, the most gratifying operation in the Pacific was the liberation of the Philippines. After the Japanese invaded the islands in early 1942, the American commander, General Douglas MacArthur, was ordered to Australia to take command of all Allied forces in the South Pacific. Japanese troops had forced the remaining defenders, under the command of General Jonathan Wainwright, to surrender on May 6, 1942.

MacArthur fought his way up the coast of New Guinea and then, in

World War II in the Pacific

October 1944, began a counterinvasion of the Philippines. The Japanese navy made one last bid for victory in the Battle of Leyte Gulf and then withdrew. American troops landed on the main island of Luzon on January 9, 1945, and fought their way to Manila. Organized Japanese resistance in the islands ended in March 1945. All told, the Japanese lost more than 400,000 men and 9,000 planes in the battle for the Philippines. The independence of the Philippine Republic was proclaimed on July 4, 1946, in accordance with the Philippine Independence Act of 1934.

Victory in Europe

The long-awaited invasion of France—code named OVERLORD—began on June 6, 1944, at Normandy. It was the greatest amphibious landing ever undertaken. Fortunately for the invaders, Hitler ignored the advice of Field Marshal Erwin Rommel—who had calculated correctly where and when the attack would take place—and had ordered the German defenders concentrated elsewhere.

For weeks the Allied armies battled against stiff German resistance. However, the Allies enjoyed complete control of the air, and the Germans had to divide their forces in expectation of attacks elsewhere. The German lines broke at Saint-Lô on about July 25, and General Patton's tanks poured through by the thousands. French underground forces rose to aid their liberators, and, up from the Mediterranean, came the American Seventh Army. Paris was freed on August 25. American troops entered Germany on September 12, 1944. Soon six Allied armies, which totaled more than 2,000,000 men, faced the great Siegfried Line which extended the length of Germany's western border.

By constitutional stipulation, the United States held its quadrennial presidential campaign in the fall of 1944, even though the time was hardly propitious for political debate. Governor Thomas E. Dewey of New York won the Republican nomination easily. The GOP adopted a platform endorsing the basic New Deal programs and promising cooperation in the creation of an international agency to preserve peace in the postwar era.

Even though Roosevelt was in failing health, he was determined to direct the war effort through to victory and to take the lead in establishing a lasting peace. The Democratic national convention had no alternative but to nominate Roosevelt for a fourth time. However, some Democratic leaders were determined to unseat Vice-President Wallace. After much skirmishing, Roosevelt and the party managers settled upon Senator Harry S Truman of Missouri. Truman, an ardent New Dealer, was acceptable to labor, Southerners, farmers, and workers. Dewey put up a good fight, but Roosevelt won a decisive victory on November 7.

Costly sacrifices were still necessary before the Germans could be beaten. Field Marshal Karl von Rundstedt launched a powerful counterattack on December 16, 1944, in the rough terrain of the Ardennes Forest. It was a final, desperate attempt to split the Allied lines and reach the Channel ports. The attack caught the Americans by surprise. The German armored divisions penetrated sixty miles before they were finally stopped. In this battle, the American 101st Airborne Division made a heroic stand at the vital transportation center of Bastogne. Counterattacking Allied forces pinched off the Bulge on about January 21, 1945. Allied losses had been high, but the battle had cost the Germans 120,000 of their best reserves and untold quantities of war supplies.

The Allies now closed in for the kill. On March 7, 1945, the American First Army crossed the Rhine River at Remagen. At this point, the Allied high command faced a difficult choice. One alternative, fervently urged by Churchill, was a drive to seize Berlin before the Russians could enter the city. The other was to let the Russians enter Berlin first.

Eisenhower chose the second alternative, largely because of military considerations. He divided his army and sent Patton into Bavaria to prevent the escape of the German army to mountain strongholds in that state. Eisenhower knew that the American, Russian, and British governments had agreed earlier on postwar occupation zones in Germany. He did not consider the capture of Berlin worth the loss of American and British lives.

Meanwhile, the Russian armies steadily advanced from the east. American units met Soviet troops at Torgau, on the Elbe River, on April 25, 1945. Soviet troops then entered Berlin. The German capital surrendered on May 2.

Hitler committed suicide in his bunker beneath the chancellery in Berlin.

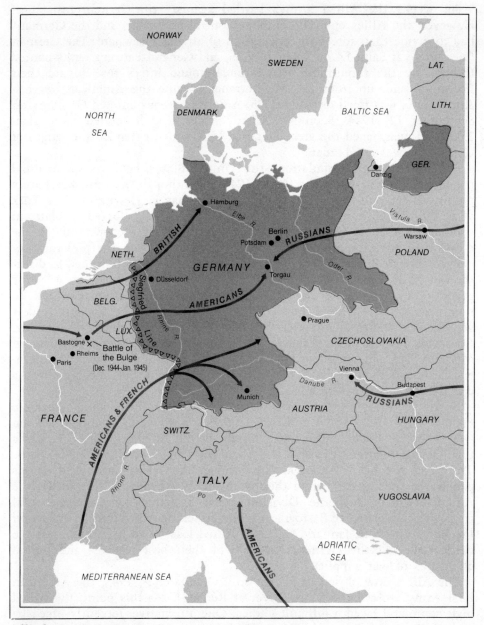

Allied Victory in Europe

Other leading Nazis who had not killed themselves or disappeared were later brought to trial before a four-power tribunal at Nuremberg. Ten German leaders were hanged, and others received long-term prison sentences for crimes against humanity. On May 8, German delegates signed terms of unconditional surrender at Eisenhower's headquarters in the French city of Rheims.

Allied War Conferences

During the Second World War, Allied heads of state met from time to time to coordinate their efforts and to plan final peace settlements. In November 1943, Roosevelt and Churchill met with the Chinese leader, Chiang Kai-shek, at Cairo. They agreed that Japan should be driven from the Asiatic mainland and from the Pacific islands which she had seized. From Cairo, Roosevelt and Churchill flew to Teheran to meet Stalin. There they discussed plans for an Anglo-American second front in Europe.

Although Roosevelt and Churchill worked well together, they did not always agree on policy. Roosevelt was always more eager than Churchill to open a second front in France. Churchill was more concerned about the protection of the Balkan countries from Soviet domination. However, both Roosevelt and Churchill agreed that one of their prime tasks was to win Russian cooperation in the postwar world. The Russians had already indicated their intention to control the countries of eastern Europe which their armies were overrunning. Consequently, Roosevelt, Churchill, and Stalin met in the Crimean city of Yalta in February 1945. The following is a brief summary of their agreements.

Defeat of Nazi Germany was close, and cooperation seemed assured between the Big Three when Churchill, Roosevelt, and Stalin met at Yalta in February 1945. Yet, undercurrents of trouble were evident. Churchill later admitted, "Our hopeful assumptions were soon to be falsified"; and Roosevelt, who was gravely ill at the time, died two months later leaving many problems unsolved. (Wide World Photos)

1. *Germany.* Roosevelt, Churchill, and Stalin approved the boundaries of the postwar zone of occupation in Germany. Germany was to be administered by an Inter-Allied Control Commission in Berlin. Russia and Poland were to receive territory in eastern Germany, and Germany was to pay reparations.

2. *Poland and eastern Europe.* The Russians had already installed a puppet Communist government in Poland. Stalin agreed to include democratic leaders in the Polish government and to permit free elections. The three leaders also signed a declaration which promised the free election of democratic governments in the other countries of eastern Europe.

3. *The United Nations.* Stalin promised to cooperate with Roosevelt and Churchill to create a new international security agency along the lines already drawn by the American government.

4. *The Far East.* Stalin secretly agreed to come into the war against Japan after the surrender of Germany and to support the government of Chiang Kai-shek. In return, Roosevelt agreed that the Russians should acquire the Kurile Islands and all territory lost to Japan at the end of the Russo-Japanese War. Roosevelt's military advisers strongly urged him to make these concessions in order to assure Russian help in subduing Japan.

Churchill believed at the time of the Yalta Conference that Roosevelt was mentally incapacitated, and that he, therefore, made too many concessions to Stalin. Churchill's belief had some justification, but in retrospect it is difficult to see how Roosevelt could have acted differently. Stalin did not intend to permit his country to be overrun by western invaders again. In establishing eastern Europe as a buffer zone, Stalin took no more than he could have taken at any time without incurring the danger of American or British interference.

A New Leader Faces Difficult Decisions

Roosevelt sought relief from his labors in a brief vacation in April 1945 at Warm Springs, Georgia. He was sitting for a portrait in his cottage there on the afternoon of April 12 when he complained of a severe headache. Two hours later he died of a cerebral hemorrhage. Most Americans, regardless of political persuasion, responded with a spontaneous expression of mourning. Roosevelt's body was brought to Washington, and he was soon afterward buried at his ancestral home at Hyde Park, New York.

The task of concluding the war in the Pacific and planning for the peace now fell to Roosevelt's successor, Harry S Truman. Truman did not conceal his anger at Russian violation of the Yalta accords, most notably those concerning Poland, when he met with Stalin, Churchill, and Clement Attlee, Churchill's successor as Prime Minister, at Potsdam, Germany, from July 17 through August 2, 1945. The Allied leaders, in spite of differences over eastern Europe, did unite in calling upon Japan to surrender unconditionally and threatening "prompt and utter destruction" if she did not.

Truman was emboldened to resist Stalin and to join in issuing the Potsdam Declaration because he knew that the United States now possessed the atomic bomb. Roosevelt had been persuaded of the vast military potential of atomic power. There were reports that Hitler was trying to develop an atomic bomb, and the American government had spent $2 billion on its development. An Anglo-American scientific team, headed by Dr. J. Robert Oppenheimer, made the first test on July 16, 1945, in a desert area near Los Alamos, New Mexico. In all of history, no such frightful weapon had been put into human hands.

We now know that the Japanese could not, in any event, have continued the war much beyond the summer of 1945. Truman, apparently unaware of this fact, decided to drop the bomb because he was convinced that, by doing so, he would end the war and save perhaps the million Japanese and American lives which would otherwise be lost in an invasion of the Japanese homeland. Some scientists argued that a demonstration of the bomb's destructiveness in an uninhabited area would end the war without further deaths; other scientists said that the United States should not bear the stigma of being the first nation to use atomic weapons. These arguments were brushed aside. Only two atomic bombs were immediately available, and military and political leaders were convinced that both might be needed to force Japan to surrender.

A lone B-29 Superfortress dropped an atomic bomb on the city of Hiroshima on the morning of August 6. A blinding explosion, followed by

Two civilians walking through the ruins of Hiroshima. In a radio address to the nation in August 1945, President Truman presented his justification for use of the atomic bomb: "We have used it against those who attacked us without warning at Pearl Harbor . . . . We have used it in order to shorten the agony of war, in order to save the lives of thousands and thousands of young Americans." (Wide World Photos)

roaring balls of fire, completely demolished four square miles of the city. It killed close to 80,000 persons and wounded at least that many more. Three days later, a second bomb was dropped on Nagasaki and turned it into an inferno, in which many thousands died immediately. Thousands more died slowly from radiation poisoning in both cities. Children conceived by survivors continue to suffer from the genetic effects of radiation. On the same day that the atomic bomb exploded over Nagasaki, Russia declared war on Japan and sent troops into Manchuria.

The Japanese government, faced with the choice of annihilation or surrender, gave up the struggle on August 14. On September 2, MacArthur received Japanese delegates aboard U.S.S. *Missouri*, in Tokyo Bay, for the formal surrender. Emperor Hirohito, although permitted to remain on his throne, was forced to renounce the ancient Japanese legend that he was of divine origin. The Supreme Commander of the Allied Powers in the Far East, MacArthur, was vested with full power over Japan until a treaty of peace had been concluded. Thus ended the most destructive war in history.

The United Nations

American leaders were determined that their country should not repeat the tragic error of refusing to participate in a postwar international organization. Roosevelt and Hull, both veterans of the Wilson administration, were also determined to avoid Wilson's mistake of making a partisan issue out of peace. Roosevelt's and Hull's first step along the road to international cooperation was the Declaration of the United Nations, signed in Washington on January 1, 1942, by representatives of twenty-six countries, including the United States, Great Britain, the Soviet Union, and China. The signatories agreed to accept the principles of the Atlantic Charter. Other nations joined the alliance until, by 1945, it represented almost the entire population of the non-Axis world.

In September 1943, the House of Representatives overwhelmingly adopted a resolution introduced by J. William Fulbright of Arkansas which endorsed American participation in the creation of international machinery "with power adequate to establish and maintain a just and lasting peace."

In October 1943, Hull flew to Moscow for a conference with the Foreign Ministers of Great Britain and the Soviet Union. They agreed on "the necessity of establishing at the earliest practical date a general international organization, based on the principle of the sovereign equality of all peace-loving states, and open to membership of all such states, large and small." This agreement was incorporated, verbatim, in a resolution approved by the Senate on November 5, 1943. The American course was, therefore, well charted by the time that American, British, Soviet, and Chinese delegates met at Dumbarton Oaks near Washington on August 21, 1944. They agreed in principle upon the basic structure of a new organization to be called the United Nations (UN).

The Conference on International Organization, approved at Yalta, opened at San Francisco on April 25, 1945, with delegates from fifty participating nations. It was not a peace conference, for the war continued on all fronts. It was, rather, a conference to help to keep the peace when it should come. The charter of the United Nations was to go into force when ratified by the United States, Great Britain, Russia, France, and China, and by a majority of the other forty-five member nations. Truman made the closing speech to the conference on June 26 and almost immediately sent the charter to the Senate. The Senate gave its consent to ratification of the charter by a vote of eighty-nine to two on July 28, 1945, and the charter went into effect about three months later.

SUGGESTED READINGS

For a fine, balanced survey of Roosevelt's foreign policy, see Robert Dallek, *Franklin D. Roosevelt and American Foreign Policy, 1932–1945* (1979). William L. Langer and S. E. Gleason, *The Challenge to Isolation* (1952) and *The Undeclared War* (1953), are excellent, comprehensive studies. For an interesting account of the debate over neutrality, see Robert Divine, *The Illusion of Neutrality* (1962). James M. Burns, *Roosevelt: The Soldier of Freedom* (1970), is a worthy sequel to his study of Roosevelt as a domestic leader.

On more specialized problems, see Bryce Wood, *The Making of the Good Neighbor Policy* (1961), and E. David Cronon, *Josephus Daniels in Mexico* (1960). Robert P. Browder, *The Origins of Soviet-American Diplomacy* (1953), is the best work on American recognition of the USSR. Dorothy Borg, *The United States and the Far Eastern Crisis of 1933–1938* (1964), is the fullest treatment of that subject. Herbert Feis, *The Road to Pearl Harbor* (1950), once the standard treatment of its subject, is now supplemented by Gordon W. Prange and others, *At Dawn We Slept: The Untold Story of Pearl Harbor* (1981). Warren Moscow, *Roosevelt and Willkie* (1968), covers their presidential campaigns and later cooperation during the war. Early sections of John Costello, *The Battle of the Atlantic* (1977), deal with the "undeclared war." Winston S. Churchill's *The Gathering Storm* (1948) and *Their Finest Hour* (1949) are helpful in placing American policy in a global context.

A. Russell Buchanan, *The United States and World War II*, 2 vols. (1964), is the most useful survey of that subject. Robert H. Connery, *Naval and Industrial Mobilization in World War II* (1951); Lester V. Chandler, *Inflation in the United States, 1940–1948* (1951); and James P. Baxter III, *Scientists against Time* (1946), are good studies of the domestic front. Jack Goodman, ed., *While You Were Gone: A Report on Wartime Life in the United States* (1946); Richard Polenberg, *War and Society: The United States, 1941–1945* (1972); and John M. Blum, *V Was for Victory: Politics and American Culture during World War II* (1976), describe American society during the war. On the status of black Americans, see N. A. Wynn, *The Afro-American and the Second World War* (1976). The tragic story of Japanese Americans is told in Roger Daniels, *Concentration Camps, U.S.A.: Japanese-Americans and*

World War II (1971), and Michi Weglyn, *The Untold Story of America's Concentration Camps* (1976).

Multivolume accounts of military, naval, and air operations have been published by the Department of the Army, Office of the Chief of Military History. A better introduction to the battles and strategies, however, would be Martha Byrd Hoyle, *A World in Flames: The History of World War II* (1970); Samuel E. Morison, *Strategy and Compromise* (1958); or Kenneth R. Greenfield, *American Strategy in World War II: A Reconsideration* (1963). For a sympathetic account of the American failure to interpret intelligence information correctly before the attacks in the Pacific, see Roberta Wohlsetter, *Pearl Harbor: Warning and Decision* (1962). The overriding role of General Marshall in devising American military strategy is described in Forrest C. Pogue, *George C. Marshall: Ordeal and Hope, 1939–1942* (1966). On the European theater, see Chester Wilmot, *The Struggle for Europe* (1952), and the memoirs of Dwight D. Eisenhower and other generals. For the Pacific theater, see Herbert Feis, *Japan Subdued* (1961); J. K. Eyre, *The Roosevelt-MacArthur Conflict* (1950); and the memoirs of Douglas MacArthur and William F. Halsey. D. Clayton James, *The Years of MacArthur*, 2 vols. (1970), is severely critical of MacArthur's general strategy in the war against Japan; William R. Manchester, *American Caesar: Douglas MacArthur, 1880–1964* (1978), in contrast, is almost wholly admiring. The war of the common soldier is described in Ernie Pyle, *The Story of G.I. Joe* (1945).

Herbert Feis has written excellent accounts of the diplomacy of the war: *Churchill, Roosevelt, Stalin* (1957); *Between War and Peace* (1960); and *The China Tangle* (1953). William L. Neuman, *After Victory* (1967), and Edward R. Stettinius, *Roosevelt and the Russians—The Yalta Conference* (1949), illustrate the complexity of the diplomacy of war and peace.

There is a large and growing literature on the atomic bomb project. Among the most valuable books are Robert Jungk, *Brighter than a Thousand Suns* (1958); Nuel Pharr Davis, *Lawrence and Oppenheimer* (1969); and Martin J. Sherwin, *A World Destroyed: The Atomic Bomb and the Grand Alliance* (1975). John Hersey's *Hiroshima* (1946) resembles a novel in its dramatic impact.

CHAPTER 28
POLITICS AND PROBLEMS
OF THE TRUMAN ERA

1. TRUMAN AND THE PROBLEMS OF DEMOBILIZATION AND RECONVERSION

The New President

Harry S Truman (1884–1972), born and reared in a small Missouri town, worked as a bank clerk and farmer after he finished high school. He served in the field artillery during the First World War and rose to the rank of major. After the war Truman went into politics with the help of the notorious Kansas City Democratic organization headed by Tom Pendergast. With Pendergast's backing, Truman was elected to the United States Senate in 1934, and again in 1940. There he gained a reputation for loyalty to the New Deal.

The country knew very little about Truman when he succeeded Roosevelt. Truman gave the appearance of a fierce partisan in the rough and tumble of politics. He often spoke impulsively—in a manner which many Americans felt was unbecoming to a President of the United States. At first, he also gave the impression of being overwhelmed and confused. But Truman was determined to provide vigorous leadership both at home and abroad; consequently he left the presidency as strong as he found it. For a while at least, he defended civil liberties at a time when ferocious assaults were being made against these cherished rights. This early stand should be kept in mind when studying the period during which Truman surrendered to political pressure and to his own fears of world communism. Also, Truman fought for a program which defended the civil rights of blacks far beyond anything that Franklin Roosevelt had ever dared to suggest. Truman soon developed a broad world view, and, once he found his bearings, he gave bold leadership to the West and its allies in Asia.

Many Democratic politicians assumed that Truman would be content to serve as caretaker in office. He startled Congress in September 1945 by calling for an expansion of the New Deal. He asked for extension of the Social Security system, an increase in the minimum wage, national health insurance, revival of the war against urban slums, and new regional developments similar to the TVA. Truman also called for federal guarantees of full employment and maintenance of economic controls throughout the period of reconversion.

Demobilization and Reconversion

To get the boys back home quickly was the reigning passion of the American people in 1945. By midsummer of 1946, the army had been reduced to 1,500,000 men and the navy to 700,000. Congress had made provision for the homeward rush of former servicemen by passing a "GI Bill of Rights" in 1944. The Veterans' Administration rapidly expanded its hospitals to care for the sick and wounded. Vocational rehabilitation centers helped disabled servicemen. Unemployed veterans received unemployment compensation for a full year. Financial assistance was given for the purchase of homes, farms, and businesses. Finally, veterans who wanted them received free tuition, books, and expenses for advanced education. Altogether, it was the largest assistance program undertaken by any government in history.

At war's end, the American economy resembled a great overheated steam engine about to explode. High wartime earnings and savings created a huge demand for consumer goods, but not enough automobiles, appliances, homes, meat, and other commodities were available to satisfy the demand.

Republicans and conservative Democrats in Congress said that American businessmen and farmers could produce in abundance only if freed from controls. However, Truman insisted upon rigorous price controls to dam up inflationary pressures until output could satisfy demand. The OPA, which still operated under wartime authority, held the line against price increases in 1945 – 1946. However, most price controls ended in November 1946. As a consequence, the consumer price index rose by almost 34 per cent between 1945 and 1948.

Troubles on the Labor Front

The end of the war found organized labor fearful of inflation and unemployment. Unions now boasted 14,600,000 members, and their leaders were determined to maintain wartime gains and to hold their own against the rising cost of living. But higher wages added to increased costs, which meant higher prices, which in turn stimulated strikes for higher wages.

A wage compromise was worked out for leading industries which set the pattern for wages elsewhere and gave hope of peaceful industrial relations. However, conflicts in two major industries upset the balance in the spring of 1946. After a nationwide railroad strike threatened to paralyze the economy, Truman seized the railroads on May 17, 1946. Truman asked Congress for power to declare a state of national emergency whenever a strike in an industry under federal control endangered national security. Workers who continued to strike would be drafted into the army, and their leaders could be fined and imprisoned. The Senate buried the bill because the striking railway workers returned to their jobs.

Meanwhile, John L. Lewis had led his United Mine Workers out on strike for higher wages and other benefits, including improved safety regulations. After fruitless negotiations, the government took over the mines. The government granted most of Lewis' demands, but he made new ones. The government, supported by a federal judge's injunction, stood firm. Lewis called a strike anyway, only to draw fines against himself and his union. A new contract, which conceded most of Lewis' demands, ended the impasse in June 1947.

Legislation and Congressional Politics, 1945–1948

Despite struggles over price controls and labor policies, Truman and the Democratic Seventy-ninth Congress cooperated to enact two epochal pieces of legislation. One, the Employment Act of 1946, established a Council of Economic Advisers to study the economy and advise the President and Congress on measures best calculated to promote prosperity. The most significant section of the Employment Act was its assertion that the federal government bore chief responsibility for maintaining prosperity. Both Truman and his successor used the Council of Economic Advisers only sparingly, but, in the 1960s, the council came to exercise vital influence in economic policymaking.

The second epochal piece of legislation was the Atomic Energy Act. Approved on August 1, 1946, this act retained the prevailing governmental monopoly on fissionable materials and vested complete control of research and production in a new five-man Atomic Energy Commission.

Popular discontent rose in the early autumn of 1946 because of skyrocketing prices and a shortage of essential commodities. Public anger against organized labor grew because of what seemed to be union irresponsibility and unfair labor practices. In 1947, more than thirty states outlawed the most important of these practices: featherbedding (demanding the employment of more labor than was necessary); jurisdictional strikes (strikes resulting from the warfare of rival unions); and secondary boycotts (refusal of members of a union to handle nonunion goods). Republicans capitalized upon this discontent and swept to victory in the mid-term elections in 1946. They controlled both houses of Congress for the first time since 1928.

The major result of the Republican landslide was the adoption of the Labor-Management Relations, or Taft-Hartley, Act, passed over Truman's angry veto in June 1947. The act outlawed the closed shop—an arrangement by which only members of a union could be hired by an employer. It forbade "unfair" union practices such as refusal to bargain in good faith, secondary boycotts, and jurisdictional strikes. The Taft-Hartley Act also permitted employers to sue unions for breach of contract and to petition the NLRB for elections to determine bargaining agents. In strikes which endangered the national safety, the act provided for cooling-off periods and for the use of temporary injunctions by the President. The measure also compelled union officers to sign anti-Communist affidavits in order to bring their cases before the NLRB. The act required unions to submit annual financial reports to the Secretary of Labor. Finally, the measure prohibited union contributions to political parties. Organized labor bitterly claimed that the Taft-Hartley Act was aimed at the destruction of the labor movement.

Truman's accusations against the Eightieth Congress during the campaign of 1948 have left the impression of constant warfare between the White House and Capitol Hill. In fact, the two branches of government cooperated during 1947 and 1948 to launch the United States upon bold leadership of the non-Communist world and to enact several important domestic measures.

The most important product of this bipartisan collaboration was the National Security Act of 1947, the result of a long struggle to overhaul America's defense structure. The act provided for a single Secretary of Defense and Joint Chiefs of Staff. It also established an independent air force and noncabinet departments of the Army, Navy, and Air Force. Finally, the measure created a National Security Council to advise the President and Congress and a new Central Intelligence Agency (CIA).

Congress also responded when Truman requested a change in the presidential succession. The Presidential Succession Act of 1947 fixed the succession after the Vice-President, first in the Speaker of the House, and then in the presiding officer of the Senate. Cabinet members were then to follow in the order of the creation of their office, beginning with the Secretary of State. On its own volition, Congress passed the Twenty-second Amendment, which limited the tenure of Presidents after Truman to two terms.

During the second session of the Eightieth Congress in 1948, Truman won approval of additional measures which strengthened the nation's military posture and expanded several New Deal programs.

2. THE BEGINNINGS OF THE COLD WAR

Deadlock after Potsdam

Efforts to draw up peace treaties with the Axis nations in Europe were crippled by conflict between the Soviet Union and the western Allies. Disagreements were particularly acute over Germany. Many of Germany's cities had been bombed into rubble and its industries crippled. Its territory had been divided into four zones, controlled by Russia, Great Britain, the United States, and France. The capital city of Berlin also had been divided among the four powers, but it was surrounded by Soviet-controlled territory. The western powers continued to call for democratically elected governments in eastern Europe, while Soviet leaders continued to fear the presence of potential adversaries along their borders. Much of the Soviet Union lay in ruins because of the second German invasion of Russia in less than thirty years. Soviet officials were determined that Germany must not be allowed to grow strong enough to try again.

The Allied Foreign Ministers finally agreed on treaties for Italy, Finland, Bulgaria, Rumania, and Hungary. These treaties, signed in February 1947, confirmed western supremacy over Italy and Soviet supremacy over the others. But on the all-important question of a settlement with Germany, there was no progress. Consequently, the western powers took steps to unify their three zones, while the Russians began to erect a separate East German government.

Russian-American differences were also acute in 1945–1946 on the international control of atomic energy. The Americans proposed the so-called Baruch Plan, which would create an International Atomic Development Authority under the UN, with a global monopoly on the production of atomic energy and the right to inspect atomic plants anywhere in the world. Moreover, the authority should not be subject to a veto in the UN Security Council. The Russians accepted all features of the plan except the one which forbade use of the veto. The United States then insisted that international control would be impossible. Hence the Baruch Plan foundered upon the shoals of Russian-American mutual suspicion.

Containment: The Truman Doctrine and the Marshall Plan

The Grand Alliance had obviously broken up by 1946, and the Soviet Union and western powers had come to an uneasy truce for the division of Europe. George F. Kennan, counselor of the American embassy in Moscow, had warned in February 1946 that Stalin's government was implacably hostile to the West. Events seemed to confirm Kennan's warnings. The Russians attempted to create a puppet regime in northern Iran, demanded that Turkey cede territory to them, and supported a Communist-led rebellion against the government of Greece.

The crisis came to a head in February 1947, when the British government informed the State Department that it could no longer maintain military and naval forces in the eastern Mediterranean. Truman quickly asked Congress to appropriate $400 million for aid to Greece and Turkey. The President announced what soon was called the Truman Doctrine: "I believe that it must be the foreign policy of the United States to support free peoples who are resisting attempted subjugation by armed minorities or by outside pressures."

Many Americans still hoped for peaceful collaboration with the Soviet Union. Truman's request, therefore, especially his request for military assistance, met strong opposition in Congress. Nevertheless, the Greek-Turkish Aid bill was approved by large majorities in both houses of Congress in May 1947. The Truman Doctrine signaled a radical new departure in American foreign policy. Henceforth, the United States would attempt to contain Soviet expansion whenever possible through cooperation with the governments of the nations involved.

The near eastern crisis paled into insignificance when compared with the crisis which was developing in western Europe. Despite the infusion of massive American aid since the end of the war, European nations were literally on the verge of bankruptcy, and there seemed to be danger of Communist takeovers in Italy and France. American planners believed that western Europe could be saved from chaos only by immense American aid. In a speech at Harvard University on June 5, 1947, Secretary of State George C. Marshall announced that the United States stood ready to help European nations (including Russia) to rebuild their economies.

The Russians condemned Marshall's offer as a cloak for American imperialism. They also forbade their satellites to participate. Delegates from sixteen non-Communist nations met at Paris in July 1947 to prepare estimates of both their needs and their abilities to contribute to European recovery. They submitted a recovery plan two months later. It called for $22.4 billion in assistance from the United States.

Congress debated the European Recovery Program (ERP), as the Marshall Plan was called, for ten months. Seizure of the government of Czechoslovakia by that country's Communists in February 1948 assured congressional approval of the ERP. Between April 1948 and December 1951, the United States poured some $12 billion into Europe. As early as 1950, western Europe had not only recovered its prewar levels of production, but it was well along the road to more substantial prosperity.

From the Berlin Crisis to the North Atlantic Treaty

West Germany, the industrial heart of Europe, was the key to European recovery. Hence the American and former Allied governments not only decided to include West Germany in the ERP but also to create a separate West German state. These plans culminated in June 1949 in the formation of a West German federal republic and its inclusion in the ERP.

The Soviet Union retaliated by limiting access to Berlin and then, on June 23, by blocking all traffic into Berlin from the west. In collaboration with the British and French governments, Truman responded with a decision to supply beleagured Berlin by airlift. Clearly, the Soviet government did not want war, for it did not intefere with the airlift. Cargo planes flew 2,500,000 tons of fuel, food, and raw materials to Berlin in defiance of the blockade. Leaders of West Germany met at Bonn on October 20, 1948, to draft a constitution for the new Federal Republic of Germany. On May 12, 1949, the blockade was lifted.

Meanwhile, representatives of Great Britain, France, Belgium, the Netherlands, and Luxembourg signed a treaty of economic cooperation and military alliance at Brussels on March 17, 1948. The Brussels Union was enlarged to include Italy, West Germany, Ireland, Denmark, Norway, and Sweden.

Leaders of western Europe now turned to the United States to fulfill its promise of 1948 of cooperation with a western European military alliance. Out of the ensuing talks came the North Atlantic Treaty, signed in April 1949 by representatives of the United States, Great Britain, France, Italy, the Netherlands, Belgium, Canada, Iceland, Luxembourg, Denmark, Norway, and Portugal. The treaty was later signed by West Germany, Turkey, and Greece. The treaty declared that an attack upon any one of the signatories would be considered an attack upon all, and would be resisted by all with armed force. Senate debate on the North Atlantic Treaty was sharp but not prolonged. The Senate gave its consent to ratification on July 21, 1949.

3. THE ELECTION OF 1948 AND THE FAIR DEAL

Republican Hopes and Democratic Quarrels

Republican hopes of capturing both Congress and the presidency were running higher in early 1948 than at any time in two decades. Republicans

North Atlantic Treaty Organization

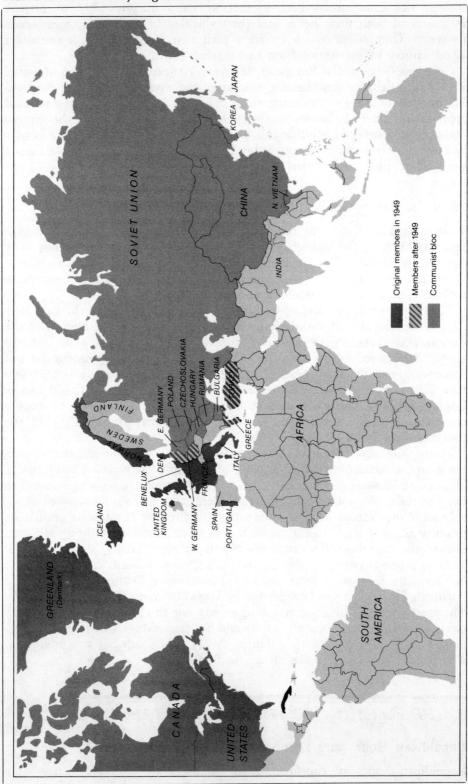

were reasonably well united, while President Truman had come under violent attack within his own party.

One revolt was brewing in the South. In 1947, Truman's Committee on Civil Rights issued an epochal report, *To Secure These Rights*. It called for a systematic legislative campaign to root out discrimination on account of race. Against the wishes of many southern congressmen, Truman endorsed the committee's legislative recommendation, but without success. Another revolt against Truman brewed in the left wing of the Democratic party. This faction had been alienated by Truman's anti-Soviet stance and by his dismissal, in 1946, of Secretary of Commerce Henry A. Wallace, a leader of the Democratic left.

With prospects for victory so alluring, many candidates wanted the Republican presidential nomination. The Republican national convention of 1948 nominated Governor Thomas E. Dewey on the third ballot. Its platform approved the basic New Deal reforms and the bipartisan foreign policy, but promised that the Republicans would run the government more efficiently.

The Democrats remained in deep gloom all through the spring of 1948. Party leaders tried to persuade Truman to withdraw, but he insisted on running. The Democratic convention could find no alternative but to renominate the incumbent. After a bitter floor fight, a liberal coalition drove through a strong civil-rights plank.

Upon the adoption of the civil-rights plank, members of the Mississippi and Alabama delegations, waving the battle flag of the Confederacy, marched out of the hall. On July 17, delegates from thirteen southern states met at Birmingham and organized the States' Rights Democratic party. The so-called Dixiecrats nominated Governor J. Strom Thurmond of South Carolina for the presidency. The Dixiecrats did not, of course, expect to win, but they did hope to carry enough southern states to throw the election into the House of Representatives.

Five days later, left-liberal Democrats met in Philadelphia and organized the Progressive party. The convention nominated Wallace on a platform which demanded further New Deal social reforms, gradual nationalization of certain basic industries, and a policy of friendship with the Soviet Union.

The Campaign and Election of 1948

Public opinion polls predicted a sweeping Republican victory, and Governor Dewey conducted a leisurely campaign while he made plans for his new administration. Truman was undaunted. He set out upon a whistle-stop campaign in which he gave 351 speeches to an estimated 12,000,000 people. Truman concentrated on the great metropolitan areas, where the New Deal coalition remained strong. He did not neglect depressed farm sections, however, where he could blame poor economic conditions on the Republican-dominated Congress. In both areas, he stressed the continuity of his own programs with the New Deal. Truman also called Congress into special session and urged it to carry out the Republican platform by adopting civil-rights and other progressive legislation. When it did not, Truman castigated the "do-nothing Congress."

On election day the outcome seemed so certain that the Chicago *Tribune* ran large headlines which hailed Dewey as the next President. In the most

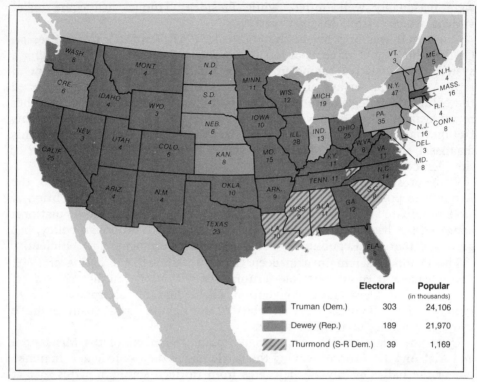

		Electoral	Popular (in thousands)
	Truman (Dem.)	303	24,106
	Dewey (Rep.)	189	21,970
	Thurmond (S-R Dem.)	39	1,169

The Election of 1948

surprising upset in American political history, Truman won 24,106,000 popular and 303 electoral votes, to 21,969,000 popular and 189 electoral votes for Dewey. Thurmond polled only 1,169,000 popular and thirty-nine electoral votes, while Wallace received 1,156,000 popular and no electoral votes. Truman held together the groups which had provided the basic support for the New Deal. Also, the country was at peace and prosperous as never before. In such happy circumstances, the voters do not usually turn out a party in power.

The Fair Deal and Governmental Reorganization

Truman interpreted his victory as proof that the American people wanted to intensify domestic reform. He outlined his program, which he called the Fair Deal, in his inaugural address in 1949. During the next two years, the President won adoption of some Fair Deal measures. They included: first, an increase in the minimum wage from forty to seventy-five cents an hour; second, extension of the Social Security system to 10,000,000 new beneficiaries; third, the extension of rent controls until March 31, 1951; fourth, a Housing Act for the construction of 810,000 units for low-income families; fifth, expansion of irrigation, water-control, and hydroelectric projects; sixth, a new Displaced Persons bill to admit 400,000 refugees; seventh, the Agricultural Act of 1949, which set price supports at 90 per cent of parity; and, eighth, incorporation of the Internal Revenue Service into the civil-service system.

Harry S Truman and Alben W. Barkley waving after their
inauguration as President and Vice President. Polls had forecast a
Republican victory, but Truman later noted: "My one-man
crusade took effect . . . I never doubted that they would vote for me."
(Wide World Photos)

Truman, however, failed to obtain other important parts of his Fair Deal
program. He failed to achieve substantial modification of the Taft-Hartley
Act by refusing to accept anything less than outright repeal. Truman's other
Fair Deal legislation—for civil rights, national health insurance, and federal
aid to education—fell victim to the opposition of powerful interest groups.
However, these programs later became the basis of Lyndon B. Johnson's
Great Society program of the 1960s. Truman did, nevertheless, use his
executive power to accomplish some of his objectives in the field of civil
rights. He strengthened the Civil Rights Division of the Justice Department,
began to abolish segregation in the federal civil service and the armed forces,
and appointed a number of blacks to high offices.

Another noteworthy accomplishment—reorganization of the executive
branch—was the product of bipartisan cooperation. Congress and Truman
had accomplished much in streamlining the government even before 1949.
The National Security Act of 1947 created a systematic defense structure for
the first time. Congress, in the Legislative Reorganization Act of 1946,
streamlined its own committee structure and instituted other reforms. Then,
in 1947, Truman appointed former President Hoover to head a blue-ribbon
commission on executive reorganization.

In the early months of 1949, the Hoover Commission issued reports which
recommended a reduction in the number of federal departments and
agencies; called for the establishment of a Department of Welfare to combine
federal activities in the fields of public health, social welfare, and education;

and advocated a reorganization of the Post Office Department. Congress responded in June 1949 with legislation which authorized the President to submit plans for reorganization which would go into effect unless Congress specifically disapproved. Truman submitted thirty-six plans within a year. Only one of them—for a Department of Welfare—was rejected.

4. THE FALL OF NATIONALIST CHINA, THE SECOND RED SCARE, AND THE KOREAN WAR

The "Fall" of Nationalist China

American confidence in the peace of the postwar world, already shaken by the onset of the Cold War in Europe, was diminished again by the fall of Nationalist China to Communist rebels. The American government had extended enormous military aid to the Nationalist government immediately after the Japanese surrender, but Chiang Kai-shek faced awesome problems of inflation, political corruption, poverty, and disorganization. His most serious problem, however, was the threat from a large and well-disciplined group of Chinese Communists led by Mao Tse-tung. Civil war broke out in late 1945. Truman sent General Marshall to persuade Chiang and Mao to form a unified government. Marshall tried hard but failed, and war soon broke out again.

The Nationalists enjoyed an initial advantage in manpower and supplies, but they collapsed under the assault of the better-disciplined Communist troops. By the summer of 1947, it was obvious that nothing less than full-scale American military participation would turn the tide in favor of the Nationalists. The Truman administration concluded that the American people would never approve participation in a Chinese civil war, and that such participation would be futile in any event. The United States Government, therefore, did not intervene directly while the Chinese Communist armies overran China and drove Chiang and his government to Formosa, or Taiwan, in October 1949.

The Second Red Scare

The fall of China occurred at a time when the American people were already in shock over revelations of Communist subversion at home. In 1946, a Canadian Royal Commission had reported the existence of a far-flung Soviet spy ring. The report set off an intense security drive in the United States. In 1947, Truman issued an Executive Order which directed the FBI and the Civil Service Commission to investigate the loyalty of all federal employees. Within the next four years, 3,000,000 employees were cleared, about 2,000 resigned, and 212 were dismissed as bad security risks.

A nationwide alarm occurred after revelation that, prior to 1947, Communist agents had infiltrated the Anglo-American team which had developed the atomic bomb. This led to the trial and conviction of three Americans as Communist couriers, two of whom—Julius and Ethel Rosenberg—were executed in 1953. Various branches of the government, evidence revealed, had been infiltrated as well. The most publicized of these cases involved

Alger Hiss, who had held a position of trust in the State Department. In 1948, Whittaker Chambers, a former Soviet courier, accused Hiss of having furnished him with valuable classified documents. Hiss denied the charges under oath. Hiss' indictment and trial, and his conviction on charges of perjury on January 21, 1950, shocked the nation.

By this time, some Republican spokesmen were already charging that the federal government was honeycombed with Communists. Senator Joseph R. McCarthy of Wisconsin took up the anti-Communist cause less than a month after Hiss' conviction. McCarthy made headlines by announcing in a speech on February 9, 1950, that he held in his hand a list with the names of 205 card-carrying Communists in the State Department. When this statement was proved false, McCarthy went on to attack a number of American political leaders; among them was General Marshall, whom McCarthy called the leading American traitor. The Wisconsin demagogue made a political blunder, however, when he turned his attacks against members of the Eisenhower administration, which had come into power in 1953, and even against Eisenhower himself. For his reckless, abusive actions, the Senate censured McCarthy in 1954.

Meanwhile, the Truman administration had been swept along in the anti-Communist hysteria. In 1948, eleven Communist leaders were tried and sentenced to prison under the Smith Act of 1940 for conspiracy to *teach* the violent overthrow of the government. In 1951, the Supreme Court, in Dennis *et al. v.* the United States, upheld their convictions and the constitutionality of the Smith Act by invoking the clear-and-present-danger doctrine of the Schenck case of 1919 (see p. 366). Nearly 100 Communist leaders were imprisoned under the Smith Act for allegedly *advocating* the violent overthrow of the government.

The chief contribution of the legislative branch to the drive against communism was the McCarran Internal Security Act of 1950. This measure required Communist organizations to register with the Attorney General and to furnish membership lists. The employment of Communists in defense plants was forbidden under this act.

The Korean War: First Phase

The explosion of the war in Korea in June 1950 drew the United States into the far eastern vortex. Korea had been surrendered by Japan to the Allies in 1945. Russian troops penetrated as far as 38° northern latitude, while American troops occupied the area south of that line. It was assumed that Korea would be united and would also be free of foreign domination. In fact, a Communist government in the north refused either to participate in elections or to permit UN personnel to enter its territory.

However, the Republic of Korea was established in the south in 1948, with dictatorial Syngman Rhee as President. The United States then withdrew its troops from Korea. On June 25, 1950, an army from North Korea invaded the Republic of Korea without warning. The move was approved by the Soviet Union on the assumption that the United States would not fight to defend South Korea.

President Truman instructed Secretary of State Dean Acheson to bring the issue before an emergency meeting of the UN Security Council. The

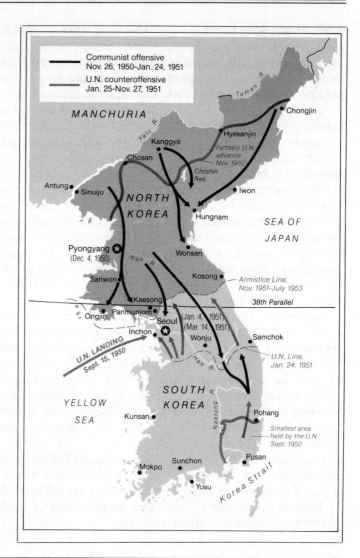

The Korean War, 1950–1953

Russians had stalked out of the council earlier, after that body had refused to seat Communist China. Free of the Russian veto, the council adopted a resolution which condemned the invasion and demanded the immediate withdrawal of North Korean troops.

Meanwhile, Truman ordered General MacArthur (still in Japan as Supreme Allied Commander) to furnish arms and air and naval support to the South Koreans. Democratic and Republican congressional leaders informally endorsed Truman's action. This precedent of going to war without congressional declaration would come back to haunt the American government during the 1960s and early 1970s. The Constitution, of course, grants to Congress, not to the President, the power to declare war.

The Security Council, on June 27, established a United Nations Command, of which MacArthur was put in charge. Nineteen nations eventually sent troops to fight under the UN flag; however, in June 1950, only two divisions of American occupation troops in Japan were quickly available. These were rushed to Korea, where they fought a brilliant delaying action around the port of Pusan. The tide turned on September 15, 1950, when MacArthur's forces made a daring flank attack by sea at Inchon. MacArthur then captured Seoul and UN forces reached the thirty-eighth parallel by about October 1.

On October 3, the Chinese People's Republic warned that, if the United States or UN forces crossed the thirty-eighth parallel, China would send troops to defend North Korea. Few leaders in the West took the warning seriously. MacArthur himself informed Truman on October 15 that there was little danger of Chinese intervention. Intelligence officials in Washington collected evidence to the contrary, but there was little that they could do about MacArthur's decision. Hence the UN forces were soon driving the North Koreans toward the Yalu River—the boundary between Korea and Manchuria. MacArthur unknowingly drove his troops into a trap set by Chinese troops already in North Korea. It required several weeks of desperate fighting before the retreating American forces could stabilize a defensive line along the thirty-eighth parallel.

General MacArthur urged that the United States blockade the Chinese coast, bomb the Chinese mainland, use atomic bombs if necessary, and help

President Truman is greeted by Douglas MacArthur upon his arrival at Wake Island where he received a firsthand briefing from the General. When Truman asked MacArthur about the chances for Soviet or Chinese interference in Korea, the General tragically miscalculated: "Very little. . . . Now that we have bases for our Air Force in Korea, if the Chinese tried to get down to Pyongyang, there would be the greatest slaughter." (Wide World Photos)

Chiang Kai-shek to invade China from Formosa. The Joint Chiefs of Staff in Washington refused. There was the danger, first, that the Soviet Union would come to the aid of China, for the two nations had signed a mutual defense alliance in early 1950. There was also the danger that the Soviets would turn against western Europe while American forces were preoccupied in the Far East. Also, even MacArthur had warned Americans against getting bogged down in a land war against a huge Asian population.

The Truman administration, meanwhile, had made its own decision to limit military operations in the Far East. MacArthur and General Matthew B. Ridgway were ordered to limit their activities to the defense of the Republic of Korea and to avoid a general war with China. MacArthur was in fundamental disagreement with this defensive strategy. In a letter to the Republican minority leader in the House of Representatives, MacArthur called for a victory offensive against China. MacArthur's letter, read to the House on April 5, 1951, was a direct challenge to the administration's foreign policy. Truman replied at once by relieving MacArthur of his command. "I could do nothing else and still be President of the United States," Truman wrote on April 10.

Truman's act was both courageous and necessary, but it set off demands for his impeachment. MacArthur came home for a triumphal tour and appearance before a joint session of Congress. Then the Senate Armed Services Committee began a long investigation of recent far eastern policies and MacArthur's recall. After listening to testimony from military as well as political leaders, the Senate hearings ended in the vindication of the administration and the discrediting of MacArthur. All three members of the Joint Chiefs of Staff had advised Truman to take exactly the positions which he had adopted, including the dismissal of MacArthur.

Security Treaties in Europe and Asia

While the war raged in Korea, Congress was in the midst of a heated debate over whether American troops should be sent to Europe. American forces were asked to participate in a North Atlantic Treaty Organization (NATO) combined army, created in 1950, with General Eisenhower as supreme commander. Truman's recommendation of United States participation evoked bitter debate in Congress. It seemed for a moment that the administration had lost control of foreign policy to its opponents in Congress led by Senator Robert A. Taft. General Eisenhower rushed to Washington from Paris to plead against the abandonment of Europe. On April 4, 1951, the Senate approved the dispatch of four divisions to support American commitments to NATO. However, the Senate warned Truman not to send additional troops without further congressional approval.

The Truman administration also worked to build a system of security pacts in the Pacific area comparable, at least in terminology, to those in the North Atlantic. A mutual defense treaty between the United States and the Philippines was concluded on August 30, 1951. Two days later, Australia, New Zealand, and the United States signed the Tripartite Security Treaty known as the ANZUS Pact.

On September 8, 1951, Japan and forty-eight of her former enemies concluded a peace treaty in San Francisco. It seemed a generous settlement. True, Japan was required to give up her overseas empire. But the treaty contained no provisions for punitive reparations or economic restrictions, and it restored full sovereignty to the Japanese people.

5. THE ELECTION OF 1952

Bitter Battles in the GOP

Republican hopes for victory in the coming presidential campaign increased in the early months of 1952. Senator McCarthy's attacks had raised doubts about the ability of the Truman administration to protect the country from internal subversion. A jump in wholesale prices between 1950 and 1952 hurt many persons who lived on fixed incomes. Finally, Americans were frustrated by the Korean War, which continued without any end in sight, even though peace talks had been going on since the summer of 1951.

The Republicans, while hopeful, were also bitterly divided. The more conservative and isolationist (or Asia-first) wing was determined to end what Senator Taft called Dewey's "metooism." Taft proposed to give the American people a clear-cut alternative to the New Deal and Fair Deal. Standing in opposition to Taft and his forces were Senator Henry Cabot Lodge, Jr., of Massachusetts, Governor Dewey, and others. They accepted the New Deal and Fair Deal and considered NATO to be the cornerstone of American foreign policy. Taft seemed irresistible. But the moderates' despair turned into elation when General Eisenhower agreed to accept the Republican presidential nomination—mainly, he said, to defeat Taft.

Eisenhower almost made his decision too late, for the Taft forces seemed to dominate the Republican national convention which opened in Chicago on July 7, 1952. However, the overconfident Taft managers made the error of permitting the seating of most of the Eisenhower delegates in contested delegations from three southern states. These delegates provided a bare majority for Eisenhower on the first ballot. For his running mate, Eisenhower chose young Senator Richard M. Nixon of California, who had gained a national reputation by helping to expose Alger Hiss. The Republican platform promised maintenance of basic New Deal-Fair Deal programs at home and a dynamic new foreign policy abroad.

The Campaign of 1952

The Democrats, assembled in Chicago on July 21, were badly split between southern opponents of civil-rights legislation and the progressive-labor forces from the large cities. Governor Adlai E. Stevenson of Illinois received the nomination on the third ballot. Stevenson chose Senator John J. Sparkman of Alabama as his running mate. Stevenson easily ranked as the most eloquent American political leader since Franklin Roosevelt. While Stevenson made few original suggestions, he did promise to extend the New Deal and the Fair Deal by further measures to expand and protect civil rights for blacks. He

Republican presidential candidate Dwight D. Eisenhower is
besieged by a crowd in Long Island, New York, on one of his many
whistle-stops during the campaign of 1952. Eisenhower's roots
lay in the rural life of a simpler era and contributed to his image as a
humble, honest American. A symbol of victory during the war,
he described his campaign as a "Great Crusade for honest
government at home and freedom throughout the world."
(United Press International)

also spoke of increasingly complicated world problems with which the
United States would have to deal.

Eisenhower's campaign was very different from Stevenson's, but it was,
politically, much more adept. Eisenhower, endowed with immense magne-
tism, went before the country like a conquering hero. He called upon
Americans to join him in a crusade and promised to clean up what he
referred to as the "mess" in Washington. Eisenhower's most effective stroke
was a promise, made on October 24, that he would go to Korea in person and
bring the Korean War to "an early and honorable end."

The general carried thirty-nine states and amassed a total of 442 electoral
votes to eighty-nine for Stevenson. The victory, however, was more a
nationwide approval of America's most popular wartime hero than a victory
for the Republican party and program. In contrast to the impressive
Eisenhower majority, the Republicans won control of Congress by the
margin of one vote in the Senate and eight in the House.

SUGGESTED READINGS

Eric F. Goldman, *The Crucial Decade, and After* (1960), is a casual survey relevant to this and the following two chapters. For the Truman administration, see Alonzo L. Hamby, *Beyond the New Deal: Harry S Truman and American Liberalism* (1973); Robert H. Ferrell, *Harry S Truman and the Modern American Presidency* (1982), a sympathetic account; and Robert J. Donovan, *Conflict and Crisis: The Presidency of Harry S Truman, 1945–1948* (1977) and *Tumultuous Years: The Presidency of Harry S Truman, 1949–1953* (1982). For a radical critique, see Barton J. Bernstein and A. J. Matusow, eds., *The Truman Administration: A Documentary History* (1966). For Truman's own story, see *Memoirs by Harry S Truman*, 2 vols. (1955–1956).

Most of the works cited on diplomacy in the preceding chapter are relevant to the origins of the Cold War. These should be supplemented by Ralph B. Levering, *The Cold War, 1945–1972* (1982); John L. Gaddis, *The United States and the Origins of the Cold War, 1941–1947* (1973), and *Strategies of Containment* (1982); Walter LaFeber, *America, Russia, and the Cold War, 1945–1980* (4th ed., 1980); Daniel Yergin, *Shattered Peace: The Origins of the Cold War and the National Security State* (1977); Lisle A. Rose, *Roots of Tragedy: The United States and the Struggle for Asia, 1945–1953* (1976); and Thomas G. Patterson, *Soviet-American Confrontation: Postwar Reconstruction and the Origins of the Cold War* (1974). Gar Alperwitz, *Atomic Diplomacy: Hiroshima and Potsdam* (1965), a New Left analysis, has been subjected to sharp scrutiny and criticism. The Truman Doctrine and the Marshall Plan are discussed in Joseph Jones, *The Fifteen Weeks* (1955). Other important memoirs and personal accounts include Dean Acheson, *Present at the Creation* (1969); Walter Millis, ed., *The Forrestal Diaries* (1951); and Arthur H. Vandenberg, Jr., ed., *The Private Papers of Senator Vandenberg* (1952).

The American occupations can be studied in Lucius C. Clay, *Decision in Germany* (1950), and Edwin O. Reischauer, *The United States and Japan* (1957). J. G. Stoessinger, *The United Nations and the Superpowers* (1965), adequately covers the early years of that organization.

Carl Berger, *The Korea Knot: A Military-Political History* (1957), and Malcolm W. Cagle and F. A. Manson, *The Sea War in Korea* (1957), are the best general surveys. The best account of the Truman-MacArthur conflict is John W. Spanier, *The Truman-MacArthur Controversy and the Korean War* (1959).

C. Vann Woodward, *The Strange Career of Jim Crow* (1957), and Arnold M. Rose, *The Negro in Postwar America* (1950), are good on the growing concern for black rights. Some of the better special studies of Truman's domestic policies are William C. Berman, *The Politics of Civil Rights in the Truman Administration* (1971); Allen Yarnell, *Democrats and Progressives* (1974); Edward S. Flash, Jr., *Economic Advice and Presidential Leadership* (1965); and R. Alton Lee, *Truman and Taft-Hartley* (1967). Irwin Ross, *The Loneliest Campaign: The Truman Victory of 1948* (1968), is good on the election of 1948. John Bartlow Martin, *Adlai Stevenson of Illinois* (1976) and *Adlai Stevenson and the World* (1977), are excellent. James T. Patterson, *Mr. Republican: A Biography of Robert A. Taft* (1972), is indispensable for Republican politics during this period.

Edward A. Shils, *The Torment of Secrecy* (1956), is a good analysis of the growth of wild fears about national security. On this topic, see Richard M. Freeland, *The Truman Doctrine and the Origins of McCarthyism* (1972); David M. Oshinsky, *A Conspiracy So Immense: The World of Joe McCarthy* (1983); Earl Latham, *The Communist Controversy in Washington: From the New Deal to McCarthy* (1966); and Robert Griffith, *The Politics of Fear* (1970). Allen Weinstein, *Perjury! The Hiss-Chambers Conflict* (1977), makes a persuasive case for Hiss' guilt.

CHAPTER 29
THE AMERICAN PEOPLE SINCE THE SECOND WORLD WAR

1. SOCIAL TRENDS

A Changing Population

The generation of young people which produced so many outspoken rebels in the 1960s became newsworthy even before most of them could talk. Both the birth and marriage rates rose sharply during the 1940s. The number of births soared when veterans returned to build homes and start families in 1945–1946. The consequence was a population increase of 14.5 per cent between 1940 and 1950 and an additional 28 per cent increase between 1950 and 1965, to a total of about 193,000,000. By the end of the 1950s, the nation was adding a population equal to that of Richmond, Virginia, every month.

Beginning in 1957, however, the rate of population growth began to slacken. By 1972, the fertility rate (the number of children per family) dropped below the point of "zero population growth." Not until 1977 did the birthrate go up, and then only very slightly. Total population stood at about 227,000,000 in 1980.

The widespread availability of contraceptives helps to explain this decline. In addition, both marriage and the birth of first children were being postponed by many persons, and it became more socially acceptable for couples to have fewer or no children. Economic expectations had a major impact on the birthrate. Couples faced with rapidly rising costs of rearing children increasingly decided to postpone or forego parenthood. The same demographic results followed when more and more married women entered the work force, either because of personal preference or because of family necessity.

Changing patterns of marriage and childbearing pointed toward a more generalized transformation of the American family. Prescribed roles within families were challenged, and even the *forms* of households became more variable. Between 1960 and 1980, the number of single-parent families rose at a rapid rate in comparison with two-parent families. Perhaps most striking was the increase in cohabitation among unmarried couples. By the end of the 1970s, there were an estimated 1,000,000 such couples. None of these developments indicated, by the beginning of the 1980s, that traditional family patterns were on the verge of extinction. Unquestionably, however, there had been major changes in sexual practices and a corresponding shift in the society's acceptance of differing life-styles.

People Still on the Move

In the decades after the Second World War, one out of every five Americans moved *each year*. Where were they all going? There was, first, a continued exodus from the farms. Between 1940 and 1980, the number of people living on farms dropped from 23.2 per cent of the population to 2.4 per cent. But the movement of people was no longer toward the center of the great cities. By the mid-1970s, more people lived in the suburbs (38 per cent) than lived in the central cities (30 per cent), and by the early 1980s, the highest rate of growth was in the "exurban" areas—the small towns and nonfarm rural areas beyond the rims of metropolitan centers.

The movement to the suburbs was partially subsidized by the federal government through low-cost loans for home construction and the building of superhighways which provided easy access to the central city via private automobiles. The new suburban rings beyond the central cities were characterized by single-family homes, community shopping centers, and a predominantly white, middle-class population. While it helped millions of Americans to fulfill their dream of homeownership, the federal government also contributed to the increased segregation of American society along both racial and economic lines. To suburbanites, poverty simply became less and less visible.

Americans also moved from region to region at a quickening pace. The Second World War accelerated the growth of the Pacific and Gulf Coast states, for here were located most of the industrial plants which produced war materiel. After the war, many servicemen returned to these areas to live, and new industries joined the defense plants in locating near the growing labor pool and markets. In the South and Southwest, new industries were lured by promises of local subsidies and prospects of nonunion work forces.

The Pacific states grew in population by about 140 per cent from 1940 to 1965; most of the migrants went to California, which became the most populous state in 1964. By 1980, 24,000,000 people—more than one tenth of the country's entire population—lived in California. The shift of jobs and population to the so-called "sunbelt" had profound political implications in the 1970s and 1980s, when the northeastern states lost and the sunbelt states gained in the reapportionment of seats in the House of Representatives.

One other population movement of major proportions was the exodus of blacks from the rural South to urban centers. The mass migration from the South, which had begun before the First World War, accelerated during the Second. It grew during the prosperous postwar era, until, in 1960, slightly more than half of all American blacks lived outside the former Confederate states, mainly in northern and midwestern cities. The regional flow reversed slightly during the 1970s, but in the South, as in the North, cities had become the magnets.

An Aging Population

Americans were also living longer by the middle decades of the twentieth century. Much of the increase in life expectancy was attributable to declining rates of infant mortality. However, the number of persons over the age of sixty-five also rose sharply, until, by 1980, 11.2 per cent of the population was in that age bracket. The increased numbers of the aged brought a host of new social and economic problems. The upsurge in pension and retirement systems, as well as the extension of Social Security coverage, reflected a new concern for elder citizens and the growing strength of "gray power" in American politics.

2. AFFLUENCE AND UNCERTAINTY IN THE AMERICAN ECONOMY

Unprecedented Economic Expansion, 1945–1965

Anyone who might have predicted in 1940 what lay ahead for the American economy during the next twenty-five years probably would have been regarded as insanely optimistic. Similarly, at the midpoint of the 1960s, anyone who suggested that the economic boom would soon end might have been thought of as sourly pessimistic. However, events at home and abroad since the late 1960s demonstrated that hopes for never-ending prosperity were premature.

By 1940, per capita income and the gross national product measured in constant dollars, had returned to 1929 levels, but it was the massive war spending from 1940 to 1945 that caused the wheels of the economy to spin at a dizzy speed. Brief business recessions occurred in 1949 and 1954, a more serious one in 1957–1958, and a brief one again in 1960–1961. However, business recovered with only moderate stimulus from governmental fiscal and monetary policies. Unemployment, which had reached 25 per cent during the Great Depression, averaged 4.6 per cent during the 1950s.

In the early 1960s, the federal government acted more aggressively than before to prevent recession. Tax reductions, increased welfare spending, and aids to business were all used to stimulate the economy. These policies followed, more or less, the precepts of John Maynard Keynes (1883–1946), the influential British economist, who had argued that, in a recession, government should stimulate the economy through deficit spending. The results of these policies were spectacularly successful. The GNP rose by 25 per cent between 1960 and 1965—the largest half-decade increase ever recorded.

During the period 1945–1965, per capita income increased by some 120 per cent, and the median income for all families doubled. Such aggregate statistics certainly mask the extreme poverty at the bottom of the economic scale, but Americans as a whole had never before known such prosperity for so long a time without a major depression. The causes of this postwar prosperity were numerous and complex, but four stand out as particularly significant:

1. In 1945, a huge, pent-up demand existed for housing and for automobiles and other consumer goods which had not been manufactured during the war. Huge savings had been accumulated by potential consumers. This gave the economy a tremendous stimulus once civilian production was resumed.

2. The new army of consumers included, by the 1950s, the first wave of the postwar baby boom. As this bumper crop of babies moved through childhood and adolescence in the 1950s and 1960s, it increased the demand for consumer goods and for services, most notably, schools.

3. Governmental spending continued to stimulate the economy after the war. Military expenditures remained high. Subsidies to farmers, veterans, and homeowners spurred growth, as did federal funding of interstate highways. Increased governmental expenditures at the state and local levels helped to raise overall governmental spending to a level which was higher than at any time during the New Deal.

4. Perhaps the most significant cause of the postwar prosperity was the high rate of increase in productivity on farms and factories from the end of the Second World War through the 1960s. We will discuss this development later in this chapter.

Uncertainties in the American Economy since 1965

By 1966, rapid expansion was straining the American economic system. One immediate source of the strain was federal fiscal policy. Under President Lyndon Johnson, the government expanded military spending to finance the war in Indochina and simultaneously increased spending on domestic social programs, without increasing taxes. The resulting deficits in the federal budget contributed to rapid inflation. During the 1950s and early 1960s, the annual inflation rate had rarely exceeded 1 per cent, but between 1965 and 1969 it jumped from 2.1 to 6 per cent; it stood at 18 per cent in early 1980. By 1980, the dollar was worth less than half its value in 1967.

Domestic inflation contributed to the weakening of the dollar as the basis of international exchange and trade. However, even before inflation had become a problem, the United States was experiencing significant deficits in its balance of payments. By 1980, the world economy had become so flooded with devalued dollars that the western European nations and the oil-rich middle eastern states were looking for alternative units of exchange.

The declining value of the dollar and the increased price of American goods sold abroad encouraged the Organization of Petroleum Exporting Countries (OPEC), an Arab-dominated cartel, to quadruple crude oil prices in

1973–1974. The price increases and the OPEC embargo of the United States during the Arab-Israeli war of 1973 demonstrated the growing dependence of the United States on foreign sources of energy and raw materials. The problem was not restricted to oil. By the mid-1970s, American industry was dependent on foreign supplies for six of the thirteen most needed raw materials.

In searching for an explanation of America's economic woes, many economists, business leaders, and politicians focused on the nation's sagging rate of productivity. The rate of increase in productivity gradually slipped in the 1970s and then actually declined in 1980. The basic reason for the decline was the decrease of investment in new plants and machinery and a drop in expenditures for research and development. Other factors contributed to the decline. The bulge of young and inexperienced workers who entered the labor force played a part, as did the fact that "service" industries accounted for an ever-increasing portion of the GNP (46 per cent in 1979 as compared to 31 per cent in 1950). It has proved more difficult to improve the efficiency of a doctor, policeman, or a college professor than that of a worker on the assembly line.

The inflationary spiral of the 1970s was particularly troubling because it was accompanied by high unemployment. The country suffered a sharp recession in 1974–1975, a milder one in 1980, and yet a third beginning in 1981, which was the most severe since the Great Depression. Throughout this era, the rate of unemployment among nonwhites was double that of the population as a whole. In December 1982, overall unemployment stood at 10.8 per cent, but among blacks the figure was 20.8 per cent, and even much higher among young black males.

The Organization of Modern American Business

During and after the Second World War, integrated multidivisional corporations, operated by salaried managers and technologists, became even more widespread in the American economy than before. Now, as in the early days of its history, the overriding concern of this kind of business organization was to replace the "invisible hand" of the market with the "visible hand" of managerial planning. In these firms, group management largely replaced the individual entrepreneur, and decision making was dispersed among a huge network of specialists. A free market continued to function in some sectors of the economy, but in such key industries as energy, steel, automobiles, and communications, a combination of corporate and governmental planning had largely replaced the dynamics of the marketplace.

A particular variant of the multidivisional firm appeared in the 1960s—the conglomerate. Unlike early diversified firms, which had typically expanded into new product lines related to their original lines, the conglomerates absorbed existing companies in unrelated fields. The conglomerates were fundamentally *financially* oriented—that is, their major concern was capital appreciation through an increase in the value of their stock.

Many multidivisional firms became multinational in their operations. By the mid-1970s, American-based multinational firms constituted the third largest economic power in the world behind the national economies of the United States and Russia. Although those firms were American in origin, they became increasingly free of the American domestic market and of control by any government.

The Continuing Technological Revolution

During and after the Second World War, research and development (R&D) were incorporated into the routine operations of large corporations and of the government itself. The wartime development of nuclear power and its subsequent commercial adaptation were prime examples of this process. Innovations in the petrochemical industry began with the wartime development of synthetic rubber and also included plastics, fertilizers, and synthetic fibers. Lightweight metals were being manufactured in such expanded quantities after 1945 that they can justly be included among the new industries.

Television sparked the growth of the electronics industry after the war. Television sets in use in the United States jumped from 7,000 in 1947 to 54,000,000 in 1960. At the end of the 1970s, expanded cable and satellite transmission increased the quantity and variety of national programming. Other innovations of the 1960s and 1970s in the field of communications included Xerography, lasers, and fiber optics.

The modern computer, born in the era of the vacuum tube, came of age after the invention of transistors in the late 1940s and of large-scale integrated circuitry (silicon chips) in the 1970s. These two electronic innovations made possible phenomenal increases in the speed and capacity of computers. They also reduced their size and cost. Consumer applications of integrated circuitry and computers burst on the scene in the 1970s in the form of pocket calculators, digital watches, and electronic games. Prior to this time, computers had already transformed business and industry through data processing. The application of computer technology to continuous flow and assembly-line manufacturing made it possible to program machines to give commands to other machines and thus carry out the production of goods in a self-contained and self-correcting system.

Stunning innovations in the biochemical and genetic realm followed the discovery of deoxyribonucleic acid (DNA) in 1953 by Francis Crick and James Watson at Cambridge University. Comprehension of the genetic "code," which their discovery entailed, had profound technological and ethical implications. Their basic breakthrough led to techniques for "splicing" genes from one organism to another (recombinant DNA), a technique through which technologists can "program" organisms to manufacture compounds as diverse as human insulin and alcohol. The full effects of genetic engineering are yet to be felt, but its impact is potentially as revolutionary as the chemical, mechanical, and electronic innovations of the period since the Second World War.

Total expenditures for R&D in the United States had reached $40 billion by the late 1970s, half of which was supplied by the federal government. But, when adjusted for inflation, the level of federal expenditures actually declined by 5 per cent between 1969 and 1979, while at the same time such expenditures increased in other industrialized nations. At the end of the 1970s, there was a growing concern about the relative decline of the United States in technological superiority. It should be noted that the decline in technology, as in productivity, was a relative one, and that the United States still led the world in overall technological innovation.

Technology and the Ecosystem

As the pace of technological development accelerated, so did the level of related social and environmental problems. The social impact of new technologies was often inadequately considered before they were implemented. Sometimes the consequences were tragic, or nearly so, as in the case of a partial "core melt-down" in a commercial nuclear reactor at Three Mile Island, Pennsylvania, in 1979. Perhaps even more threatening than the potential for individual catastrophies was the pervasive pollution of air and water by chemical effluents. At the same time, predictions of the depletion of nonrenewable resources sounded to some like the death knell of the affluent, mobile life-style which most Americans enjoyed.

In response to these signs of impending ecological disaster, there emerged an environmental movement which heightened public awareness of the problems and helped to mobilize support for new governmental action. In the 1960s and 1970s, Congress passed laws designed to clean up the nation's air and water and to curtail future pollution. Despite constraints on both federal and state environmental programs, substantial gains were made in some areas. Automobile emissions of carbon monoxide and hydrocarbons declined, and some heavily polluted waterways were reclaimed.

However, the cost of the antipollution campaign was substantial. Direct costs were passed along to consumers in the form of higher prices. Regulations curtailed individual and corporate freedom. And efforts to protect the environment and to conserve natural resources triggered conflicting claims for use of the nation's land and water and the store of riches beneath them.

Environmentalism evoked a critique of "high" technology and a search for alternatives to large-scale, energy-intensive systems of production. Proponents of "appropriate" or "alternative" technologies stressed the need for renewable, nonpolluting sources of energy and for a reduction in scale of production. Clearly, this movement represented more than a dissenting opinion about the "how-to" of modern technology. It also articulated values which clashed with prevailing views about economic growth and mankind's relations with the natural environment.

The American Worker

The technological innovations described above, along with the bureaucratization of work, changed the profile of the American work force in the postwar period. The number of farmers and farm laborers continued to decline in the face of mechanization. The number of production workers stayed fairly constant after 1950. The greatest change in the labor force from 1940 to 1980 was the enormous expansion of employment in "service industries" such as trade, finance, and government. Clerical jobs in the huge bureaucracies of both the public and private sectors of the economy multiplied. Although clerical workers were formally categorized as "white collar," many of the jobs in the modern, factorylike offices were routine and low paying. Another important change in the work force was the increased participation of women. By 1979, their percentage had risen to 41.7 per cent of the total work force.

By the time of the Second World War, labor unions had achieved considerable political and economic power. In the Truman era, the AFL and the CIO won new objectives such as automatic annual wage increases, improved pensions, more paid holidays, longer vacations, and medical insurance. In December 1955, the great division that had split the labor movement in 1935 was finally healed when the AFL and CIO came together to form the AFL-CIO, with more than 15,000,000 members. George Meany, head of the AFL, became president, and Walter Reuther, president of the CIO, was elected vice-president.

By 1974, all of organized labor counted about 19,000,000 members in its ranks, but only 26.2 per cent of all nonfarm workers belonged to unions. Organized labor suffered from the *relative* decline in the number of production workers and from the migration of firms to the South, where antiunionism was strong. Also, the unions failed to make large inroads among the expanding body of professional and service personnel.

How well off were American workers in the postwar era? Real wages of factory workers increased steadily between the 1940s and 1960s. Just before the Great Depression, about 60 per cent of Americans lived at or below the subsistence level. By 1979, that figure had been reduced to 9.6 per cent. Moreover, after the Second World War there was an increase in the percentage of minority group members in the middle class and in professional and managerial positions.

Yet chronic and systematic inequities persisted. The percentage of non-whites who lived at or below the poverty level remained almost three times as high as the percentage of whites throughout the 1970s. Sex-based wage differentials also persisted, despite laws which prohibited them. Since the war, the distribution of before-tax income had changed very little: the top one fifth of American families received over 40 per cent of the income and the bottom one fifth received about 5 per cent.

3. AN AGE OF SOCIAL PROTEST

The "Silent" Generation

Most Americans from the Second World War through the 1950s accepted the direction in which their society seemed headed. This sense of well-being sprang from the relative affluence of postwar America and the rise of a mass culture which the advent of television accentuated. Social scientists who examined American social behavior in the 1950s concluded that Americans were increasingly concerned with social acceptance and less inclined to take chances. College students allegedly were concerned only with personal gain. Women had accepted the "cult of domesticity" instead of continuing the struggle for equal rights. These characterizations were certainly overdrawn and hardly applicable to the 1950s alone. But they had some basis in fact: young people did give the impression of a silent, uncommitted generation. This impression did not last long, for young people, ethnic minorities, and

The plight of such children as these, the real victims of poverty
in Appalachia, was brought to national attention in the 1960s. This
home is near Hazard, Kentucky, in Appalachia, an area largely
bypassed by economic development. (Wide World Photos)

women transformed the 1960s into a period of social protest. The roots of
their various protest movements lay precisely in the era of the so-called
silent generation.

The Afro-American Revolution: From Civil Rights to Black Power

A new movement among Afro-Americans broke the silence of the 1950s. In
fact, the drive for racial equality had never died since Reconstruction, but it
gained new momentum in the 1940s and 1950s. Blacks participated in both
the military hardships and economic gains of the Second World War, albeit
on an unequal basis. Out of that experience came rising expectations for an
end to discrimination.

Postwar prosperity enlarged the black middle class, and the courts chipped
away at the wall of legalized discrimination. In 1954, the Supreme Court
handed down an epochal decision which required an end to school segregation, and during the 1950s both Congress and Presidents took some steps to
end discrimination (see pp. 457, 459, 489, 492–94). But the pace of change
was slow. The court's rulings produced only token integration of public
schools, and other public facilities in the South remained segregated.

In 1955, nonviolent direct protest became a major tactic in the struggle
against segregation. In Montgomery, Alabama, a black woman, Rosa Parks,
refused to give up her seat on a bus to a white passenger and was arrested for

violating a city ordinance which required her to do so. This touched off a boycott against the bus line which was led by a young Baptist minister, Martin Luther King, Jr. This boycott was the beginning of a sustained effort by southern blacks to end segregation by their own efforts. Nonviolent civil disobedience was for King and others a philosophical imperative. It was also an effective tactic for dramatizing grievances. Again and again, Americans witnessed on their television sets confrontations between passive resisters and enforcers of segregationist laws.

The direct protest movement caught fire in 1960, when four black college students in Greensboro, North Carolina, sat down at a lunch counter reserved for whites and refused to move. During the following months there were many such "sit-ins" throughout the urban South. In 1961, black and white youths began taking "freedom rides" to test segregation on interstate buses in the Deep South. Violent opposition from whites attracted national attention to the freedom rides and contributed to a decision by the Interstate Commerce Commission to enforce its own regulations against segregation.

The movement gained additional momentum in 1962 and 1963. King lent his prestige and leadership to a campaign in Birmingham to end discrimination in public accommodations and employment. The movement filled the streets with peaceful protesters, young and old. Local police arrested thousands and dispersed even more with dogs and fire hoses. The spectacle forced President Kennedy to support federal legislation to bar discrimination.

Disfranchisement of southern blacks also came under fire from the civil-rights movement. Laborious efforts to register blacks to vote paid some dividends, despite violent resistance in the form of beatings and the murder of civil-rights workers. However, it was the mass demonstrations in Selma, Alabama, in 1965 that riveted national attention on the issue of the right to vote. With national support for the movement running at full tide, President Johnson endorsed voting-rights legislation which would finally end the legal disfranchisement of southern blacks.

Just as the movement seemed to be sweeping away centuries of racial discrimination, the fragile coalition of black and white reformers was jolted by the cry of "black power," and black ghettos in several cities erupted into flames. The causes of this dramatic turn of events were to be found in places as different as the rural communities of the South and the inner cities of the North.

Out of the first wave of sit-ins in 1960 came a new protest organization, the Student Nonviolent Coordinating Committee (SNCC). SNCC members participated in the sit-ins and freedom rides and then shifted their energies to the mass registration of voters in the Deep South. The resistance which these college students encountered, coupled with the failure of federal authorities to intervene, convinced many of them that King's dream of peaceful integration was unattainable. The enthusiastic response of some blacks in 1966 to the militant Stokely Carmichael's cry of "black power" stemmed from the radicalizing experience of SNCC's voter-registration drive.

Other voices, many of them outside the South, were also demanding black self-determination and the celebration of Afro-American culture. The black novelist James Baldwin predicted in *The Fire Next Time* (1962) that, unless the nation granted "the unconditional freedom of the Negro," there would be violence. Baldwin's words were prophetic. Between 1964 and 1968, the

Malcolm X speaking before a convention of Black Muslims in Chicago, February 1963. Malcolm X broke away from the "Lost Nation of Islam" in 1964 to form the Organization of African-American Unity. Possibly because of his departure from total separatism, he was shot and killed on February 21, 1965. (Wide World Photos)

nation's large cities were swept by rioting; beginning in Harlem, they spread to Los Angeles, Detroit, Cleveland, Washington, and Newark. President Johnson appointed a Commission on Civil Disorders to find the causes of the violence. Early in 1968, the commission reported:

This is our basic conclusion: Our nation is moving toward two societies, one black, one white—separate and unequal. Segregation and poverty have created in the racial ghetto a destructive environment totally unknown to most Americans.

Georgia State Senator Julian Bond, was one of the founders of the Student Nonviolent Coordinating Committee in 1960. Though blacks are still represented in token numbers, such organizations as the Southern Elections Fund in Atlanta, chaired by Bond, have been instrumental in significant election victories. (Photo © Lionel Delevingnel/ Picture Group)

Indeed, the civil-rights movement and the legislation which it spawned had left untouched the basic economic problems of the inner city. In an age of rising expectations, the lack of jobs and lack of control over the economic institutions which govern everyday life made the ghetto a tinderbox, ready to be ignited by the smallest spark.

Martin Luther King, Jr., was assassinated in April 1968. In the aftermath of that tragedy, one more wave of rioting erupted. King's objectives of gaining access to public accommodations and to the ballot box had been largely achieved. But the more stubborn problems of segregated urban housing and lack of economic opportunity for the mass of black people remained unsolved. In the 1970s, the use of busing to desegregate urban schools and of affirmative action programs to improve job opportunities for blacks triggered a backlash on the part of some whites. Many underlying causes of racial discrimination remained unresolved, but substantial gains had been made. The civil-rights movement and the drive for black identity had swept away the legal barriers of segregation and had contributed to a new awareness by

Two major figures in education, each in his own way. Professor John Hope Franklin, (Above), preeminent scholar, teacher, and author. One of the Reverend Jesse Jackson's (Right) programs developed under the educational branch of his Operation PUSH honors Professor Franklin. The John Hope Franklin Club draws high school students together to interview black celebrities and newsmakers from across the country. (Photo of Professor Franklin, courtesy of the University of Chicago, photo of Rev. Jackson © 1979 Robert J. Izzo/Picture Group

Afro-Americans of their rich cultural heritage. Also, the struggles of the 1960s brought political power to southern blacks for the first time in the twentieth century.

The Emergence of the Hispanic Community

The struggle for black equality was paralleled by the rising aspirations of Hispanic Americans. By 1979, this group numbered about 18,000,000. It included (natives and their descendants) 1,000,000 Cubans, 2,000,000 Puerto Ricans, and 15,000,000 Mexicans. Although they were linked by similar cultures, the American experience of these groups had differed in significant respects.

The vast majority of the Cubans in the United States emigrated after the rise to power of Fidel Castro in 1959. The first wave came predominantly from the middle and upper classes and saw themselves as political exiles. They became a self-conscious ethnic community, but also blended into American economic life to a considerable extent. A second wave of 100,000 came in 1980 when Castro temporarily loosened his ban on emigration.

Relatively few Puerto Ricans migrated to the mainland until the Second World War, when poor economic conditions on the island and the lure of jobs set off a large migration. Puerto Ricans, like American blacks, migrated to the cities just when the number of available jobs was declining. In the 1960s, the concentration of Puerto Ricans in New York gave them, like earlier immigrant groups, some political leverage. For example, Herman Badillo, a Puerto Rican American, was elected borough president of the Bronx in 1965.

The Mexican-American community grew rapidly in the twentieth century, despite major efforts in the 1930s and 1950s to expel Mexicans suspected of being illegal immigrants. The federal *bracero* program brought in over 5,000,000 Mexican workers on a temporary basis between 1942 and 1964, mainly for seasonal labor in agriculture. A much larger number of *mojados* (illegal aliens) immigrated after the 1940s.

Ninety per cent of the Mexican-American people, called Chicanos, remained clustered in the Southwest. There, particularly since the 1940s, Chicano protest movements sought to preserve the Hispanic cultural heritage and to combat various forms of discrimination. As with blacks, rising expectations created a new sense of purpose, even militancy, as was evidenced in the 1960s by the emergence of groups which demanded the return of lands seized long ago from Mexican Americans in violation of the Treaty of Guadalupe Hidalgo.

The most influential Mexican-American leader of the 1960s and 1970s was César Chavez, who formed a union of California agricultural laborers, the United Farm Workers, in 1962. Chavez used strikes and national boycotts against the fruit- and vegetable-raising agribusinesses and won a contract with California grape growers in 1970.

By the 1970s, Mexican Americans were the fastest growing ethnic group in the nation. With roots in Hispanic and Indian cultures, the Chicano spirit was taking its place along with black pride as a major manifestation of the new ethnicity in American life.

Apprehension of Mexicans attempting to immigrate to the United States. U.S. Border Patrol agents used 2-way radios and a helicopter for this arrest in San Ysidro, California. (Copyright © 1980 by Len Lahman)

César Chavez, the charismatic farmworker organizer and human rights activist, delivers a speech at a rally. (United Farm Workers of America, Photograph by Cathy Murphy.)

Student Protest

The struggle for racial equality helped to generate the student movement of the 1960s known as the "New Left." These protesters shared with the civil-rights workers an idealistic commitment to righting the injustices of American society. The movement was self-consciously youth-oriented. The youths in question were part of the huge postwar generation, who, by the 1960s, were extending their education (and their "youth") beyond high school in unprecedented numbers.

Although the New Left movement could attract mass attendance at rallies, probably no more than 5 per cent of college students were directly involved in New Left organizations. However, the movement was concentrated in the nation's more prestigious universities. At first, the movement viewed universities as havens from which to attack injustice. But student protesters came to view the universities themselves as part of the oppressive "system." This transformation occurred first in the events which shook the University of California at Berkeley in 1964 and 1965. In the fall of 1964, the administration blocked student efforts to disseminate political materials on the campus. Student radicals mobilized a mass protest and used the confrontation tactics of the civil-rights movement. The protests, which were sparked by the specific issue of freedom of speech, escalated to a more general challenge. American universities, the dissidents said, had become impersonal, socially irresponsible institutions, which served the needs of the "military-industrial complex" more than they did the educational needs of the students.

Over the next half decade, the battle of Berkeley was fought again on campuses across the country, most notably at Columbia University. In 1968, disputes over issues, which ranged from Columbia's involvement in military research to its relations with the adjacent black community, led to a bloody protest.

Beginning in 1968, the New Left's principal institution, the Students for a Democratic Society (SDS), was splintered by ideological factionalism. Its vision of a student-worker coalition was in shambles; the SDS, confronted with governmental persecution, disintegrated into competing bands of ideologues and urban guerrillas.

The New Left's ideology overlapped with the movement to end American involvement in Vietnam. When President Johnson escalated American involvement in the war in 1965, there were teach-ins and campus rallies, followed by massive public demonstrations, most notably in Chicago in 1968 and Washington in 1969. In 1970, after the American incursion into Cambodia, there was one last wave of campus demonstrations and strikes (see p. 533−35).

The Women's Movement

Like the civil-rights crusade, the women's movement was spurred by profound social and economic changes since the 1940s. The popular literature of the 1950s had nurtured a "cult of domesticity" which conditioned women to accept passive roles as wives and mothers rather than to challenge men for positions in the world of work and politics. Yet, by the 1960s, fully 40 per cent of all adult women had entered the work force, including half of those with school-age children. Middle-class boys and girls who grew up in postwar America were more likely than their forebears to have a "working" mother. By the 1970s, that cohort of young people had been conditioned to accept even greater changes in the traditional role of the mother and father.

In addition to changes in the status and expectations of many women, there appeared a cogent feminist assessment of sexual inequality and a demand for change. That assessment began in earnest with the publication of Betty Friedan's *The Feminine Mystique* in 1963. The women's movement which emerged in the mid-1960s was far from monolithic. The National Organization for Women (NOW) was founded in 1966, with Friedan as president. A moderate reformist group, NOW fought institutionalized discrimination and fostered "consciousness raising" among women and men. Other participants in the movement sought not just an end to formal discrimination but also a revolution in the relationships between men and women. Marriage and the family, they argued, were a form of slavery from which women had to liberate themselves.

The women's movement had a substantial political impact in the 1960s. Many states liberalized abortion statutes and laws which governed property rights of women. The federal government took some steps to end sex-based discrimination. The Equal Rights Amendment to the Constitution (ERA), which had been tied up in a congressional committee for forty-seven years, was finally passed by Congress in 1970–1971. However, the amendment still fell three states short of adoption on the extended deadline for ratification, June 30, 1982.

Resistance to the ERA from women as well as men, along with the controversy over legalized abortion in the 1970s and 1980s, demonstrated the complexities of the liberation movement. In the 1960s, that movement had primarily attracted white, middle-class college students and graduates. Although the movement encountered apathy and resistance from many people in the 1970s, its base of support expanded dramatically. The struggle over the ERA educated many women on how to use political instrumentalities and economic pressure.

4. THE SEARCH FOR IDENTITY IN A MASS SOCIETY

From Youth Culture to Counterculture

Social and political protest was by no means the sole source of personal and cultural identity during the unsettling postwar era. Amid the pervasive mass culture of the television age, there flourished a diversity of life-styles, religions, and ethnic communities. At its worst, this diversity bred polarization and bigotry; at its best, it nurtured a robust cultural pluralism. The particular rebelliousness of youth in the 1960s was expressed not only through the political upheavals of the decade but also in cultural terms—in a rejection of prevailing values. Popular music was the principal transmitter of the youth-oriented cultural revolution. Beginning early in the 1950s, many young Americans adopted the rock-and-roll style which fused elements of black rhythm-and-blues with white southern folk music. The new music suited a populous generation of teenagers who were increasingly conscious of themselves as a cultural minority. Whether the new popular singers were black, like Chuck Berry and Otis Redding, or white, like Elvis Presley and Jerry Lee Lewis, parents and teachers found their stage movements and lyrics very threatening to moral standards.

In the early 1960s, folk music, although a less threatening genre than rock-and-roll, served as a vehicle for social protest. Bob Dylan's "The Times They Are a-Changing" expressed the growing alienation of many young people.

Rock-and-roll again dominated popular music after 1964 when the Beatles burst on the American scene. The message which they conveyed was not one of political radicalism, but the Beatles did express an infectious cultural rebelliousness. That was even truer of groups such as the Rolling Stones, the Jefferson Airplane, and the Doors, whose overt sexuality and identification with the drug culture made them the symbols of a small but highly publicized counterculture. Public expressions of this culture included rock music, long hair, communal living, sexual promiscuity, and the use of drugs. Unlike the New Left, the counterculture reflected a withdrawal from public action. The admonition to "tune in, turn on, and drop out" was heeded by many who despaired of reforming the "system."

This "hippie" culture which emerged in 1965 and 1966 was too fragile to survive the combined assaults of repression by authorities, coverage by the news media, and commercialization of its life-style. The counterculture faded from public view after the late 1960s. Yet this cultural rebellion altered the life-styles of millions of persons who had not been part of the counterculture itself. By the early 1970s, long hair, blue jeans, and the use of marijuana had become commonplace.

Religion in Modern America

There have been two periods of intensified religious fervor in America since the Second World War. Between 1940 and 1955, membership in churches and synagogues rose from 43 per cent to 61 per cent of the total population. The religiosity of the 1950s involved an increase in church membership but did not alter traditional *forms* of religious expression. Among evangelical Protestants, growth was spurred by itinerant revivalists such as Billy Graham.

Many church leaders were alarmed by what they described as unfortunate side effects of this renewed enthusiasm. Organized religion, some feared, deified the American way of life. However, the tradition of the Social Gospel also remained alive after the Second World War. During the 1960s, religious leaders of many persuasions participated in movements for social justice, in particular the civil-rights crusade. Their social action was accompanied by a renewed ecumenical spirit which swept through American Christianity, partially as an outgrowth of the Second Vatican Council, which Popes John XXIII and Paul VI convened in Rome in 1962 and 1965.

In the 1970s, there was a wave of interest in eastern mystical religions, and new sects emerged, as did a host of introspective "human potential groups" which functioned more or less as religions. Within established Christian bodies, ranging from Catholic and Episcopalian to evangelical Protestant churches, there appeared charismatic movements which featured speaking in tongues and faith healing. One other feature of the religious revival of the 1970s was increased political activism, on religious grounds, for culturally conservative causes and candidates. Militant lobbying campaigns were mobilized in opposition to legalized abortion, the ERA, and aspects of modern school curricula, particularly sex education and the teaching of evolution.

The New Ethnicity

The persistence of ethnic identity in modern America is perhaps surprising, given the forces of assimilation which have been at work even among relatively recent immigrant groups. Nevertheless, ethnic ties persisted, and there were even renewed signs of ethnic militancy and conflict in the 1970s.

Native Americans sought to renew their tribal identities, which had been weakened in the 1950s by yet another effort at assimilation. Some militant Indian groups fought for the return of tribal lands.

A sense of community remained strong among many white ethnic groups, including those from southern and eastern Europe. In the 1970s, several of these groups clashed with blacks in northern cities over such issues as school busing, open housing, and job quotas. Even a recent immigrant group, the Vietnamese, found themselves in conflict. More than 100,000 Vietnamese were resettled in the United States after 1975, and a second wave arrived in 1979. These new arrivals sometimes encountered hostility and even violence.

The new awakening of ethnicity in the 1970s led Americans to fill the reading rooms of libraries and archives in search of information about long-lost ancestors. In the 1980s, ethnicity remained a vital component of self-understanding for many Americans.

The Crisis of Identity and the Renewal of Community

The term "identity crisis" is, appropriately, a creation of the postwar era. Erik Erikson, a psychologist, applied it to the personal anxieties which accompany the transition from one stage of human development to another. The concept could also be applied to much of American society during the tumultuous postwar epoch.

Much of the popular literature of the time voiced longings for personal identity and freedom in a world governed by large and impersonal forces. Norman Mailer's powerful novel of the Second World War, *The Naked and the Dead* (1948); J. D. Salinger's story of rebellious adolescence, *The Catcher in the Rye* (1951); and Joseph Heller's *Catch-22* (1960) all described a human condition in which freedom is circumscribed and personal identity is impossible to maintain in the "sane" world.

The search for selfhood in this kind of world has given rise to what some scholars have called a "psychiatric world view," one characterized by constant self-examination and self-doubt and by a preoccupation with self-gratification in the present moment. Not all Americans would agree with such a gloomy assessment. Many were either more satisfied with their own lives or more certain about the objects of their dissatisfaction than such an analysis would suggest. Furthermore, many Americans, although no longer optimistic about saving the whole world from its various maladies, were busily engaged in efforts of reform and reconstruction on a more modest scale.

In the 1970s, participants in a "neighborhood movement," which one observer has called "a kind of invisible saga of the decade," were engaged in cooperative action of all sorts. The neighborhood movement included groups engaged in such disparate activities as opposing school busing, encouraging interracial cooperation, fighting governmental and corporate bureaucracies, and resisting increases in property taxes. The direction and impact of this movement for the remainder of the twentieth century are impossible to predict, but its vitality is a hopeful sign for the future of democracy at the grass roots in America.

SUGGESTED READINGS

The standard reference for up-to-date social and economic data is the *American Almanac* (formerly *Statistical Abstracts of the United States*), which is published annually. See also summary volumes of the decennial census.

The scholarship on the American family is voluminous. See especially Kenneth Keniston *et al.*, *All Our Children: The American Family under Pressure* (1977), and Joseph F. Kett, *Rites of Passage: Adolescence in America, 1790 to the Present* (1979).

Economic trends can be followed in W. Elliot Brownlee, *Dynamics of Ascent: A History of the American Economy* (1979). The structure of economic life is discussed in Alfred D. Chandler, Jr., *The Visible Hand: The Managerial Revolution in American Business* (1977), and John Kenneth Galbraith, *The New Industrial State* (2nd ed., 1972). The underside of economic development is described in an influential study, Michael Harrington, *The Other America: Poverty in the United States* (1963). Elting E. Morison, *From Know-How to Nowhere: The Development of American Technology* (1974), is useful.

Changing sex roles and the women's movement are discussed in William H. Chafe, *The American Woman: Her Changing Social, Economic, and Political Roles, 1920 – 1970* (1972); Betty Friedan, *The Feminine Mystique* (1963); and Peter Filene, *Him/Her/Self: Sex Roles in Modern America* (1975).

Of the general treatments of Afro-American history, the best is John Hope Franklin, *From Slavery to Freedom* (5th ed., 1978). Important studies of black leaders and black movements include Martin Luther King.

Jr., *Stride toward Freeedom* (1958); David L. Lewis, *King: A Critical Biography* (2nd ed., 1978); and Peter Goldman, *The Death and Life of Malcolm X* (1973). The urban upheavals of the 1960s are analyzed in Joe R. Feagin and Harlan Hahn, *Ghetto Riots: The Politics of Violence in American Cities* (1973).

The Hispanic experience in America is summarized in James S. Olsen, *The Ethnic Dimension in American History* (1979). The largest segment of the nation's Hispanic population is the subject of Matt S. Meier and Feliciano Rivera, *The Chicanos: A History of Mexican Americans* (1972).

The search for the "American character" has not lacked its chroniclers. David Reisman, *The Lonely Crowd* (1950), and W. H. Whyte, Jr., *The Organization Man* (1956), decried the conformity of the 1950s. William L. O'Neill, *Coming Apart: An Informal History of American Life in the 1960s* (1971), gives a good account of the counterculture. In *The Culture of Narcissism: American Life in an Age of Diminishing Expectations* (1979), Christopher Lasch describes a debilitating cultural malaise, but for a contrary view of the 1970s, see Harry C. Boyte, *The Backyard Revolution: Understanding the New Citizen Movement* (1980).

The best general treatment of religion after the Second World War is found in Sidney E. Ahlstrom, *A Religious History of the American People* (1972). Literary trends can be followed in Robert E. Spiller *et al.*, *Literary History of the United States,* 3 vols. (1963), and Alfred Kazin, *Bright Book of Life: American Novelists and Storytellers from Hemingway to Mailer* (1973).

CHAPTER 30
THE MIDDLE OF THE ROAD UNDER EISENHOWER

1. THE MIDDLE ROAD

Eisenhower and the Presidency

The election of Dwight David Eisenhower in 1952 proved that the American people still loved military heroes. Eisenhower was born in Texas in 1890 and grew up in Kansas. His military career culminated in leadership of the forces which defeated Germany on the western front in 1945. No American was more popular than "Ike" at the end of the Second World War. Eisenhower remained in the army as Chief of Staff until 1948 and three years later was called back into service as the first commander of NATO forces in Europe. He resigned in June 1952 to campaign for the Republican presidential nomination. The American people elected him because they admired him as a person who stood above ordinary political conflict. They also trusted his judgment in an era when charges of corruption and even treason reverberated throughout the land.

Eisenhower was not an active domestic leader. He wasted opportunities for constructive leadership unparalleled since the Great Depression. He resisted appeals to take action in critical areas ranging from civil rights to air and water pollution. He refused to recommend governmental action to counter industrial stagnation, or to relieve hard-core unemployment. And he declined to change the Cold War assumptions which governed foreign policy. He had at his disposal a reservoir of goodwill such as few Presidents ever possessed. His presidency coincided with a period of general prosperity. Yet Eisenhower was convinced that Roosevelt and Truman had concentrated too much power in their own hands; hence, he never tried to establish personal leadership over Congress, nor even over his own party. Moreover, Eisenhower maintained the style of leadership which he had employed so successfully as Allied commander—that of conciliating differing points of view rather than of initiating programs. But the most important reason for Eisenhower's failure as an active leader was his fundamental lack of interest in American politics. Politicians bored him. He far preferred golf games with businessmen. Therefore, he failed to rebuild the Republican party, although associates urged him to lead the progressive and internationalist wing which had obtained his nomination in 1952.

Nevertheless, Eisenhower made some important contributions. In foreign policy, he guided the government through a series of crises without resort to violence and maintained continuity with the American diplomatic policies of the 1940s. He helped to heal deep wounds in the body politic by his own decency and fair play. Finally, Eisenhower helped to consolidate and strengthen the New Deal's economic and social programs. Some Democrats rather gloomily predicted that Republicans, once in power, would try to turn the clock back to the 1920s. However, throughout his eight years as President, Eisenhower tried to follow domestic policies which would appeal to the moderate majorities in both parties. The evidence shows that Eisenhower protected New Deal and Fair Deal programs for human welfare and even extended some. His "dynamic conservatism" implied caution in financial affairs, not the use of those policies to choke established social-welfare programs.

Promises and Performances

As a candidate in 1952, Eisenhower had proclaimed a great crusade to clean up the "mess" in Washington. Yet he arrived in Washington only to discover that his predecessor had thoroughly cleaned up whatever "mess" existed. Eisenhower did not mention the crusade again, particularly since he suffered embarrassment from minor scandals in his own administration. Eisenhower also talked much in 1952 about the evils of centralization in government. However, he took not a single effective step as President toward diffusing federal power. The presidential candidate in 1952 discoursed on "fiscal integrity." And yet the federal deficit in 1959 bulged to the largest in American peacetime history to that time. There was much Republican talk in 1952 about cleaning the Communists out of Washington. Yet frantic investigations discovered only one Communist on the federal payroll, a typesetter in the Government Printing Office.

One promise—to reverse the tide of governmental participation in business —Eisenhower carried out to a considerable degree. He quickly ended price and wage controls imposed during the Korean War. In 1953, Eisenhower obtained authority from Congress to sell government-owned synthetic rubber manufacturing plants to private industry, and in 1954 he obtained amendment of the Atomic Energy Act to permit private industry to participate in the development and use of atomic energy.

These actions passed without much notice. What did stir great controversy were Eisenhower's efforts to halt governmental development of natural resources. These efforts led to three major conflicts:

1. *Offshore oil lands.* The discovery of vast oil deposits off the coasts of California and the Gulf states raised the question of who owned these coastal areas. Twice, Congress passed bills giving title to the states. Truman vetoed them both. Eisenhower signed a compromise measure in 1953 which transferred title to submerged coastal lands to the states, but only within their historical boundaries.

2. *The development of Hell's Canyon.* Between 1953 and 1955, a battle raged between the Idaho Power Company and advocates of public-power development. The power company wanted to build three dams in the Hell's Canyon area of the Snake River. Advocates of public power wanted one large dam to be built and operated by the federal government. Eisenhower supported the power company, which won approval of its plans in 1955.

3. *The Tennessee Valley Authority.* In 1953, Eisenhower referred to the TVA as an example of "creeping socialism." Although he later retracted the remark, it revealed his basic opposition to governmental development when private utilities could do the job. In 1954, he directed the Atomic Energy Commission to permit private power companies to supply 600,000 kilowatts of power to the TVA. The opposition grew so strong, and the evidence of irregularities in the contract negotiations so pervasive, that the contract was canceled.

One of the most stubborn problems facing the Eisenhower administration was the decline in farm income which occurred after 1952. Between then and 1960, farm income fell 23 per cent, while the national income as a whole increased by 43 per cent. The most important reason for this agricultural distress was a huge increase in production resulting from the use of machinery, hybrid seed, and fertilizers.

Farm spokesmen pleaded for maintenance of high price supports and suggested that the government should use surpluses to combat world hunger. In contrast, the Secretary of Agriculture, Ezra Taft Benson, favored low and flexible price supports. The government, Benson insisted, must stop paying farmers to overproduce. This tug of war continued throughout the Eisenhower era. The Benson program drove more and more farmers out of the GOP.

Neither side had its way completely by the end of the 1950s. Price supports dropped from 90 to 65 per cent of parity, and Congress initiated programs to use American agricultural surpluses abroad. But the problem remained. Farmers produced more every year, and farm income continued to decline, in spite of federal subsidies.

As we have said, Eisenhower never contemplated turning back the clock of economic and social reform. Repeal of the New Deal-Fair Deal laws would not have been possible anyway, for the Democrats controlled both houses of Congress from 1955 to 1961, and conservatives did not have a working majority in the Republican-controlled Congress from 1953 to 1955. The President and Congress agreed to increase Social Security benefits and broaden the system to include 10,000,000 new workers. In 1955, a new minimum-wage law raised the minimum from seventy-five cents to $1 an hour. Greater disagreement took place between the two branches of government over public housing. Democrats wanted generous measures and were disappointed when forced to accept administration bills. However, between

1953 and 1961, the federal government spent some $1.3 billion for slum clearance and public housing.

In health and medical welfare, as in housing, Eisenhower carried forward the programs begun by Roosevelt and Truman. In 1953, Eisenhower signed a bill (proposed by Truman) which established the Department of Health, Education, and Welfare. Although Eisenhower opposed Truman's plan for national health insurance, measures which provided federal funds for medical research and hospital construction were adopted throughout the 1950s.

The Civil-Rights Crusade Gains Momentum

Truman, who failed to win civil-rights legislation, used his executive power to fight segregation. Eisenhower carried this program forward, but with no great enthusiasm. Only Congress could strengthen civil rights by law, and southern senators prevented civil-rights bills even from coming to a vote before 1957. The log jam was finally broken in that year when Lyndon B. Johnson of Texas, Democratic majority leader in the Senate, pushed through a limited bill which sought to protect black Americans' right to vote in the southern states. Johnson had national political ambitions, a genuine wish to help poor blacks and Mexican Americans, and a genius for persuading fellow legislators to vote his way.

The Civil Rights Act of 1957 created a Commission on Civil Rights with authority to investigate violations of civil rights. The act authorized federal courts to issue injunctions and begin civil contempt proceedings to end discrimination. The Civil Rights Act of 1957, although limited in scope, was the first federal civil-rights legislation passed since 1875. In 1960, Congress adopted a second bill to provide additional protection for blacks who attempted to vote.

Beginnings of the Judicial Revolution under the Warren Court

In 1953, Eisenhower unwittingly ushered in a new era in the history of the Supreme Court by appointing Earl Warren as Chief Justice. It was, Eisenhower later said, the "biggest damnfool mistake I ever made." The appointment, however, appeared, in 1953, to be eminently safe. Warren, a Republican in predominantly Democratic California, had won a reputation as the most popular governor in the history of the state. As state Attorney General in 1941, he had approved the internment of the Japanese Americans. Warren had also opposed reapportionment plans which would have given large cities representation in the legislature consistent with their population. Finally, Warren had accused the Truman administration of "coddling" Communists.

However, Warren's record masked a burning passion for social justice. Moreover, Warren was a skillful politician who used his personal moral force to persuade the court to follow his lead. Consequently, from 1953 until his retirement in 1969, Warren forged a liberal majority on the supreme bench which made the court the most important instrumentality for political and social change in the United States during the 1950s and 1960s.

The Warren Court moved in cases relating to internal security to restore traditional constitutional protection to individuals. In 1957, the court struck

The United States Supreme Court in 1962. Front row, left to right: William O. Douglas, Hugo Black, Earl Warren, Felix Frankfurter, Tom C. Clark. Back row: Potter Stewart, John M. Harlan, William J. Brennan, Jr., and the newly appointed Byron White. Three of the major figures behind the early landmark decisions of what is called the "Warren Court" were Justices Douglas, Black, and Frankfurter, all appointed by President Roosevelt in the late 1930s. The judicial revolution that Warren presided over and helped to expand during his sixteen years as Chief Justice involved critical cases in the areas of race relations, free speech, fairness in the criminal justice system, and fairness in legislative apportionment. (Historical Pictures Service, Inc., Chicago)

boldly in defense of civil rights in Yates *v.* United States. In this decision, the court overturned the decision in the Dennis case of 1951, and in effect invalidated the Smith Act.

The Supreme Court, from 1944 to 1953, had already begun to undercut the legal bases of segregation. The court had ruled, first, that blacks could not be excluded from state primary elections on account of race; second, that persons could not be excluded from jury service on account of race; third, that so-called restrictive covenants (agreements by home buyers not to sell them to persons of certain races and religions) were unenforceable; and, fourth, that segregation was illegal in the District of Columbia, in interstate transportation, and in public recreational facilities.

The Supreme Court, under steady pressure from lawyers representing the NAACP, had also begun to reexamine the constitutionality of enforced segregation in public schools and colleges. For example, in 1950, the court had ruled in Sweatt *v.* Painter that a recently established state law school for blacks in Texas could never provide training equal to that offered by the Law

School of the University of Texas and had ordered the latter to admit the claimant, Herman M. Sweatt. However, the court refused to overturn Plessy v. Ferguson, the bastion of legal segregation (see p. 318).

However, the day of reckoning on the "separate but equal" doctrine could not have been postponed for long. That day came when Brown v. Board of Education of Topeka and several related cases, all involving segregation in public schools, came before the court in 1953. The Chief Justice read the unanimous decision in the Brown case on May 17, 1954. It decreed that compulsory segregation in public schools on account of race violated the Fourteenth Amendment's guarantee of equal rights to all citizens. Segregated schools, Warren said, specifically repudiating Plessy v. Ferguson, were inherently unequal because they stamped black children as inferior. It was a landmark in American constitutional history. A year later the Supreme Court clarified the application of Brown v. Board of Education and instructed

Elizabeth Eckford, fifteen-year-old black girl, braves the insults of white students as she marches down a line of National Guardsmen, who blocked the main entrances of Little Rock's Central High School and would not let her enter, September 1957. (Wide World Photos)

federal district courts to require local authorities to move with "all deliberate speed" toward desegregation of all public schools. In practice, the rate of change was more deliberate than speedy. Nevertheless, school desegregation was fairly well accomplished in the District of Columbia and the Border States by 1957. By then, a beginning toward school desegregation had been made in North Carolina, Tennessee, Arkansas, and Texas. However, massive resistance developed at the same time in Virginia and the states of the Deep South. Their legislatures denounced the Supreme Court's rulings and enacted laws which closed their public schools if desegregation was forced upon them. The first outright defiance of the federal courts occurred in Little Rock, Arkansas. In September 1957, Governor Orval E. Faubus used the National Guard to prevent desegregation of the high school. However, Eisenhower, who privately deplored the Brown decision, could not brook such defiance of federal authority. He called the National Guard of Arkansas into federal service and sent in regular army troops to reopen the school. For the first time since Radical Reconstruction, the federal government demonstrated that blacks' constitutional rights would be protected by military might, if necessary. By the end of the Eisenhower administration in 1961, only South Carolina, Alabama, and Mississippi still maintained all-out resistance to any desegregation. But elsewhere in the South the actual pace of change remained painfully slow.

2. THE "NEW LOOK" IN FOREIGN POLICY

Secretary Dulles and the "New Look"

From 1953 until 1959, John Foster Dulles was one of the most controversial Secretaries of State in American history. Dulles was supremely confident both of his abilities and of his moral righteousness. Dulles, nephew of Wilson's Secretary of State, Robert Lansing, had played a role in American foreign policy during the Paris Peace Conference and between the two world wars. Dulles had long believed that a monolithic "world Communist movement" represented, in his words, "an unholy alliance of Marx's communism and Russia's imperialism."

Some of the controversy which Dulles provoked arose because of his flare for catchy slogans. He talked about the liberation of "captive peoples" under Soviet domination and about the use of "massive retaliation"—presumably nuclear—against the Soviet Union or Communist China if they committed serious aggression. In some cases, Dulles talked about carrying the country to the "brink of war" (giving rise to the term "brinkmanship") in order to preserve the peace of the world.

Dulles' slogans obscured the central facts about the foreign policies of the Eisenhower administration. First, Eisenhower, not Dulles, made almost all the important decisions. However, the two men shared the fundamental beliefs that underlay American foreign policy in this era—commitment to a continuation of the Cold War, certainty of America's moral superiority in this conflict, and the precedence of European affairs over problems elsewhere. Second, Eisenhower and Dulles carried forward policies initiated by Roosevelt and Truman. Third, Dulles, in spite of his bombast, was a

As U.S. delegates to the United Nations, John Foster Dulles and
Eleanor Roosevelt here listen to Russian Foreign Minister Andrei
Vishinsky call Dulles one of the nine leading "warmongers" in
the United States, September 9, 1947. Despite Dulles' gift for
forceful speech, he later proved to be capable of both restraint and
diplomacy as Secretary of State. Eleanor Roosevelt's distinguished
service as delegate to the UN included a major role in drafting
and securing the adoption of the Universal Declaration of Human
Rights in 1948. After she resigned her post in 1952, she promoted
the work of the UN and other causes in her constant travels over the
next decade. (Acme Photo)

resourceful diplomat, and his accomplishments were considerable. Among
them was the protection of Eisenhower from political criticism from the
Republican right wing.

The Korean Armistice and New Crises in the Far East

The first task in foreign policy which faced the Eisenhower administration
was the conclusion of the war in Korea. The Chinese and North Koreans had
opened armistice negotiations with General Ridgway in the summer of 1951
and then broken them off in October 1952. Dulles sent a message to the
Chinese leaders that the United States would open a wholesale offensive,
perhaps against China as well as North Korea, if the North Koreans did not
bargain in good faith. Negotiations were indeed reopened, and the comba-
tants finally signed an armistice at Panmunjom, Korea, on July 27, 1953. It
provided for the return of prisoners on a voluntary basis and established a

demilitarized zone along the battle line not far from the thirty-eighth parallel.

At the same time, another crisis was brewing in Indochina. Vietnamese Communists under Ho Chi Minh had been leading an independence movement against French colonial authority since 1946. The United States had been providing the French with financial aid and supplies since 1950. In the spring of 1954, the French, on the verge of a major defeat, appealed to the United States for direct military support. Dulles, supported by Vice-President Nixon, favored American air strikes against the insurgents (called Viet Minh). With public opinion clearly lukewarm for American military participation, Eisenhower vetoed plans for the air strike at Dien Bien Phu, a French fortification in northern Vietnam under siege by the Viet Minh. After the fall of Dien Bien Phu, France agreed to withdraw from all of Indochina. Terms were arranged at a Foreign Ministers' conference already in progress at Geneva in May 1954. Dulles left the meeting when it became evident that Vietnam, one of the new independent states created out of what had been French Indochina, would be divided—temporarily, according to the terms of the agreement—between a Communist North and a non-Communist South.

Dulles, who feared that all of Asia might soon fall under Communist control, called a conference of non-Communist nations to meet in Manila. Delegates from Australia, Great Britain, France, New Zealand, Pakistan, the Philippines, Thailand, and the United States signed the Manila Pact on September 8, 1954, which created the Southeast Asia Treaty Organization (SEATO). Like the North Atlantic Treaty, the Manila Pact pledged joint action in the event of aggression against any member nation, and it provided special protection for Cambodia, Laos, and South Vietnam.

German Rearmament and the First Summit Conference

Just as crises shook the Far East, so a controversy in the West threatened to split NATO. It involved the question of whether to rearm Germany and incorporate this former enemy state into the western defense system. Truman had made such a suggestion as early as 1950. France, Italy, Belgium, the Netherlands, Luxembourg, and West Germany had agreed in 1952 to form a European Defense Community (EDC). The EDC featured a tightly integrated western European army with German contingents.

The French Chamber of Deputies balked at German rearmament. Dulles entered the fray by warning that French refusal to ratify the EDC treaty might force the United States to reconsider its support of NATO. The threat only further angered the French who rejected the EDC treaty again in August 1954.

A solution proposed by the British Foreign Secretary, Anthony Eden, resulted in the signing of the Paris Pact in October 1954. In this treaty, the western powers gave full sovereignty to the Federal Republic of Germany. West Germany was admitted to NATO and permitted an army of 500,000 men to serve under NATO command. Finally, the United States and Britain promised to keep troops on the continent so long as the Brussels Treaty Organization wanted them to remain.

The Soviet dictator, Stalin, died in 1953. For a time, the new rulers of the Soviet Union seemed to want to reduce the tensions of the Cold War.

Eisenhower accepted suggestions for a summit conference. Like Roosevelt, Eisenhower believed that he could accomplish much by personal diplomacy. The conference met at Geneva in July 1955, in an atmosphere of strained cordiality. Although the chiefs of state (of the United States, Russia, Great Britain, and France) adopted no concrete measures to end the Cold War, they did refer four major European problems to their Foreign Ministers for further discussion. However, the Foreign Ministers' conference broke up without a single agreement.

3. POLITICS STILL IN MODERATION

1956: The Eisenhower Landslide

Two events caused Democrats to look to the presidential election of 1956 with increasing confidence. The first was the election in 1954 of a Congress with small Democratic majorities in both houses. The second event shocked the country. On September 24, 1955, Eisenhower suffered a heart attack. Observers assumed that he would not run again. However, the President's recovery was almost complete by 1956, and he announced that he would be a candidate for reelection. The President and Vice-President Nixon were renominated by acclamation. Adlai E. Stevenson easily won the Democratic nomination on the first ballot. Senator Estes Kefauver of Tennessee, Stevenson's chief preconvention rival, obtained Stevenson's endorsement as his running mate.

Both parties conducted short, intensive campaigns with much use of television. The Republicans had the advantage of Eisenhower's enormous popularity and of continuing prosperity. Democratic hopes lay in better local organization and in support from labor and blacks. In the final analysis, the campaign was an unevenly matched popularity contest. The differences on issues were narrow, indeed.

Eisenhower's victory was never in doubt, and the explosion of war in the Middle East in late October (see pp. 500–501) turned many wavering voters to the President's side. He carried forty-one states to Stevenson's seven. It was an endorsement, however, only of Eisenhower and not of his party. The Democrats actually increased their majorities in Congress.

Crises on the Economic and National Security Fronts

The most urgent problem confronting Eisenhower and Congress was a business recession which threatened to turn into a full-fledged depression. It began with a drop in the stock market in the summer of 1957. The recession deepened because of a cutback in spending for new plants and machinery and a worldwide decline in trade. By January 1958, unemployment in the United States had reached a postwar high of nearly 4,500,000.

The President and Congress agreed that the government should act to reverse the slump. Gone were the days when Americans would accept depressions as inevitable. However, sharp disagreement existed over the weapons to be used. Many Democrats urged drastic tax reductions and large federal spending to increase consumer purchasing power. However, Eisenhower and his Council of Economic Advisers insisted on a more limited program of increased credit, encouragement to home construction, increase in Social Security benefits, extension of unemployment insurance payments, and some expansion of federal spending for construction projects. The administration had its way, mainly because Senate Majority Leader Lyndon Johnson also favored moderate policies.

By May 1958, the economic downturn had ended, and the economy was growing at normal speed again by the beginning of 1959. However, some Democrats pointed to a retarded growth rate in the 1950s and to persistently high unemployment of about 6 per cent as proof that stronger countercyclical devices should have been used.

The development of missiles had been proceeding in Russia and the United States since the end of the Second World War, and Americans believed that they were far ahead in the race for new weapons. Then, in October 1957, Russia launched *Sputnik I*, the first earth-launched satellite. Americans suddenly realized that the Russians possessed rockets powerful enough to bombard the United States with nuclear weapons. The Russians had exploded a hydrogen bomb in 1953, not long after the first American hydrogen bomb had been detonated. The launching of the first American satellite, *Explorer I*, in January 1958 did not quiet American fears. And Democrats and aerospace corporations encouraged fear of a "missile gap" between the United States and the Soviet Union.

In January 1958, Eisenhower presented to Congress the largest peacetime budget in American history—nearly $74 billion. Congress increased this sum to more than $76 billion and added $4 billion more for rocket and missile development and the conquest of outer space. In addition, at Eisenhower's request, the lawmakers amended the Atomic Energy Act of 1946 to permit the sharing of atomic secrets with America's allies; created a National Aeronautics and Space Administration (NASA) to coordinate research and development; and adopted the National Defense Education Act, which granted funds to schools for special programs in science, mathematics, and foreign languages.

Alaska and Hawaii were especially important to American defenses. Bases in Alaska stood guard to signal possible attacks across the Arctic. The great naval base at Pearl Harbor controlled the Pacific to Formosa Strait. Nevertheless, Alaskan and Hawaiian pleas for statehood had repeatedly died in Congress; but now the rocket and jet plane had annihilated the "too far from the mainland" argument, and both were admitted: Alaska in January 1959 and Hawaii in August of that year.

1958: The Democratic Landslide and Its Aftermath

Three developments in 1958 caused a Democratic congressional landslide. First, a congressional committee discovered that Eisenhower's chief assistant, Sherman Adams, had been receiving gifts from a businessman in return for favors rendered. Second, Republicans made open-shop laws the main issues in many states and thus aroused the vigorous opposition of organized labor. Third, farmers blamed Republicans for the Agricultural Act of 1958, which cut price supports. The resulting landslide victory gave Deomcrats two-to-one majorities in both houses of Congress.

Democrats who expected to ride roughshod over the President in the Eighty-sixth Congress, which met in January 1959, underestimated Eisen-

This ceremony took place in front of Iolani Palace, the seat of
Hawaii's government in March 1959 after Congress took action that
would make Hawaii the fiftieth state within five months. Honor
Guards of the Army, Navy, Marines, Coast Guard, and Air Force
lined up with flags while spectators joined in the National
Anthem. (Wide World Photos)

hower's skill, popularity, and veto power. By the end of the first session of
the new Congress, the President could claim as many victories as could his
Democratic opponents.

The most important legislation of the last two years of the Eisenhower era
was the Labor-Management Reporting and Disclosure, or Landrum-Griffin,
Act of 1959. It grew out of the recommendations of a special Senate
committee headed by Senator John F. Kennedy of Massachusetts which had
been probing into corruption in some labor unions, especially the Teamsters'
Union. The new law required union officials to submit detailed financial
reports to the Secretary of Labor, established other safeguards against union
corruption, and strengthened previous restrictions on secondary boycotts and
picketing.

4. TO THE SECOND SUMMIT AND BACK AGAIN

Middle Eastern Crises and Threats to Western Unity

The last four years of the Eisenhower administration were full of reversals
for the United States abroad. Even in Latin America, developments turned

unfavorable after 1955. Vice-President Nixon's goodwill tour of Latin America in 1958 was marred by an outbreak of violence in Caracas, Venezuela. Moreover, in Cuba the victory of Fidel Castro's revolution in early 1959 brought to power a regime soon bitterly hostile to the United States. A repetition of the State Department's and CIA's coup, which ousted a pro-Communist government in Guatemala in 1954, could not be carried out immediately in Cuba, but planning for intervention began with Eisenhower's approval.

A chain of troubling events in the Middle East began just before Eisenhower's second election. Israel, goaded by Arab border raids and threats of destruction, attacked Egypt on October 29, 1956. The Israelis quickly smashed the armies of President Gamal Abdel Nasser and seized the Sinai Peninsula. France and Great Britain had been angered by Nasser's aid to rebels in French-ruled Algeria and by his seizure of the Suez Canal. The British and French governments resolved to overthrow Nasser and regain control of the Suez lifeline. By a prearranged understanding with Israel, Britain and France demanded that Egypt and Israel stop fighting and withdraw from the Suez. When Nasser refused, the British destroyed what remained of his air force and occupied the northern third of the canal.

The Soviet government was at this moment suppressing an anti-Communist revolution in Budapest. Soviet leaders sought to draw the spotlight of world opinion away from Hungary by condemning Great Britain, France, and Israel as aggressors in Egypt.

The United States did not rush to defend its allies. Eisenhower and Dulles were angered by the Anglo-French military action, which they feared might drive the entire Arab world, with its great petroleum resources, into the arms of the Russians. Therefore, the United States supported a resolution which demanded withdrawal of British, French, and Israeli forces from Egyptian territory. The three powers decided to comply. In contrast, the Soviets ignored a UN resolution which called upon them to withdraw their troops from Hungary.

The Suez affair shook the western alliance to its foundations. France proceeded to reconsider its dependence upon American military protection. The American government supplied economic aid to clear the canal and to enable Britain and France to purchase oil from the United States until the Suez route was restored. Next, Eisenhower conferred with the new British Prime Minister, Harold Macmillan. They agreed that the United States should build missile sites in Great Britain. And, when disarmament talks with Russia failed, the NATO Council agreed that the United States should negotiate with other NATO members for construction of more missile sites in western Europe.

In the aftermath of the Suez crisis, American policymakers searched for a way to recover United States influence in the Middle East. In January 1957, Eisenhower enunciated what was soon called the Eisenhower Doctrine. The United States, he announced, would help any middle eastern country to resist Communist military aggression and, in addition, would undertake aid programs for economic development.

The main threat in the Middle East was not open Communist aggression, but the subversion of existing governments. Also, the Eisenhower Doctrine could not be enforced unless one government asked for help. By sending

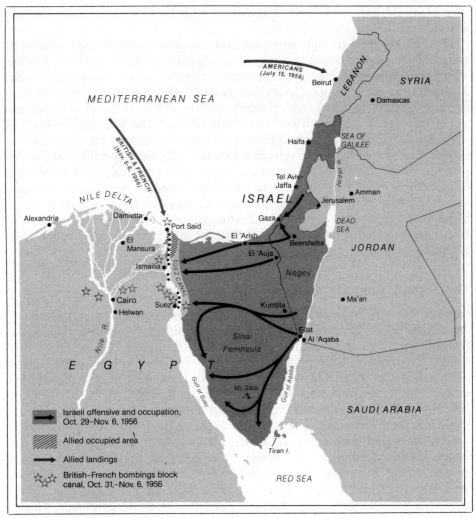

MEDITERRANEAN SEA

AMERICANS
(July 15, 1958)

BRITISH & FRENCH
(Nov. 5-6, 1956)

NILE DELTA

Alexandria

Damietta

Port Said

El Mansura

El 'Arish

Ismailia

SUEZ CANAL

Cairo

Helwan

Suez

Nile R.

E G Y P T

Sinai
Peninsula

Gulf of Suez

Mt. Sinai

Tiran I.

RED SEA

Beirut

LEBANON

SYRIA

Damascas

Haifa

SEA OF
GALILEE

Tel Aviv-
Jaffa

ISRAEL

Jerusalem

Gaza

Beersheba

El 'Auja

Negev

Kuntilla

Jordan R.

Amman

DEAD
SEA

JORDAN

Ma'an

Eilat

Al 'Aqaba

Gulf of Aqaba

SAUDI ARABIA

Israeli offensive and occupation,
Oct. 29–Nov. 6, 1956

Allied occupied area

Allied landings

British-French bombings block
canal, Oct. 31,–Nov. 6, 1956

The Suez Crisis, 1956

marines into Lebanon at the request of the President of that country in July 1958, Eisenhower helped to prevent the overthrow of a friendly government. But the Eisenhower Doctrine provided no remedy when a more serious crisis erupted in Iraq within the same week. There a group of army officers murdered the King and Prime Minister and wrecked the West's defensive system in the Middle East.

The Berlin Crisis

On November 27, 1958, the Soviet government proposed that West Berlin be evacuated by Allied troops and be made a free city. Russia warned that it would sign a separate peace treaty with the East Germans unless the western Allies pulled out of Berlin within six months. If this happened, the western powers would have to make arrangements with East Germany for entry into Berlin.

The French, British, and American governments rejected Soviet demands and suggested a four-power meeting to consider the German problem. Dulles, who opposed a second summit meeting, proposed a conference of Foreign Ministers. Soviet Premier Nikita Khrushchev, on the other hand, insisted upon a meeting of the heads of state.

The impasse was soon broken in a dramatic way. Dulles died of cancer on May 24, 1959. He had been succeeded a month earlier by Christian A. Herter. Eisenhower now took personal direction of foreign policy, and there were immediate results. In August, Eisenhower announced that he and Khrushchev would exchange visits. In mid-September, he received Khrushchev. Their meeting seemed to promise an early end to the Berlin crisis: Khrushchev agreed to settle the Berlin question by negotiations, while Eisenhower made it plain that he would go to a summit meeting in the near future.

The Second Summit and Afterward

During late 1959 and early 1960, all signs seemed to point to a solution of the Berlin crisis and a revival of American influence around the world. Eisenhower made triumphal tours of fifteen European, Asian, and Latin American countries. Leaders of the western powers met in Paris in December 1959 and invited Khrushchev to join them in a meeting during the coming spring. The conference was set for May 16 in Paris.

At this point, bungling, bad luck, and bad temper spoiled all chances for an East-West understanding. On May 5, 1960, Khrushchev announced that Soviet forces had shot down an American U-2 observation plane over the Soviet Union. Authorities in Washington declared that the plane, on a routine meteorological mission, had strayed off course. Khrushchev, who may have expected a prompt apology, now charged that the plane had been on an espionage mission. The pilot had been captured and had confessed. Herter admitted the charge and implied that the flights would continue. Eisenhower accepted personal responsibility for the aerial spying and, moreover, defended it. The atmosphere, consequently, was highly charged when the heads of state assembled in Paris for the summit meeting.

That conference actually never occurred. Khrushchev was genuinely upset by the U-2 incident. At the first meeting on May 16, Khrushchev made a violent personal attack on Eisenhower for continuing the spy-plane trips over the Soviet Union. Khrushchev withdrew his earlier invitation to the President to visit Russia and announced that he would attend no more meetings until Eisenhower apologized for the U-2 incident. Eisenhower refused either to engage in personal recrimination or to apologize, and the conference broke up before it could begin.

More bad news came in the months ahead. Eisenhower set out upon a visit of goodwill to Japan on June 12 and got as far as Manila. The Japanese government felt compelled to ask Eisenhower to cancel the tour after rioting mobs seemed to threaten his personal safety if he came to Tokyo. In the following month, a civil war rocked the Republic of the Congo. The dispatch of a UN task force prevented threatened Russian intervention but brought no

Enraged by repeated booing from the audience, a furious Nikita Khrushchev shakes his fist while delivering an abusive tirade during a press conference in Paris in May 1960. Referring to the U-2 incident earlier that month, the Soviet Premier compared President Eisenhower to "a thief caught red-handed in his theft." (United Press International)

long-term solution to the new nation's problems. Soviet-American tension was intensified when the Russians shot down an American reconnaissance plane in the area of the Barents Sea on July 1, 1960. The pilot of the U-2 plane shot down over Russia was sentenced to a ten-year term in August 1960, after a trial in which he confessed to all charges.

5. THE ELECTION OF 1960

Candidates and Conventions

During the turmoil just described, the parties began to prepare for the presidential campaign of 1960. There were only two serious Republican contenders, Governor Nelson A. Rockefeller of New York and Nixon. Rockefeller represented the progressive elements in the GOP, but he withdrew from the race in December 1959. The road was now cleared for Nixon.

Meanwhile, four candidates openly contended for the Democratic nomina-

*Senator John F. Kennedy and Vice President Richard M. Nixon as
they appeared in the fourth and final television debate in New York
City. The 1960 presidential campaign was marked by a series of
televised debates during which the candidates were asked questions
by newsmen before an estimated audience of 70,000,000 viewers.
Self-confident and well-informed, Kennedy was able to cast aside
his image of being too young and inexperienced in comparison
to Nixon. (Wide World Photos)*

tion, while several others, including Stevenson, would not have refused a
call. At first, the contest seemed to lie between Senator Hubert H.
Humphrey of Minnesota, who hoped to rally liberals, and Senator John F.
Kennedy of Massachusetts, a young leader of the eastern, urban wing, and
the first Roman Catholic to make a serious bid for the presidency since 1928.
The turning point of their battle came in the West Virginia primary on May
10. Kennedy polled 60 per cent of the votes in that predominantly Protestant
state, and Humphrey withdrew from the race. From this point on, it was a
question of whether Lyndon B. Johnson and favorite-son candidates could
prevent Kennedy's nomination.

The question was quickly answered at the Democratic national convention
on July 11. The Democrats adopted the strongest civil-rights platform in
their history and then proceeded to nominate Kennedy on the first ballot. In
a surprising move, Kennedy requested Johnson's nomination as his running
mate.

Republicans convened ten days later. For a moment conflict loomed over
the platform, for Rockefeller threatened a floor fight if Nixon did not support
a more progressive platform than had been drafted. Rockefeller had his way,
and Nixon was named for the presidency on the first ballot. Henry Cabot
Lodge, Jr., Ambassador to the UN, was drafted as his running mate.

The presidential campaign of 1960 became an exciting affair. Nixon

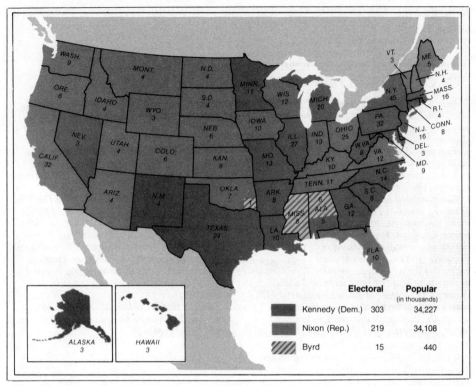

The Election of 1960

	Electoral	Popular (in thousands)
Kennedy (Dem.)	303	34,227
Nixon (Rep.)	219	34,108
Byrd	15	440

benefited from Eisenhower's active support. His backers claimed that his experience made him the logical man to "stand up" to Khrushchev. Also, a huge amount of anti-Catholic literature was distributed by Nixon supporters. Kennedy enjoyed the advantage of greater party strength, better organization, and an electric personality. Also, Catholics, angered at the campaign against Kennedy's religion, returned in large numbers to the Democratic fold.

The turning point in the campaign came in a series of four television debates between September 26 and October 24. It was the first time that presidential candidates had ever been brought face to face. The two men found it hard to grapple with issues, both for lack of time and because they agreed so much on fundamental principles. Even so, Kennedy demolished the Republican charges that he was inexperienced and badly informed. Moreover, Kennedy succeeded far better than his opponent in giving an impression of boldness, imagination, and poise.

No one, not even the pollsters, could safely predict what the result would be on election day, since there was a surge in Nixon's strength at the end of the campaign. First returns from the eastern states indicated a Kennedy landslide. But as election night passed, Nixon was seen to have carried most of the Middle West and West and was whittling away at Kennedy's lead in the crucial states of Illinois, Texas, and California. Kennedy carried Illinois and Texas—and the election—by the thinnest of margins. All told, Kennedy's popular majority was two-tenths of 1 per cent. The vote in the Electoral

College was 303 to 219. The next Congress would have large Democratic majorites in both houses.

SUGGESTED READINGS

Robert A. Divine, *Eisenhower and the Cold War* (1981); Herbert S. Parmet, *Eisenhower and the American Crusades* (1972); and Charles C. Alexander, *Holding the Line: The Eisenhower Era, 1952 – 1961* (1975), are good surveys. The most complete accounts are by Eisenhower himself—*Mandate for Change* (1963) and *Waging Peace* (1965). Fred L. Greenstein, *The Hidden-Hand Presidency: Eisenhower as Leader* (1982), tries hard to make Eisenhower into an active, aggressive leader. Emmet J. Hughes, *The Ordeal of Power* (1963), is a revealing discussion of the President and his administration as well. Richard Kluger, *Simple Justice: The History of Brown* v. *Board of Education and Black America's Struggle for Racial Equality* (1975), is an excellent book. On the period's legislation, the most valuable work is James L. Sundquist, *Politics and Policy: The Eisen-*

hower, Kennedy, and Johnson Years (1968).

The defense policy of the Eisenhower administration has been analyzed in numerous works. The best are Henry A. Kissinger, *Nuclear Weapons and Foreign Policy* (1956), and Samuel P. Huntington, *Changing Patterns of Military Politics* (1962). Conflicting opinions on John Foster Dulles can be found in Emmet J. Hughes, *America the Vincible* (1959); John R. Beal, *John Foster Dulles: A Biography* (1957); Michael A. Hugin, *John Foster Dulles: A Statesman and His Times* (1972); and Townsend Hoopes, *The Devil and John Foster Dulles* (1973). For the problem of the underdeveloped nations, see Barbara Ward, *The Rich Nations and the Poor Nations* (1962).

The election of 1960 is the subject of Theodore H. White, *The Making of the President, 1960* (1961).

CHAPTER 31
NEW FRONTIERS,
THE GREAT SOCIETY,
AND THE VIETNAM WAR

1. THE KENNEDY ERA BEGINS

The New President

On January 20, 1961, tens of millions of Americans watched John Fitzgerald Kennedy deliver his inaugural address. He began by reminding his fellow countrymen that they were heirs to the first successful constructive revolution in history. "Let the word go forth from this time and place, to friend and foe alike," he continued, "that the torch has been passed to a new generation of Americans." He called for a "grand and global alliance" against "the common enemies of man: tyranny, poverty, disease, and war itself"; he also pledged strong support to the United Nations and generous assistance to underdeveloped countries. He concluded with these words: "And so, my fellow Americans: ask not what your country can do for you—ask what you can do for your country."

John F. Kennedy was born in Brookline, Massachusetts, in 1917, into a large Irish-American, Roman Catholic family. Both his grandfathers had been prominent in Irish Democratic politics in Boston. His father, Joseph P. Kennedy, had made a fortune in business and finance and had served as ambassador to Great Britain from 1937 to 1940. Young John F. Kennedy was graduated with honors from Harvard in 1940. After distinguished war service, he was elected to the House of Representatives in 1946 and to the Senate in 1952 and 1958. Kennedy ran unsuccessfully for the Democratic vice-presidential nomination in

1956. No sooner had he failed in this bid than he began to campaign for the presidential nomination in 1960.

Kennedy was the youngest man ever elected to the presidency and one of the most fascinating. With reporters, he was relaxed, candid, and witty. To the people at large, he gave the impression of youthful vigor infused with intelligence. To young Americans, especially, Kennedy seemed imaginative and unconventional enough to receive new ideas and to try new approaches.

Kennedy had weaknesses as well as strengths. Inexperience in foreign affairs caused him to make costly blunders. His most striking weakness was his inability to establish leadership of Congress, although circumstances over which he had no control were in part responsible for that. The Eighty-seventh Congress, which sat in 1961 and 1962, appeared to be solidly Democratic. However, Kennedy never had a reliable majority because many southern Democrats voted with Republicans on crucial bills. Kennedy and his aids never trusted Vice-President Johnson sufficiently to make good use of his remarkable legislative skills.

In addition, Kennedy suffered the consequences both of his own political philosophy and of his political past. Despite the rhetoric of his inaugural address, he believed that the day of passionate commitment to causes was over. The United States, he thought, had reached a consensus on domestic policies. Therefore, his chief role as President was to help work out details of

This photograph was taken following President-elect John F. Kennedy's announcement that his brother Robert, who had served as his campaign manager, was to be Attorney General in his cabinet. In an early effort to unite the nation, John Kennedy urged: "I call upon you to join us in a journey to the new frontier. The voyage is a long and hazardous one, but we are all partners in a great and historic journey." (United Press International)

legislation, not to head a new reform movement. Moreover, as a representative and senator, Kennedy had never been a member of the inner congressional circle. As President, he failed to use the techniques and powers that a President must master in order to lead the Congress. Kennedy was not a strong domestic leader, finally, because he was preoccupied with foreign affairs.

Furthermore, Kennedy accepted most of the premises on which American foreign policy in the Cold War were based. If anything, he seemed more attached to aggressive anticommunism than Eisenhower. Kennedy was entranced, especially, by the possibilities of war conducted quietly by expertly trained counterinsurgency units.

It is only fair to add that this evaluation is based upon Kennedy's brief tenure as President. Kennedy was giving evidence of greater mastery of foreign affairs and domestic politics before his untimely death in 1963.

Slow Progress toward New Frontiers

In outlining his domestic program in 1961, Kennedy called for measures to "get the country moving again," but he soon discovered that unexpected circumstances have a way of defeating even the best-laid plans. Perhaps his most ironical defeat was the failure of his ambitious federal aid-to-education bill. Kennedy proposed to spend more than $5.6 billion to enrich and equalize educational opportunities. The bill easily passed the Senate. Then Roman Catholic leaders insisted that the measure be amended to aid parochial schools. Kennedy would not agree, and enough Roman Catholic Democratic congressmen joined the bipartisan conservative opposition to defeat the bill in the House. Opposition arose to other administrative measures. An ambitious plan called Medicare—to provide medical care for the aged through the Social Security system—was killed because of opposition from the American Medical Association.

But the new President had some legislative successes. The Housing Act of 1961 authorized the expenditure of $4.9 billion over four years for urban renewal projects. Under Kennedy's prodding, the Democrats also raised the minimum wage from $1 to $1.25 an hour and extended protection to an additional 3,624,000 workers. The Area Redevelopment Act of 1961 provided $300 million in loans and grants for new industries and the retraining of workers in areas of high unemployment. The Twenty-fourth Amendment, which outlawed the poll tax as a requirement for voting in federal elections, was approved by Congress in 1962 and ratified in January 1964.

The Eighty-seventh Congress agreed with Kennedy about maintaining powerful defenses. Congress appropriated a total of $95 billion in 1961 and 1962 for defense. It also authorized the President to call 250,000 reserves into active duty for a year. Leaders in Washington continued to push the missile program because it seemed to offer the best hope of enabling the United States to deter a major war. By 1965 the United States had a fleet of twenty-nine nuclear submarines armed with Polaris nuclear missiles, an arsenal of Atlas intercontinental missiles, and more than 500 new Minuteman missiles in underground "silos."

Congress also supported Kennedy's recommendation to expand the space program. Congress appropriated generously when Kennedy, in May 1961, requested approval of a program aimed at putting a task force on the moon by 1970. Progress in space flight accelerated. The *Gemini* series of orbital flights was completed in 1966 with successful docking of two *Gemini* capsules. In July 1969, Neil Armstrong and Edwin Aldrin made a historic landing on the moon, which was witnessed by television viewers around the world.

But on earth, after a year and a half of Kennedy's administration, Congress was deadlocked on important domestic issues, much as it had been since the Truman administration. To be sure, there was excitement on some fronts. Under pressure from the government, the steel companies and the United Steel Workers concluded a new contract on March 31, 1962, which provided modest wage increases. Then, on April 10, the president of United States Steel Corporation announced a price increase of $6 a ton, and other companies followed suit. Kennedy denounced the action and moved to prosecute the steel companies for illegal price fixing. They retreated at once, but Kennedy's attack shook the confidence of the business community. Kennedy later acquiesced in other increases in steel prices.

In the mid-term election of 1962, Kennedy campaigned hard for Democratic candidates, and it seemed that the Democrats would just about hold their

A fifty-foot cross blazes against the sky at a rally of the Ku Klux Klan in Tuscaloosa, Alabama, in June 1963. The meeting was held outside this college city where two blacks were scheduled to enroll in the University of Alabama, an event which Governor George Wallace vowed he would try to prevent. (United Press International)

Dr. Martin Luther King, Jr., addressing a crowd of thousands
gathered in front of the Lincoln Memorial during the civil rights
march on Washington, August 1963. The tragic assassination of
this charismatic preacher of nonviolence in April 1968 was preceded
and followed by devastating urban rioting. (Wide World Photos)

own. Then the missile crisis with Russia exploded in late October (see pp.
513 – 14) and caused a general disposition to stand by the President. This
helped the Democrats to increase their majorities in both houses of
Congress.

Although the Eighty-eighth Congress had large Democratic majorities,
Kennedy still could not push through his program. It is clear in retrospect
that Congress was fiddling while the country burned. Most Americans were
aroused by the brutal police suppression, in April and May 1963, of black
civil-rights demonstrations in Birmingham led by the Rev. Martin Luther
King, Jr., and, in September, by the bombing of churches and the murder of
black children in that same city. Blacks and whites joined in sympathetic
demonstrations across the country to protest segregation.

Kennedy heretofore had shown no great zeal for bold new civil-rights
legislation. He had used troops to suppress a bloody riot in Oxford,
Mississippi, in September 1962, when a federal court had compelled the
admission of a black student by the University of Mississippi. In addition,

Kennedy sent a mild civil-rights bill to Congress in February 1963. But he did not press the measure for fear of imperiling southern support in Congress for other New Frontier bills.

Kennedy finally was galvanized into action by the Birmingham demonstrations. He spoke to the nation by television on June 11, 1963, and then sent a strong new civil-rights bill to Congress. The response throughout the country was electric. Religious leaders joined hands with civil-rights and labor groups in a grass-roots lobbying campaign. On August 28, more than 200,000 blacks and whites gathered before the Lincoln Memorial in Washington in a peaceful demonstration for the civil-rights bill. In October, the President and his brother, Attorney General Robert F. Kennedy, worked with congressional leaders of both parties to submit a revised bill.

2. THE COLD WAR CONTINUES

The Same Frontiers Abroad

The style of American diplomacy changed somewhat after the succession in 1961. However, in substance, the foreign policies of the early 1960s were marked by an almost complete continuity with the policies of the 1950s. Acheson, Dulles, and Kennedy's Secretary of State, Dean Rusk, had practically interchangeable ideas, values, and goals. One fact, to be sure, had not yet changed: the global struggle between Russia and the United States for the loyalty of the uncommitted majority of the world and for predominance along the perimeters of the two great powers.

The European area in greatest peril was still Germany, and in Asia, Vietnam. Khrushchev's main target in Germany remained West Berlin. Kennedy, in order to explore any possibility that the Russian leader might moderate his threats against Berlin, flew to Vienna for a meeting with the Soviet Premier in June 1961. Kennedy was shocked by Khrushchev's belligerence and threats against Allied rights in Berlin. Kennedy announced his determination to stand and fight for Berlin, if necessary, in a televised address on June 28. A month later he asked Congress for an additional $3.25 billion for the armed forces, especially to meet the Soviet challenge to Berlin.

Khrushchev announced that he was willing to seek a negotiated settlement of the Berlin question. Meanwhile, to prevent the escape of thousands of East Germans to the West, the Communists, in August 1961, walled off their part of Berlin. American and Russian troops faced each other across this barrier. The negotiations failed, as earlier ones had, and West Berlin continued to be a powder keg. However, after 1961 the Communists did not seriously endanger the western position, and the powder keg, at least for a time, was without a fuse.

The hardest blows to American prestige and the gravest threat to world peace during the early 1960s occurred not in Europe, but in the Caribbean, where Cuban-American relations were strained to the breaking point. It was obvious by the end of 1960 that a Soviet ally existed ninety miles off American shores.

Eisenhower, in September 1960, approved a CIA plan to dislodge Cuban President Fidel Castro. The plan involved the supply of arms and money to anti-Castro Cubans in Guatemala. They would invade Cuba and rally the mass of supposedly disaffected Cubans. American planes would protect the landing force.

Kennedy gave his approval for the invasion in early April 1961, but he would not agree to American air cover for the invaders. Some 1,400 armed Cuban refugees embarked on April 17. Castro's forces easily captured the little army in the marshes of the Bay of Pigs on the southern coast of Cuba.

Khrushchev, on April 18, threatened to go to Cuba's assistance if the United States did not stop "the aggression against the Republic of Cuba." Kennedy replied that the United States would not permit the Russians to establish a military foothold in Cuba.

The Cuban fiasco and Kennedy's conference with Khrushchev in Vienna made it clear that the struggle with Russia might be prolonged and dangerous. Kennedy's main reply to the Soviet challenge consisted of a foreign-aid program to help peoples in underdeveloped countries, particularly in poverty-stricken Latin America. In August 1961, the United States, working through an Inter-American Conference, launched the Alliance for Progress. This program envisaged the extension of some $20 billion in United States economic aid over a ten-year period. The administration hoped that this aid would improve the relations of the United States with unaligned countries and would prop up the governments of these nations against revolution. Unfortunately, many of the governments to which the United States sent this aid were repressive dictatorships, and some were so corrupt that little aid reached the poor.

Meanwhile, other signs indicated that the United States was seizing the initiative in its foreign policy. One such effort was the creation of the Peace Corps to train thousands of young people for voluntary educational, medical, and technical services to people in underdeveloped countries. The enthusiastic response of young people showed that idealism remained very much alive on American college and university campuses. Kennedy replied to the Soviet show of military might also by asking for and receiving from Congress higher military appropriations than Eisenhower had requested.

All during the summer and autumn of 1962, the American government became increasingly alarmed at the buildup of Soviet arms in Cuba. In October, aerial reconnaissance revealed that the Russians were installing sites in Cuba for missiles capable of hitting targets in the United States. The Russian ambassador denied that missile sites were being built. Kennedy and his advisers then decided to force a showdown at the risk of war. In a dramatic television address on October 22, 1962, Kennedy denounced "this secret, swift, and extraordinary buildup of Communist missiles" and said that he had already ordered the United States Navy to begin a blockade of Cuba against Russian ships which carried offensive military equipment. "It shall be the policy of this nation," Kennedy went on, "to regard any nuclear missile launched from Cuba against any nation in the Western Hemisphere as an attack by the Soviet Union on the United States requiring a full retaliatory response upon the Soviet Union." What was more, "Any hostile move anywhere in the world against the safety or freedom of peoples to whom we are committed—including in particular the brave people of West Berlin—will be met by whatever action is needed."

American naval vessels then began to turn back Soviet ships approaching

Cuba. Khrushchev responded promptly in a conciliatory tone. This led to an exchange between the President and the Premier; Khrushchev promised to remove the offensive missiles (which he did), and Kennedy promised to launch no attack against Cuba. The bargain salvaged some Russian prestige and the peace of the world. However, it led also to vast increases in Soviet expenditures for naval vessels and nuclear missiles so that American threats could not force the USSR to back down under superior force in the future.

The Weakening of the Great Alliances and the Beginnings of Russian-American Détente

The Cuban missile crisis and subsequent arms buildup revealed that the two superpowers soon would be tied in a nuclear deadlock. Neither would be able to inflict serious injury on the other without suffering grave damage in return. The approaching nuclear standoff had important consequences.

For one thing, the coming stalemate, along with rapid economic progress throughout Europe, gave greater diplomatic freedom to the smaller powers within the two alliance systems. Fear of Russian attack had drawn the western powers into close alliance, and fear of German resurgence had kept eastern Europe dependent upon Russia. The waning of these fears encouraged nations hitherto under the shadow of the superpowers to assert independent policies.

Few persons in Washington read these signs correctly in 1961 and 1962. On the contrary, the Kennedy administration was working on what was called a Grand Design to draw the western community into closer association. The United States, Kennedy declared, should join in economic partnership with the European Common Market by a mutual slashing of tariffs.

The Common Market, established in 1957 by France, Germany, Italy, and the Benelux countries (Belgium, the Netherlands, and Luxembourg), had been working toward a customs union and had already stimulated the rapid economic growth of its members. Congress, in October 1962, authorized the President to reduce tariffs generally by 50 per cent, and to remove tariffs altogether on articles heavily traded by the United States and western Europe. The latter provision depended upon the entry of Great Britain into the Common Market.

However, President De Gaulle interpreted the Grand Design as a plan to fasten Anglo-American control on western Europe. He vetoed Britain's entrance into the Common Market in January 1963. De Gaulle hoped to create a new power bloc under French leadership; thus he proceeded to build his own nuclear weapons and reduced French participation in NATO. Kennedy, who sought to prevent any widening of the breach, offered to give Polaris missiles to France and proposed to create a NATO naval force with nuclear weapons. Both De Gaulle and the British disliked this proposal.

At the same time that NATO was coming apart at the seams, a similar loosening of bonds proceeded apace within the Communist world. Poland and Rumania, following Yugoslavia's earlier example, initiated their own projects of internal development and began to show economic and diplomatic independence. But the great rupture in the Communist world took place between the Soviet Union and China. Chinese leaders ended their dependence on Soviet arms and equipment and thereby on Soviet political orders. A series of subsequent quarrels led to the withdrawal of all Russian advisers from China in 1960. During the next two years, the two powers glowered at each other along their long common border. Beginning in the late 1960s, reports reached the West of sporadic fighting along the Chinese-Russian border.

Tensions between the United States and Russia lessened as their respective alliance systems were weakening. The leaders of both superpowers seemed to acquire a new respect for each other during the missile crisis. They now realized that coexistence was the only alternative to mutual annihilation. The first sign of what diplomats call a détente, or relaxation of tensions, came in 1963. Kennedy appealed to Khrushchev for a ban on all above-ground nuclear testing. After months of negotiations, such a treaty was signed and approved by the Senate. But neither France, which recently had exploded an atomic bomb, nor China, which soon would, agreed to sign the treaty.

By the autumn of 1963, a dark cloud on the American diplomatic horizon appeared in the form of a resumption of the revolution in South Vietnam. The United States had aided the government of that rump republic since Vietnam's partition in 1954. Sporadic attacks by a South Vietnamese insurgent force, the National Liberation Front (NLF),* supported by Ho Chi Minh's Communist government in North Vietnam, had burgeoned into full-scale civil war by 1961. This occurred despite the announcement by the South Vietnamese dictator, Ngo Dinh Diem, that his "political reeducation" program had "entirely destroyed the predominant Communist influence."

The American government sent thousands of military personnel to train the South Vietnamese army. By 1963, some 16,000 American military "advisers" served in South Vietnam. More and more of them were becoming directly involved in combat. However, the political situation in South Vietnam was chaotic, and the war against the NLF made little progress. Sooner or later, Kennedy would be forced either to withdraw or else greatly to increase American commitments to South Vietnam. His friends claimed later that he had planned to withdraw American forces altogether from Vietnam after his reelection in 1964. But, while he lived, Kennedy continued to build up American forces in South Vietnam.

The Death of President Kennedy

During the summer and early autumn of 1963, Kennedy worked to repair some badly broken political fences at home. To do this, he embarked upon a speaking tour in mid-November, traveling first to Florida, then to Texas. The crowds were large and enthusiastic everywhere that he went, including Dallas, where he arrived just before noon on November 22, 1963.

The presidential entourage passed through cheering throngs until, just as the presidential car turned into an expressway, bullets from a high-powered rifle ripped through Kennedy's body and also seriously wounded Governor

---

* Called the Viet Cong by the South Vietnamese dictatorship and then by the Americans to imply that all NLF members were Communists.

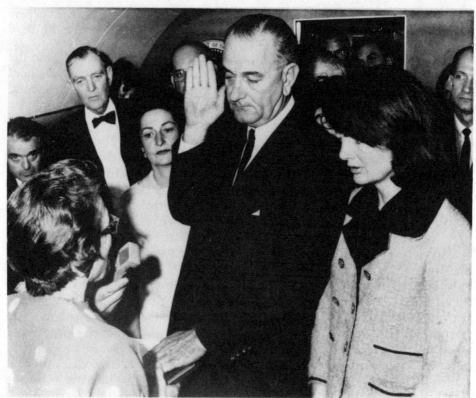

*Lyndon B. Johnson is being sworn in as President by Judge Sarah
T. Hughes on November 22, 1963, aboard the presidential airplane at
Dallas, Texas, with Mrs. Johnson and Mrs. Kennedy at his side.
He returned to Washington and expressed his intention to follow the
whole agenda of the New Frontier with the theme "let us
continue." (Wide World Photos)*

John B. Connally, who was riding with him. Kennedy died before his car
reached a hospital. The assassin was Lee Harvey Oswald, a neurotic, solitary
miscreant. Oswald was murdered in front of a television camera on
November 24 by a Dallas nightclub owner. John F. Kennedy was the fourth
American President to die at the hands of an assassin.

3. A NEW PRESIDENT MOVES TOWARD THE GREAT SOCIETY

The New President

Lyndon Baines Johnson, who took the presidential oath in Dallas soon after
Kennedy's death, was born near Stonewall, Texas, in 1908. Johnson entered
public life as director of the WPA's National Youth Administration for Texas
in 1935. He served in the House of Representatives from 1937 until 1949 and
in the Senate from 1949 to 1960. He was elected minority leader of the
Senate in 1953 and majority leader in 1955. Kennedy asked Johnson to be his

running mate in part because the Texan's support was essential to victory in the South and Southwest. Johnson accepted because he wanted to be a national, not merely regional, leader.

Politically, Johnson was a New Dealer: Franklin D. Roosevelt had been the idol of his young manhood. This heritage, in addition to his own experiences in the Great Depression, gave him the strong conviction that governmental power should be used to improve the human condition.

Johnson also was a master manipulator of other politicians. No man ever came to the presidency with greater knowledge of Congress. In addition, he strongly believed that politics is the art of the possible. He willingly accepted half a loaf if he could not obtain a whole one. His greatest deficiency was lack of experience in foreign affairs. Johnson lacked Kennedy's suavity and wit; his ruggedness and his Texan manners reflected American frontier traditions. The energy which drove him, in spite of a severe heart attack in 1957, to herculean labors might have made him a great President. However, he was hypersensitive to criticism, and his mental rigidity prevented him from changing courses. Johnson, who was eager for approval and determined to earn a high place in the annals of the presidency, failed to earn that place. But he did not fail because he lacked lofty ambitions or political skills—except in the crucial area of foreign policy.

More Rapid Movement toward New Frontiers

Johnson urged rapid completion of Kennedy's unfinished legislative agenda— tax reduction and adoption of the pending civil-rights bill. In February 1964, with elections coming soon, Congress approved a bill which reduced taxes by $11.5 billion over two years. Congress also provided funds for public housing, continued the National Defense Education Act of 1958, and established a food-stamp plan for families who received welfare assistance. After he brought all these Kennedy measures to fruition, Johnson submitted one of his own—the Economic Opportunity Act. This measure authorized the expenditure of about $1 billion in the following year alone to launch a national war against poverty.

The most significant legislation of 1964 was the Civil Rights Act, which was passed in July after the Senate broke an eighty-three day filibuster by southern senators. The Civil Rights Act of 1964 forbade racial discrimination in most places of public accommodation; attempted to protect the right of blacks to vote; forbade discrimination on account of race or sex by employers and unions; created an Equal Employment Opportunity Commission; forbade discrimination in the use of federal funds by state and local authorities; empowered the Attorney General to initiate school desegregation cases; and created a Community Relations Service to deal with racial problems on the local level.

The Presidential Campaign of 1964

These mighty events on Capitol Hill served as a prelude to the battle for control of Congress and the presidency. The Democrats nominated Johnson by acclamation and adopted a platform which promised mobilization of national resources to create what the President called "the Great Society."

Johnson picked Senator Hubert H. Humphrey of Minnesota as his running mate.

The Republicans, meanwhile, had been torn by dissension. Only two serious candidates eagerly challenged the Texan in the White House. They were Governor Nelson A. Rockefeller of New York and Senator Barry M. Goldwater of Arizona. Goldwater, popular with most of the state Republican organizations and with conservative groups, won the presidential nomination with ease on the first ballot. Conservative delegates heckled and booed progressive leaders when they tried to persuade the convention to denounce extremist groups. Goldwater replied in his acceptance speech that "extremism in the defense of liberty is no vice."

Not since 1936 had there been a presidential campaign in which the contenders were so unevenly matched. Concerning foreign affairs, Johnson gave the impression of restraint and warned that Goldwater's proposals about Vietnam might involve the nation in an Asian war. On domestic issues, Johnson stood behind the Civil Rights Act of 1964, the war against poverty, Medicare, and federal aid to education. The public response was overwhelmingly favorable.

Goldwater, on the other hand, had promised "a choice, not an echo." He had voted against the civil-rights bill, the Test Ban Treaty, and most of the Kennedy-Johnson welfare measures. During the campaign, he intimated that he would like to repeal the Social Security Act, sell the TVA to private investors, and wipe out as much progressive legislation as possible.

Goldwater hoped to carry the segregationist South and what he believed to be the conservative Middle West and Far West. His strategy failed. Johnson amassed 486 electoral votes to fifty-two for Goldwater. The Arizonan carried only five states in the Deep South and his home state. In the Eighty-ninth Congress (1965–1966), Democrats had two-thirds majorities in both houses.

Toward the Great Society

Johnson seized the opportunity presented by his own landslide and the Democratic majorities in Congress. With furious energy, he pushed through Congress the most comprehensive domestic program since the high tide of the New Deal. The President finally broke the logjam which had prevented a comprehensive education bill. The Education Act of 1965, adopted and approved in mid-April, authorized $1.3 billion for direct federal assistance to public schools. In addition, a Higher Education Act of 1965 authorized $650 million in federal aid to colleges and universities for scholarships, teaching, and research.

An Appalachian Regional Development Act, approved in March 1965, provided $1.1 billion for highways, health centers, and development to the poverty-stricken region which stretched from Pennsylvania to Alabama and Georgia. A Medicare bill, enlarged to include low-cost insurance against doctors' bills as well as hospital and nursing expenses for all persons over sixty-five, was overwhelmingly approved by Congress. Medicare effected the first fundamental change in the Social Security Act since its adoption in 1935. The Housing and Urban Development Act of 1965 provided assistance for the construction of low-rent public housing and for urban renewal. In addition, Congress created a Department of Housing and Urban Development. Robert C. Weaver, the first black ever named to the cabinet, was sworn in as its head in January 1966.

Johnson and Congress also responded to growing demands for improvement of the ecological conditions in which Americans lived. Legislation enacted in 1966 attempted to control both air and water pollution. Another measure gave the government authority to set highway and automobile safety standards.

The Immigration Act of 1965 signified a fundamental change in American immigration policy. The act of 1965 reversed the National Origins Act of 1924 (see pp. 392 – 93) and put all nations on an equal footing.

Johnson, meanwhile, responded to new convulsions on the civil-rights front with additional voting-rights legislation. Various organizations had worked to encourage black registration and voting throughout the South in 1964. But white reaction in the Deep South had been violent. Whites and blacks were murdered. Black churches had been bombed or burned, and local registrars had prevented most blacks from registering, often with the help of local police.

National indignation at these developments intensified in March, when Alabama state troopers used clubs and tear gas to break up a voter registration demonstration in Selma, led by Martin Luther King, Jr. Johnson went before Congress to denounce the denial of basic constitutional rights. He demanded adoption of a bill for federal registrars in all counties where blacks did not vote in normal numbers. This measure, called the Voting Rights Act of 1965, was put on its way to passage even while thousands of Americans flocked to join the marchers from Selma. Passage of the bill was made inevitable by the murder of three civil-rights workers near Selma.

Johnson's Great Society programs obtained wide support at the time of their enactment. That support ranged from business leaders worried about deterioration in housing and smog in downtown urban areas, to blacks who demanded voting rights and access to decent homes and schools. Johnson, early in his elected term, seemed to have put together a progressive coalition as powerful as the one which kept Franklin Roosevelt in office. Then, in two years, controversial decisions in foreign policy stripped needed funds from his domestic programs, shattered the consensus behind Johnson, and bitterly divided the country. The Johnsonian consensus was also undermined, as early as 1966, by a rising tide of conservatism on domestic, social, and economic issues.

The Supreme Court Continues Its Own Revolution

In the 1960s, the Supreme Court, under the influence of Chief Justice Warren, completed the revolution in constitutional interpretation which it had begun in the 1950s. The court effected a fundamental reinterpretation of laws which involved individual rights.

The Supreme Court threw the weight of the American judiciary behind the civil-rights revolution. In Heart of Atlanta Motel *v.* the United States (1964), the court upheld the Civil Rights Act of 1964 in sweeping language. In other cases, the court upheld the Voting Rights Act of 1965 and outlawed the poll tax as a requirement for voting in local and state elections.

The Warren Court also struck death blows at another ancient political inequity—rural control of state legislatures in urban states. Citizens of Tennessee brought suit to compel their legislature to grant equal representation to Tennessee's urban citizens. The Supreme Court, in Baker v. Carr (1962), in effect declared that the federal courts should intervene in such cases to guarantee equal representation to all citizens in all states. Subsequent rulings compelled all state legislatures to reapportion themselves and their congressional districts on the principle of "one man, one vote."

In Engel v. Vitale (1962) and School District of Abington Township v. Schempp (1963), the court more clearly defined the principle of separation of church and state. These decisions outlawed requirements for Bible reading and prayers in public schools on the ground that they violated the First Amendment.

Finally, the court threw up new safeguards for individuals accused of crime. In Gideon v. Wainwright (1963), the court ruled that a defendant too poor to hire an attorney had to be furnished one at public expense. The court, in Escobedo v. Illinois (1964), and Miranda v. Arizona (1966), extended the right of arrested persons to be informed of their constitutional rights in most categories of offenses. Some public officials complained that these decisions severely handicapped law enforcement. However, statistics since these decisions indicate a steady level of convictions and even of confessions.

Johnson and Latin America

Since the 1930s, United States intervention in Latin America depended more on dollars than on bullets, and the United States used friendly native leaders and American-trained armed forces rather than the marines. That pattern changed in 1965, when civil war broke out in the Dominican Republic between forces committed to the deposed democratic President, Juan Bosch, and other elements of the army led by conservative generals. Johnson decided that Communists were about to take over the small Caribbean nation. He quickly sent in more than 20,000 United States troops to intercede. When it became obvious that Communists played hardly any role in the quarrel, and that the United States was attempting to install an unpopular military regime, the United States helped to work out a compromise between the warring factions. Meanwhile, Latin Americans in general were furious and many liberals in the United States began to worry that Johnson was trigger happy.

Vietnam: Into the Quagmire

Johnson reinforced these fears with his decision in favor of a massive land war in Asia. During the presidential campaign of 1964, he had assured the voters: "We are not going to send American boys nine or ten thousand miles away from home to do what Asian boys ought to be doing for themselves."

Early in 1965, the army of South Vietnam outnumbered its guerrilla enemies, the NLF, by six to one. Nevertheless, thousands of American advisers and enormous amounts of American financial and military aid barely enabled the South Vietnamese forces to hold their own. Johnson and his chief policy planners feared that if Vietnam fell, then what they perceived to be a monolithic Communist enemy would be encouraged to undertake further expansion. Many commentators referred to this idea as the "domino theory"—that is, if South Vietnam fell, neighboring countries inevitably would topple also. Johnson was impressed, too, with the arguments of military theorists, who confidently predicted that a calculated escalation of the conflict would force an enemy to ask for peace. In February 1965, Johnson ordered the bombing of North Vietnam and sent American combat units to South Vietnam. He had received, in August 1964, congressional approval in a joint resolution adopted after North Vietnamese attacked American destroyers in the Gulf of Tonkin, off the coast of North Vietnam. The resolution pledged congressional support for military action by the United States in Vietnam.

The Vietnam Conflict, 1966

A steady buildup of forces followed. But, just as steadily, reinforcements streamed down from North Vietnam to combat the Americans. Previously, the North Vietnamese had given the southern rebels little but training and moral support. By the time that Johnson left office, 535,000 United States soldiers were stationed in Vietnam and were assisted by 1,000,000 South Vietnamese and 72,000 allied troops. They opposed about 320,000 North Vietnamese soldiers and the remnant of the NLF. The tonnage of bombs dropped on North and South Vietnam by American planes by 1970 had already exceeded by over 50 per cent the total dropped in all theaters during the Second World War. Attempts to starve and expose the guerrillas included chemical defoliation of almost 1,000,000 acres, which transformed South Vietnam from a major rice exporter into an impoverished, large-scale importer of rice by 1968.

Despite these measures, no end to the war was in sight. Promises of victory from American officials accompanied each stage of the escalation. Critics pointed to the danger of continuing the costly war. Even old friends of the President such as Clark Clifford and Dean Acheson found that Johnson refused to take their advice to deescalate the war, and that he reacted with

Helicopters, a distinctive feature in the Vietnam War, proved extremely useful for carrying infantrymen to remote and inaccessible points of the war front. In this 1968 photograph, U.S. infantrymen have landed on a dirt road southwest of Saigon and are wading into a rice paddy in search of Viet Cong. Intensive patrols of suspected hiding places were aimed at preventing another attack on the South Vietnamese capital. (Wide World Photos)

hypersensitivity to suggestions that he had made any kind of mistake. High officials who made such suggestions—like Secretary of Defense Robert McNamara—were forced to resign.

Since the Vietnam War was costing over $20 billion annually, Johnson was obliged to reduce expenditures on domestic programs designed to alleviate poverty and urban unrest. Not only were Americans reluctant to tax themselves further, but international bankers and speculators began to exchange dollars for gold and more stable currencies because of the inflation caused by the seemingly endless war.

Then, in January 1968, two separate incidents further exacerbated Johnson's problems. The NLF launched a major offensive during Tet, the Vietnamese New Year, against South Vietnamese towns and cities. They even invaded the center of Saigon and shelled the United States embassy there. The NLF failed to hold the principal cities, but their offensive further weakened American support for the war. Late in the month, a United States intelligence ship, U.S.S. *Pueblo*, was captured by North Korean patrol boats off the coast of that country. American officials angrily denounced the action, but Johnson backed away from an additional conflict with Korea. Johnson's decision not to contest the seizure of *Pueblo* provided him with an opportunity to contemplate the overextended and vulnerable position in which he had placed the United States.

4. THE ELECTION OF 1968

McCarthy and the Peace Platform

In November 1967, Senator Eugene McCarthy of Minnesota announced his candidacy for the Democratic presidential nomination on a peace platform. At the time, McCarthy's action seemed a token gesture on behalf of the peace advocates, or "doves," within the Democratic party. McCarthy was virtually unknown in much of the country. His campaign suffered further from his subdued, whimsical speaking style, and from his refusal to dramatize his differences with the administration or to appeal to ethnic groups.

Nevertheless, thousands of young Americans, mostly college students, grasped at the opportunity presented by McCarthy's candidacy to oppose Johnson's policies. Students on the East Coast descended upon New Hampshire, site of the earliest presidential primary, and, with little help from professional politicians, organized a thorough campaign. Young men and women systematically canvassed the state and spoke to almost every registered Democrat and many Republicans. Americans were startled in mid-March 1968 when McCarthy won 42 per cent of the Democratic vote to 48 per cent for Johnson.

Politicians in Washington understood immediately the meaning of McCarthy's showing. National polls also reported widespread disenchantment with Johnson's policies. After the Tet offensive, influential newspapers and magazines began severely to criticize American participation in the war.

Robert F. Kennedy, now senator from New York and heir to his brother's political organization and popularity, had refused for months to run against

Johnson. Until the Tet offensive, Kennedy had opposed the Vietnam War strongly, but privately. After Tet, however, Kennedy decided to speak out. As evidence mounted of Johnson's political vulnerability, Kennedy announced his active candidacy. Not only did Kennedy thus provide Johnson with truly formidable opposition, but Johnson also now faced a man who had treated him with humiliating condescension when he had served as Vice-President.

McCarthy's campaign workers had already moved to Wisconsin, where hordes of midwestern college students helped to organize a statewide canvass similar to the one in New Hampshire. Polls in Wisconsin indicated that the Minnesota senator would swamp the President. Two days before the Wisconsin primary election on April 2, Johnson announced that, in the interest of national unity, he would not be a candidate for reelection. During the same speech, Johnson also announced a partial halt of American bombing in North Vietnam. An American mission met with North Vietnamese delegates in Paris in May for preliminary talks. Following a total cessation of the bombing of North Vietnam in October, the negotiators in Paris began formal discussions in early 1969. However, peace remained as elusive as ever at the end of the Johnson administration.

Meanwhile, in the Democratic preconvention contest, Kennedy won every presidential primary which he entered except for Oregon, which went to McCarthy. On June 5, Kennedy won the crucial California primary, but during the evening of that day, at a victory celebration, he was shot by a young Palestinian, Sirhan Sirhan, who was infuriated by Kennedy's statements favorable to Israel. Kennedy died on June 6, 1968.

The Campaign and Election of 1968

Kennedy's supporters and delegates drifted into the camp of either Vice-President Hubert Humphrey or Senator George S. McGovern, neither of whom had directly participated in the primaries. At the Democratic national convention in Chicago, Humphrey won the presidential nomination on the first ballot; he chose Senator Edmund Muskie of Maine as his running mate.

The attention of most observers at the Democratic convention focused less on floor votes than on the battles which raged outside the hall between young people and police. Words were exchanged with police; objects were thrown by demonstrators; then police used night sticks and tear gas indiscriminately to disperse the throngs. Members of the press and onlookers were assaulted along with the demonstrators, while events were captured by the ubiquitous eyes of the television cameras.

The struggle for the Republican nomination in 1968 did not even last until the first primary. Republicans opposed to former Vice-President Nixon backed Governor George Romney of Michigan. However, Romney withdrew before New Hampshire, and the other possible candidates, Governors Nelson Rockefeller of New York and Ronald Reagan of California, did not campaign actively until just before the Republican convention. They acted too late, and Nixon won on the first ballot. Nixon chose Spiro T. Agnew, governor of Maryland, as his vice-presidential nominee. George C. Wallace, former governor of Alabama, founded the American Independent party, a southern-based conservative organization, which obligingly nominated him for the presidency.

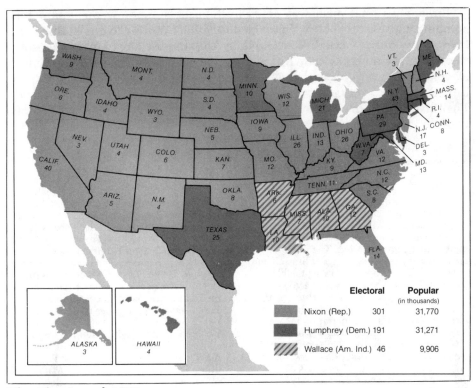

The Election of 1968

The fall campaign opened with Humphrey trailing far behind Nixon in the polls. To many young people, Humphrey represented the Vietnam War and the suppression of the Chicago demonstrations. On the first major issue of the campaign—crime in the streets—Humphrey spoke of the need for "order and justice," rather than "law and order," and stressed that discrimination against black Americans had to end. On the second major issue—Vietnam—he encountered almost insurmountable difficulties. He badly needed the antiwar vote, but he dared not repudiate Johnson. Not until late September, in a speech in Salt Lake City, did the Vice-President appear to move away from the administration's position by calling for an end to all bombing of North Vietnam in order to make possible meaningful peace talks. By that time, however, Johnson also had decided that peace could best be attained by ending the bombing, as he publicly announced late in October. This declaration, coupled with Muskie's increasingly effective campaign, infused new vigor into the Democratic campaign.

The Republicans began their campaign confidently. Nixon and Agnew talked of the need to stop crime in the streets. Nixon also declared that he had a "plan for peace" in Vietnam, but he refused to divulge any particulars. Meanwhile, Wallace made law and order his major issue. Despite all the excitement generated by his flailing attacks, it soon became apparent that he would poll a significant vote only in the South and would hurt Nixon more than Humphrey.

Humphrey's final push was aided by Johnson's announcement of a total bombing pause over North Vietnam on October 31. Indeed, it seemed that Humphrey might actually accomplish the impossible. Americans spent election night much as they had eight years before. By the early morning of November 6 it was clear that Nixon had carried the crucial states of Ohio, Illinois, and California by small margins and had barely won the presidency. The final tally in the Electoral College was Nixon, 301; Humphrey, 191; and Wallace, forty-six—all from the Deep South.

SUGGESTED READINGS

Arthur M. Schlesinger, Jr., *A Thousand Days: John F. Kennedy in the White House* (1965), although distinctly partisan, remains the most comprehensive and lively account of that administration. The literature on the assassinated President himself and his brief administration is growing rapidly. The only full-scale biography, but a good one, is Herbert S. Parmet, *Jack: The Struggles of John F. Kennedy,* 2 vols. (1980, 1983). Special works on Kennedy's administration include: Haynes B. Johnson, *The Bay of Pigs* (1964); Robert F. Kennedy, *Thirteen Days: The Cuban Missile Crisis* (1969); Lewis J. Paper, *The Promise and the Performance: The Leadership of John F. Kennedy* (1975); Carl M. Brauer, *John F. Kennedy and the Second Reconstruction* (1977); and Arthur M. Schlesinger, Jr., *Robert Kennedy and His Times* (1978). The official account of the Kennedy assassination is the Warren Commission, *Report* (1964). Among the many criticisms of this report, E. J. Epstein, *Inquest* (1966), remains the best.

The election of 1964 is the subject of Theodore H. White, *The Making of the President, 1964* (1965). For an analysis of the problems of the Republican party, see Robert D. Novak, *The Agony of the G.O.P. 1964* (1965).

Conflicting opinions on Johnson are offered by Rowland Evans and Robert Novak, *Lyndon B. Johnson: The Exercise of Power* (1966); William S. White, *The Professional: Lyndon B. Johnson* (1964); and Eric F. Goldman, *The Tragedy of Lyndon Johnson* (1969). Doris Kearns, *Lyndon Johnson and the American Dream* (1976), is a highly personal analysis; Johnson gives his own version in *The Vantage Point* (1971). Sar A. Levitan and

Robert Taggart analyze the effects of Johnson's Great Society programs in *The Promise of Greatness* (1976), but see also Patterson, *America's Struggle against Poverty,* cited earlier. Eugene McCarthy has offered his own history of his presidential campaign in *Year of the People* (1969). Norman Mailer has written a fascinating account of the confrontations at the Democratic national convention of 1968 in *Miami and the Siege of Chicago* (1968).

A blueprint for the Nixon administration was presented by a young member of Attorney General John Mitchell's staff: Kevin P. Phillips, *The Emerging Republican Majority* (1969). A perceptive account of the election of 1968 can be found in Joseph McGinnis, *The Selling of the President* (1969).

There is a large literature on the origins and early years of American intervention in Vietnam. Among the most important are Bernard B. Fall, *Viet-Nam Witness* (1966); Frances FitzGerald, *Fire in the Lake: The Vietnamese and the Americans in Vietnam* (1972); and Guenter Lewy, *America in Vietnam* (1978). The combat soldiers' view of the war is described vividly in Al Santoli, *Everything We Had* (1981). An invaluable documentary source is Neil Sheehan et al., *The Pentagon Papers* (1971).

Anthony Lewis, *Gideon's Trumpet* (1964), is a provocative analysis of Gideon v. Wainwright, while Robert G. Dixon, Jr., *Democratic Representation: Reapportionment in Law and Politics* (1968), is an important work on that aspect of judicial history in the 1960s. For general studies of the Warren Court, see Stanley Kutler, *The Supreme Court and the Constitution* (1969), and Archibald Cox, *The Warren Court* (1968).

CHAPTER 32
THE PRESIDENCY
ON TRIAL

1. THE NIXON
ADMINISTRATION BEGINS

The Tragedy of Richard M. Nixon

Richard Milhous Nixon was born on a small farm in California in 1913 and grew up in nearby Whittier, where his father owned a modest grocery store. Nixon worked his way through Whittier College and attended Duke University Law School on a scholarship. Then followed federal employment and service during the Second World War as a naval supply officer. Back in California after the war, Nixon entered politics as a Republican and defeated a prominent Democratic liberal for the House of Representatives in 1946. Then came, as we have seen, election to the Senate in 1948, election as Vice-President in 1952 and 1956, and, finally, election as President in 1968.

Republicans had nominated Nixon for Vice-President in the 1950s to placate the right wing of the GOP. During the presidential campaigns of 1960 and 1968, Nixon seemed eager to retain that conservative image, since he criticized Democrats as reckless liberals, soft on the threat of communism. Democratic politicians viewed Nixon as the relentless prosecutor of Alger Hiss and as the tireless campaigner who attempted to tie Democratic opponents to years of alleged treason in high places.

Actually, Nixon was an opportunist who had adopted many right-wing positions because they served him well during a period of intense public concern about the Cold War. In 1960, it was Nixon, rather than Kennedy, who suggested that attitudes of the

Cold War might be outmoded. Nixon actually did want to bring an end to the era of severe Cold War tension. He realized that, as a proved extreme patriot, he enjoyed unique protection from rightist criticism if he pursued such policies, and he intended to take full advantage of this position.

Nixon's efforts toward reconciliation met with remarkable success. And yet, when Nixon departed from the White House, he left behind a nation bitterly divided. The damage that he inflicted, or permitted others to inflict, on the office of the presidency, placed his successors in almost impossible positions.

The New Administration

Nixon appointed mostly moderate or conservative Republicans to the cabinet and other key posts. John Mitchell, his Attorney General, was the most influential. Mitchell, Nixon's former law partner and manager of his presidential campaign, had formed the "brain trust" which had planned Nixon's campaign strategy. This group spoke of a "new Republican majority" of middle-class white Southerners, midwestern and western conservatives, and conservatives in the labor movement.

During the campaign of 1968, upon the advice of these men, Nixon continually attacked Johnson's Attorney General, Ramsey Clark, for what he

President Nixon waves from his helicopter after his arrival in Washington from his world trip in August 1969. After his election, Nixon returned to a theme he had frequently touched upon during the campaign and asserted that "the great objective of this Administration at the outset" was "to bring the American people together." (Wide World Photos)

called softness toward criminals of all sorts—from muggers to antiwar dissidents. Now, to Mitchell, was entrusted the task of carrying out Nixon's promise to bring "law and order" to the country. Nixon persuaded his longtime California aide, Robert H. Finch, to take charge of the Department of Health, Education, and Welfare (HEW). Finch, a liberal on civil rights, provided some counterweight to the animosity aroused by Nixon's "southern strategy" (see pp. 539–41). As Secretary of the Interior, Walter J. Hickel, former governor of Alaska, perhaps surprised Nixon by his enthusiasm for conservation and environmental protection.

In 1968, Nixon could and did remain vague about his proposed domestic policies as President. At the time, he appeared to be trying to project an image of a judicious "new Nixon." It now seems clear that this vagueness resulted also from a lack of deep concern about domestic policy, except to the extent that it might significantly affect future elections.

Foreign policy fascinated Nixon. He intended to use American power as a bargaining weapon for a reduction in the tensions of the Cold War. He also intended to take personal charge of these negotiations. Nixon had declared in 1968: "No Secretary of State is really important. The President makes foreign policy."

Thus Nixon appointed as Secretary of State one of his early close advisers, William P. Rogers, and then proceeded to ignore him. Nixon's actual partner in making foreign policy was Henry A. Kissinger, whom he appointed as head of the National Security Council and Special Assistant to the President for National Security Affairs. Kissinger, a former Harvard professor, had written books which criticized American Cold War foreign policies which he said were outdated by events such as the split between China and the Soviet Union—an attitude that Nixon shared. Nixon also shared Kissinger's view that the Soviet Union remained a dangerous enemy. The Sino-Soviet rupture merely presented an opportunity to shift the global balance of power. After Nixon's reelection in 1972, Kissinger was rewarded with the post of Secretary of State, which he held thereafter concurrently with the position of National Security Adviser.

Gyrating Domestic Policies

Nixon surprised both liberals and conservatives by advocating or accepting from Congress a wide variety of innovative legislation. Despite his unexpectedly open mind, Nixon's own policies seldom enjoyed success. He was not really interested in domestic legislation Moreover, he was secluded behind a small group of trusted but inexperienced assistants, most notably his chief aides, H. R. ("Bob") Haldeman and John Ehrlichman.

The experiences of Finch and Hickel illustrate how Nixon's domestic policy was formulated. Early in his administration, Nixon had permitted Finch great leeway in running HEW. Finch announced that HEW would withhold federal aid from school districts which made only token efforts at integration. Finch rejected every plan to slow school integration. When protests from southern politicians increased, Nixon called a halt to rapid integration and specifically granted Mississippi more time to end its dual system. Mitchell brought suits to delay integration in Mississippi. Within a few weeks, the Supreme Court decided that Mississippi had to integrate its schools "at once." Finch prepared to comply with the court's decision. Nixon then ordered Finch to permit delays in integration, the Supreme Court notwithstanding. Finch and his top aides resigned in frustration. However, federal judges obeyed the Supreme Court's rulings and ordered prompt integration. By the end of Nixon's first term, the percentage of southern blacks in all-black schools had declined from 80 to less than 20 per cent. Nevertheless, Nixon had made his own sympathies clear.

Hickel issued a series of regulations to protect the environment, including one that halted the construction of the trans-Alaskan oil pipeline until a route less destructive to Alaska's terrain and wildlife could be found. Hickel also halted oil drilling in the Santa Barbara Channel after a well blowout filled the area's water and beaches with petroleum. Nixon not only permitted Hickel to undertake such initiatives but also called for an environmental program in his State of the Union message in 1970. By late 1970, however, business complaints persuaded Nixon to withdraw his support. Hickel promptly followed Finch into private life. Both former cabinet members complained that they had been unable to present their cases to Nixon because Haldeman and Ehrlichman had refused to give them appointments with the President and had evidently failed even to pass on their messages to Nixon.

Nixon's adviser on urban affairs, Daniel Patrick Moynihan, a sociologist who had served as an adviser to both Kennedy and Johnson, for a while enjoyed better access to Nixon than Finch or Hickel. Nixon responded favorably when Moynihan suggested a Family Assistance Plan (FAP), which would guarantee to a family of four an income of $1,600 a year, plus $800 in food stamps (a total equal to more than double that income in 1983 dollars). The amount suggested by Moynihan exceeded welfare payments in over twenty states, most of them in the South. Moynihan pleased Nixon by pointing out that he could thus aid the poor without interference from federal bureaucrats, and that Nixon could then end certain Great Society programs. These included the "Head Start" educational program and free legal assistance to the poor.

Criticism erupted from both liberals and conservatives. Liberals complained that no family of four could live decently in an American city on $40 a week. Conservatives objected to such payments to persons who refused to work. Despite the misgivings of liberals, the Democratic House of Representatives approved the FAP early in 1973. However, Nixon announced that he no longer supported it. Both Democratic and Republican senators, already doubtful about the FAP, dropped the measure also. Thus, the welfare system, which satisfied almost no one, continued in operation. And once again, Nixon, after showing a surprisingly open mind to new ideas, discarded the FAP when opposition aroused his caution and that of his close advisers.

The most heralded part of Nixon's domestic program—revenue sharing by the federal government with the cities and states—also failed to meet any reasonable expectations. Congress approved the transfer of funds so that cities and states could take over responsibility for federal programs, and revenue sharing began in 1973 with the shift from Washington of about $5 billion. However, mayors and governors soon began to complain. Under revenue sharing, they said, their constituents received less money than they had previously received for specific programs which the Nixon administration now reduced in size or ended, such as the Job Corps training centers.

Nixon's attempts to reduce domestic expenditures were motivated in part by the need to control high rates of inflation. This problem had arisen largely because Johnson had vastly increased federal expenditures for the Great Society and the Vietnam War and had not increased taxes. When reduced spending and higher interest rates caused rising unemployment without checking inflation, Nixon asked Congress for authorization to impose wage and price controls. Although he received this authority in the Economic Stabilization Act of 1970, Nixon promised, "I will not take this nation down the road of wage and price controls, however politically expedient that may seem."

Nevertheless, when inflation continued, Nixon invoked his powers, in August 1971, to freeze wages and prices for six months. Then, when he began decontrol, prices rose again. With the presidential campaign of 1972 only months ahead, Nixon adopted policies that added fuel to the flames. He urged a willing Congress to reduce taxes and persuaded the Federal Reserve Board to lower interest rates. Spending by government agencies increased by about $1 billion a month. The federal deficit for 1972 exceeded that of any year since the Second World War. Nixon's new policies had created tremendous pressure for another inflationary surge.

Nixon came closer to giving a free rein to Attorney General John Mitchell than to any other member of his cabinet. Mitchell built up a record of attempting to stifle civil liberties and civil rights which was unmatched since the actions of Attorney General A. Mitchell Palmer during the Red Scare of 1919–1920. Mitchell attempted to prevent congressional extension of the Voting Rights Act of 1965. He even persuaded Finch to discharge the HEW official in charge of enforcing integration regulations because of that official's zeal for the task.

Mitchell's main objective was to stamp out dissent in the country. He insisted that the Department of Justice could use wiretaps without obtaining court orders. He urged "preventive detention" for criminal suspects when evidence was insufficient for an arrest and persuaded Congress to grant authority for "no-knock" searches. He also instituted prosecution, under various "conspiracy" laws, of antiwar demonstrators.

The "Nixon Court"

Nixon promised to appoint southern justices to the Supreme Court. He also promised to appoint strict constructionists who would "interpret the law, not make the law." Chief Justice Earl Warren resigned in 1969, and Nixon appointed as his successor Warren Burger of Minnesota, a member of the United States Court of Appeals for the District of Columbia. Burger had publicly criticized the Supreme Court's concern for what he called the rights of criminals.

Soon thereafter, however, Nixon encountered unprecedented opposition in trying to fill vacancies on the high bench. Two conservative southern nominees—Clement Haynsworth of South Carolina and G. Harrold Carswell of Florida, were rejected by the Senate. Haynsworth was accused of bigotry and conflict of interest, while legal authorities questioned Carswell's professional qualifications. Nixon then prudently nominated another experienced and competent Minnesota conservative, Judge Harry A. Blackmun, whose views on most subjects apparently resembled those of Burger. The Senate accepted Blackmun. Nixon then replaced two liberal justices, Hugo Black and John M. Harlan, with Lewis F. Powell, Jr., of Virginia and William H. Rehnquist, a leading intellectual of the far right from Arizona. These four new judges greatly slowed the activism of the Warren Court.

Those groups which had benefited most from the Warren Court's activism now lost some aid which they had received previously from the Supreme Court. In a series of decisions, the Burger Court decreased the rights of criminal suspects; indeed, that court stopped just short of reversing the Miranda decision altogether. The court also approved police raids on newspaper offices in search of evidence and denied to reporters the right to keep their sources and notes confidential. The court reduced the rights of poor people to appeal state and local welfare regulations and decisions. The court also permitted Congress to forbid Medicaid payments for abortion and thereby practically ended the former right of poor women to have legal abortions.

However, the court refused to reverse the Warren Court's major decisions. The central concept of the Brown decision—that segregation in public education had to end—was not repudiated. In 1980, the court explicitly approved federal affirmative action programs. The justices required the government to obtain court orders before employing wiretapping against suspected subversives. The justices whom Nixon appointed retained greater independence than he had expected. Furthermore, the choice by Gerald R. Ford (Nixon's successor) of John Paul Stevens to replace the liberal William O. Douglas produced surprising results—for Ford and other conservatives, at least. They had evidently failed to note that Stevens held many liberal opinions, which he soon began to express as a Supreme Court justice.

2. NIXON'S VIETNAM WAR

Futile Efforts for Peace

Nixon promised the American people peace in Vietnam. He failed to explain exactly what he meant. However, events soon made it clear that Nixon, like Johnson, hoped to end the war without further large American casualties and without the surrender of any part of Southeast Asia to the Communists. Ho Chi Minh and the National Liberation Front in South Vietnam, of course, refused to accept Nixon's definition of peace. Negotiations in Paris dragged on without evidence of progress.

Meanwhile, Nixon adopted a policy of "Vietnamization"—that is, of providing the South Vietnamese military forces with huge supplies of American military equipment so that South Vietnam could take over completely the task of fighting. As part of this program, Nixon withdrew American troops. Compared to the 543,000 American soldiers in Vietnam in 1968, only 39,000 remained in the autumn of 1972. Nixon responded in part to massive demonstrations for peace and public opinion polls which showed that most Americans wanted the war ended.

View of Washington, D.C., on Moratorium Day, November 15, 1969. The peace parade is passing along Pennsylvania Avenue from the Capitol to the Washington Monument for a rally. Mass protests such as this symbolized widespread opposition throughout the country to the Vietnam War. (Wide World Photos)

However, Nixon was also responding to congressional action which limited his abiity to continue the fighting. Congress, in December 1970 and January 1971, repealed the Gulf of Tonkin resolution of 1964. When Nixon continued to order new American military activity, particularly in Cambodia and Laos, Congress passed a measure which set August 15, 1973, as the deadline for ending all United States military action in Indochina.

Although Nixon, Kissinger, and Secretary of Defense Melvin R. Laird announced periodically that Vietnamization was proceeding successfully, South Vietnam's dictator, Nguyen Van Thieu, actually enjoyed little support outside the capital city of Saigon and a few provincial capitals. As the failure of Vietnamization became obvious, Nixon and Kissinger decided to use massive bombing attacks to persuade the North Vietnamese and the leaders of the NLF to negotiate seriously. The American leaders believed that their enemies would prefer a peace treaty which permitted them to occupy part of South Vietnam, rather than endure the terrible damage that huge amounts of American bombs could inflict.

The Cambodian Affair

When NLF and North Vietnamese raids from border areas of neutral Cambodia threatened the Saigon government, Nixon, in April 1970, ordered

American troops to invade Cambodia. Enemy forces simply moved deeper into Cambodia. Kissinger then suggested increased bombing. The elusive North Vietnamese suffered hardly at all either from the invasion or the tremendous bombing. However, the Cambodian government (at that point anti-Communist) and the Cambodian economy were wrecked. This mass destruction enabled a small but dedicated group of Communists—the Khmer Rouge—to take over the country and to start a bloody purge of both middle-class and pro-North Vietnamese Cambodians.

Nixon's announcement of the invasion (but not the bombing) of Cambodia set the American peace movement in motion. Protesters demanded "strikes"

A South Vietnamese Ranger keeps his finger on the trigger of his weapon as he watches a Cambodian woman and baby girl emerge from a bunker entrance following American air strikes near Cau Sap in Cambodia in early May 1970. The invasion of Cambodia by U.S. troops to clear out "sanctuaries" used by North Vietnamese and National Liberation Front forces increased opposition to the war at home, particularly as the devastating effects upon the Cambodian people and economy became known. (Wide World Photos)

to close down colleges as evidence of opposition to the war. A more violent fringe of students burned and bombed buildings and interrupted Reserve Officers Training Corps (ROTC) programs, and recruiting efforts by corporations involved in war-related production. Police and national guardsmen called to protect campuses often met angry, rock-throwing mobs of students.

Ohio National Guardsmen shot and killed four students and wounded eleven at Kent State University, and policemen killed two and wounded eleven students at Jackson State University in Mississippi. These events led to larger demonstrations, which closed down over 200 colleges.

Nixon seems to have thought that a revolution was in the making. He arranged for taps on the telephones of reporters and of high governmental officials whom he suspected of leaking news of the Cambodian bombing. He tried to establish a national security committee led by J. Edgar Hoover, which would seek to end dissent with the aid of electronic surveillance, secret break-ins, and infiltration of "subversive" groups. This plan alarmed even Hoover, and it was abandoned.

A demonstration by students on the College Park, Maryland, campus of the University of Maryland on May 4, 1970. The antiwar demonstrators were dispersed by state police who threw tear gas into the crowd. (Wide World Photos)

A wounded student on the campus of Kent State University,
Kent, Ohio, receives help from other students following a
confrontation between national guardsmen and antiwar
demonstrators on May 4, 1970. National guardsmen, who had been
called to the campus to control a series of demonstrations that
had culminated in the burning of an ROTC building, resorted to tear
gas and bullets. Four students were killed and several others were
injured. (Wide World Photos)

Peace of a Sort

Despite the combat failure of Vietnamization, Nixon and Kissinger got their
main point across to the North Vietnamese and the NLF. If their resistance
to American peace proposals continued, the United States would use
saturation bombing to end the war. By 1971 the United States had already
dropped far more bombs on Indochina than it had used during the Second
World War. Now Nixon ordered further escalation of the bombing, aimed at
South Vietnamese villages reportedly controlled by the NLF and at military
installations in North Vietnam.

Meanwhile, South Vietnamese and American troops also understood that
Nixon and Kissinger no longer hoped to win the war; they only hoped to get

out without obviously losing. Desertions from the South Vietnamese army rose to 12,000 a month. American troops, an increasing proportion of whom were black or Hispanic draftees, realized that they risked death and mutilation in a futile war, and they carried on their own rebellion. Racial strife increased and enlisted men killed or disabled the officers who tried to push them too hard. United States commanders acknowledged in the spring of 1971 that at least 10 per cent of American troops in Vietnam used heroin.

In these circumstances, Nixon and Kissinger put still more pressure on the North Vietnamese and NLF negotiators. On May 8, 1972, Nixon ordered the mining of the chief North Vietnamese port of Haiphong and other North Vietnamese ports. Nixon's objective was to stop or slow drastically the shipment of military supplies from China and the Soviet Union. Nixon also ordered B-52 bombing strikes at targets in Hanoi and Haiphong—clearly a warning that no part of North Vietnam would escape destruction unless peace came soon.

On October 26, Kissinger announced that, as a result of talks which he had conducted with the North Vietnamese Foreign Secretary, Le Duc Tho, "Peace is at hand." The North Vietnamese government accepted the agreements reached by Kissinger and Le Duc Tho. However, after the election, South Vietnam's President Thieu demanded major changes in the treaty. Hanoi then demanded further concessions in an effort to force the Americans back to the October agreement.

On December 17, without warning, Nixon ordered the heaviest and most savage bombing of the entire war, aimed mainly at targets in North Vietnamese cities. General Alexander Haig, Kissinger's military adviser, accurately described the bombing as the "brutalizing" of North Vietnam. On December 30, Nixon announced that the North Vietnamese had agreed to reopen negotiations and that the bombing would cease. The negotiations finally produced a cease-fire agreement signed on January 27, 1973.

The peace agreement—what Nixon called "peace with honor"—stipulated that the remaining American troops would leave and that all prisoners of war would be returned within sixty days. The agreement left the future of South Vietnam vague. Secretly, Nixon had promised Thieu renewed military aid if fighting resumed. To discourage further participation by American troops, Congress passed, over Nixon's veto, the war-powers resolution of 1973. It stated that a President could not order troops into action unless he reported the fact to Congress; that he had to halt the military action at once if Congress voted its disapproval; and that he had to do so within ninety days unless Congress voted its approval.

In 1975, the North Vietnamese launched a powerful offensive across their border and sent the South Vietnamese army into hasty retreat. Kissinger urged Congress to honor Nixon's secret pledge to Thieu, but Congress refused. Before enemy troops occupied Saigon, the 5,000 Americans who remained in Vietnam were evacuated, along with more than 100,000 South Vietnamese.

After more than a decade of American fighting in Southeast Asia, all of Vietnam, Cambodia, and half of Laos were in Communist hands. Casualties included 56,000 Americans and over 1,000,000 North and South Vietnamese killed. Millions of refugees crowded camps for displaced persons.

The war also left deep divisions in American society. When Assistant Secretary of Defense John T. McNaughton suggested to McNamara in 1967

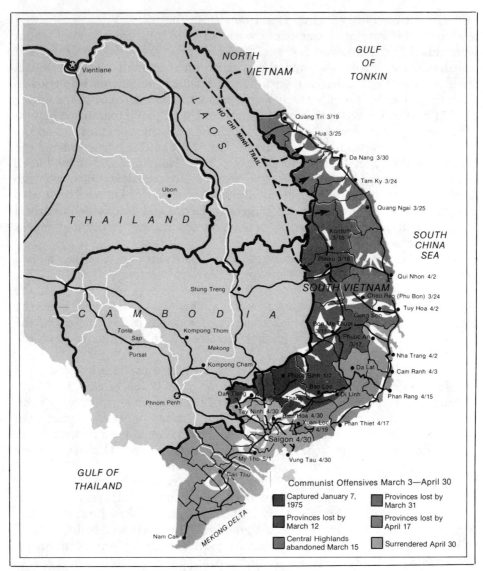

The Collapse of South Vietnam, 1975

the "objective and encyclopedic" study of events connected with Vietnam (published as *The Pentagon Papers*), he had written: "A feeling is widely and strongly held that 'the Establishment' is out of its mind." This feeling intensified during Nixon's Vietnam War.

3. NEW INITIATIVES IN FOREIGN POLICY

Opening the Door to China

The achievement of friendlier relations with the People's Republic of China and the Soviet Union was one reason for Nixon's confidence that the United

States could mine and bomb North Vietnam with safety. Nixon and Kissinger, both advocates of balance-of-power global politics, grasped the strategic significance of the Sino-Soviet rift and understood the advantage that improved relations with China would give the United States in dealing with the Soviet Union.

The Chinese dropped numerous hints of their change in attitude before Nixon returned a favorable sign in 1971. Then in response to an invitation by the Chinese Premier, Chou En-lai, Nixon sent Kissinger secretly to Peking, where he arranged for a visit to China by Nixon.

Nixon announced in July 1971 that he would visit the People's Republic of China. That visit, which occurred in February 1972, succeeded as a theatrical as well as a diplomatic event. Officials of the two countries agreed on various cultural, commercial, journalistic, and diplomatic exchanges but postponed formal diplomatic relations, which would necessitate recognition of the People's Republic rather than Taiwan as the legitimate government of China.

Détente with the Soviet Union

Nixon had wished to visit the Soviet Union in 1970. He expected to make North Vietnamese leaders more willing to sign a peace treaty by showing them that Soviet decision makers considered them expendable when larger matters were involved. Four weeks after Nixon announced his forthcoming visit to China, Soviet officials invited him to visit Moscow.

The agreements reached by Nixon in Moscow in May 1972 indicated that both the Soviet leaders and the American President wanted to reduce tensions between the two countries. Nixon and the Communist party leader, Leonid Brezhnev, signed the SALT agreement, already hammered out by their subordinates. It restricted emplacement of antiballistic missile systems and froze the deployment of additional missile launchers by each side. The Soviet Union received the right to buy large quantities of American wheat, which American farmers eagerly sold to them. After the presidential election, these sales produced sharply higher grain prices in the United States.

Brezhnev came to Washington in June 1973 for further bargaining. In a new agreement, Brezhnev and Nixon promised to hasten negotiations toward SALT II, which would halt the construction of offensive nuclear weapons. Nixon, in the area of what he considered the President's foremost responsibility—foreign policy—had tried, in dealing with China and the Soviet Union, to work for future peace and had enjoyed significant success.

4. WATERGATE AND THE DOWNFALL OF NIXON

The Campaign and Election of 1972

During the campaign of 1968, Nixon's advisers had decided that a new majority coalition could be formed among the American electorate. Its basis would be a combination of the regular conservative Republican minority and George Wallace's American party constituency of 1968.

Some Nixon aides had spoken freely during the campaign of 1968 about presidential policies which would shift Wallace's supporters to Nixon during his first term in office. One of Nixon's strategists, Kevin Phillips, used the term "middle Americans" to describe the former Democrats, Wallace supporters, and the regular Republicans who would form the new Republican majority in support of Nixon. Phillips further identified the members of the new majority as "the unyoung, the unblack, and the unpoor."

Nixon and Mitchell aimed their "southern strategy" largely at middle-class southern whites. To the former southern Democrats and the dependable conservative Republicans, Nixon strategists expected to add millions of votes from northern and western workers. Nixon and Mitchell used both rhetoric and policies to assure these particular "middle Americans" that the Nixon administration shared their distress about crime in the streets, the integration of their ethnic neighborhoods, school busing, welfare cheating, peace demonstrations, and certain life-styles associated with young people in the 1960s. Although these attitudes within the administration would antagonize many blacks and some moderate Republicans, Nixon and his advisers concluded that the next presidential election could be won easily without them. Their new coalition, they believed, would destroy the Democratic majority created during the New Deal and make the Republican party dominant in the United States.

The Nixon strategists received unexpected aid in May 1972, when an attempted assassination left George Wallace partially paralyzed and eliminated Nixon's chief competitor for the votes of "middle Americans." The Democratic convention provided further help. It nominated for President George S. McGovern, senator from South Dakota and the favorite of the party's antiwar and left wing. Blacks, women, and young people constituted a much higher proportion of the delegates in the Democratic convention in Miami than in previous Democratic conventions on account of the adoption of new rules for choosing delegates. The rejection of Chicago's Mayor Daley as a delegate by the Democratic convention of 1972 revealed both the shift in power within the party and the alienation of traditional sources of Democratic votes. When Democrats such as Daley and George Meany, president of the AFL-CIO, withheld their active support from McGovern, they increased the chances for the successful execution of the plan of the Nixon strategists to form a new Republican majority coalition.

Nevertheless, McGovern attacked Nixon for continuing the war in Vietnam, which had claimed 15,000 lives since Nixon's inauguration. McGovern also made charges of corruption against Nixon. Most of them were accurate but ignored.

In 1971, Nixon and his campaign leaders had formed the Committee to Reelect the President (commonly called CREEP once its activities became known), under the leadership of John Mitchell, who resigned as Attorney General. CREEP collected a record $55 million to $60 million, much of it in large illegal contributions from corporations and individuals who had received or expected special favors from the government. During the preconvention campaign, CREEP used this money to finance "dirty tricks" intended to demoralize potentially strong opponents such as Wallace and the early leader for the Democratic nomination, Senator Edmund S. Muskie of Maine.

Five CREEP agents broke into Democratic National Committee headquarters in the Watergate complex in Washington in May 1972, copied files, and placed a tap on the telephones. On June 17, 1972, policemen arrested the same five men in the act of a second burglary of Democratic headquarters. Two accomplices were arrested soon afterward. One of them, James McCord, a former CIA agent, was a well-known official of CREEP.

Mitchell swiftly denied that the burglars had acted under orders from CREEP, and Nixon's press secretary called the break-in a "third-rate burglary." Nixon denied that he knew anything about the break-in. McGovern attempted to tie Nixon to the Watergate burglary, but few American voters took McGovern's charges seriously. Nixon left most of the Republican campaigning to Vice-President Agnew, who railed against peace demonstrators and spoke in favor of law and order. The only remaining question about the election was the dimension of the Nixon victory. Nixon won 60.8 per cent of the popular votes and 521 electoral votes—both the second largest majorities in history. However, Democrats retained control of both houses of Congress.

The Downfall of Nixon

Meanwhile, the outwardly jubilant Nixon was trying desperately to keep his administration from falling apart. His personal counsel, John Dean, had told his closest aide, Haldeman, almost every detail about the Watergate break-in two days after it occurred. On the following day, June 20, Nixon and Haldeman evidently discussed the arrests, their possible legal and political repercussions, and methods to prevent those consequences. During the remainder of the campaign, Nixon and his chief assistants devoted time almost daily to efforts to cover up the Watergate affair.

On June 23, Haldeman reported to Nixon: "We're back in the problem area because the FBI is out of control." Nixon ordered Haldeman to tell the acting director of the FBI, L. Patrick Gray, "Don't go any further into this case, period." Gray and officials of CREEP destroyed huge quantities of records which related to the administration's illegal campaign activities. The leading Watergate defendants received promises of presidential pardons if they would agree quietly to serve short prison terms; over $400,000 was distributed to the defendants from CREEP campaign funds to pay legal fees, support families, and to buy their silence. Thus Nixon kept the matter fairly quiet during the campaign.

Nixon's administration and his political career began to disintegrate almost immediately after his second inauguration. The trial judge for the Watergate burglars, John J. Sirica of the district court of the District of Columbia, was a tough law-and-order judge. The trial of the Watergate burglars began in January 1973; on February 2, Sirica declared that he was "not satisfied" that the whole story was being told. Partly as a result of Sirica's demand for further investigation, the Senate established a special investigatory committee. Another law-and-order advocate, Senator Sam Ervin, Jr., of North Carolina, was chairman of the committee.

After the prosecution had presented its case before Sirica, the Watergate defendants declined to testify and all pleaded guilty. Sirica then gave each the maximum sentence allowed; however, he added that he would show leniency to any defendant who told the truth. McCord broke first. He wrote to Sirica that high administration officials had been involved, and he offered to testify before the Ervin committee. Dean, who had been involved in the cover-up, began to fear that he was being groomed for the role of scapegoat. He, too, began to confess to the Watergate prosecutors. As evidence accumulated of widespread criminal behavior within the Nixon administration, the President sacrificed one aide after another to the investigators. However, he continued to maintain his own innocence.

Gray resigned on April 27, 1973, after he admitted that he had burned documents concerning Watergate. Three days later, Nixon announced the resignation of Haldeman, Ehrlichman, Dean, and Attorney General Richard Kleindienst. Nixon also promised to continue to ferret out the facts.

Ervin's committee began televised hearings on May 17. A parade of witnesses connected with the administration confessed to criminal acts which aimed, first, to win the election of 1972 and, second, to cover up these acts by perjury and destruction of evidence. In addition, there were revelations of attempts to interfere with judicial proceedings and of bribery, blackmail, promises of presidential pardons, and numerous other offenses. "It's beginning to be like Teapot Dome," exclaimed Senator Goldwater.

During testimony before the Ervin committee, a White House official revealed that Nixon routinely taped his conversations in the Oval Office. All through the following year, the Senate, Sirica, and federal prosecutors fought with Nixon for possession of these tapes. Although he continued to maintain, as he stated in one news conference, that he was not "a crook," Nixon knew that the tapes would prove otherwise.

Special Watergate prosecutor Archibald Cox obtained an order from Sirica on August 29 for nine sections of tapes which would have incriminated Nixon. Nixon offered instead transcripts, which he would edit himself. Cox refused to accept the edited transcripts. Nixon then ordered Attorney General Elliot Richardson to discharge Cox. Richardson resigned on Saturday, October 20, rather than carry out this order. William Ruckelshaus, recently appointed Deputy Attorney General, also declined to discharge Cox, and Nixon dismissed Ruckelshaus. The Nixon appointee next in line for the position of Attorney General, Robert Bork, finally discharged Cox on Saturday night.

This, the so-called Saturday Night Massacre, aroused serious doubts about Nixon's innocence even among his close supporters. The House Judiciary Committee began to discuss whether the President should be impeached, and Republican congressional leaders warned Nixon that Republicans as well as Democrats were prepared to approve impeachment.

Another blow to the administration came on October 10, 1973. Vice-President Agnew, critic of judges who meted out lenient sentences to criminals, was allowed to plead *nolo contendere* (no contest) on one count of income-tax evasion and surrendered the vice-presidency in exchange for an agreement by the government not to prosecute charges of soliciting, extorting, and accepting bribes. Evidence released by the Justice Department appeared sufficient to indict Agnew on at least fifty counts. Congress quickly confirmed Nixon's choice, Gerald R. Ford, the House minority leader, to succeed Agnew under the terms of the Twenty-fifth Amendment.

Nixon delivered one emotional appeal after another over the heads of his tormentors to the American people. However, these appeals became less and less effective as new evidence came to light of Nixon's personal involvement in criminal activities.

Nixon toured the Middle East in mid-1974 and visited Moscow soon afterward. He received enthusiastic public receptions, but Kissinger complained later that diplomacy "was getting more and more difficult because it involved the question of whether we could, in fact, carry out what we were negotiating."

By June 1974, Nixon had listened to all his tapes and realized that they provided evidence for criminal prosecution as well as impeachment. Therefore, when Cox's successor, Leon Jaworski, demanded access to sixty-four tapes, Nixon refused on grounds of the constitutional privileges of the executive branch in its dealings with the judiciary and Congress. Nixon expected the Supreme Court to concur in his refusal.

Impeachment and Resignation

Contrary to Nixon's expectation, on July 24, 1974, the Supreme Court unanimously ruled that the Watergate events were "criminal proceedings" and that Nixon had to turn over the sixty-four tapes to Judge Sirica immediately. By July 30, the House Judiciary Committee had voted to impeach Nixon on three counts. The first article of impeachment charged him with obstruction of justice through the use of false statements, payment

After hearing testimony for several weeks on impeachment charges against President Nixon, the House Judiciary Committee opened debate on the articles of impeachment on July 24, 1974, before a nationwide television audience. Three days later, the Committee voted by a margin of 27 to 11 to recommend the impeachment of Richard M. Nixon, 37th President of the United States. (Wide World Photos).

*Former President Richard M. Nixon waves farewell from the
presidential helicopter after his resignation. It is a crushing
historical irony that the Nixon administration succeeded beyond
belief in its campaign promise to unify the American people. The
Watergate crisis not only brought the American public together
in common outrage, but led to some of the most concerted
congressional action in the country's history. (Wide World
Photos)*

of bribes, withholding of evidence, interference with investigations, and lying
in addresses to the American people. The second article accused Nixon of
misusing the FBI, CIA, and Internal Revenue Service to spy on the public.
The third article dealt with Nixon's refusal to turn over the tapes and other
evidence to Congress, despite subpoenas to do so. Nixon finally turned over
the last of the tapes demanded by Jaworski on August 5. Nixon admitted that
he had concealed their existence from his own lawyers, but he still insisted
that he was innocent. Nevertheless, he did not wait to find out whether
Congress would agree (which was highly unlikely). Instead, on August 9,
1974, he resigned from office, the first President to do so.

Members of the Nixon administration began a parade to grand juries,
courts, and federal prisons. In addition to the seven men connected directly
to the Watergate burglary, over ten other Nixon administration and CREEP
officials received jail sentences. The most prominent of these included
former Attorney General John Mitchell and Nixon's closest aides, Haldeman
and Ehrlichman. Still the nation waited for the truth about Nixon's role in
crimes already discussed in court cases and signed confessions. Meanwhile,
for the first time, the American people had a President whom they had not
elected.

SUGGESTED READINGS

A comprehensive analysis of the Nixon presidency remains to be written. Richard Nixon, *Six Crises* (1962), offers self-revelations about the man, some of which are unintentional. Nixon's autobiography is *RN: The Memoirs of Richard Nixon* (1978). Garry Wills, *Nixon Agonistes* (1970), is perceptive, but lacks the perspective that knowledge of the rest of Nixon's presidency would have brought.

On Agnew, see Jules Witcover and R. M. Cohen, *Heartbeat Away* (1974). Kevin Phillips' book on the Nixon-Mitchell political strategy, *The Emerging Republican Majority*, already cited, is also cited in the text. Other volumes on politics during the Nixon administration include Arthur M. Schlesinger, Jr., *The Imperial Presidency* (1973), and Theodore H. White, *The Making of the President, 1972* (1973), which is the least competent of White's series of books on presidential elections. The best general study of the entire Nixon presidency is Jonathan Schell, *The Time of Illusion* (1976).

Members of the Nixon administration have written about it in almost unprecedented numbers. Among the more informative is Henry Kissinger, *White House Years* (1979), which should be read as the work of a man still ambitious for a leading role in foreign policy. Among the useful memoirs dealing with Watergate are John W. Dean, *Blind Am-*bition (1976); Leon Jaworski, *The Right and the Power: The Prosecution of Watergate* (1976); and John J. Sirica, *To Set the Record Straight* (1979).

In addition to the memoirs mentioned above, the Watergate scandals have given rise to numerous books. Carl Bernstein and Bob Woodward, *All the President's Men* (1974), will remain a classic journalistic account of the uncovering of the Watergate scandal —in part—by the two *Washington Post* reporters who played major roles in that process. Bernstein and Woodward's *The Final Days* (1976) completes their particular story.

In addition to Kissinger's memoir, mentioned above, other informative volumes on Nixon's foreign policy include Marvin and Bernard Kalb, *Kissinger* (1974); John G. Stoessinger, *Henry Kissinger: The Anguish of Power* (1976); and John Newhouse, *Cold Dawn* (1973), which relates the shift in the relations between the United States and the USSR. William Shawcross, *Sideshow: Kissinger, Nixon, and the Destruction of Cambodia* (1979), is a devastating indictment which Kissinger tried, unsuccessfully, to refute in *White House Years*. Finally, Seymour Hersh, *The Price of Power: Kissinger in the Nixon White House* (1983), portrays Kissinger as a person with no principles, who lusted after power.

CHAPTER 33
SINCE WATERGATE

1. THE FORD PRESIDENCY

The Legacy of Watergate

Vice-President Ford took the oath of office as President of the United States on August 9, 1974. On that same day, Ford announced reassuringly: "Our long national nightmare is over." Ford's awareness of the country's turmoil and of his own limitations immediately established a favorable comparison of Ford and Nixon. Ford's selection of the veteran moderate Republican, Nelson Rockefeller, as his Vice-President seemed to demonstrate a desire to heal the nation's wounds. The new President appeared open, amiable, and eager to compromise rather than to fight with opponents. Actually, Ford held much more conservative political views than Nixon, and his Cold-War attitudes were more rigid.

Only one month after his inauguration, Ford suddenly issued to his predecessor and benefactor a "full, free, and absolute" pardon for "all offenses against the United States" which Nixon had committed while President. Nixon continued to deny that he had committed any crimes, yet he hastily accepted the pardon. A majority of Americans found unsatisfactory Ford's explanation of the pardon—that he wanted only to end "an American tragedy in which we have all played a part." Was he blaming the American people for the behavior exposed in the Nixon tapes? For what crimes had Nixon been pardoned? Why were Nixon's chief assistants on trial, while the man who had issued their orders was absolved? Public confidence in Ford plunged.

Meanwhile, a Senate committee uncovered a long history of violations of constitutional rights and of international law by the CIA and the FBI. This evidence implicated the CIA in assassinations of a number of foreign political leaders and revealed, too, that the CIA had spied on over 10,000 American citizens—including congressmen, governmental officials, and antiwar and civil-rights leaders. The CIA had thus violated the National Security Act of 1947, which forbade it to undertake domestic internal security operations.

FBI misdeeds shocked the nation even more. Clearly illegal efforts to injure the reputations of individuals disliked by J. Edgar Hoover were disclosed; so, too, were attempts to destroy organizations which had fitted Hoover's very broad definition of "subversive." Directives from Washington had ordered field officers of the FBI to attempt to discredit the New-Left movement and the Black Muslims. Hoover had directed a vicious FBI campaign against Martin Luther King, Jr. An FBI offensive against the Black Panthers coincided with the shooting, evidently while they slept, of Chicago's Panther leaders by Chicago police who acted in cooperation with the FBI.

Persistent Problems, Foreign and Domestic

Ford retained Henry Kissinger as Secretary of State, and Kissinger continued the balance-of-power politics which had been his trademark. In the Middle East, his efforts contributed to some easing of tensions, but not to a resolution of the Arab-Israeli conflict. With regard to Southeast Asia, Kissinger argued that the "fall" of Indochina in 1975 reflected an American failure of will. But there was much evidence that it reflected changed world conditions in which the power of the United States was more limited than at any time since the Second World War.

The foreign policies of Kissinger and Nixon had put great emphasis on détente with the two major Communist powers. These efforts were partially frustrated during the Ford presidency. China balked at establishing formal relations so long as the United States maintained diplomatic and military ties with Taiwan. Negotiations with the Soviet Union for SALT II dragged on. In July 1975, the United States and the Soviet Union, and thirty-one other nations, did sign a European Security Treaty in Helsinki. The pact recognized the territorial status quo in Europe and pledged the signatories to protect human rights. However, the United States remained troubled by Soviet violations of the human-rights agreement, particularly the persecution of dissidents and of Jews, and by indirect Russian intervention in Africa and elsewhere.

In domestic affairs, as in foreign relations, old problems brought new troubles to the Ford administration. The Arab oil embargo prompted by the Yom Kippur War in 1973 led to the quadrupling of OPEC oil prices in early 1974. Subsequent price increases saddled the world economy with another major inflationary force. The sources of the oil crisis of the 1970s were many and complex, but underlying all of them was the fact that the world's finite reserves were being consumed at a prodigious rate. The United States alone, with 6 per cent of the world's population, consumed 33 per cent of the energy used worldwide. In the short term, parties which shared responsibility for the jump in prices included the OPEC nations, which had seen their

earnings dwindle amidst worldwide inflation; the multinational oil companies, which had developed mechanisms for controlling world production and
benefited from the new world market prices; and even the United States
Government, whose oil policies had exacerbated the problem.

Nixon, in November 1973, had proposed a "Project Independence" designed to make America self-sufficient in energy by 1980. But as the decade
waned the nation actually became more dependent on imported oil than it
had been in 1973. Not until 1979 did American oil consumption begin to
decline. By the time that Ford took office, the shortages of oil had
disappeared (although the prices continued to climb), and there was little
public support for conservation or for diversion of public funds to energy
research.

Oil price increases aggravated inflation rates in the Nixon-Ford years. Ford,
unlike Nixon, relied on tight fiscal and monetary policy and on voluntary
wage and price guidelines to combat inflation. These measures had little
effect. Inflation did decline, but only because of the worst recession to that
point since the Second World War. The overall unemployment rate exceeded
9 per cent by the end of 1975—the highest since the 1930s—and Ford was
forced to stimulate the economy despite the inflationary risks.

In economic affairs, and in other areas as well, Ford found himself at odds
with a Democratic Congress which was flexing its muscles in the aftermath
of Watergate. During his brief tenure, Ford vetoed fifty bills. Congress failed
to override most of the vetoes, but it was able to block many of Ford's
legislative proposals. By 1976, this legislation stalemate gave the impression
of a government unable to deal with pressing affairs of state. There was
blame enough to go around, but Ford became the most convenient target of
such faultfinding.

The Presidential Election of 1976

When Ford succeeded to the presidency, he seemed to have no further
ambition than to serve out Nixon's term. But by early 1975, he was a
presidential candidate in all but name. Ford was challenged for the Republican nomination by Ronald Wilson Reagan, the champion of the party's
conservative wing. Ford won, but the narrow margin of his victory in the
convention demonstrated his vulnerability.

The Democrats, excluded from the White House for eight years, smelled
victory at last. The legacy of the Nixon-Agnew scandals, the lack of unity in
the GOP, and the economic malaise of the nation made the Democratic
party's chances bright indeed. The prospect of victory attracted many well-
known Democratic contenders for the nomination. But in an astonishing
upset, the nomination went to an "outsider," Jimmy Carter, former governor
of Georgia.

Like McGovern in 1972, Carter had campaigned tirelessly for four years.
He and his small staff mastered the complex procedures for selecting
delegates to the Democratic convention of 1976 and then set out on a
grueling grass-roots campaign. Carter made *himself* the issue by emphasizing
the need for honesty, managerial competency, and fresh ideas in Washington.
Carter's strategy paid off with victories in the early caucuses and primaries.
Following these successes, Carter's campaign attracted the kind of media

coverage which can anoint candidates as "front runners" in modern campaigns. Carter amassed enough delegates to lock up the nomination before the convention, despite a late challenge by Governor Edmund G. Brown, Jr., of California.

Ford spent much of his time in the White House carrying out the duties of his office—and attracting the news coverage that goes with such activities. Meanwhile, Ford and his associates jabbed at his opponent by questioning the wisdom of electing a man of unknown abilities. Ford's strategy seemed to work, for Carter's initial lead in the public opnion polls had melted away by October. That month a series of televised "debates" between the incumbent and the challenger shed little light on substantive differences between them. However, they did reassure many voters that Carter was at least as well qualified as Ford to be President.

The outcome was extremely close. Carter won 51 per cent of the popular vote and 297 electoral votes; Ford, 48 per cent and 241 electoral votes. The sectional distribution of the electoral vote seemed to indicate a revival of traditional voting patterns. The Republican nominee carried every state west of Missouri, except Texas and Hawaii, while the Democrat carried the entire South, except Virginia, and won enough of the big industrial states of the East and Midwest to eke out a narrow victory. Closer examination, however, revealed something new about Carter's "Solid South." His triumph in the South and elsewhere would have been impossible without overwhelming support from blacks. Ironically, the Voting Rights Act of 1965 helped to elect

The Election of 1976

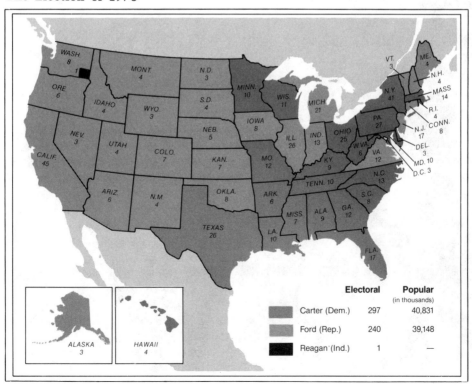

	Electoral	Popular (in thousands)
Carter (Dem.)	297	40,831
Ford (Rep.)	240	39,148
Reagan (Ind.)	1	—

the first President from the Deep South since Zachary Taylor. Carter also benefited from the aura of corruption which, fairly or not, still clung to the party of Richard Nixon. As an outsider, Carter was also free to capitalize on the public perception that the federal government was not coping with the country's great social and economic problems.

2. THE NEW PRESIDENT

"Jimmy Who?"

Jimmy Carter entered the White House virtually unknown to most Americans. In part, the uncertainty about Carter stemmed from his lack of prior visibility in Washington. But the confusion also reflected the contradictory images which he had projected during the campaign. On the one hand, Carter called himself a "Populist" and championed the interests of the average citizen against the "special interests." On the other hand, he stressed his experiences as an engineer (naval officer), businessman, and efficiency-minded governor. Who was the *real* Jimmy Carter—the "Populist" reformer or the efficiency-minded engineer/manager?

President Carter and his family walking from the Capitol to the White House following his inauguration in 1977. Like Thomas Jefferson's unceremonious walk to his first inauguration in 1801, President Carter's gesture was an intentional contrast to the "imperial Presidency" of the recent past. (United Press International)

Carter's folksiness and his campaign denunciations of special interests gave him something of a Populist aura. But his personal background, record as governor of Georgia, and policies as President all suggest greater ties with the southern progressive tradition than with Populism. Progressivism in the South was predominantly a movement of the middle and upper classes, and its goals had included "businesslike" administration of government. Jimmy Carter, for all the talk of his humble origins, was the son of a small-town rich man. The Carters of Sumter County occupied a position of prestige. They had a sense of social responsibility, albeit a paternalistic one.

Carter's training at the United States Naval Academy broadened but did not fundamentally alter his notion of social responsibility. His engineer's training, reinforced by service in the elite nuclear submarine service, instilled in Carter habits of management and problem solving which encouraged diligent personal effort and systematic analysis. Once the "right" answer was determined in this engineering world, one need only explain it to others to persuade them of its correctness. This style of leadership had its limitations when transferred to the political and governmental arenas.

In the Georgia statehouse and in the White House, Carter's actions were shaped by a moderate, morally grounded reformism, coupled with an engineer's zeal for efficiency and rational problem solving. In the former respect, he resembled his southern predecessor, Woodrow Wilson. In the latter, he resembled his fellow engineer, Herbert Hoover.

The Carter Presidency

Once in the White House, Carter's inclination was to forego new spending programs (he promised a balance budget by 1980) and to set about reforming the *structure* of government. In January 1978, Carter proposed comprehensive reforms of the tax and welfare systems. All of these were long-needed changes, but Carter was unable to steer them through the legislative maze.

In the post-Watergate era, Congress was determined to establish a strong position relative to the President, *any* President. Furthermore, party discipline was weak among the unwieldy Democratic majority. The Carter administration also proved unable or unwilling to play the game of legislation as it was customarily played on Capitol Hill. Carter vetoed "pet" water and flood-control projects in the name of economy and prudence. His staff slighted and infuriated, influential congressmen with real or imagined intent. More damaging still, Carter and his staff devised comprehensive legislative programs without giving adequate attention to the task of shepherding them through Congress.

In 1977–1978, Carter offered comprehensive legislative proposals relating to energy, welfare, and taxes; none of them was enacted as proposed. Carter's energy program featured a substantial tax on crude oil. Although it passed the House more or less intact, it was gutted in the Senate. The bills which emerged from Congress in October 1978 gave Carter no more than a symbolic victory in his energy war. An even worse fate awaited the tax bill submitted in January 1978. Promoted as a plan to reduce taxes for the poor and to close "loopholes" for the rich, the income-tax cuts were offset by increases in Social Security taxes, while the taxes on capital gains were actually reduced.

Carter's major accomplishments came in foreign affairs. He completed negotiations on two Panama Canal treaties in September 1977. The first provided that after the year 2000, ownership of the canal would go to Panama. The Senate gave its consent to ratification in the spring of 1978 with only one vote to spare and only after adding a "clarifying" amendment that safeguarded the right of the United States to protect the canal, by the use of force if necessary.

In early 1979, the United States and the People's Republic of China entered into formal diplomatic relations. Carter also withdrew recognition of the Republic of China in Taiwan and renounced the mutual defense treaty between the United States and the Republic of China. Negotiations also continued with the Soviet Union on the SALT II treaty. Carter and Brezhnev signed the treaty in Vienna on June 18, 1979. Its most important provision set a limit on long-range missiles which each country might possess and provided for a decrease in these awesome weapons by 1981.

Carter's most stunning achievement was a peace treaty between Israel and Egypt. Under pressure from Washington, President Anwar el-Sadat of Egypt and Prime Minister Menachem Begin of Israel exchanged visits in late 1977. The two leaders tried to reach an agreement, but negotiations were at an end by the early summer of 1978. Then Carter invited Sadat and Begin to Camp David, the presidential retreat in Maryland, in September and patiently brought the two antagonists together. In spite of the opposition of the rest of the Arab world, Sadat signed with Begin a treaty of peace at the White House on March 26, 1979. It provided for gradual Israeli evacuation of the Sinai and for the establishment of normal diplomatic relations. The treaty left unsettled the troubling question of the fate of Palestinians in the Gaza Strip and on the West Bank of the Jordan River. However, the Israeli-Egyptian Treaty did guarantee the security of Israel, at least for a time, and it gave

President Anwar el-Sadat of Egypt, President Jimmy Carter of the United States, and Prime Minister Menachem Begin of Israel at the signing of the peace treaty between Egypt and Israel on March 29, 1979. Carter's influential role in this tentative but significant step toward peace in the Middle East marked this occasion as a high point of his presidency. (Wide World Photos)

Sadat an opportunity, with the assistance of the United States, to address himself to urgent economic problems in his own country.

These were impressive achievements, but many Americans were still frustrated by the realization that the United States no longer dominated world affairs as it had for a generation. Many were particularly disturbed by their nation's inability to influence events in the Middle East (except for Egypt), Africa, and other parts of the third world—areas which in an age of scarce natural resources had taken on new significance for the United States.

Foreign affairs again intruded into the domestic economy in 1979 in the form of shrinking supplies and skyrocketing prices of imported oil and in the continued decline of the dollar overseas. Carter had come to view inflation, not unemployment, as the nation's number one economic problem. But Carter's voluntary guidelines had little effect on inflation. To deal with the renewed oil crisis, Carter proposed a $142.2 billion program which concentrated on the development of alternative sources of energy and on price-induced conservation. Funds for development were to be derived from a "windfall profits" tax levied against oil companies when prices were decontrolled. Carter finally won most of his energy program in the spring of 1980. It provided for gradual deregulation of the prices of oil produced in the United States and a "windfall profits" tax on domestic production.

Oil price increases in 1979 triggered still higher inflation. By the end of 1979, the consumer price index was rising at an annual rate of almost 18 per cent. Carter resisted the imposition of wage and price controls. Instead, with its wage and price guidelines in shambles, the administration turned increasingly to budget cutting and restrictions on credit and the money supply. The clampdown on credit immediately depressed the housing and automobile industries. Layoffs in these and related industries led the surge in unemployment, which by July 1980 exceeded 8 per cent for the first time since the major downturn of 1974–1975.

3. THE PRESIDENTIAL CAMPAIGN AND ELECTION OF 1980

Presidential Politics and International Crises

Carter had never left much doubt about his intentions to run for a second term. Not only would he face strong Republican opposition, but he also faced an uphill fight for the Democratic nomination. A poll of Democratic voters taken on November 1, 1979, showed Senator Edward M. Kennedy of Massachusetts leading Carter by 54 per cent to 20 per cent. One week later, both Kennedy and Governor Edmund G. Brown, Jr., of California announced their candidacies.

Even before the campaign began, it was transformed by events halfway around the world. On November 4, 1979, 500 young Iranians occupied the American embassy in Teheran and seized American diplomats as hostages. Two weeks later, they released some hostages but continued to hold more than fifty Americans. Relations between the United States and Iran had been strained since the Islamic revolution, led by the Moslem fundamentalist, the Ayatollah Ruhollah Khomeini, which toppled the Pahlavi regime of the Shah early in 1979. Now the two nations were on a collision course. While Carter demanded the release of the hostages, the Iranians demanded the return of the Shah from the United States, to which he was admitted in October 1979 for medical treatment.

As often happens during an international crisis, the President's popularity rose after the occupation of the embassy. Presidential contestants, most notably Kennedy, who openly criticized his stand, suffered politically as a result. In December 1979, another crisis—a Soviet invasion of Afghanistan— also worked to Carter's political advantage. His decisions to place an embargo on grain sales to Russia and to discourage American athletes from participating in the Olympic games in Moscow in the summer of 1980 were at first well received.

Carter defeated Kennedy in the early primaries and caucuses, and Brown trailed far behind. But Kennedy hung on by winning major eastern primaries. As the crises abroad dragged on and the economy weakened, Carter's popularity sagged once again.

Carter publicly pursued diplomatic options and pressed for worldwide economic sanctions against Iran. Privately, Carter authorized a military operation which he hoped would free the hostages. On April 24, 1980, a daring commando raid was launched, but the mission failed with eight lives lost before the would-be rescuers could reach Teheran. The United States seemed helpless to end the crisis.

At least for a time, Carter had been the beneficiary of international events which seemingly pointed to weaknesses in his own foreign policy. The United States Government had misjudged the Iranian Revolution. Similarly, the Soviet invasion of Afghanistan showed that, despite Carter's interest in easing East-West tensions, the Russians were still willing to advance their own interests by military force. Carter acknowledged that his perception of Soviet intentions had changed. So, too, had the mood of Congress. Senate action on the SALT II treaty was suspended, and Congress increased the military budget amidst talk of a new Cold War.

The Republican Challenge

Even before the election year began, Carter's political vulnerability had attracted a large field of would-be Republican challengers. As the primary season progressed, Ronald Reagan's drive for the nomination began to look invincible, despite early losses to the Texan, George Bush, and despite the highly publicized candidacy of John B. Anderson, congressman from Illinois. Anderson staked out a claim as the "moderate" alternative among the conservatives in the Republican field. In March, Reagan delivered a knockout blow to Anderson by defeating him in the Illinois primary. One month later, Anderson announced that he would run for President on an independent ticket. Public opinion polls taken at the time showed that he would have the support of about 20 per cent of the voters in a three-way race with Reagan and Carter.

Meanwhile, Reagan's juggernaut forced his rivals from the field one by one. Despite his age (sixty-eight at the beginning of 1980), Reagan had campaigned vigorously. In fact, he had never stopped running since his loss to Ford in 1976. In 1980, Reagan was able to maintain his base of support among the Republican right wing, while he added to that group an impressive number of voters who had never before been associated with the Republican party. Many of these new Reagan supporters were attracted by his conservative positions on social issues, his pithy attacks on big government, and his straightforward appeal to restore the presumed moral integrity and world leadership of an older United States.

With Reagan's nomination secure before the Republican convention, only the question of Reagan's running mate remained as a point of contention. Reagan tried to resolve that dilemma by enticing former President Ford to join the ticket. Ford demanded something like a "co-presidency." When this unprecedented and constitutionally dubious arrangement did not materialize, Reagan turned to his former rival, George Bush, who eagerly accepted the nomination.

The Race for the White House

While Reagan was basking in his convention triumph, Jimmy Carter was still struggling for his own renomination. By the summer of 1980, Carter's political windfall from the Iranian crisis had disappeared. Rising unemployment had caused wholesale defections among blue-collar workers. By early August, Carter trailed Reagan in the polls and faced an intraparty challenge from Kennedy supporters and others who wished to nominate someone other than Carter.

When the Democratic convention opened in New York on August 11, the "open-convention" movement was quickly snuffed out, and Senator Kennedy conceded the nomination to Carter. But the party unity which Carter so desperately sought still eluded him. Carter accepted most of Kennedy's liberal platform planks in an effort to win the senator's active support. In the end, Kennedy's endorsement seemed halfhearted, and some of his backers vowed to support Anderson rather than Carter, who they said had turned his back on the heritage of the New Deal.

The Democratic and Republican conventions reflected, in different ways, the changing nature of the presidential nominating process. Between 1960 and 1980, the percentage of delegates selected by primary vote had doubled. Political "insiders," including an incumbent President, could no longer control the selection of delegates as easily as they once could. Victory in the all-important primaries required not only intensive organizing efforts in the states but also cooperation with newly powerful single-issue groups, whose grass-roots strength and ability to deliver votes could be crucial.

Pressure groups were very much in evidence at both conventions. At the Republican gathering, "Right to Life" and "Moral Majority" advocates helped to secure the adoption of an antiabortion plank and the omission of approval of the Equal Rights Amendment in the platform. At the Democratic convention, feminists led a successful floor fight for platform planks which endorsed federally funded abortions and called for the Democratic National Committee to withhold campaign funds from candidates who did not support the ERA.

Although both these platforms were largely ignored after Labor Day, the conventions did set the tone for the autumn campaign in another respect. To an even greater extent than is usually the case, the speechmakers at both conventions attempted to make the other party's candidate the central issue

Rosalynn Carter (left), then first lady, and former first lady, Betty Ford, address a fundraising gathering in support of the equal rights amendment on the eve of the National Women's Conference in November 1977. (United Press International)

in the campaign. The Republicans charged Carter with incompetence and wrongheaded economic and foreign policies, while the Democrats suggested that Reagan would dismantle the New Deal and lead the nation to war. Widespread dissatisfaction with the two major party candidates seemed at first to work in John Anderson's favor. But by mid-October his standing in the polls had dropped below 10 per cent.

By October the two major candidates were virtually even in the polls, with one third or more of the voters undecided. As had often been the case in the past century, the election could be won or lost in the belt of industrial states stretching from New York to Illinois. These six states accounted for 157

Opening session of the National Women's Conference at the Houston Coliseum, November 19, 1977. (United Press International)

electoral votes, 58 per cent of the total needed for victory. The battle for the industrial heartland in 1980 shaped up as more than a contest between two candidates. It was a test of the vitality of the New Deal coalition which had kept the Democratic party preeminent in American politics since the 1930s. Shifts in voting patterns among blue-collar workers in that region in the 1890s and the 1930s had been crucial factors in the major political realignments of the past century.

In 1968 and 1972, George Wallace and Richard M. Nixon had made inroads among blue-collar Democrats in the region, primarily through conservative appeals on social issues. Now, in 1980, Reagan not only repeated those appeals but also challenged an incumbent Democrat on the bread-and-butter issues which had tied industrial workers to the party of Franklin D. Roosevelt for half a century. Regardless of whether Reagan's claims had any basis in fact, they were politically potent in a time of economic stagnation.

In the final days of the campaign, the balance tipped dramatically toward Reagan. One week before the election, the two leading candidates met in the "one-on-one" debate which Carter had sought. But the televised confrontation actually stalled the President's drive to take the lead from Reagan. Reagan displayed a relaxed demeanor which seemed to belie the Democrats' characterization of him as a bumbling, right-wing ideologue. It was later revealed that aides who briefed Reagan for the debate had secretly acquired materials which Carter was using to prepare for their televised confrontation.

Along with the debate, the issue of the hostages gave Reagan a last-minute boost. Election day, November 4, was the anniversary of the capture of the American embassy in Teheran, and the stalemate epitomized for many Americans the loss of national power in world affairs. Carter, the incumbent, was the obvious target of such frustration.

Reagan's victory was more decisive than any pollster had predicted. He captured 489 electoral votes to Carter's forty-nine. Reagan won 51 per cent of the popular vote to 41 per cent for Carter. Anderson received about 7 per cent of the popular vote. The twenty-year decline in voter turnout continued: only 52 per cent of those eligible to vote cast a ballot.

All across the United States, the venerable New Deal coalition, which Carter had patched together in 1976, seemed finally to be coming apart. Reagan made huge inroads into the union labor vote; among blue-collar workers as a whole, he actually outpolled Carter. More Catholics voted for Reagan than for Carter, and Carter barely outpolled Reagan among Jews. Among the voting blocs which had historically constituted the New Deal

The Election of 1980

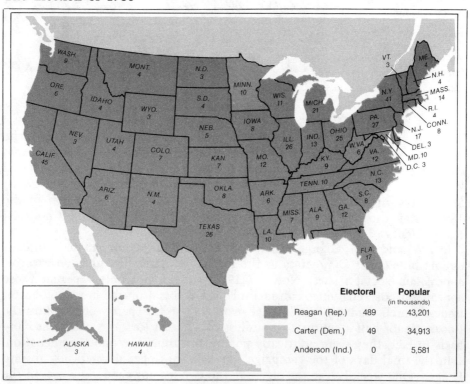

	Electoral	Popular (in thousands)
Reagan (Rep.)	489	43,201
Carter (Dem.)	49	34,913
Anderson (Ind.)	0	5,581

coalition, only blacks remained solidly behind Carter. Reagan had succeeded in making Carter's lack of leadership in foreign policy and his economic record the central issues. Significantly, over half of those questioned in one poll said that they had little faith in *any* President's ability to deal with these problems.

At a more fundamental level, the rejection of Carter, like the defeat of Gerald R. Ford, reflected the anxiety felt by many Americans throughout the 1970s about the nation's inability to shape its own future. Carter had argued with no little justification that, in the years ahead, the freedom to act, both as a nation and as individuals, would be more circumscribed than had been the case in the boom years since 1945. Reagan, on the other hand, asserted that it was within the power of the United States to reestablish its global economic and strategic superiority. In the end, his appeal to get America "moving again" probably contributed more to the Californian's success than any of his specific conservative proposals.

The Reagan victory was only part of the political upheaval of 1980. Republicans gained twelve seats in the Senate, giving them control of that body for the first time since 1954. Democrats retained nominal control of the House, but lost thirty-three seats in that body. Reagan's victory undoubtedly explained some of the Republican gains in Congress. However, an anti-

President-elect Ronald Reagan and his wife, Nancy, wave to supporters November 4 after President Jimmy Carter conceded that Reagan had won the presidential election. Promising to "get America moving again," Reagan's campaign helped swing a nationwide move to the right among all levels of election. (United Press International Photo)

incumbent tide was running which transcended the presidential race. A number of liberal Democratic senators had been "targeted" for defeat by various "nonpartisan" conservative groups. Three veteran liberal senators— Frank Church of Idaho, George McGovern of South Dakota, and Birch Bayh of Indiana—as well as freshman John Culver of Iowa, were obvious victims. Republicans also won four additional governorships. Democrats still controlled a sizable majority of state legislatures and a more modest majority of governorships, but the Republican advances, following on the heels of similar gains in 1978, left Democrats in fear of losing control of statehouses everywhere but in the South. Even there, the "presidential Republicanism" of the last sixteen years was having some impact on state and local races.

Ronald Reagan and the American Presidency

Whereas Jimmy Carter had entered the White House as an enigma, in 1980 Ronald Reagan's position on the political spectrum seemed clear. Since 1964 he had been the leading spokesman for the conservative western wing of the Republican party, and he had risen to national prominence on the strength of the growing conservative movement.

However straightforward Reagan's conservatism might have seemed in 1980, his own political journey had taken some surprising turns. An ardent New Dealer as a young man, Reagan had campaigned actively for liberal Democratic candidates as late as 1948 (Harry Truman for President) and 1950 (Helen Gahagan Douglas against Richard Nixon for United States senator). Reagan's record as governor of California between 1967 and 1975 is difficult to categorize. In campaigning for that office in 1966, he had preached a crusade against big government and against student protests at the state universities. But in office, particularly in his second term, Reagan practiced the art of compromise with the state legislature. He attempted to hold the line on spending (although in the end both spending and taxes increased), but he did not dismantle state agencies wholesale, as his critics had feared he would do.

Similarly, the first years of Reagan's presidency, although in some ways sharply more conservative than that of his predecessors', hardly constituted the transformation of government which his more ardent supporters had hoped for. In particular, Reagan's social conservatism on such issues as abortion and prayer in schools did not translate into vigorous presidential support for legal or constitutional change.

Economic matters dominated Reagan's first two years in office, and even here the Reagan revolution was less than complete. As a candidate, Reagan had promised to balance the budget, lower taxes, and raise military spending, all by means of a "new" set of policies called "supply-side" economics. This school of thought was in fact a new version of orthodox economics as practiced by men such as Andrew W. Mellon before the Great Depression (see p. 391).

In 1981, after an assassination attempt which nearly claimed his life, Reagan pushed through Congress budget and tax bills which, in the first instance, reduced the level of spending for some social programs while sharply increasing military expenditures, and, in the second instance, enacted a supply-side tax program which featured a 25 per cent reduction in tax rates over a three-year period and other measures designed to stimulate savings and investment by high-income taxpayers. In shepherding the budget and tax bills through Congress, the Reagan administration showed remarkable skill, reminiscent of the legislative feats of Lyndon Johnson, Franklin Roosevelt, and Woodrow Wilson. However, as a cure for the nation's economic ills, the Reagan program was far from successful.

Despite deep cuts in some social programs, the federal budget deficit increased at an alarming rate. Furthermore, the tax "cut" did not produce the economic stimulus which supply-side economists had predicted. In fact, by the end of 1981, the nation was sliding into yet another recession. By late 1982 more than 12,000,000 Americans (almost 11 per cent of the work force) were unemployed. Inflation declined to the lowest level since 1972 (a year of wage and price controls), but the drop was due in large measure to the worst unemployment since the Great Depression. Simultaneously, federal deficits mushroomed, reaching $110 billion in fiscal 1982 (nearly twice the previous high), and exceeding $200 billion in 1983.

In response to these ominous developments, Reagan backed away from parts of his supply-side policy, accepting first a tax increase and then job-training and public-works bills. By mid-1983, the jobless rate had begun to decline, and recovery seemed actually to have begun, but huge pockets of unemployment remained, especially in the nation's chronically depressed basic industries, such as steel, textiles, and automobiles.

Even though domestic economic concerns dominated Reagan's first two years in office, the nation continued to struggle with the fundamental issues of foreign policy since 1945: the relationship between the United States and the Soviet Union and the People's Republic of China, America's position in the fragmented western alliance and in the war-torn Middle East, and the nation's role in the internal affairs of third-world countries, particularly the troubled nations of Central America. Rhetorically, American foreign policy was more militantly anti-Communist than at any time since the days of John Foster Dulles, but Reagan's actions were more complex than his words. America's military buildup continued, and arms negotiations with the Soviet Union remained stalled. However, Reagan lifted Jimmy Carter's grain embargo against the Soviets and accepted the Nixon-Ford-Carter framework for normalizing relations with the People's Republic of China. Perhaps the sharpest departure from immediate past policies came in Central America, where Carter's emphasis on human rights gave way to American-backed military efforts to support anti-Communist regimes.

In the aftermath of Republican political victories in 1980, some experts announced that a "critical realignment" was under way in the two-party system, with a staunchly conservative Republican party supplanting the liberal Democrats who had dominated national politics since the days of Franklin D. Roosevelt. That announcement was at the same time tardy and premature. On the one hand, a rising conservative tide in domestic politics could be traced back to the last years of Lyndon B. Johnson's administration, and it certainly influenced the administration of Carter, a self-styled "fiscal conservative." On the other hand, the demise of the Democratic party was prematurely announced. Mid-term congressional elections in 1982 gave the Democrats a net gain of twenty-six seats in the House of Representatives, and many of the new Democrats were decidedly more liberal than the young "boll weevil" Democrats who had cooperated with Reagan in the legislative battles of 1981. Of course the party which controls the White House often loses ground in Congress at midterm, but such a turn of events hardly confirms a critical realignment in favor of the Republican party. Perhaps historians will look back on those years as a watershed in the nation's political development, but the shape of any new political synthesis is not yet fully formed.

SUGGESTED READINGS

Historical analysis of the Ford and Carter years is just beginning. Much of the material for this chapter came from contemporary journalistic sources, including *Congressional Quarterly, The National Journal,* and major newspapers.

Several general studies of recent United States history include material on national politics and government in the late 1970s. The best brief account of energy and economic policies under Ford and Carter is found in Arthur S. Link and William B. Catton, *American Epoch, 1938–1980,* 5th ed. (1980).

Gerald R. Ford describes his own brief presidency in *A Time to Heal: An Autobiography* (1979). Jimmy Carter tells his story in *Keeping Faith: Memories of a President* (1982), and in *Why Not the Best?* (1975). The first study by a historian of Carter's gubernatorial career is Gary M. Fink, *Prelude to the Presidency: The Political Character and Legislative Style of Governor Jimmy Carter* (1980).

The most comprehensive journalistic account of the election campaign of 1976 is Jules Witcover, *Marathon: The Pursuit of the Presidency, 1972–1976* (1977). The political upheaval which was so evident in the election of 1980 reflected trends which had been emerging over the past several years. William N. Chambers and Walter D. Burnham, *The American Party Systems,* 2nd ed. (1975), puts the electoral changes of the 1970s and 1980 in historical perspective. Also valuable in this regard is William E. Leuchtenburg, *In the Shadow of F.D.R.: From Harry Truman to Ronald Reagan* (1983).

Memoirs by leaders of the Carter administration are just beginning to appear. In addition to Carter's *Keeping Faith,* Hamilton Jordan, *Crisis: The Last Year of the Carter Presidency* (1982), reveals the degree to which the administration was traumatized by the Iranian hostage crisis. Carter's first Secretary of State, Cyrus R. Vance, tells his story somewhat blandly in *The Choice Is Ours* (1983). For a different view, see Zbigniew Brzezinski, *Power & Principle: Memoirs of the National Security Advisor, 1977–1981* (1983).

APPENDICES

THE DECLARATION OF INDEPENDENCE

When in the Course of human events, it becomes necessary for one people to dissolve the political bands which have connected them with another, and to assume among the Powers of the earth, the separate and equal station to which the Laws of Nature and of Nature's God entitle them, a decent respect to the opinions of mankind requires that they should declare the causes which impel them to the separation.

We hold these truths to be self-evident, that all men are created equal, that they are endowed by their Creator with certain unalienable Rights, that among these are Life, Liberty and the pursuit of Happiness. That to secure these rights, Governments are instituted among Men, deriving their just powers from the consent of the governed, That whenever any Form of Government becomes destructive of these ends, it is the Right of the People to alter or to abolish it, and to institute new Government, laying its foundation on such principles and organizing its powers in such form, as to them shall seem most likely to effect their Safety and Happiness. Prudence, indeed, will dictate that Governments long established should not be changed for light and transient causes; and accordingly all experience hath shown, that mankind are more disposed to suffer, while evils are sufferable, than to right themselves by abolishing the forms to which they are accustomed. But when a long train of abuses and usurpations, pursuing invariably the same Object evinces a design to reduce them under absolute Despotism, it is their right, it is their duty, to throw off such Government, and to provide new Guards for their future security. – Such has been the patient sufferance of these Colonies; and such is now the necessity which constrains them to alter their former Systems of Government. The history of the present King of Great Britain is a history of repeated injuries and usurpations, all having in direct object the establishment of an absolute Tyranny over these States. To prove this, let Facts be submitted to a candid world.

He has refused his Assent to Laws, the most wholesome and necessary for the public good.

He has forbidden his Governors to pass Laws of immediate and pressing importance, unless suspended in their operation till his Assent should be obtained; and when so suspended, he has utterly neglected to attend to them.

He has refused to pass other Laws for the accommodation of large districts of people, unless those people would relinquish the right of Representation in the Legislature, a right inestimable to them and formidable to tyrants only.

He has called together legislative bodies at places unusual, uncomfortable, and distant from the depository of their Public Records, for the sole purpose of fatiguing them into compliance with his measures.

He has dissolved Representative Houses repeatedly, for opposing with manly firmness his invasions on the rights of the people.

He has refused for a long time, after such dissolutions, to cause others to be elected; whereby the Legislative Powers, incapable of Annihilation, have returned to the People at large for their exercise; the State remaining in the mean time exposed to all the dangers of invasion from without, and convulsions within.

He has endeavoured to prevent the population of these States; for that purpose obstructing the Laws of Naturalization of Foreigners; refusing to pass others to encourage their migration hither, and raising the conditions of new Appropriations of Lands.

He has obstructed the Administration of Justice, by refusing his Assent to Laws for establishing Judiciary Powers.

He has made Judges dependent on his Will alone, for the tenure of their offices, and the amount and payment of their salaries.

He has erected a multitude of New Offices, and sent hither swarms of Officers to harass our People, and eat out their substance.

He has kept amoung us, in times of peace, Standing Armies without the Consent of our legislature.

He has affected to render the Military independent of and superior to the Civil Powers.

He has combined with others to subject us to a jurisdiction foreign to our constitution, and unacknowledged by our laws; giving his Assent to their acts of pretended legislation.

For quartering large bodies of armed troops among us:

For protecting them, by a mock Trial, from Punishment for any Murders which they should commit on the Inhabitants of these States:

For cutting off our Trade with all parts of the world:

For imposing taxes on us without our Consent:

For depriving us in many cases, of the benefits of Trial by Jury:

For transporting us beyond Seas to be tried for pretended offenses:

For abolishing the free System of English Laws in a neighbouring Province, establishing therein an Arbitrary government, and enlarging its Boundaries so as to render it at once an example and fit instrument for introducing the same absolute rule into these Colonies:

For taking away our Charters, abolishing our most valuable Laws, and altering fundamentally the Forms of our Governments:

For suspending our own Legislature, and declaring themselves invested with Power to legislate for us in all cases whatsoever.

He has abdicated Government here, by declaring us out of his Protection and waging War against us.

He has plundered our seas, ravaged our Coasts, burnt our towns, and destroyed the lives of our people.

He is at this time transporting large armies of foreign mercenaries to compleat the works of death, desolation and tyranny, already begun with circumstances of Cruelty & perfidy scarcely paralleled in the most barbarous ages, and totally unworthy the Head of a civilized nation.

He has constrained our fellow Citizens taken Captive on the high Seas to bear Arms against their Country, to become the executioners of their friends and Brethren, or to fall themselves by their Hands.

He has excited domestic insurrections amongst us, and has endeavoured to bring on the inhabitants of our frontiers, the merciless Indian Savages, whose known rule of warfare, is an undistinguished destruction of all ages, sexes and conditions.

In every stage of these Oppressions We have Petitioned for Redress in the most humble terms: Our repeated Petitions have been answered only by repeated injury. A Prince, whose character is thus marked by every act which may define a Tyrant, is unfit to be the ruler of a free People.

Nor have We been wanting in attention to our British brethren. We have warned them from time to time of attempts by their legislature to extend an unwarrantable jurisdiction over us. We have reminded them of the circumstances of our emigration and settlement here. We have appealed to their native justice and magnanimity, and we have conjured them by the ties of our common kindred to disavow these usurpations, which, would inevitably interrupt our connections and correspondence. They too have been deaf to the voice of justice and of consanguinity. We must, therefore, acquiesce in the necessity, which denounces our Separation, and hold them, as we hold the rest of mankind, Enemies in War, in Peace Friends.

We, therefore, the Representatives of the United States of America, in General Congress, Assembled, appealing to the Supreme Judge of the world for the rectitude of our intentions, do, in the Name, and by Authority of the good People of these Colonies, solemnly publish and declare, That these United Colonies are, and of Right ought to be Free and Independent States; that they are Absolved from all Allegiance to the British Crown, and that all political connection between them and the State of Great Britain, is and ought to be totally dissolved; and that as Free and Independent States, they have full Power to levy War, conclude Peace, contract Alliances, establish Commerce, and to do all other Acts and Things which Independent States may of right do. And for the support of this Declaration, with a firm reliance on the Protection of Divine Providence, we mutually pledge to each other our Lives, our Fortunes and our sacred Honor.

THE CONSTITUTION OF THE UNITED STATES

We the people of the United States, in Order to form a more perfect Union, establish Justice, insure domestic Tranquility, provide for the common defence, promote the general Welfare, and secure the Blessings of Liberty to ourselves and our Posterity, do ordain and establish This CONSTITUTION for the United States of America.

Article I

Section 1. All legislative Powers herein granted shall be vested in a Congress of the United States, which shall consist of a Senate and House of Representatives.

Section 2. The House of Representatives shall be composed of Members chosen every second Year by the People of the several States, and the Electors in each State shall have the Qualifications requisite for Electors of the most numerous Branch of the State Legislature.

No Person shall be a Representative who shall not have attained to the Age of twenty-five Years, and been seven Years a Citizen of the United States, and who shall not, when elected, be an Inhabitant of that State in which he shall be chosen.

Representatives and direct Taxes shall be apportioned among the several States which may be included within this Union, according to their respective Numbers, which shall be determined by adding to the whole Number of free Persons, including those bound to Service for a Term of Years, and excluding Indians not taxed, three fifths of all other Persons. The actual Enumeration shall be made within three Years after the first Meeting of the Congress of the United States, and within every subsequent Term of ten Years, in such Manner as they shall by Law direct. The Number of Representatives shall not exceed one for every thirty Thousand, but each State shall have at Least one Representative; and until such enumeration shall be made, the State of New Hampshire shall be entitled to chuse three, Massachusetts eight, Rhode-Island and Providence Plantations one, Connecticut five, New-York six, New Jersey four, Pennsylvania eight, Delaware one, Maryland six, Virginia ten, North Carolina five, South Carolina five, and Georgia three.

When vacancies happen in the Representation from any State, the Executive Authority thereof shall issue Writs of Election to fill such Vacancies.

The House of Representatives shall chuse their Speaker and other Officers; and shall have the sole Power of Impeachment.

Section 3. The Senate of the United States shall be composed of two Senators from each State, chosen by the Legislature thereof, for six Years; and each Senator shall have one Vote.

Immediately after they shall be assembled in Consequence of the first Election, they shall be divided as equally as may be into three Classes. The Seats of the Senators of the first Class shall be vacated at the Expiration of the second Year, of the second Class at the Expiration of the fourth Year, and of the third Class at the Expiration of the sixth Year, so that one-third may be chosen ever second Year; and if Vacancies happen by Resignation, or otherwise, during the Recess of the Legislature of any State, the Executive thereof may make temporary Appointments until the next Meeting of the Legislature, which shall then fill such Vacancies.

No Person shall be a Senator who shall not have attained to the age of thirty Years, and been nine Years a Citizen of the United States, and who shall not, when elected, be an Inhabitant of that State in which he shall be chosen.

The Vice President of the United States shall be President of the Senate, but shall have no vote, unless they be equally divided.

The Senate shall chuse their other Officers, and also a President pro tempore, in the absence of the Vice President, or when he shall exercise the Office of the President of the United States.

The Senate shall have the sole Power to try all Impeachments. When sitting for that purpose, they shall be on Oath or Affirmation. When the President of the United States is tried, the Chief Justice shall preside: And no person shall be convicted without the Concurrence of two thirds of the Members present.

Judgment in Cases of Impeachment shall not extend further than to removal from Office, and disqualification to hold and enjoy any Office of honor, Trust, or Profit under the United States: but the Party convicted shall nevertheless be liable and subject to Indictment, Trial, Judgment, and Punishment, according to Law.

Section 4. The Times, Places and Manner of holding Elections for Senators and Representatives, shall be prescribed in each state by the Legislature thereof; but the Congress may at any time by Law make or alter such Regulations, except as to the Places of Chusing Senators.

The Congress shall assemble at least once in every Year, and such Meeting shall be on the first Monday in December, unless they shall by Law appoint a different Day.

Section 5. Each House shall be the Judge of the Elections, Returns and Qualifications of its own Members, and a Majority of each shall constitute a Quorum to do Business; but a smaller number may adjourn from day to day, and may be authorized to compel the Attendance of absent Members, in such Manner, and under such Penalties, as each House may provide.

Each House may determine the Rules of its Proceedings, punish its Members for disorderly Behavior, and, with the Concurrence of two thirds, expel a Member.

Each House shall keep a Journal of its Proceedings, and from time to time publish the same, excepting such Parts as may in their Judgment require Secrecy; and the Yeas and Nays of the Members of either House on any question shall, at the Desire of one fifth of those Present, be entered on the Journal.

Neither House, during the Session of Congress, shall, without the Consent of the other, adjourn for more than three days, nor to any other Place than that in which the two Houses shall be sitting.

Section 6. The Senators and Representatives shall receive a Compensation for their Services, to be ascertained by Law, and paid out of the Treasury of the United States. They shall in all Cases, except Treason, Felony, and Breach of the Peace, be privileged from arrest during their Attendance at the Session of their respective Houses, and in going to and returning from the same; and for any Speech or Debate in either House, they shall not be questioned in any other Place.

No Senator or Representative shall, during the Time for which he was elected, be appointed to any civil Office under the Authority of the United States, which shall have been created, or the Emoluments whereof shall have been increased, during such time; and no Person holding any Office under the United States shall be a Member of either House during his continuance in Office.

Section 7. All Bills for raising Revenue shall originate in the House of Representatives; but the Senate may propose or concur with Amendments as on other bills.

Every Bill which shall have passed the House of Representatives and the Senate, shall, before it become a Law, be presented to the President of the United States; If he approve he shall sign it, but if not he shall return it, with his Objections, to that House in which it shall have originated, who shall enter the Objections at large on their Journal, and proceed to reconsider it. If after such Reconsideration two thirds of that House shall agree to pass the bill, it shall be sent, together with the objections, to the other House, by which it shall likewise be reconsidered, and if approved by two thirds of that House, it shall become a Law. But in all such Cases the Votes of both Houses shall be determined by Yeas and Nays, and the Names of the Persons voting for and against the Bill shall be entered on the Journal of each House respectively. If any Bill shall not be returned by the President within ten days (Sundays excepted) after it shall have been presented to him, the Same shall be a Law, in like Manner as if he had signed it, unless the Congress by their Adjournment prevent its Return, in which Case it shall not be a Law.

Every Order, Resolution, or Vote to which the Concurrence of the Senate and House of Representatives may be necessary (except on a question of Adjournment) shall be presented to the President of the United States; and before the Same shall take Effect, shall be approved by him, or being disapproved by him, shall be repassed by two thirds of the Senate and House of Representatives, according to the Rules and Limitations prescribed in the Case of a Bill.

Section 8. The Congress shall have Power To lay and collect Taxes, Duties, Imposts and Excises, to pay the Debts and provide for the common Defence and general Welfare of the United States; but all Duties, Imposts and Excises shall be uniform throughout the United States;

To borrow money on the credit of the United States;

To regulate Commerce with foreign Nations, and among the several States, and with the Indian Tribes;

To establish a uniform Rule of Naturalization, and uniform Laws on the subject of Bankruptcies throughout the United States;

To coin Money, regulate the Value thereof, and of foreign Coin, and fix the standard of Weights and Measures;

To provide for the Punishment of counterfeiting the Securities and current Coin of the United States;

To establish Post Offices and post Roads;

To promote the Progress of Science and useful Arts, by securing for limited Times to Authors and Inventors the exclusive Right to their respective Writings and Discoveries;

To constitute Tribunals inferior to the Supreme Court;

To define and punish Piracies and Felonies committed on the high Seas, and Offenses against the Law of Nations;

To declare War, grant Letters of Marque and Reprisal, and make Rules concerning Captures on Land and Water;

To raise and support Armies, but no Appropriation of Money to that Use shall be for a longer Term than two Years;

To provide and maintain a Navy;

To make Rules for the Government and Regulation of the land and naval forces;

To provide for calling forth the Militia to execute the Laws of the Union, suppress Insurrections and repel Invasions;

To provide for organizing, arming, and disciplining the Militia, and for governing such Part of them as may be employed in the Service of the United States, reserving to the States respectively, the Appointment of the Officers, and the Authority of training the Militia according to the discipline prescribed by Congress;

To exercise exclusive Legislation in all Cases whatsoever, over such District (not exceeding ten Miles square) as may, by Cession of particular States, and the acceptance of Congress, become the Seat of Government of the United States, and to exercise like Authority over all Places purchased by the consent of the Legislature of the State in which the Same shall be, for the Erection of Forts, Magazines, Arsenals, dock-Yards, and other needful Buildings; – And

To make all Laws which shall be necessary and proper for carrying into Execution the foregoing Powers, and all other Powers vested by this Constitution in the Government of the United States, or in any Department or Officer thereof.

Section 9. The Migration or Importation of such Persons as any of the States now existing shall think proper to admit, shall not be prohibited by the Congress prior to the Year one thousand eight hundred and eight, but a tax or duty may be imposed on such Importation, not exceeding ten dollars for each Person.

The privilege of the Writ of Habeas Corpus shall not be suspended, unless when in Cases of Rebellion or Invasion the public Safety may require it.

No Bill of Attainder or ex post facto Law shall be passed.

No capitation, or other direct, Tax shall be laid unless in Proportion to the Census or Enumeration herein before directed to be taken.

No Tax or Duty shall be laid on Articles exported from any State.

No Preference shall be given by any Regulation of Revenue to the Ports of one State over those of another: nor shall Vessels bound to, or from, one State, be obliged to enter, clear, or pay Duties in another.

No Money shall be drawn from the Treasury, but in Consequence of Appropriations made by Law; and a regular Statement and Account of the Receipts and Expenditures of all public Money shall be published from time to time.

No Title of Nobility shall be granted by the United States: And no Person holding any Office of Profit or Trust under them, shall, without the Consent of the Congress, accept of any present, Emolument, Office, or Title, of any kind whatever, from any King, Prince, or foreign State.

Section 10. No State shall enter into any Treaty, Alliance, or Confederation; grant Letters of Marque and Reprisal; coin Money; emit Bills of Credit; make any Thing but gold and silver Coin a Tender in Payment of Debts; pass any Bill of Attainder, ex post facto Law, or Law impairing the Obligation of Contracts, or grant any Title of Nobility.

No State shall, without the Consent of the Congress, lay any Imposts or Duties on Imports or Exports, except what may be absolutely necessary for executing its inspection Laws: and the net Produce of all Duties and Imposts, laid by any State on Imports or Exports, shall be for the Use of the Treasury of the United States; and all such Laws shall be subject to the Revision and Control of the Congress.

No State shall, without the Consent of Congress, lay any duty of Tonnage, keep Troops, or Ships of War in time of Peace, enter into any Agreement or Compact with another State, or with a foreign Power, or engage in War, unless actually invaded, or in such imminent Danger as will not admit of delay.

Article II

Section 1. The executive Power shall be vested in a President of the United States of America. He shall hold his Office during the Term of four years, and, together with the Vice-President, chosen for the same Term, be elected, as follows:

Each State shall appoint, in such Manner as the Legislature thereof may direct, a Number of

Electors, equal to the whole Number of Senators and Representatives to which the State may be entitled in the Congress: But no Senator or Representative, or Person holding an Office or Trust or Profit under the United States, shall be appointed an Elector.

The Electors shall meet in their respective States, and vote by Ballot for two persons, of whom one at least shall not be an Inhabitant of the same State with themselves. And they shall make a List of all the Persons voted for, and of the Number of Votes for each; which List they shall sign and certify, and transmit sealed to the Seat of the Government of the United States, directed to the President of the Senate. The President of the Senate shall, in the Presence of the Senate and House of Representatives, open all the Certificates, and the Votes shall then be counted. The Person having the greatest Number of Votes shall be the President, if such Number be a Majority of the whole Number of Electors appointed; and if there be more than one who have such Majority, and have an equal Number of Votes, then the House of Representatives shall immediately chuse by Ballot one of them for President; and if no Person have a Majority, then from the five highest of the List the said House shall in like Manner chuse the President. But in chusing the President, the Votes shall be taken by States, the Representation from each State having one Vote; a quorum for this Purpose shall consist of a Member or Members from two-thirds of the States, and a Majority of all the States shall be necessary to a Choice. In every Case, after the Choice of the President, the Person having the greatest Number of Votes of the Electors shall be the Vice President. But if there should remain two or more who have equal votes, the Senate shall chuse from them by Ballot the Vice-President.

The Congress may determine the Time of chusing the Electors, and the Day on which they shall give their Votes; which Day shall be the same throughout the United States.

No person except a natural-born Citizen, or a Citizen of the United States, at the time of the Adoption of this Constitution, shall be eligible to the Office of President; neither shall any Person be eligible to that Office who shall not have attained to the Age of thirty-five years, and been fourteen Years a Resident within the United States.

In Case of the Removal of the President from Office, or of his Death, Resignation, or Inability to discharge the Powers and Duties of the said Office, the same shall devolve on the Vice President, and the Congress may by Law provide for the Case of Removal, Death, Resignation, or Inability, both of the President and Vice President, declaring what Officer shall then act as President, and such Officer shall act accordingly, until the disability be removed, or a President shall be elected.

The President shall, at stated Times, receive for his Services a Compensation, which shall neither be increased nor diminished during the Period for which he shall have been elected, and he shall not receive within that Period any other Emolument from the United States, or any of them.

Before he enter on the execution of his Office, he shall take the following Oath or Affirmation: – "I do solemnly swear (or affirm) that I will faithfully execute the Office of President of the United States, and will, to the best of my Ability, preserve, protect, and defend the Consittution of the United States."

Section 2. The President shall be Commander in Chief of the Army and Navy of the United States, and of the Militia of the several States, when called into the actual Service of the United States; he may require the Opinion, in writing, of the principal Officer in each of the executive Departments, upon any subject relating to the Duties of their respective Offices, and he shall have Power to Grant Reprieves and Pardons for Offenses against the United States, except in Cases of Impeachment.

He shall have Power, by and with the Advice and Consent of the Senate, to make Treaties, provided two thirds of the Senators present concur; and he shall nominate, and by and with the Advice and Consent of the Senate, shall appoint Ambassadors, other public Ministers and Consuls, Judges of the supreme Court, and all other Officers of the United States, whose Appointments are not herein otherwise provided for, and which shall be established by Law: but the Congress may by Law vest the Appointment of such inferior Officers, as they think proper, in the President alone, in the Courts of Law, or in the Heads of Departments.

The President shall have Power to fill up all Vacancies that may happen during the Recess of the Senate, by granting Commissions which shall expire at the End of their next Session.

Section 3. He shall from time to time give to the Congress Information of the State of the Union, and recommend to their Consideration such Measures as he shall judge necessary and expedient; he may, on extraordinary occasions, convene both Hourse, or either of them, and in Case of Disagreement between them, with respect to the Time of Adjournment, he may adjourn them to such Time as he shall think proper; he shall receive Ambassadors and other public Minsters; he shall take Care that the Laws be faithfully executed, and shall Commission all the Officers of the United States.

Section 4. The President, Vice President and all civil Officers of the United States, shall be removed from Office on Impeachment for, and Conviction of, Treason, Bribery, or other high Crimes and Misdemeanors.

Article III

Section 1. The judicial Power of the United States, shall be vested in one supreme Court, and in such inferior Courts as the Congress may from time to time ordain and establish. The Judges, both of the supreme and inferior Courts, shall hold their Offices during good Behaviour, and shall, at stated Times, receive for their Services, a Compensation, which shall not be diminished during their Continuance in Office.

Section 2. The judicial Power shall extend to all Cases, in Law and Equity, arising under this Constitution, the Laws of the United States, and treaties made, or which shall be made, under their authority;—to all Cases affecting ambassadors, other public ministers and consuls;—to all cases of admiralty and maritime Jurisdiction;—to Controversies to which the United States shall be a Party;—to Controversies between two or more States;—between a State and Citizens of another State;—between Citizens of different States,—between Citizens of the same State claiming Lands under Grants of different States, and between a State, or the Citizens thereof, and foreign States, Citizens or Subjects.

In all Cases affecting Ambassadors, other public Ministers and Consuls, and those in which a State shall be Party, the supreme court shall have original Jurisdiction. In all the other Cases before mentioned, the supreme Court shall have appellate Jurisdiction, both as to Law and Fact, with such Exceptions, and under such Regulations as the Congress shall make.

The trial of all Crimes, except in Cases of Impeachment, shall be by Jury; and such Trial shall be held in the State where the said Crimes shall have been committed; but when not committed within any State, the Trial shall be at such Place or Places as the Congress may by Law have directed.

Section 3. Treason against the United States, shall consist only in levying War against them, or in adhering to their Enemies, giving them Aid and Comfort. No Person shall be convicted of Treason unless on the Testimony of two Witnesses to the Same overt Act, or on Confession in open Court.

The Congress shall have power to declare the Punishment of Treason, but no Attainder of Treason shall work Corruption of Blood, or Forfeiture except during the Life of the Person attainted.

Article IV

Section 1. Full Faith and Credit shall be given in each State to the public Acts, Records, and judicial Proceedings of every other State. And the Congress may by general Laws prescribe the Manner in which such Acts, Records and Proceedings shall be proved, and the Effect thereof.

Section 2. The Citizens of each State shall be entitled to all Privileges and Immunities of Citizens in the several States.

A Person charged in any State with Treason, Felony, or other Crime, who shall flee from Justice, and be found in another State, shall on demand of the executive authority of the State from which he fled, be delivered up, to be removed to the State having Jurisdiction of the crime.

No Person held to Service or Labour in one State, under the Laws thereof, escaping into another, shall, in Consequence of any Law or Regulation therein, be discharged from such Service or Labour, but shall be delivered up on Claim of the Party to whom such Service or Labour may be due.

Section 3. New States may be admitted by the Congress into this Union; but no new State shall be formed or erected within the Jurisdiction of any other State; nor any State be formed by the Junction of two or more States, or parts of States, without the Consent of the Legislatures of the States concerned as well as of the Congress.

The Congress shall have Power to dispose of and make all needful Rules and Regulations respecting the Territory or other Property belonging to the United States; and nothing in this Constitution shall be so construed as to Prejudice any Claims of the United States, or of any particular State.

Section 4. The United States shall guarantee to every State in this Union a Republican Form of Government, and shall protect each of them against Invasion; and on Application of the Legislature, or of the Executive (when the Legislature cannot be convened) against domestic Violence.

Article V

The Congress, whenever two-thirds of both Houses shall deem it necessary, shall propose Amendments to this Constitution, or, on the Application of the Legislatures of two-thirds of the several States, shall call a Convention for proposing Amendments, which, in either Case, shall be valid to all Intents and Purposes, as part of this Constitution, when ratified by the Legislatures of three-fourths of the several States, or by Conventions in three-fourths thereof, as the one or the other Mode of Ratification may be proposed by the Congress; Provided that no Amendment which may be made prior to the Year One thousand eight hundred and eight shall in any Manner affect the first and fourth Clauses in the Ninth Section of the first Article; and that no State, without its Consent, shall be deprived of its equal Suffrage in the Senate.

Article VI

All Debts contracted and Engagements entered into, before the Adoption of this Constitution, shall be as valid against the United States under this Constitution, as under the Confederation.

This Constitution, and the Laws of the United States which shall be made in Pursuance thereof; and all Treaties made, or which shall be made, under the Authority of the United States, shall be the supreme Law of the Land; and the Judges in every State shall be bound thereby, any Thing in the Constitution or Laws of any State to the Contrary notwithstanding.

The Senators and Representatives before mentioned, and the Members of the several State Legislatures, and all executive and judicial Officers, both of the United States and of the several States, shall be bound by Oath or Affirmation to support this Constitution; but no religious Test shall ever be required as a qualification to any Office or public Trust under the United States.

Article VII

The Ratification of the Conventions of nine States shall be sufficient for the Establishment of this Constitution between the States so ratifying the same.

Done in Convention by the Unanimous Consent of the States present the Seventeenth Day of September in the Year of our Lord one thousand seven hundred and Eighty seven, and of the Independence of the United States of America the Twelfth. In Witness whereof We have hereunto subscribed our Names.

Articles in Addition to, and Amendment of, the Constitution of the United States of America, Proposed by Congress, and Ratified by the Legislatures of the Several States, Pursuant to the Fifth Article of the Original Constitution.

Amendment I [1791]

Congress shall make no law respecting an establishment of religion, or prohibiting the free exercise thereof; or abridging the freedom of speech, or of the press; or the right of the people peaceably to assemble, and to petition the Government for a redress of grievances.

Amendment II [1791]

A well regulated Militia, being necessary to the security of a free State, the right of the people to keep and bear arms shall not be infringed.

Amendment III [1791]

No Soldier shall, in time of peace, be quartered in any house, without the consent of the Owner, nor in time of war, but in a manner to be prescribed by law.

Amendment IV [1791]

The right of the people to be secure in their persons, houses, papers, and effects, against unreasonable searches and seizures, shall not be violated, and no Warrants shall issue, but upon probable cause, supported by Oath or affirmation, and particularly describing the place to be searched, and the persons or things to be seized.

Amendment V [1791]

No person shall be held to answer for a capital or otherwise infamous crime, unless on a presentment or indictment of a Grand Jury, except in cases arising in the land or naval forces, or in the Militia, when in actual service in time of War or public danger; nor shall any person be subject for the same offence to be twice put in jeopardy of life or limb; nor shall be compelled in any criminal case to be a witness against himself, nor be deprived of life, liberty, or property, without due process of law; nor shall private property be taken for public use, witout just compensation.

Amendment VI [1791]

In all criminal prosecutions, the accused shall enjoy the right to a speedy and public trial, by an impartial jury of the State and district wherein the crime shall have been committed, which district shall have been previously ascertained by law, and to be informed of the nature and cause of the accusation; to be confronted with the witnesses against him; to have compulsory process for obtaining witnesses in his favor, and to have the Assistance of Counsel for his defense.

Amendment VII [1791]

In suits at common law, where the value in controversy shall exceed twenty dollars, the right of trial by jury shall be preserved, and no fact tried by a jury, shall be otherwise reexamined in any Court of the United States, than according to the rules of the common law.

Amendment VIII [1791]

Excessive bail shall not be required, not excessive fines imposed, nor cruel and unusual punishments inflicted.

Amendment IX [1791]

The enumeration in the Constitution, of certain rights, shall not be construed to deny or disparage others retained by the people.

Amendment X [1791]

The powers not delegated to the United States by the Constitution, nor prohibited by it to the States, are reserved to the States respectively, or to the people.

Amendment XI [1798]

The Judicial power of the United States shall not be construed to extend to any suit in law or equity, commenced or prosecuted against one of the United States by Citizens of another State, or by Citizens or Subjects of any Foreign State.

Amendment XII [1804]

The Electors shall meet in their respective States and vote by ballot for President and Vice-President, one of whom, at least, shall not be an inhabitant of the same State with themselves; they shall name in their ballots the person voted for as President, and in distinct ballots the person voted for as Vice-President, and they shall make distinct lists of all persons voted for as President, and of all persons voted for as Vice-President, and of the number of votes for each, which lists they shall sign and certify, and transmit sealed to the seat of the government of the United States, directed to the President of the Senate; – The President of the Senate shall, in the presence of the Senate and House of Representatives, open all the certificates and the votes shall then be counted; – The person having the greatest number of votes for President, shall be the President, if such number be a majority of the whole number of Electors appointed; and if no person have such majority, then from the persons having the highest numbers vote exceeding three on the list of those voted for as President, the House of Representatives shall choose immediately, by ballot, the President. But in choosing the president, the votes shall be taken by states, the representation from each state having one vote; a quorum for this purpose shall consist of a member or members from two-thirds of the states, and a majority of all the states shall be necessary to a choice. And if the House of Representatives shall not choose a President whenever the right of choice shall devolve upon them, before the fourth day of March next following, then the Vice-President shall act as President, as in the case of the death or other constitutional disability of the President. – The person having the greatest number of votes as Vice-President, shall be the Vice-President, if such number be a majority of the whole number of Electors appointed, and if no person have a majority, then from the two highest numbers on the list, the Senate shall choose the Vice-President; a quorum for the purpose shall consist of two-thirds of the whole number of Senators, and a majority of the whole number shall be necessary to a choice. But no person constitutionally ineligible to the office of President shall be eligible to that of Vice-President of the United States.

Amendment XIII [1865]

Section 1. Neither slavery nor involuntary servitude, except as a punishment for crime whereof the party shall have been duly convicted, shall exist within the United States, or any place subject to their jurisdiction.

Section 2. Congress shall have power to enforce this article by appropriate legislation.

Amendment XIV [1868]

Section 1. All persons born or naturalized in the United States, and subject to the jurisdiction thereof, are citizens of the United States and of the State wherein they reside. No State shall make or enforce any law which shall abridge the privileges or immunities of citizens of the United States; nor shall any State deprive any person of life, liberty, or property, without due process of law; nor deny to any person within its jurisdiction the equal protection of the laws.

Section 2. Representatives shall be apportioned among the several States according to their respective numbers, counting the whole number of persons in each State, excluding Indians not taxed. But when the right to vote at any election for the choice of electors for President and Vice-President of the United States, Representatives in Congress, the Executive and Judicial officers of a State, or the members of the Legislature thereof, is denied to any of the male inhabitants of such State, being twenty-one years of age, and citizens of the United States, or in any way abridged, except for participation in rebellion, or other crime, the basis of representation therein shall be reduced in the proportion which the number of such male citizens shall bear to the whole number of male citizens twenty-one years of age in such State.

Section 3. No person shall be a Senator or Representative in Congress, or elector of President and Vice-President, or hold any office, civil or military, under the United States, or under any State, who, having previously taken an oath, as a member of Congress, or as an officer of the United States, or as a member of any State legislature, or as an executive or judicial officer of any State, to support the Constitution of the United States, shall have engaged in insurrection or rebellion against the same, or given aid or comfort to the enemies thereof. But Congress may by a vote of two-thirds of each House, remove such disability.

Section 4. The validity of the public debt of the United States, authorized by law, including debts incurred for payment of pensions and bounties for services in suppressing insurrection or rebellion, shall not be questioned. But neither the United States nor any State shall assume or pay any debt or obligation incurred in aid of insurrection or rebellion against the United States, or any claim for the loss or emancipation of any slave; but all such debts, obligations, and claims shall be held illegal and void.

Section 5. The Congress shall have the power to enforce, by appropriate legislation, the provisions of this article.

Amendment XV [1870]

Section 1. The right of citizens of the United States to vote shall not be denied or abridged by the United States or by any State on account of race, color, or previous condition of servitude –

Section 2. The Congress shall have power to enforce this article by appropriate legislation.

Amendment XVI [1913]

The Congress shall have power to lay and collect taxes on incomes, from whatever source derived, without apportionment among the several States, and without regard to any census or enumeration.

Amendment XVII [1913]

The Senate of the United States shall be composed of two Senators from each State, elected by the people thereof, for six years; and each Senator shall have one vote. The electors in each State shall have the qualifications requisite for electors of the most numerous branch of the State legislatures.

When vacancies happen in the representation of any State in the Senate, the executive authority of such State shall issue writs of election to fill such vacancies: *Provided,* That the legislature of any State may empower the executive thereof to make temporary appointments until the people fill the vacancies by election as the legislature may direct.

This amendment shall not be so construed as to affect the election to term of any Senator chosen before it becomes valid as part of the Constitution.

Amendment XVIII [1919]

Section 1. After one year from the ratification of this article the manufacture, sale, or transportation of intoxicating liquors within, the importation thereof into, or the exportation thereof from the United States and all territory subject to the jurisdiction thereof for beverage purposes is hereby prohibited.

Section 2. The Congress and the several States shall have concurrent power to enforce this article by appropriate legislation.

Section 3. This article shall be inoperative unless it shall have been ratified as an amendment to the Constitution by the legislatures of the several States, as provided in the Constitution, within seven years from the date of the submission hereof to the States by the Congress.

Amendment XIX [1920]

The right of citizens of the United States to vote shall not be denied or abridged by the United States or by any State on account of sex.

Congress shall have power to enforce this article by appropriate legislation.

Amendment XX [1933]

Section 1. The terms of the President and Vice-President shall end at noon on the 20th day of January, and the terms of Senators and Representatives at noon on the 3d day of January, of the years in which such terms would have ended if this article had not been ratified; and the terms of their successors shall then begin.

Section 2. The Congress shall assemble at least once in every year, and such meeting shall begin at noon on the 3d day of January, unless they shall by law appoint a different day.

Section 3. If, at the time fixed for the beginning of the term of the President, the President elect shall have died, the Vice-President elect shall become President. If a President shall not have been chosen before the time fixed for the beginning of his term, or if the President elect shall have failed to qualify, then the Vice-President elect shall act as President until a President shall have qualified; and the Congress may by law provide for the case wherein neither a President elect nor a Vice-President elect shall have qualified, declaring who shall then act as President, or the manner in which one who is to act shall be selected, and such person shall act accordingly until a President or Vice-President shall have qualified.

Section 4. The Congress may by law provide for the case of the death of any of the persons from whom the House of Representatives may choose a President whenever the right of choice shall have devolved upon them, and for the case of the death of any of the persons from whom the Senate may choose a Vice-President whenever the right of choice shall have devolved upon them.

Section 5. Sections 1 and 2 shall take effect on the 15th day of October following the ratification of this article.

Section 6. This article shall be inoperative unless it shall have been ratified as an amendment to the Constitution by the legislatures of three-fourths of the several States within seven years from the date of its submission.

Amendment XXI [1933]

Section 1. The eighteenth article of amendment to the constitution of the United States is heareby repealed.

Section 2. The transportation or importation into any State, Territory, or possession of the United States for delivery or use therein of intoxicating liquors, in violation of the laws thereof, is hereby prohibited.

Section 3. This article shall be inoperative unless it shall have been ratified as an amendment to the Constitution by conventions in the several States, as provided in the Constitution, within seven years from the date of the submission hereof to the States by the Congress.

Amendment XXII [1951]

No person shall be elected to the office of the President more than twice, and no person who has held the office of President, or acted as President, for more than two years of a term to which some other person was elected President shall be elected to the office of the President more than once.

But this Article shall not apply to any person holding the office of President when this Article was proposed by the Congress, and shall not prevent any person who may be holding the office of President, or acting as President, during the term within which this Article becomes operative from holding the office of President or acting as President during the remainder of such term.

Amendment XXIII [1961]

Section 1. The District constituting the seat of Government of the United States shall appoint in such manner as the Congress may direct:

A number of electors of President and Vice President equal to the whole number of Senators and Representatives in Congress to which the District would be entitled if it were a State, but in no event more than the least populous State; they shall be in addition to those appointed by the States, but they shall be considered, for the purposes of the election of President and Vice

President, to be electors appointed by a State; and they shall meet in the District and perform such duties as provided by the twelfth article of amendment.

Section 2. The Congress shall have power to enforce this article by appropriate legislation.

Amendment XXIV [1966]

Section 1. The right of citizens of the United States to vote in any primary or other election for President or Vice President, for electors for President or Vice President, or for Senator or Representative in Congress, shall not be denied or abridged by the United States or any State by reason of failure to pay any poll tax or other tax.

Section 2. The Congress shall have the power to enforce this article by appropriate legislation.

Amendment XXV [1967]

Section 1. In case of the removal of the President from office or his death or resignation, the Vice President shall become President.

Section 2. Whenever there is a vacancy in the office of the Vice President, the President shall nominate a Vice President who shall take office upon confirmation by a majority vote of both Houses of Congress.

Section 3. Whenever the President transmits to the President pro tempore of the Senate and the Speaker of the House of Representatives his written declaration that he is unable to discharge the powers and duties of his office, and until he transmits to them a written declaration to the contrary, such powers and duties shall be discharged by the Vice President as Acting President.

Section 4. Whenever the Vice President and a majority of either the principal officers of the executive department or of such other body as Congress may by law provide, transmit to the President pro tempore of the Senate and the Speaker of the House of Representatives their written declaration that the President is unable to discharge the powers and duties of his office, the Vice President shall immediately assume the powers and duties of the office as Acting President.

Thereafter, when the President transmits to the President pro tempore of the Senate and the Speaker of the House of Representatives his written declaration that no inability exists, he shall resume the powers and duties of his office unless the Vice President and a majority of either the principal officers of the executive department or of such other body as Congress may by law provide, transmit within four days to the President pro tempore of the Senate and the Speaker of the House of Representatives their written declaration that the President is unable to discharge the powers and duties of his office. Thereupon Congress shall decide the issue, assembling within forty-eight hours for that purpose if not in session. If the Congress, within twenty-one days after receipt of the latter written declaration, or, if Congress is not in session, within twenty-one days after Congress is required to assemble, determines by two-thirds vote of both Houses that the President is unable to discharge the powers and duties of this office, the Vice President shall continue to discharge the same as Acting President; otherwise, the President shall resume the powers and duties of this office.

Amendment XXVI [1971]

Section 1. The right of citizens of the United States, who are eighteen years of age or older, to vote shall not be denied or abridged by the United States or by any State on account of age.

Section 2. The Congress shall have power to enforce this article by appropriate legislation.

PRESIDENTS OF THE UNITED STATES AND TERMS OF OFFICE

No.	Name	Life Dates	Term of Office
1	George Washington	1732 – 1799	1789 – 1797
2	John Adams	1735 – 1826	1797 – 1801
3	Thomas Jefferson	1743 – 1826	1801 – 1809
4	James Madison	1751 – 1836	1809 – 1817
5	James Monroe	1758 – 1831	1817 – 1825
6	John Quincy Adams	1767 – 1848	1825 – 1829
7	Andrew Jackson	1767 – 1845	1829 – 1837
8	Martin Van Buren	1782 – 1862	1837 – 1841
9	William H. Harrison	1773 – 1841	1841
10	John Tyler	1790 – 1862	1841 – 1845
11	James K. Polk	1795 – 1849	1845 – 1849
12	Zachary Taylor	1784 – 1850	1849 – 1850
13	Millard Fillmore	1800 – 1874	1850 – 1853
14	Franklin Pierce	1804 – 1869	1853 – 1857
15	James Buchanan	1791 – 1868	1857 – 1861
16	Abraham Lincoln	1809 – 1865	1861 – 1865
17	Andrew Johnson	1808 – 1875	1865 – 1869
18	Ulysses S. Grant	1822 – 1885	1869 – 1877
19	Rutherford B. Hayes	1822 – 1893	1877 – 1881
20	James A. Garfield	1831 – 1881	1881
21	Chester A. Arthur	1829 – 1886	1881 – 1885
22	Grover Cleveland*	1837 – 1908	1885 – 1889
23	Benjamin Harrison	1833 – 1901	1889 – 1893
24	Grover Cleveland	1837 – 1908	1893 – 1897
25	William McKinley	1843 – 1901	1897 – 1901
26	Theodore Roosevelt	1858 – 1919	1901 – 1909
27	William H. Taft	1857 – 1930	1909 – 1913
28	Woodrow Wilson	1856 – 1924	1913 – 1921
29	Warran G. Harding	1865 – 1923	1921 – 1923
30	Calvin Coolidge	1872 – 1933	1923 – 1929
31	Herbert C. Hoover	1874 – 1964	1929 – 1933
32	Franklin D. Roosevelt	1882 – 1945	1933 – 1945
33	Harry S Truman	1884 – 1972	1945 – 1953
34	Dwight D. Eisenhower	1890 – 1969	1953 – 1961
35	John F. Kennedy	1917 – 1963	1961 – 1963
36	Lyndon B. Johnson	1908 – 1973	1963 – 1969
37	Richard M. Nixon	1913 –	1969 – 1974
38	Gerald R. Ford	1913 –	1974 – 1977
39	Jimmy Carter	1924 –	1977 – 1981
40	Ronald W. Reagan	1911 –	1981 –

*See also 24.

PRESIDENTIAL ELECTIONS/1789–1980

Year	Candidates	Party	Popular Vote	Electoral Vote
1789	**George Washington**			69
	John Adams			34
	Others			35
1792	**George Washington**			132
	John Adams			77
	George Clinton			50
	Others			5
1796	**John Adams**	Federalist		71
	Thomas Jefferson	Democratic-Republican		68
	Thomas Pinckney	Federalist		59
	Aaron Burr	Democratic-Republican		30
	Others			48
1800	**Thomas Jefferson**	Democratic-Republican		73
	Aaron Burr	Democartic-Republican		73
	John Adams	Federalist		65
	Charles C. Pinckney	Federalist		64
	John Jay	Federalist		1
1804	**Thomas Jefferson**	Democratic-Republican		162
	Charles C. Pinckney	Federalist		14
1808	**James Madison**	Democratic-Republican		122
	Charles C. Pinckney	Federalist		47
	Geroge Clinton	Independent-Republican		6
1812	**James Madison**	Democratic-Republican		128
	DeWitt Clinton	Federalist		89
1816	**James Monroe**	Democratic-Republican		183
	Rufus King	Federalist		34
1820	**James Monroe**	Democratic-Republican		231
	John Quincy Adams	Independent-Republican		1
1824	**John Quincy Adams**	Democratic-Republican	108,740 (30.5%)	84
	Andrew Jackson	Democratic-Republican	153,544 (43.1%)	99
	Henry Clay	Democratic-Republican	47,136 (13.2%)	37
	William H. Crawford	Democratic-Republican	46,618 (13.1%)	41
1828	**Andrew Jackson**	Democratic	647,231 (56.0%)	178
	John Quincy Adams	National-Republican	509,097 (44.0%)	83
1832	**Andrew Jackson**	Democratic	687,502 (55.0%)	219
	Henry Clay	National-Republican	530,189 (42.4%)	49
	William Wirt	Anti-Masonic }	33,108 (2.6%)	7
	John Floyd	National-Republican		11
1836	**Martin Van Buren**	Democratic	761,549 (50.9%)	170
	William H. Harrison	Whig	549,567 (36.7%)	73
	Hugh L. White	Whig	145,396 (9.7%)	26
	Daniel Webster	Whig	41,287 (2.7%)	14
	W. P. Mangum	Whig		11
1840	**William H. Harrison**	Whig	1,275,017 (53.1%)	234
	Martin Van Buren	Democratic	1,128,702 (46.9%)	60
1844	**James K. Polk**	Democratic	1,337,243 (49.6%)	170
	Henry Clay	Whig	1,299,068 (48.1%)	105
	James G. Birney	Liberty	62,300 (2.3%)	

Because only the leading candidates are listed, popular vote percentages do not always total 100.

PRESIDENTIAL ELECTIONS/1789–1980

Year	Candidates	Party	Popular Vote	Electoral Vote
1848	**Zachary Taylor**	Whig	1,360,101 (47.4%)	163
	Lewis Cass	Democratic	1,220,544 (42.5%)	127
	Martin Van Buren	Free Soil	291,263 (10.1%)	
1852	**Franklin Pierce**	Democratic	1,601,474 (50.9%)	254
	Winfield Scott	Whig	1,386,578 (44.1%)	42
	John P. Hale	Free Soil	155,825 (5.0%)	
1856	**James Buchanan**	Democratic	1,838,169 (45.4%)	174
	John C. Frémont	Republican	1,335,264 (33.0%)	114
	Millard Fillmore	American	874,534 (21.6%)	8
1860	**Abraham Lincoln**	Republican	1,865,593 (39.8%)	180
	Stephen A. Douglas	Democratic	1,382,713 (29.5%)	12
	John C. Breckinridge	Democratic	848,356 (18.1%)	72
	John Bell	Constitutional Union	592,906 (12.6%)	39
1864	**Abraham Lincoln**	Republican	2,206,938 (55.0%)	212
	George B. McClellan	Democratic	1,803,787 (45.0%)	21
1868	**Ulysses S. Grant**	Republican	3,013,421 (52.7%)	214
	Horatio Seymour	Democratic	2,706,829 (47.3%)	80
1872	**Ulysses S. Grant**	Republican	3,596,745 (55.6%)	286
	Horatio Greeley	Democratic	2,843,446 (43.9%)	66
1876	**Rutherford B. Hayes**	Republican	4,036,572 (48.0%)	185
	Samuel J. Tilden	Democratic	4,284,020 (51.0%)	184
1880	**James A. Garfield**	Republican	4,449,053 (48.3%)	214
	Winfield S. Hancock	Democratic	4,442,035 (48.2%)	155
	James B. Weaver	Greenback-Labor	308,578 (3.4%)	
1884	**Grover Cleveland**	Democratic	4,874,986 (48.5%)	219
	James G. Blaine	Republican	4,851,981 (48.2%)	182
	Benjamin F. Butler	Greenback-Labor	175,370 (1.8%)	
1888	**Benjamin Harrison**	Republican	5,444,337 (47.8%)	233
	Grover Cleveland	Democratic	5,540,050 (48.6%)	168
1892	**Grover Cleveland**	Democratic	5,554,414 (46.0%)	277
	Benjamin Harrison	Republican	5,190,802 (43.0%)	145
	James B. Weaver	People's	1,027,329 (8.5%)	22
1896	**William McKinley**	Republican	7,035,638 (50.8%)	271
	William J. Bryan	Democratic: People's	6,467,946 (46.7%)	176
1900	**William McKinley**	Republican	7,219,530 (51.7%)	292
	William J. Bryan	Democratic: Populist	6,356,734 (45.5%)	155
1904	**Theodore Roosevelt**	Republican	7,628,834 (56.4%)	336
	Alton B. Parker	Democratic	5,084,401 (37.6%)	140
	Eugene V. Debs	Socialist	402,460 (3.0%)	
1908	**William H. Taft**	Republican	7,679,006 (51.6%)	321
	William J. Bryan	Democratic	6,409,106 (43.1%)	162
	Eugene V. Debs	Socialist	420,820 (2.8%)	
1912	**Woodrow Wilson**	Democratic	6,286,820 (41.8%)	435
	Theodore Roosevelt	Progressive	4,126,020 (27.4%)	88
	William H. Taft	Republican	3,483,922 (23.2%)	8
	Eugene V. Debs	Socialist	897,011 (6.0%)	

PRESIDENTIAL ELECTIONS/1789–1980

Year	Candidates	Party	Popular Vote	Electoral Vote
1916	**Woodrow Wilson**	Democratic	9,129,606 (49.3%)	277
	Charles E. Hughes	Republican	8,538,221 (46.1%)	254
	A. L. Benson	Socialist	585,113 (3.2%)	
1920	**Warren G. Harding**	Republican	16,152,200 (61.0%)	404
	James M. Cox	Democratic	9,147,353 (34.6%)	127
	Eugene V. Debs	Socialsit	919,799 (3.5%)	
1924	**Calvin Coolidge**	Republican	15,725,016 (54.1%)	382
	John W. Davis	Democratic	8,385,586 (28.8%)	136
	Robert M. LaFollette	Progressive	4,822,856 (16.6%)	13
1928	**Herbert C. Hoover**	Republican	21,392,190 (58.2%)	444
	Alfred E. Smith	Democratic	15,016,443 (40.8%)	87
1932	**Franklin D. Roosevelt**	Democratic	22,809,638 (57.3%)	472
	Herbert C. Hoover	Republican	15,758,901 (39.6%)	59
	Norman Thomas	Socialist	881,951 (2.2%)	
1936	**Franklin D. Roosevelt**	Democratic	27,757,333 (60.8%)	523
	Alfred M. Landon	Republican	16,684,231 (36.5%)	8
	William Lemke	Union	891,858 (1.9%)	
1940	**Franklin D. Roosevelt**	Democratic	27,243,466 (54.7%)	449
	Wendell L. Willkie	Republican	22,304,755 (44.8%)	82
1944	**Franklin D. Roosevelt**	Democratic	25,602,505 (52.8%)	432
	Thomas E. Dewey	Republican	22,006,278 (44.5%)	99
1948	**Harry S Truman**	Democratic	24,105,812 (49.5%)	303
	Thomas E. Dewey	Republican	21,970,065 (45.1%)	189
	J. Strom Thurmond	States' Rights	1,169,063 (2.4%)	39
	Henry A. Wallace	Progressive	1,157,172 (2.4%)	
1952	**Dwight D. Eisenhower**	Republican	33,936,234 (55.2%)	442
	Adlai E. Stevenson	Democratic	27,314,992 (44.5%)	89
1956	**Dwight D. Eisenhower**	Republican	35,590,472 (57.4%)	457
	Adlai E. Stevenson	Democratic	26,022,752 (42.0%)	73
1960	**John F. Kennedy**	Democratic	34,227,096 (49.9%)	303
	Richard M. Nixon	Republican	34,108,546 (49.6%)	219
1964	**Lyndon B. Johnson**	Democratic	43,126,233 (61.1%)	486
	Barry M. Goldwater	Republican	27,174,989 (38.5%)	52
1968	**Richard M. Nixon**	Republican	31,770,237 (43.4%)	301
	Hubert H. Humphrey	Democratic	31,270,533 (42.7%)	191
	George C. Wallace	American Independent	9,906,141 (13.5%)	46
1972	**Richard M. Nixon**	Republican	46,740,323 (60.7%)	520
	George S. McGovern	Democratic	28,901,598 (37.5%)	17
	John G. Schmitz	American Independent	993,199 (1.4%)	
1976	**Jimmy Carter**	Democratic	40,828,929 (50.1%)	297
	Gerald R. Ford	Republican	39,148,940 (47.9%)	240
	Eugene McCarthy	Independent	739,256	
1980	**Ronald Reagan**	Republican	43,201,220 (50.9%)	489
	Jimmy Carter	Democratic	34,913,332 (41.2%)	49
	John B. Anderson	Independent	5,581,379 (6.6%)	

THE VICE-PRESIDENCY AND THE CABINET/1789-1983

Vice-President

John Adams	1789-1797
Thomas Jefferson	1797-1801
Aaron Burr	1801-1805
George Clinton	1805-1813
Elbridge Gerry	1813-1817
Daniel D. Tompkins	1817-1825
John C. Calhoun	1825-1833
Martin Van Buren	1833-1837
Richard M. Johnson	1837-1841
John Tyler	1841
George M. Dallas	1845-1849
Millard Fillmore	1849-1850
William R. King	1853-1857
John C. Breckinridge	1857-1861
Hannibal Hamlin	1861-1865
Andrew Johnson	1865
Schuyler Colfax	1869-1873
Henry Wilson	1873-1877
William A. Wheeler	1877-1881
Chester A. Arthur	1881
Thomas A. Hendricks	1885-1889
Levi P. Morton	1889-1893
Adlai E. Stevenson	1893-1897
Garret A. Hobart	1897-1901
Theodore Roosevelt	1901
Charles W. Fairbanks	1905-1909
James S. Sherman	1909-1913
Thomas R. Marshall	1913-1921
Calvin Coolidge	121-1923
Charles G. Dawes	1925-1929
Charles Curtis	1929-1933
John Nance Garner	1933-1941
Henry A. Wallace	1941-1945
Harry S Truman	1945
Alben W. Barkley	1949-1953
Richard M. Nixon	1953-1961
Lyndon B. Johnson	1961-1963
Hubert H. Humphrey	1965-1969
Spiro T. Agnew	1969-1973
Gerald R. Ford	1973-1974
Nelson A. Rockefeller	1974-1977
Walter F. Mondale	1977-1981
George Bush	1981-

Secretary of State (1789-)

Thomas Jefferson	1789
Edmund Randolph	1794
Timothy Pickering	1795
John Marshall	1800
James Madison	1801
Robert Smith	1809
James Monroe	1811
John Q. Adams	1817
Henry Clay	1825
Martin Van Buren	1829
Edward Livingston	1831
Louis McLane	1833
John Forsyth	1834
Daniel Webster	1841
Hugh S. Legare	1843
Abel P. Upshur	1843
John C. Calhoun	1844
James Buchanan	1845
John M. Clayton	1849
Daniel Webster	1850
Edward Everett	1852
William L. Marcy	1853
Lewis Cass	1857
Jeremiah S. Black	1860
William H. Seward	1861
E. B. Washburne	1869
Hamilton Fish	1869
William M. Evarts	1877
James G. Blaine	1881
F. T. Frelinghuysen	1881
Thomas F. Bayard	1885
James G. Blaine	1889
John W. Foster	1892
Walter Q. Gresham	1893
Richard Olney	1895
John Sherman	1897
William R. Day	1898
John Hay	1898
Elihu Root	1905
Robert Bacon	1909
Philander C. Knox	1909
William J. Bryan	1913
Robert Lansing	1915
Bainbridge Colby	1920
Charles E. Hughes	1921
Frank B. Kellogg	1925
Henry L. Stimson	1929
Cordell Hull	1933
E. R. Stettinius, Jr.	1944
James F. Byrnes	1945
George C. Marshall	1947
Dean Acheson	1949
John Foster Dulles	1953
Christian A. Herter	1959
Dean Rusk	1961
William P. Rogers	1969
Henry A. Kissinger	1973
Cyrus R. Vance	1977
Edmund Muskie	1980
Alexander M. Haig, Jr.	1981
George P. Shultz	1982

Secretary of the Treasury (1789-)

Alexander Hamilton	1789
Oliver Wolcott	1795
Samuel Dexter	1801
Albert Gallatin	1801
G. W. Campbell	1814
A. J. Dallas	1814
William H. Crawford	1816
Richard Rush	1825
Samuel D. Ingham	1829
Louis McLane	1831
William J. Duane	1833
Roger B. Taney	1833
Levi Woodbury	1834
Thomas Ewing	1841
Walter Forward	1841
John C. Spencer	1843
George M. Bibb	1844
Robert J. Walker	1845
William M. Meredith	1849
Thomas Corwin	1850
James Guthrie	1853
Howell Cobb	1857
Philip F. Thomas	1860
John A. Dix	1861
Salmon P. Chase	1861
Wm. P. Fessenden	1864
Hugh McCulloch	1865
George S. Boutwell	1869
William A. Richardson	1873
Benjamin H. Bristow	1874
Lot M. Morrill	1876
John Sherman	1877
William Windom	1881
Charles J. Folger	1881
Walter Q. Gresham	1884
Hugh McCulloch	1884
Daniel Manning	1885
Charles S. Fairchild	1887
William Windom	1889
Charles Foster	1891
John G. Carlisle	1893
Lyman J. Gage	1897
Leslie M. Shaw	1902
George B. Cortelyou	1907
Franklin MacVeagh	1909
William G. McAdoo	1913
Carter Glass	1919
David F. Houston	1920
Andrew W. Mellon	1921
Ogden L. Mills	1932
William H. Woodin	1933
Henry Morgenthau, Jr.	1934
Fred M. Vinson	1945
John W. Snyder	1946
George M. Humphrey	1953
Robert B. Anderson	1957
C. Douglas Dillon	1961
Henry H. Fowler	1965
David M. Kennedy	1969
John B. Connally	1971
George P. Shultz	1972
William E. Simon	1974
W. Michael Blumenthal	1977
G. William Miller	1979
Donald T. Regan	1981

Secretary of War (1789-1947)

Henry Knox	1789
Timothy Pickering	1795
James McHenry	1796
John Marshall	1800
Samuel Dexter	1800
Roger Criswold	1801
Henry Dearborn	1801
William Eustis	1809
John Armstrong	1813
James Monroe	1814
William H. Crawford	1815
Isaac Shelby	1817
George Graham	1817
John C. Calhoun	1817

THE VICE-PRESIDENCY AND THE CABINET/1789-1983

Name	Year
James Barbour	1825
Peter B. Porter	1828
John H. Eaton	1829
Lewis Cass	1831
Benjamin F. Butler	1837
Joel R. Poinsett	1837
John Bell	1841
John McLean	1841
John C. Spencer	1841
James M. Porter	1843
William Wilkins	1844
William L. Marcy	1845
George W. Crawford	1849
Charles M. Conrad	1850
Jefferson Davis	1853
John B. Floyd	1857
Joseph Holt	1861
Simon Cameron	1861
Edwin M. Stanton	1862
Ulysses S. Grant	1867
Lorenzo Thomas	1868
John M. Schofield	1868
John A. Rawlins	1869
William T. Sherman	1869
William W. Belknap	1869
Alphonso Taft	1876
James D. Cameron	1876
George W. McCrary	1877
Alexander Ramsey	1879
Robert T. Lincoln	1881
William C. Endicott	1885
Redfield Proctor	1889
Stephen B. Elkins	1891
Daniel S. Lamont	1893
Russell A. Alger	1897
Elihu Root	1899
William H. Taft	1904
Luke E. Wright	1908
J. M. Dickinson	1909
Henry L. Stimson	1911
L. M. Garrison	1913
Newton D. Baker	1916
John W. Weeks	1921
Dwight F. Davis	1925
James W. Good	1929
Patrick J. Hurley	1929
George H. Dern	1933
H. H. Woodring	1936
Henry L. Stimson	1940
Robert P. Patterson	1945
Kenneth C. Royall	1947

Secretary of the Navy (1798-1947)

Name	Year
Benjamin Stoddert	1798
Robert Smith	1801
J. Crowninshield	1805
Paul Hamilton	1809
William Jones	1813
B. W. Crowninshield	1814
Smith Thompson	1818
S. L. Southard	1823
John Branch	1829
Levi Woodbury	1831
Mahlon Dickerson	1834
James K. Paulding	1838
George E. Badger	1841
Abel P. Upshur	1841
David Henshaw	1843
Thomas W. Gilmer	1844
John Y. Mason	1844
George Bancroft	1845
John Y. Mason	1846
William B. Preston	1849
William A. Graham	1850
John P. Kennedy	1852
James C. Dobbin	1853
Isaac Toucey	1857
Gideon Welles	1861
Adolph E. Borie	1869
George M. Robeson	1869
R. W. Thompson	1877
Nathan Goff, Jr.	1881
William H. Hunt	1881
William E. Chandler	1881
William C. Whitney	1885
Benjamin F. Tracy	1889
Hilary A. Herbert	1893
John D. Long	1897
William H. Moody	1902
Paul Morton	1904
Charles J. Bonaparte	1905
Victor H. Metcalf	1907
T. H. Newberry	1908
George von L. Meyer	1909
Josephus Daniels	1913
Edwin Denby	1921
Curtis D. Wilbur	1924
Charles F. Adams	1929
Claude A. Swanson	1933
Charles Edison	1940
Frank Knox	1940
James V. Forrestal	1944

Secretary of Defense (1947-)

Name	Year
James V. Forrestal	1947
Louis A. Johnson	1949
George C. Marshall	1950
Robert A. Lovett	1951
Charles E. Wilson	1953
Neil H. McElroy	1957
Thomas S. Gates, Jr.	1959
Robert S. McNamara	1961
Clark Clifford	1968
Melvin R. Laird	1969
Elliot L. Richardson	1973
James R. Schlesinger	1973
Donald Rumsfeld	1975
Harold Brown	1977
Caspar W. Weinberger	1981

Postmaster General (1789-) (since 1971 appointed by Postal Service Board of Governors)

Name	Year
Samuel Osgood	1789
Timothy Pickering	1791
Joseph Habersham	1795
Gideon Granger	1801
Return J. Meigs, Jr.	1814
John McLean	1823
William T. Barry	1829
Amos Kendall	1835
John M. Niles	1840
Francis Granger	1841
Charles A. Wickliffe	1841
Cave Johnson	1845
Jacob Collamer	1849
Nathan K. Hall	1850
Samuel D. Hubbard	1852
James Campbell	1853
Aaron V. Brown	1857
Joseph Holt	1859
Horatio King	1861
Montgomery Blair	1861
William Dennison	1864
Alexander W. Randall	1866
John A. J. Creswell	1869
James W. Marshall	1874
Marshall Jewell	1874
James N. Tyner	1876
David M. Key	1877
Horace Maynard	1880
Thomas L. James	1881
Timothy O. Howe	1881
Walter Q. Gresham	1883
Frank Hatton	1884
William F. Vilas	1885
Don M. Dickinson	1888
John Wanamaker	1889
Wilson S. Bissell	1893
William L. Wilson	1895
James A. Gary	1897
Charles E. Smith	1898
Henry C. Payne	1902
Robert J. Wynne	1904
George B. Cortelyou	1905
George von L. Meyer	1907
F. H. Hitchcock	1909
Albert S. Burleson	1913
Will H. Hays	1921
Hubert Work	1922
Harry S. New	1923
Walter F. Brown	1929
James A. Farley	1933
Frank C. Walker	1940
Robert E. Hannegan	1945
J. M. Donaldson	1947
A. E. Summerfield	1953
J. Edward Day	1961
John A. Gronouski	1963
Lawrence F. O'Brien	1965
Marvin Watson	1968
Winton M. Blount	1969
Elmer T. Klassen	1971
Benjamin F. Bailar	1975
William F. Bolger	1978

Attorney General (1789-)

Name	Year
Edmund Randolph	1789
William Bradford	1794
Charles Lee	1795
Theophilus Parsons	1801

THE VICE-PRESIDENCY AND THE CABINET/1789–1983

Levi Lincoln	1801
Robert Smith	1805
John Breckinridge	1805
Caesar A. Rodney	1807
William Pinckney	1811
Richard Rush	1814
William Wirt	1817
John M. Berrien	1829
Roger B. Taney	1831
Benjamin F. Butler	1833
Felix Grundy	1838
Henry D. Gilpin	1840
John J. Crittenden	1841
Hugh S. Legare	1841
John Nelson	1843
John Y. Mason	1845
Nathan Clifford	1846
Isaac Toucey	1848
Reverdy Johnson	1849
John J. Crittenden	1850
Caleb Cushing	1853
Jeremiah S. Black	1857
Edwin M. Stanton	1860
Edward Bates	1861
Titian J. Coffey	1863
James Speed	1864
Henry Stanbery	1866
William M. Evarts	1868
Ebenezer R. Hoar	1869
Amos T. Ackerman	1870
George H. Williams	1871
Edward Pierrepont	1875
Alphonso Taft	1876
Charles Devens	1877
Wayne MacVeagh	1881
Benjamin H. Brewster	1881
A. H. Garland	1885
William H. H. Miller	1889
Richard Olney	1893
Judson Harmon	1895
Joseph McKenna	1897
John W. Griggs	1897
Philander C. Knox	1901
William H. Moody	1904
Charles J. Bonaparte	1907
G. W. Wickersham	1909
J. C. McReynolds	1913
Thomas W. Gregory	1914
A. Mitchell Palmer	1919
H. M. Daugherty	1921
Harlan F. Stone	1924
John G. Sargent	1925
William D. Mitchell	1929
H. S. Cummings	1933
Frank Murphy	1939
Robert H. Jackson	1940
Francis Biddle	1941
Tom C. Clark	1945
J. H. McGrath	1949
J. P. McGranery	1952
H. Brownell, Jr.	1953
William P. Rogers	1957
Robert F. Kennedy	1961
Nicholas Katzenbach	1964
Ramsey Clark	1967

John N. Mitchell	1969
Richard G. Kleindienst	1972
Elliot L. Richardson	1973
Robert H. Bork (acting)	1973
William B. Saxbe	1974
Edward H. Levi	1975
Griffin Bell	1977
Benjamin R. Civiletti	1979
William French Smith	1981

Secretary of the Interior (1849–   )

Thomas Ewing	1849
Alexander H. H. Stuart	1850
Robert McClelland	1853
Jacob Thompson	1857
Caleb B. Smith	1861
John P. Usher	1863
James Harlan	1865
O. H. Browning	1866
Jacob D. Cox	1869
Columbus Delano	1870
Zachariah Chandler	1875
Carl Schurz	1877
Samuel J. Kirkwood	1881
Henry M. Teller	1881
L. Q. C. Lamar	1885
Willaim F. Vilas	1888
John W. Noble	1889
Hoke Smith	1893
David R. Francis	1896
Cornelius N. Bliss	1897
E. A. Hitchcock	1899
James R. Garfield	1907
R. A. Ballinger	1909
Walter L. Fisher	1911
Franklin K. Lane	1913
John B. Payne	1920
Albert B. Fall	1921
Hubert Work	1923
Roy O. West	1928
Ray L. Wilbur	1929
Harold L. Ickes	1933
Julius A. Krug	1946
Oscar L. Chapman	1949
Douglas McKay	1953
Fred A. Seaton	1956
Stewart L. Udall	1961
Walter J. Hickel	1969
Rogers C. B. Morton	1971
Stanley K. Hathaway	1975
Thomas Kleppe	1975
Cecil D. Andrus	1977
James G. Watt	1981
William P. Clark, Jr.	1983

Secretary of Agriculture (1889–   )

Norman J. Colman	1889
Jeremiah M. Rusk	1889
J. Sterling Morton	1893
James Wilson	1897
David F. Houston	1913
Edward T. Meredith	1920
Henry C. Wallace	1921

Howard M. Gore	1924
William M. Jardine	1925
Arthur M. Hyde	1929
Henry A. Wallace	1933
Claude R. Wickard	1940
Clinton P. Anderson	1945
Charles F. Brannan	1948
Ezra Taft Benson	1953
Orville L. Freeman	1961
Clifford M. Hardin	1969
Earl L. Butz	1971
John A. Knebel	1976
Robert Bergland	1977
John R. Block	1981

Secretary of Commerce and Labor (1903–1913)

George B. Cortelyou	1903
Victor H. Metcalf	1904
Oscar S. Straus	1906
Charles Nagel	1909

Secretary of Commerce (1913–   )

William C. Redfield	1913
Joshua W. Alexander	1919
Herbert Hoover	1921
William F. Whiting	1928
Robert P. Lamont	1929
Roy D. Chapin	1932
Daniel C. Roper	1933
Harry L. Hopkins	1939
Jesse Jones	1940
Henry A. Wallace	1945
W. A. Harriman	1946
Charles Sawyer	1948
Sinclair Weeks	1953
Lewis L. Strauss	1958
Frederick H. Mueller	1959
Luther Hodges	1961
John T. Connor	1965
A. B. Trowbridge	1967
Maurice H. Stans	1969
Peter G. Peterson	1972
Frederick B. Dent	1973
Rogers C. B. Morton	1975
Elliot L. Richardson	1975
Juanita M. Kreps	1977
Philip M. Klutznick	1979
Malcolm Baldridge	1981

Secretary of Labor (1913–   )

William B. Wilson	1913
James J. Davis	1921
William N. Doak	1930
Frances Perkins	1933
L. B. Schwellenbach	1945
Maurice J. Tobin	1948
Martin P. Durkin	1953
James P. Mitchell	1953
Arthur J. Goldberg	1961
W. Willard Wirtz	1962
George P. Shultz	1969

THE VICE-PRESIDENCY AND THE CABINET/1789–1983

James D. Hodgson	1970	Forrest D. Mathews	1975	**Secretary of Transportation**	
Peter J. Brennan	1973	Joseph A. Califano	1977		
John T. Dunlop	1975	Patricia R. Harris	1979	John A. Volpe	1969
W. J. Usery	1976			Claude S. Brinegar	1973
F. Ray Marshall	1977	**Secretary of Health and**		William T. Coleman	1975
Raymond J. Donovan	1981	**Human Services**		Brock Adams	1977
				Neil E. Goldschmidt	1979
		Patricia R. Harris	1980	Andrew L. Lewis, Jr.	1981
Secretary of Health,		Richard S. Schweiker	1981		
Education, and Welfare				**Secretary of the Department**	
(1953–1980)		**Secretary of Housing and**		**of Energy**	
		Urban Development			
Oveta Culp Hobby	1953			James R. Schlesinger	1977
Marion B. Folsom	1955	Robert C. Weaver	1966	Charles W. Duncan	1979
Arthur S. Flemming	1958	Robert C. Wood	1968	James B. Edwards	1981
Abraham A. Ribicoff	1961	George M. Romney	1969		
Anthony J. Celebrezze	1962	James T. Lynn	1973	**Secretary of the Department**	
John W. Gardner	1965	Carla A. Hills	1975	**of Education**	
Robert H. Finch	1969	Patricia R. Harris	1977		
Elliot L. Richardson	1970	Moon Landrieu	1979	Shirley M. Hufstedler	1980
Caspar W. Weinberger	1973	Samuel R. Pierce, Jr.	1981	T. H. Bell	1981

THE STATES

1. Delaware	7 Dec. 1787	18. Louisiana	30 Apr. 1812	35. West Virginia	19 June 1863
2. Pennsylvania	12 Dec. 1787	19. Indiana	11 Dec. 1816	36. Nevada	31 Oct. 1864
3. New Jersey	18 Dec. 1787	20. Mississippi	10 Dec. 1817	37. Nebraska	1 Mar. 1867
4. Georgia	2 Jan. 1788	21. Illinois	3 Dec. 1818	38. Colorado	1 Aug. 1876
5. Connecticut	9 Jan. 1788	22. Alabama	14 Dec. 1819	39. North Dakota	2 Nov. 1889
6. Massachusetts	6 Feb. 1788	23. Maine	15 Mar. 1820	40. South Dakota	2 Nov. 1889
7. Maryland	28 Apr. 1788	24. Missouri	10 Aug. 1821	41. Montana	8 Nov. 1889
8. South Carolina	23 May 1788	25. Arkansas	15 June 1836	42. Washington	11 Nov. 1889
9. New Hampshire	21 June 1788	26. Michigan	26 Jan. 1837	43. Idaho	3 July 1890
10. Virginia	25 June 1788	27. Florida	3 Mar. 1845	44. Wyoming	10 July 1890
11. New York	26 July 1788	28. Texas	29 Dec. 1845	45. Utah	4 Jan. 1896
12. North Carolina	21 Nov. 1789	29. Iowa	28 Dec. 1846	46. Oklahoma	16 Nov. 1907
13. Rhode Island	29 May 1790	30. Wisconsin	29 May 1848	47. New Mexico	6 Jan. 1912
14. Vermont	4 Mar. 1791	31. California	9 Sept. 1850	48. Arizona	14 Feb. 1912
15. Kentucky	1 June 1792	32. Minnesota	11 May 1858	49. Alaska	3 Jan. 1959
16. Tennessee	1 June 1796	33. Oregon	14 Feb. 1859	50. Hawaii	21 Aug. 1959
17. Ohio	1 Mar. 1803	34. Kansas	29 Jan. 1861		

TERRITORIAL EXPANSION

Louisiana Purchase	1803	Gadsden Purchase	1853	Guam	1899
Florida	1819	Alaska	1867	Amer. Samoa	1900
Texas	1845	Hawaii	1898	Canal Zone	1904
Oregon	1846	The Philippines	1898–1946	U.S. Virgin Islands	1917
Mexican Cession	1848	Puerto Rico	1899	Pacific Islands Trust Terr.	1947

POPULATION/1790–1980

1790	3,929,214	1840	17,069,453	1890	62,947,714	1940	131,669,275
1800	5,308,483	1850	23,191,876	1900	75,994,575	1950	151,325,798
1810	7,239,881	1860	31,443,321	1910	91,972,266	1960	179,323,175
1820	9,638,453	1870	39,818,449	1920	105,710,620	1970	203,235,298
1830	12,866,020	1880	50,155,783	1930	122,775,046	1980	225,478,656

THE CONGRESS/1789–1983

Congress	Term	Senate Maj.	Senate Min.	Senate Other	House Maj.	House Min.	House Other	Administration
1	1789–1791	Adm. 17	Op. 9		Adm. 38	Op. 26		Washington
2	1791–1793	Adm. 16	Op. 13		Adm. 37	Op. 33		Washington
3	1793–1795	Adm. 17	Op. 13		Adm. 57	Op. 48		Washington
4	1795–1797	Adm. 19	Op. 13		Adm. 54	Op. 52		Washington
5	1797–1799	F 20	DR 12		F 58	DR 48		J. Adams (F)
6	1799–1801	F 19	DR 13		F 64	DR 42		J. Adams (F)
7	1801–1803	DR 18	F 14		DR 69	F 36		Jefferson (DR)
8	1803–1805	DR 25	F 9		DR 102	F 39		Jefferson (DR)
9	1805–1807	DR 27	F 7		DR 116	F 25		Jefferson (DR)
10	1807–1809	DR 28	F 6		DR 118	F 24		Jefferson (DR)
11	1809–1811	DR 28	F 6		DR 94	F 48		Madison (DR)
12	1811–1813	DR 30	F 6		DR 108	F 36		Madison (DR)
13	1813–1815	DR 27	F 9		DR 112	F 68		Madison (DR)
14	1815–1817	DR 25	F 11		DR 117	F 65		Madison (DR)
15	1817–1819	DR 34	F 10		DR 141	F 42		Monroe (DR)
16	1819–1821	DR 35	F 7		DR 156	F 27		Monroe (DR)
17	1821–1823	DR 44	F 4		DR 158	F 25		Monroe (DR)
18	1823–1825	DR 44	F 4		DR 187	F 26		Monroe (DR)
19	1825–1827	Adm. 26	Op. 20		Adm. 105	Op. 97		J. Q. Adams (DR)
20	1827–1829	Op. 28	Adm. 20		Op. 119	Adm. 94		J. Q. Adams (DR)
21	1829–1831	D 26	NR 22		D 139	NR 74		Jackson (D)
22	1831–1833	D 25	NR 21	2	D 141	NR 58	14	Jackson (D)
23	1833–1835	D 20	NR 20	8	D 147	AM 53	60	Jackson (D)
24	1835–1837	D 27	W 25		D 145	W 98		Jackson (D)
25	1837–1839	D 30	W 18	4	D 108	W 107	24	Van Buren (D)
26	1839–1841	D 28	W 22		D 124	W 118		Van Buren (D)
27	1841–1843	W 28	D 22	2	W 133	D 102	6	{ W. H. Harrison (W) / Tyler (W)
28	1843–1845	W 28	D 25	1	D 142	W 79	1	Tyler (W)
29	1845–1847	D 31	W 25		D 143	W 77	6	Polk (D)
30	1847–1849	D 36	W 21	1	W 115	D 108	4	Polk (D)
31	1849–1851	D 35	W 25	2	D 112	W 109	9	{ Taylor (W) / Fillmore (W)
32	1851–1853	D 35	W 24	3	D 140	W 88	5	Fillmore (W)
33	1853–1855	D 38	W 22	2	D 159	W 71	4	Pierce (D)
34	1855–1857	D 40	R 15	5	R 108	D 83	43	Pierce (D)
35	1857–1859	D 36	R 20	8	D 118	R 92	26	Buchanan (D)
36	1859–1861	D 36	R 26	4	R 114	D 92	31	Buchanan (D)
37	1861–1863	R 31	D 10	8	R 105	D 43	30	Lincoln (R)
38	1863–1865	R 36	D 9	5	R 102	D 75	9	Lincoln (R)
39	1865–1867	R 42	D 10		R 149	D 42		{ Lincoln (R) / A. Johnson (R)
40	1867–1869	R 42	D 11		R 143	D 49		A. Johnson (R)
41	1869–1871	R 56	D 11		R 149	D 63		Grant (R)
42	1871–1873	R 52	D 17	5	D 134	R 104	5	Grant (R)
43	1873–1875	R 49	D 19	5	R 194	D 92	14	Grant (R)
44	1875–1877	R 45	D 29	2	D 169	R 109	14	Grant (R)

THE CONGRESS/1789–1983

Congress	Term	Senate Maj.	Senate Min.	Senate Other	House Maj.	House Min.	House Other	Administration
45	1877–1879	R 39	D 36	1	D 153	R 140		Hayes (R)
46	1879–1881	D 42	R 33	1	D 149	R 130	14	Hayes (R)
47	1881–1883	R 37	D 37	1	R 147	D 135	11	Garfield (R) / Arthur (R)
48	1883–1885	R 38	D 36		D 197	R 118	10	Arthur (R)
49	1885–1887	R 43	D 34		D 183	R 140	2	Cleveland (D)
50	1887–1889	R 39	D 37		D 169	R 152	4	Cleveland (D)
51	1889–1891	R 39	D 37		R 166	D 159		B. Harrison (R)
52	1891–1893	R 47	D 39	2	D 235	R 88	9	B. Harrison (R)
53	1893–1895	D 44	R 38	3	D 218	R 127	11	Cleveland (D)
54	1895–1897	R 43	D 39	6	R 244	D 105	7	Cleveland (D)
55	1897–1899	R 47	D 34	7	R 204	D 113	40	McKinley (R)
56	1899–1901	R 53	R 26	8	R 185	D 163	9	McKinley (R)
57	1901–1903	R 55	D 31	4	R 197	D 151	9	McKinley (R) / T. Roosevelt (R)
58	1903–1905	R 57	D 33		R 208	D 178		T. Roosevelt (R)
59	1905–1907	R 57	D 33		R 250	D 136		T. Roosevelt (R)
60	1907–1909	R 61	D 31		R 222	D 164		T. Roosevelt (R)
61	1909–1911	R 61	D 32		R 219	D 172		Taft (R)
62	1911–1913	R 51	D 41		D 228	R 161	1	Taft (R)
63	1913–1915	D 51	R 44		D 291	R 127	17	Wilson (D)
64	1915–1917	D 56	R 40		D 230	R 196	9	Wilson (D)
65	1917–1919	D 53	R 42		D 216	R 210	6	Wilson (D)
66	1919–1921	R 49	D 47		R 240	D 190	3	Wilson (D)
67	1921–1923	R 59	D 37		R 303	D 131	1	Harding (R)
68	1923–1925	R 51	D 43	2	R 225	D 205	5	Harding (R) / Coolidge (R)
69	1925–1927	R 56	D 39	1	R 247	D 183	4	Coolidge (R)
70	1927–1929	R 49	D 46	1	R 237	D 195	3	Coolidge (R)
71	1929–1931	R 56	D 39	1	R 267	D 167	1	Hoover (R)
72	1931–1933	R 48	D 47	1	D 220	R 214	1	Hoover (R)
73	1933–1935	D 60	R 35		D 310	R 117	5	F. D. Roosevelt (D)
74	1935–1937	D 69	R 25	2	D 319	R 103	10	F. D. Roosevelt (D)
75	1937–1939	D 76	R 16	4	D 331	R 89	13	F. D. Roosevelt (D)
76	1939–1941	D 69	R 23	4	D 261	R 164	4	F. D. Roosevelt (D)
77	1941–1943	D 66	R 28	2	D 268	R 162	5	F. D. Roosevelt (D)
78	1943–1945	D 58	R 37	1	D 218	R 208	4	F. D. Roosevelt (D) / Truman (D)
79	1945–1947	D 56	R 38	1	D 242	R 190	2	Truman (D)
80	1947–1949	R 51	D 45		R 246	D 188	1	Truman (D)
81	1949–1951	D 54	R 42		D 263	R 171	1	Truman (D)
82	1951–1953	D 49	R 47		D 235	R 199	1	Truman (D)
83	1953–1955	R 48	D 47	1	R 221	D 212	1	Eisenhower (R)
84	1955–1957	D 48	R 47	1	D 232	R 203		Eisenhower (R)
85	1957–1959	D 49	R 47		D 232	R 199		Eisenhower (R)
86	1959–1961	D 62	R 34		D 280	R 152		Eisenhower (R)

THE CONGRESS/1789–1983

Congress	Term	Senate Maj.	Min.	Other	House Maj.	Min.	Other	Administration
87	1961–1963	D 65	R 35		D 261	R 176		Kennedy (D)
88	1963–1965	D 67	R 33		D 258	R 177	1	Kennedy (D) / L. B. Johnson (D)
89	1965–1967	D 68	R 32		D 295	R 140		L. B. Johnson (D)
90	1967–1969	D 64	R 36	1	D 247	R 187		L. B. Johnson (D)
91	1969–1971	D 58	R 42		D 243	R 192		Nixon (R)
92	1971–1973	D 54	R 45	1	D 254	R 180	1	Nixon (R)
93	1973–1975	D 56	R 42	2	D 240	R 192	3	Nixon-Ford (R)
94	1975–1977	D 61	R 37	2	D 291	R 144		Ford (R)
95	1977–1979	D 61	R 38	1	D 292	R 143		Carter (D)
96	1979–1981	D 58	R 41	1	D 276	R 159		Carter (D)
97	1981–1983	R 53	D 46	1	D 242	R 191	2	Reagan (R)
98	1983–1985	R 55	D 45		D 269	R 166		Reagan (R)

INDEX